ULTIMATE FANTASTIC FOUR

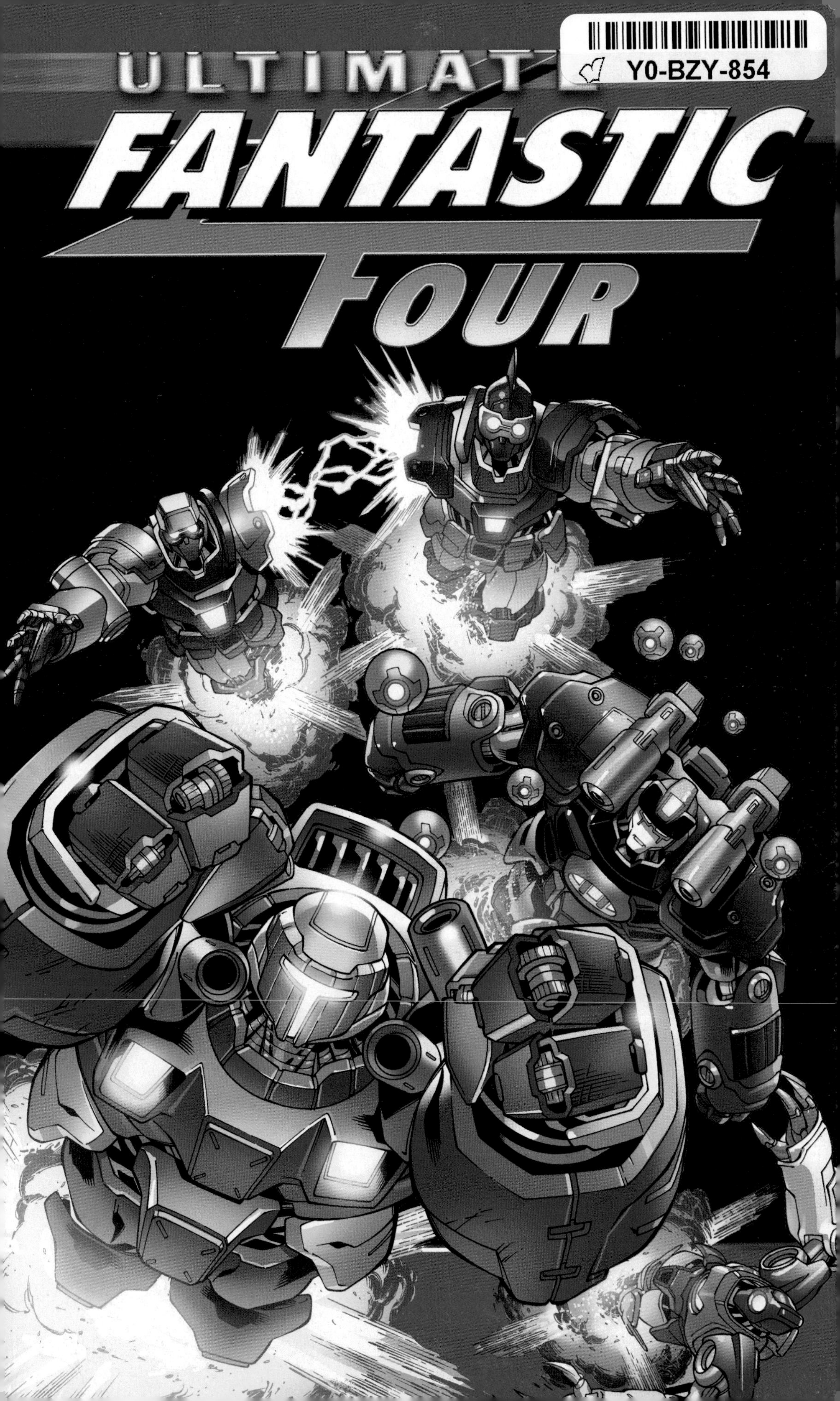

ULTIMATE FANTASTIC FOUR
GHOSTS

writer: **MIKE CAREY**

ART, ISSUES #47-49
penciler: **MARK BROOKS**
inker: **JAIME MENDOZA**
colorists: **JUSTIN PONSOR & ANDREW CROSSLEY**

ART, ISSUES #50-53
BY TOP COW PRODUCTIONS, INC.
penciler: **TYLER KIRKHAM**
inker: **SAL REGLA**
colorist: **BLOND**

letterer: **VIRTUAL CALLIGRAPHY'S RUS WOOTON**

cover artists: **MARK BROOKS, JAIME MENDOZA & CHRISTINA STRAIN (ISSUE #47 & #49);
MARK BROOKS (ISSUE #48); MARKO DJURDJEVIC (ISSUE #50); NIC KLEIN (ISSUE #51);
GREG LAND, JAY LEISTEN, & STEPHANE PERU (ISSUE #52);
AND GABRIELE DELL'OTTO (ISSUE #53)**

SPECIAL THANKS TO TOP COW'S ROB LEVIN

assistant editor: **LAUREN SANKOVITCH**
editor: **BILL ROSEMANN**
senior editor: **RALPH MACCHIO**

collection editor:
CORY LEVINE
editorial assistant:
JODY LEHEUP
assistant editor:
JOHN DENNING
editors, special projects:
JENNIFER GRÜNWALD & MARK D. BEAZLEY
senior editor, special projects:
JEFF YOUNGQUIST

senior vice president of sales:
DAVID GABRIEL
production:
JERRON QUALITY COLOR
vice president of creative:
TOM MARVELLI

editor in chief:
JOE QUESADA
publisher:
DAN BUCKLEY

eviously:

er an interdimensional accident, young Reed Richards, Sue Storm, Johnny Storm, and Ben
nm are changed forever. The quartet's genetic structures are scrambled and recombined in
antastically strange way. Reed's body stretches and flows like water. Ben looks like a thing
ved from desert rock. Sue can become invisible. Johnny generates flame. Together, they are
Fantastic Four!

weeks, Reed has been obsessing over plans for a mysterious cosmic cube — plans that were
nted in his mind by an alien force. When Reed attempted to fuel the cube by harnessing the
power of a star, he accidentally drew to Earth the Silver Surfer and the Surfer's king, the
cho-Man!

er defeating the Psycho-Man and his metallic minions, Reed has once again retreated into
fixation on the cosmic cube…much to the dismay of his friends and family…and most
portantly, his girlfriend, Sue.

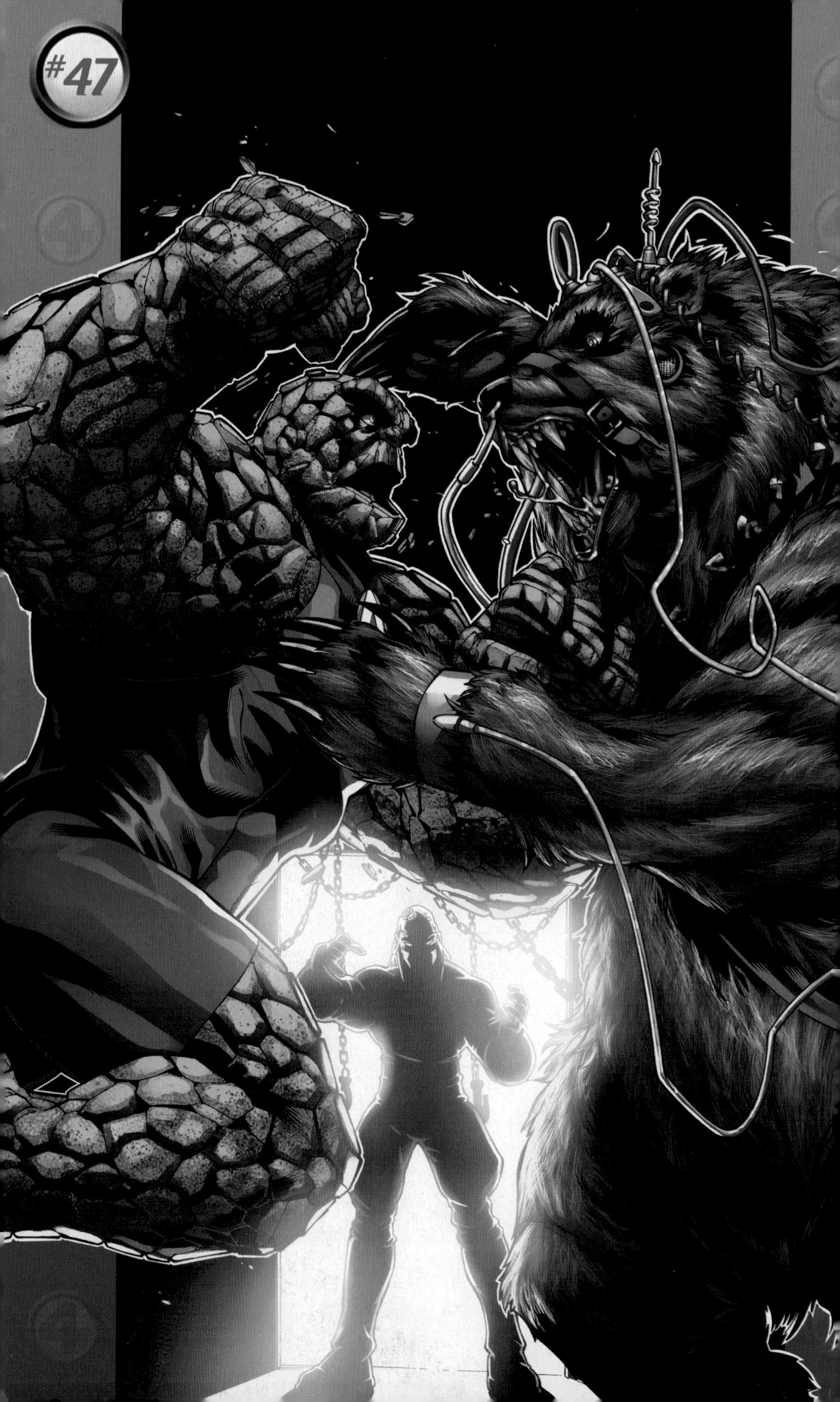
#47

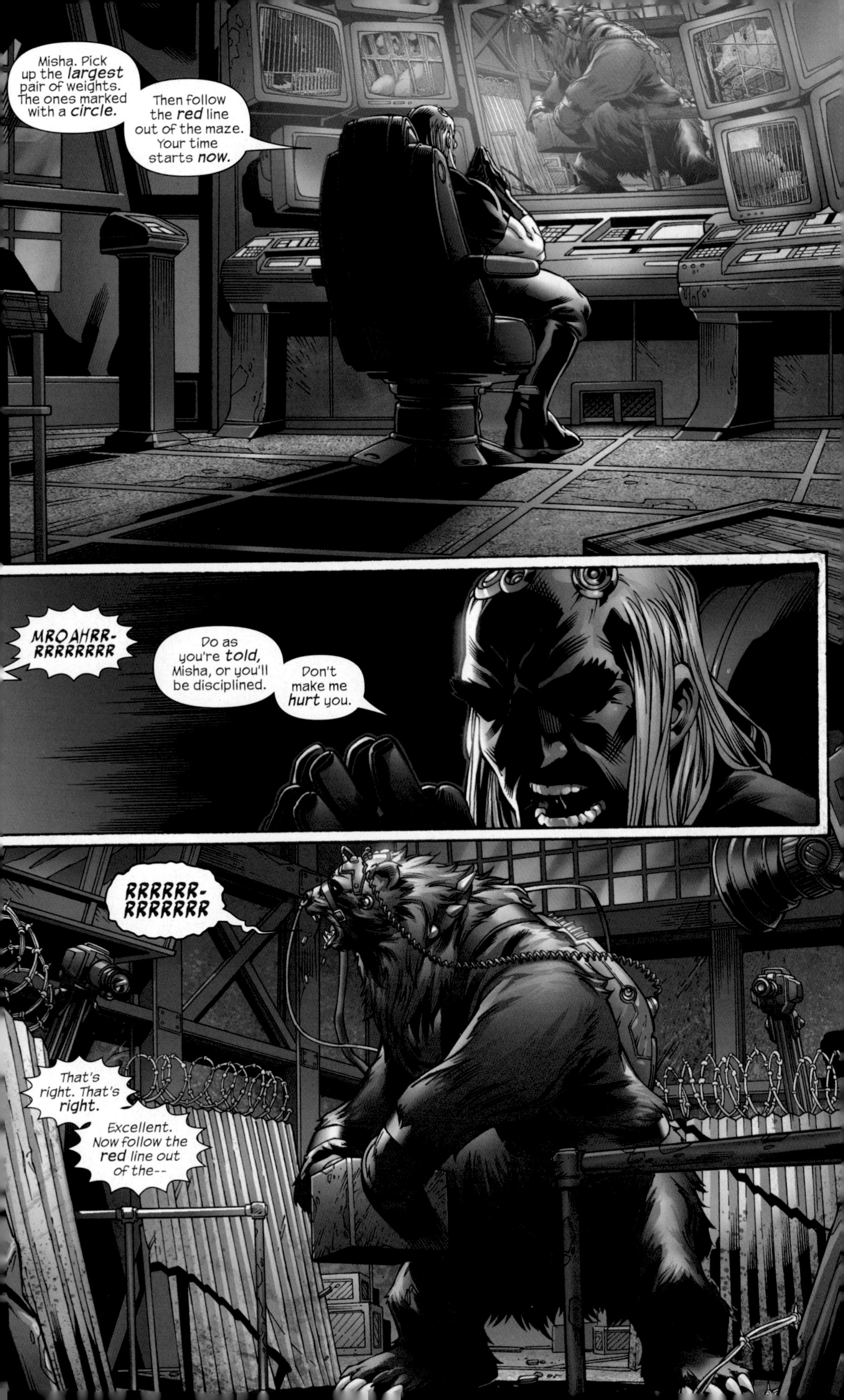
Misha. Pick up the largest pair of weights. The ones marked with a circle.
Then follow the red line out of the maze. Your time starts now.
MROAHRR-RRRRRRRR
Do as you're told, Misha, or you'll be disciplined.
Don't make me hurt you.
RRRRRR-RRRRRRR
That's right. That's right.
Excellent. Now follow the red line out of the--

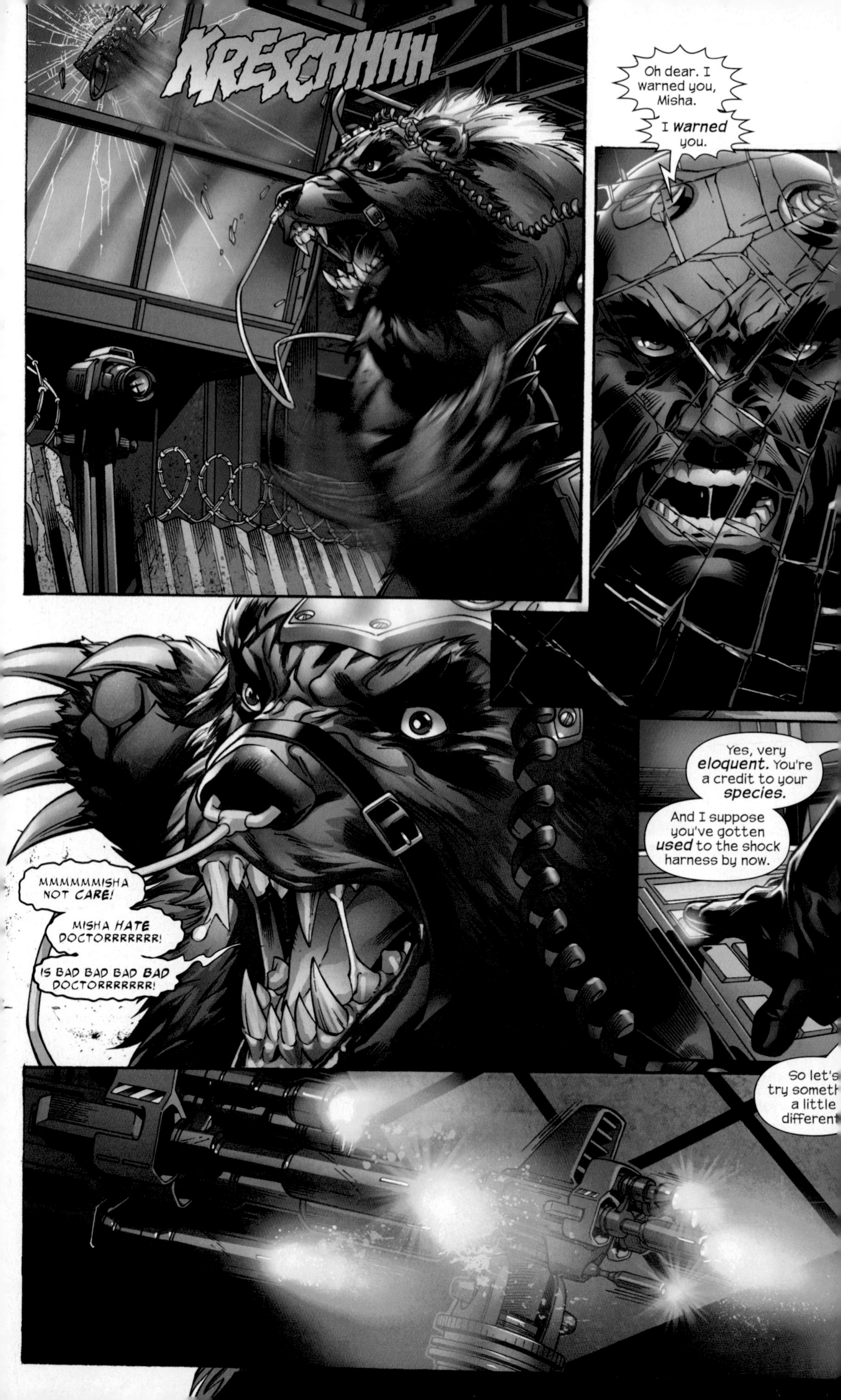
KRESCHHHH
Oh dear. I warned you, Misha.
I warned you.
MMMMMMISHA NOT CARE!
MISHA HATE DOCTORRRRRRR!
IS BAD BAD BAD BAD DOCTORRRRRRR!
Yes, very eloquent. You're a credit to your species.
And I suppose you've gotten used to the shock harness by now.
So let's try someth a little different

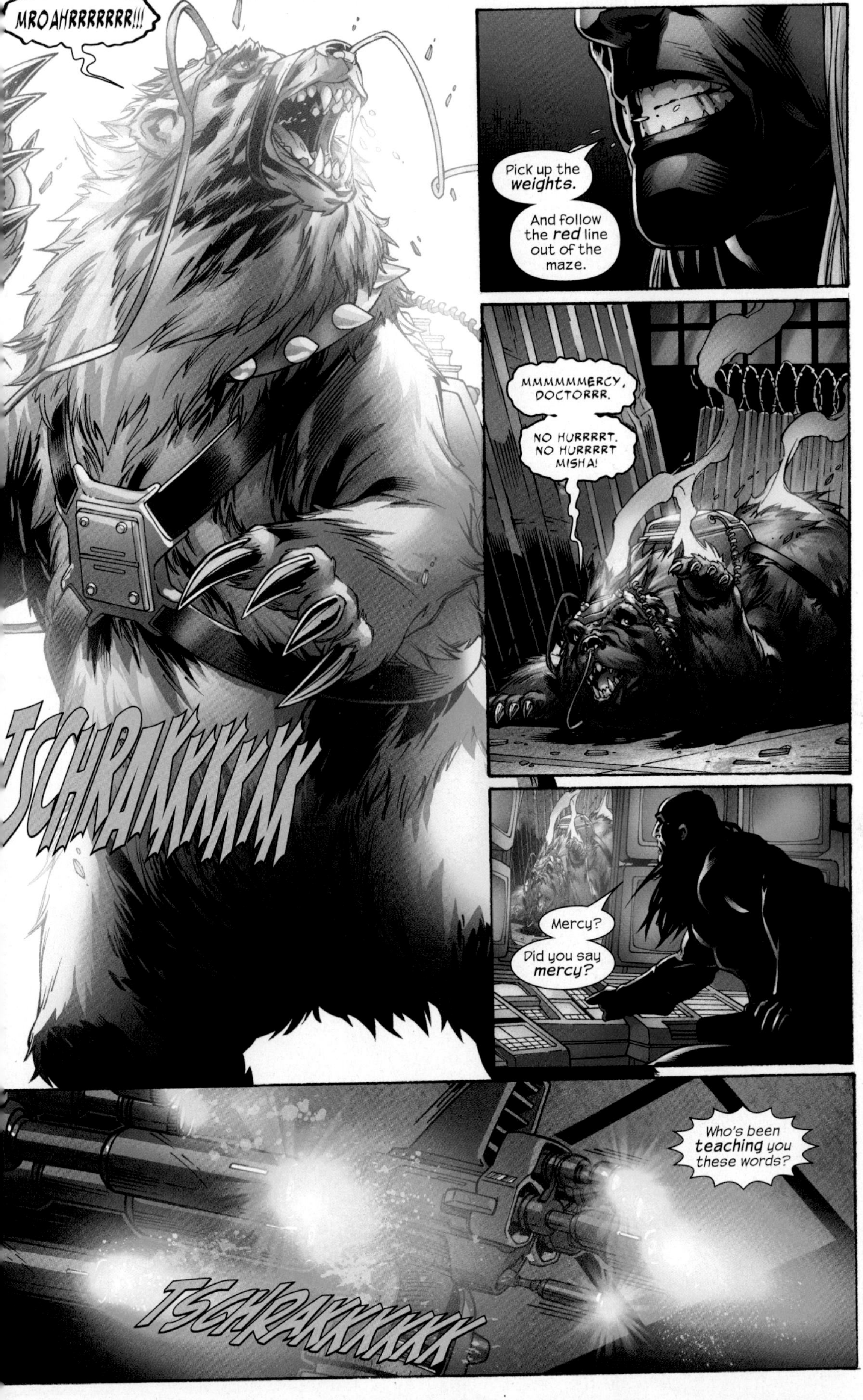
MROAHRRRRRRR!!!
Pick up the weights.
And follow the red line out of the maze.
MMMMMMERCY, DOCTORRR.
NO HURRRRT. NO HURRRRT MISHA!
TSCHRAKKKKK
Mercy?
Did you say mercy?
Who's been teaching you these words?
TSCHRAKKKKKKK

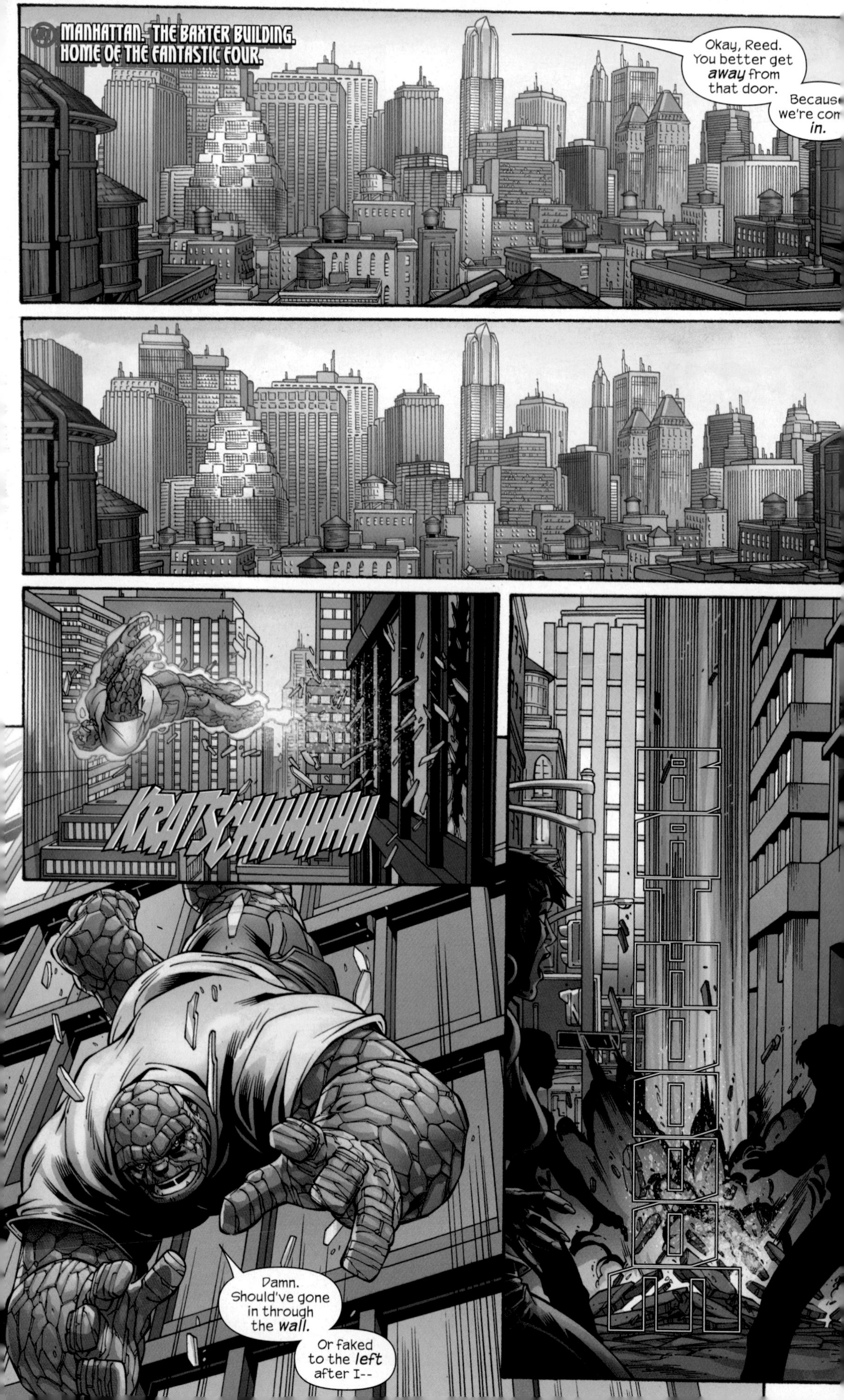
MANHATTAN. THE BAXTER BUILDING. HOME OF THE FANTASTIC FOUR.
Okay, Reed. You better get *away* from that door.
Becaus we're com *in.*
KRATSCHHHHHH
Damn. Should've gone in through the *wall.*
Or faked to the *left* after I--

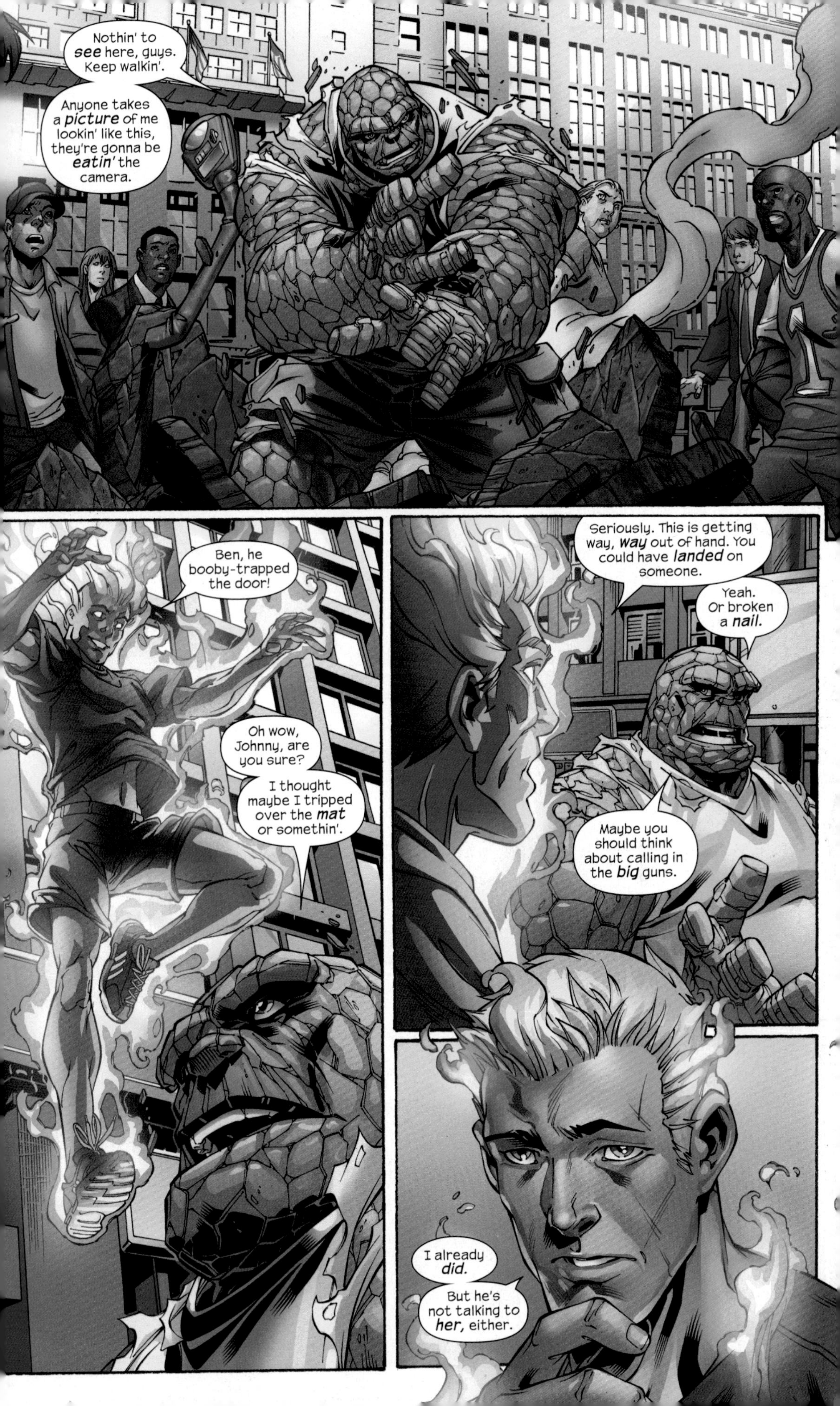
Nothin' to see here, guys. Keep walkin'.
Anyone takes a picture of me lookin' like this, they're gonna be eatin' the camera.
Ben, he booby-trapped the door!
Oh wow, Johnny, are you sure?
I thought maybe I tripped over the mat or somethin'.
Seriously. This is getting way, way out of hand. You could have landed on someone.
Yeah. Or broken a nail.
Maybe you should think about calling in the big guns.
I already did.
But he's not talking to her, either.

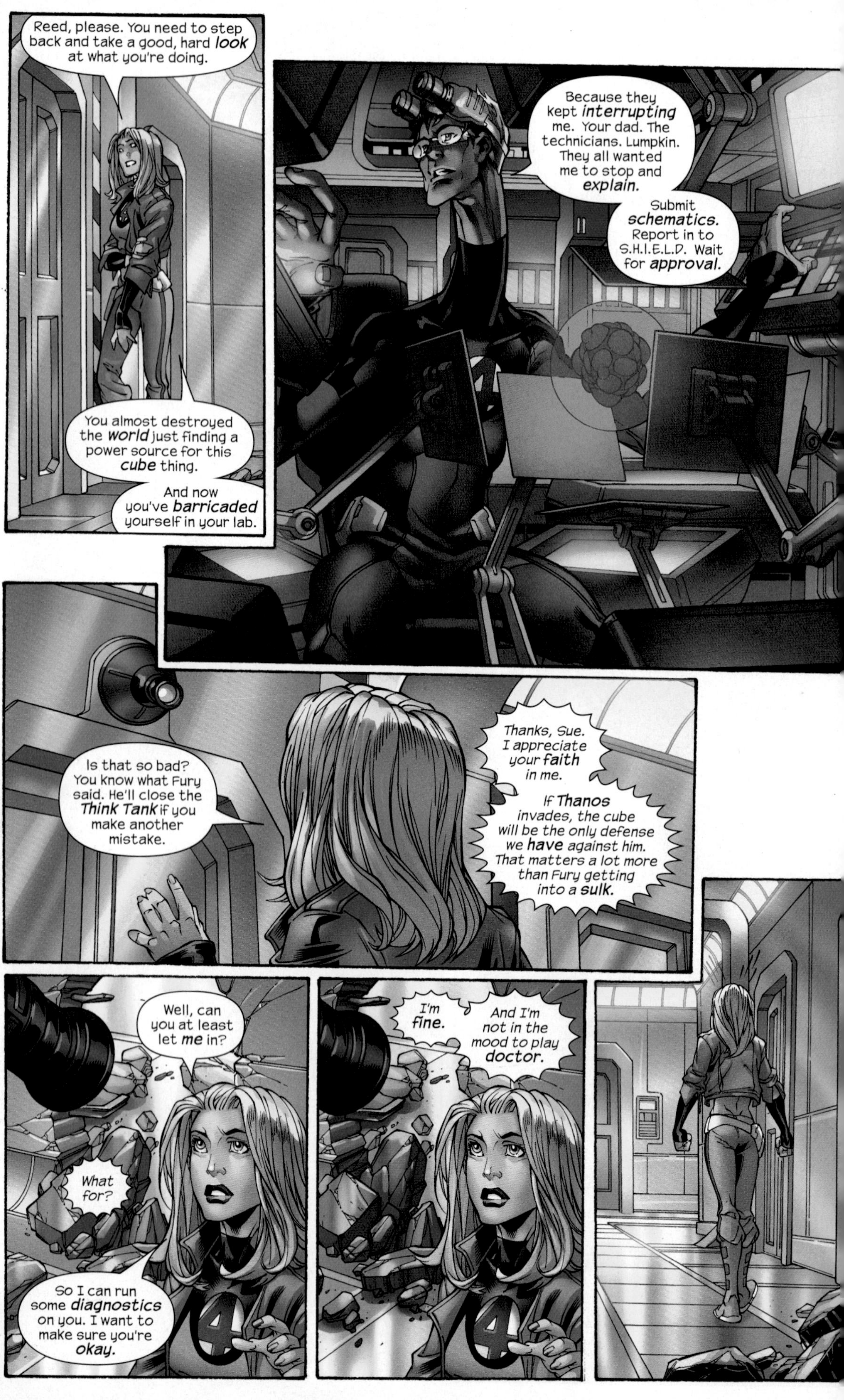
Reed, please. You need to step back and take a good, hard *look* at what you're doing.
You almost destroyed the *world* just finding a power source for this *cube* thing.
And now you've *barricaded* yourself in your lab.
Because they kept *interrupting* me. Your dad. The technicians. Lumpkin. They all wanted me to stop and *explain.*
Submit *schematics.* Report in to S.H.I.E.L.D. Wait for *approval.*
Is that so bad? You know what Fury said. He'll close the *Think Tank* if you make another mistake.
Thanks, Sue. I appreciate your *faith* in me.
If *Thanos* invades, the cube will be the only defense we *have* against him. That matters a lot more than Fury getting into a *sulk.*
Well, can you at least let *me* in?
What for?
So I can run some *diagnostics* on you. I want to make sure you're *okay.*
I'm *fine.*
And I'm not in the mood to play *doctor.*

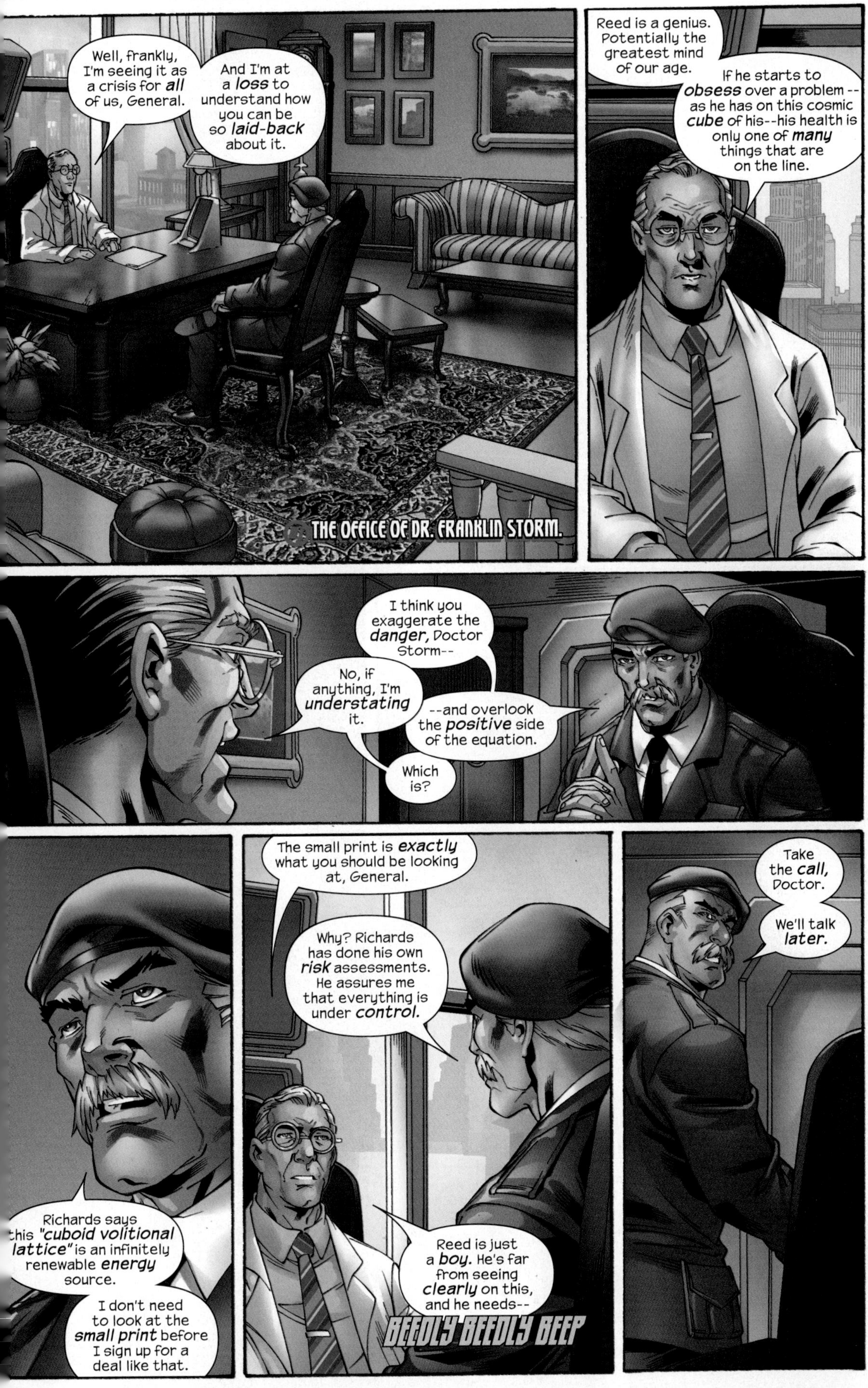
THE OFFICE OF DR. FRANKLIN STORM.
Well, frankly, I'm seeing it as a crisis for all of us, General.
And I'm at a loss to understand how you can be so laid-back about it.
Reed is a genius. Potentially the greatest mind of our age.
If he starts to obsess over a problem -- as he has on this cosmic cube of his--his health is only one of many things that are on the line.
I think you exaggerate the danger, Doctor Storm--
No, if anything, I'm understating it.
--and overlook the positive side of the equation.
Which is?
Richards says this "cuboid volitional lattice" is an infinitely renewable energy source.
I don't need to look at the small print before I sign up for a deal like that.
The small print is exactly what you should be looking at, General.
Why? Richards has done his own risk assessments. He assures me that everything is under control.
Reed is just a boy. He's far from seeing clearly on this, and he needs--
BEEDLY BEEDLY BEEP
Take the call, Doctor.
We'll talk later.

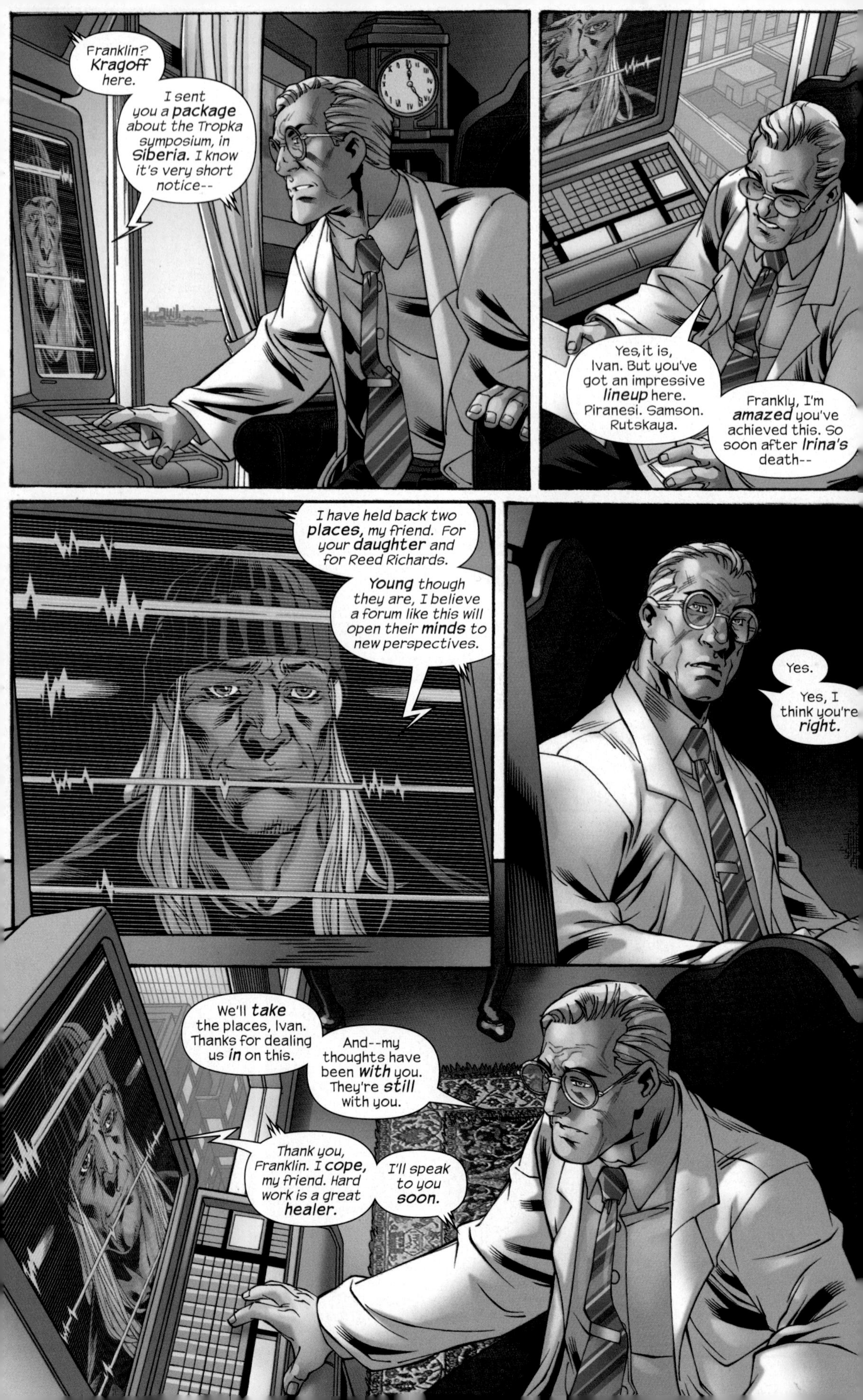

Franklin? Kragoff here.
I sent you a package about the Tropka symposium, in Siberia. I know it's very short notice--
Yes, it is, Ivan. But you've got an impressive lineup here. Piranesi. Samson. Rutskaya.
Frankly, I'm amazed you've achieved this. So soon after Irina's death--
I have held back two places, my friend. For your daughter and for Reed Richards.
Young though they are, I believe a forum like this will open their minds to new perspectives.
Yes.
Yes, I think you're right.
We'll take the places, Ivan. Thanks for dealing us in on this.
And--my thoughts have been with you. They're still with you.
Thank you, Franklin. I cope, my friend. Hard work is a great healer.
I'll speak to you soon.

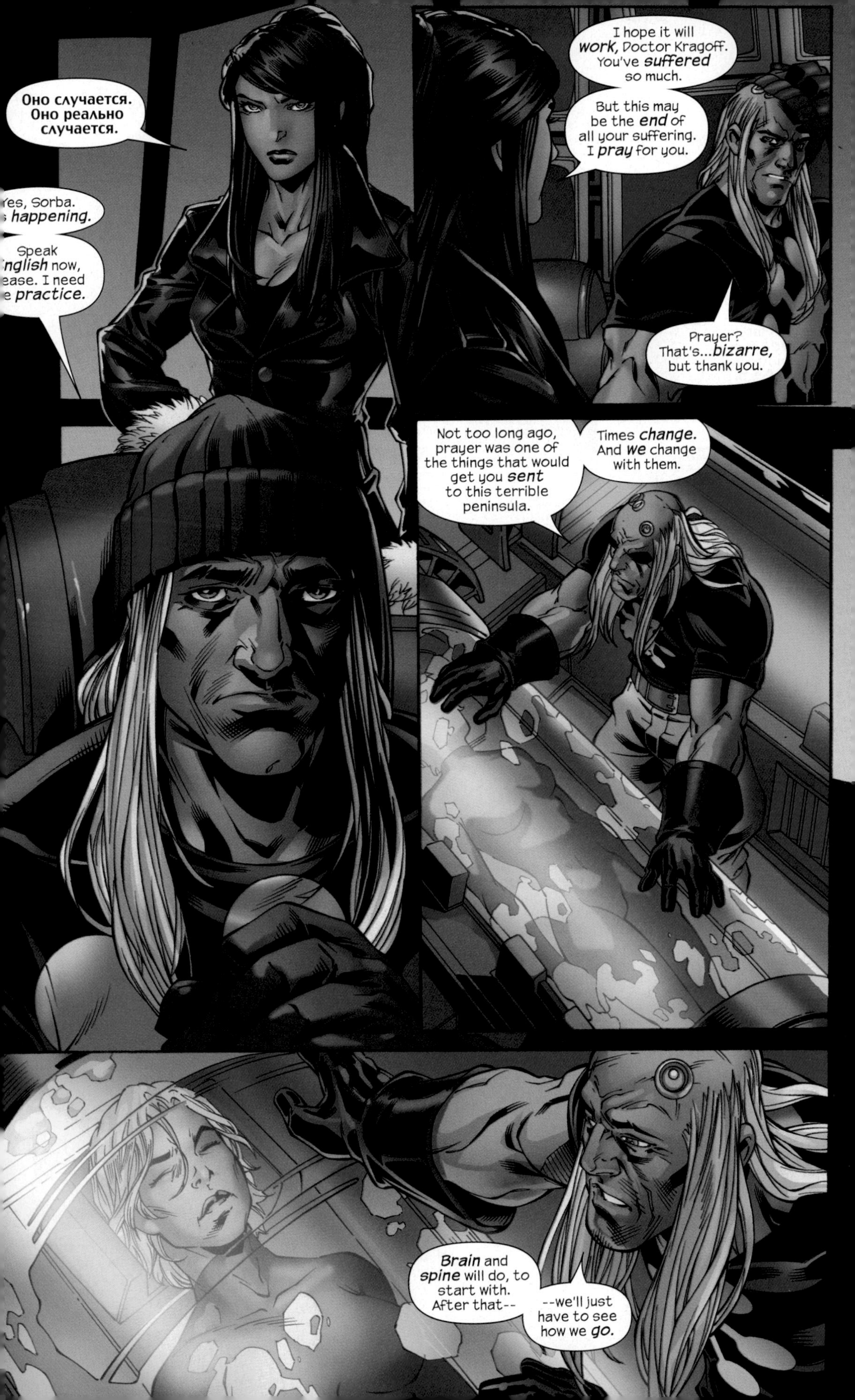

Оно случается. Оно реально случается.
Yes, Sorba. s happening.
Speak English now, ease. I need e practice.
I hope it will work, Doctor Kragoff. You've suffered so much.
But this may be the end of all your suffering. I pray for you.
Prayer? That's...bizarre, but thank you.
Not too long ago, prayer was one of the things that would get you sent to this terrible peninsula.
Times change. And we change with them.
Brain and spine will do, to start with. After that--
--we'll just have to see how we go.

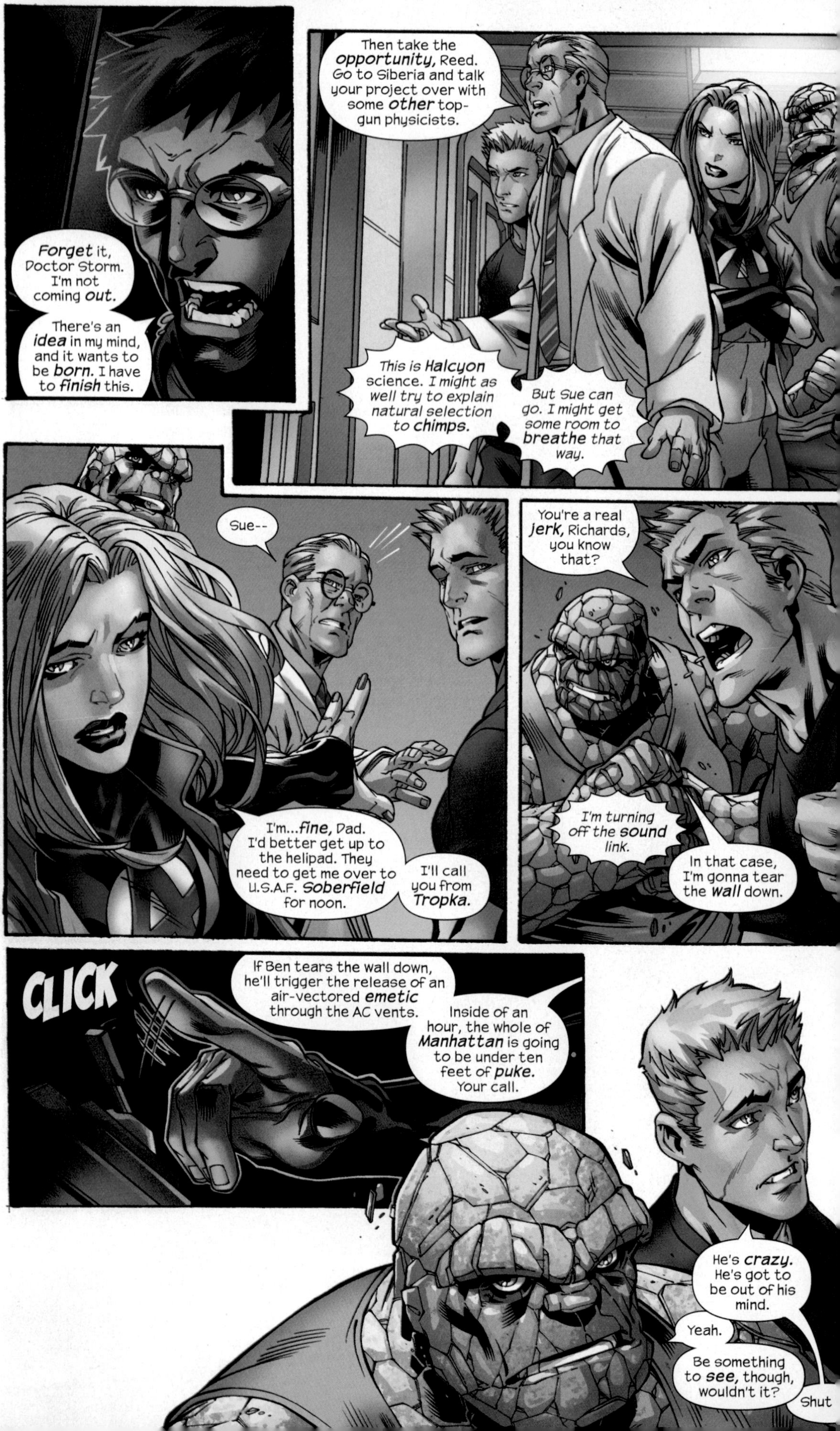

Forget it, Doctor Storm. I'm not coming out.
There's an idea in my mind, and it wants to be born. I have to finish this.
Then take the opportunity, Reed. Go to Siberia and talk your project over with some other top-gun physicists.
This is Halcyon science. I might as well try to explain natural selection to chimps.
But Sue can go. I might get some room to breathe that way.
Sue--
I'm...fine, Dad. I'd better get up to the helipad. They need to get me over to U.S.A.F. Soberfield for noon.
I'll call you from Tropka.
You're a real jerk, Richards, you know that?
I'm turning off the sound link.
In that case, I'm gonna tear the wall down.
CLICK
If Ben tears the wall down, he'll trigger the release of an air-vectored emetic through the AC vents.
Inside of an hour, the whole of Manhattan is going to be under ten feet of puke. Your call.
He's crazy. He's got to be out of his mind.
Yeah.
Be something to see, though, wouldn't it?
Shut

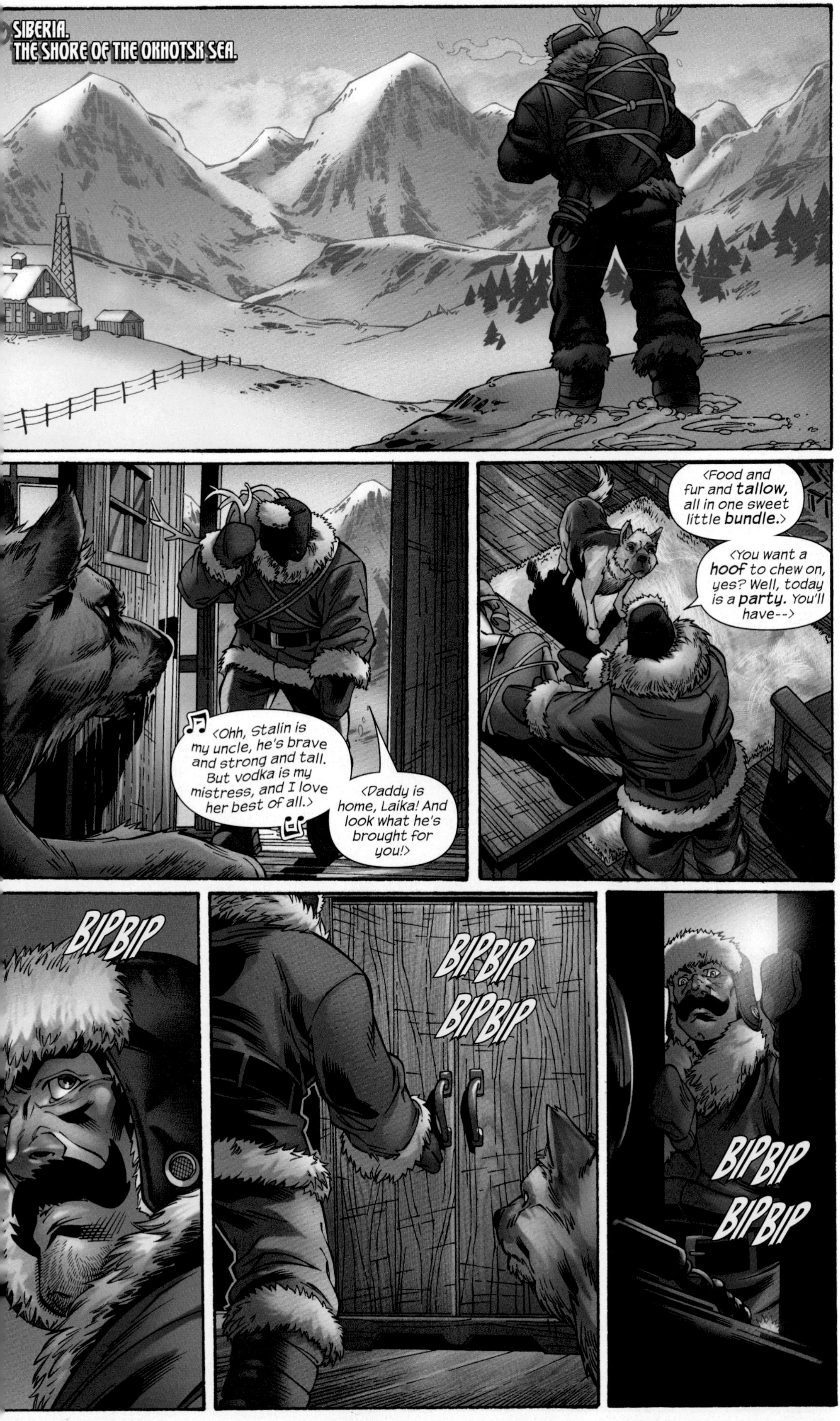
SIBERIA.
THE SHORE OF THE OKHOTSK SEA.
<Ohh, Stalin is my uncle, he's brave and strong and tall. But vodka is my mistress, and I love her best of all.>
<Daddy is home, Laika! And look what he's brought for you!>
<Food and fur and tallow, all in one sweet little bundle.>
<You want a hoof to chew on, yes? Well, today is a party. You'll have-->
BIPBIP
BIPBIP
BIPBIP
BIPBIP
BIPBIP

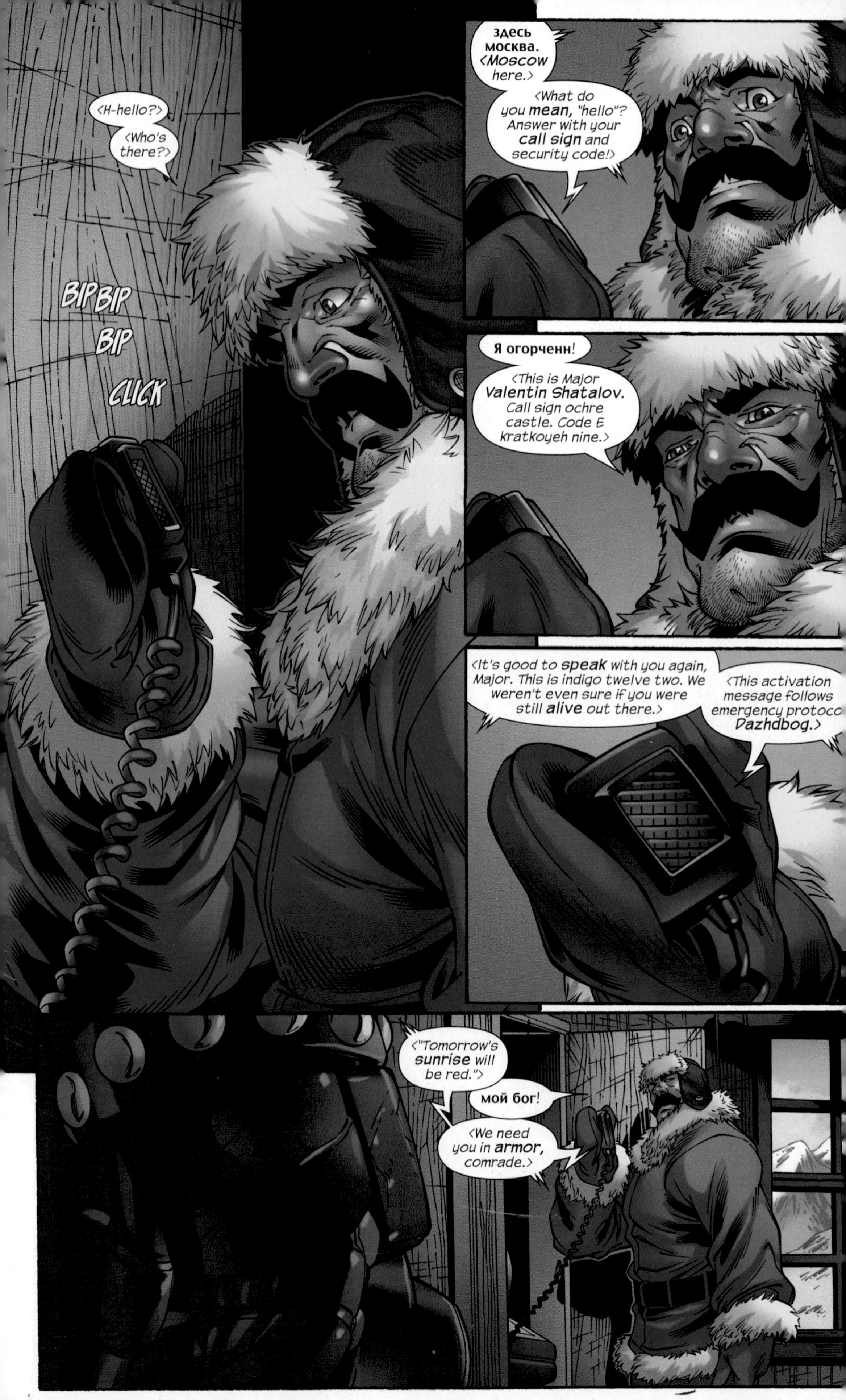

<H-hello?>
<Who's there?>
BIP BIP
BIP
CLICK
здесь москва. <Moscow here.>
<What do you mean, "hello"? Answer with your call sign and security code!>
Я огорченн!
<This is Major Valentin Shatalov. Call sign ochre castle. Code E kratkoyeh nine.>
<It's good to speak with you again, Major. This is indigo twelve two. We weren't even sure if you were still alive out there.>
<This activation message follows emergency protoco Dazhdbog.>
<"Tomorrow's sunrise will be red.">
мой бог!
<We need you in armor, comrade.>

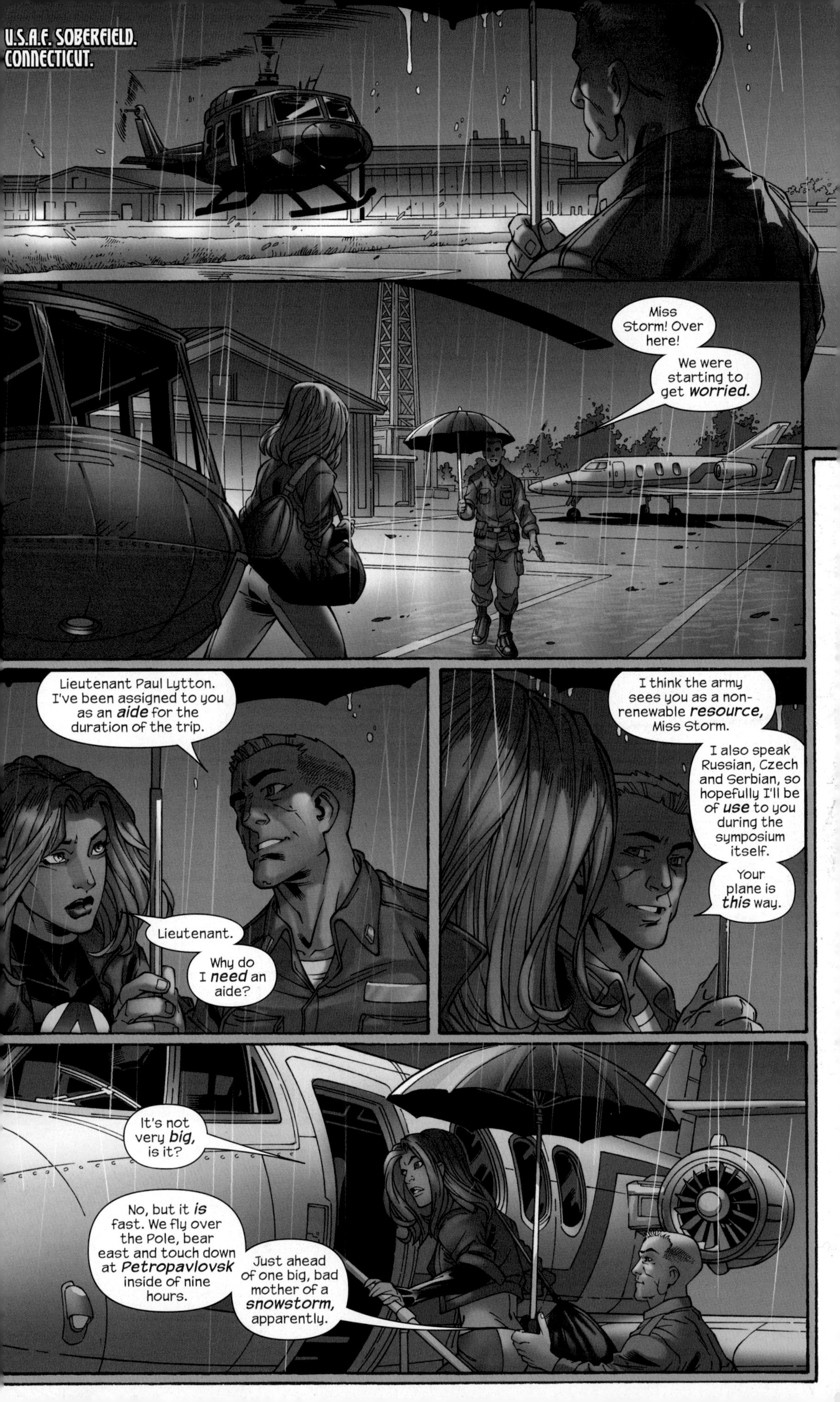
U.S.A.F. SOBERFIELD. CONNECTICUT.
Miss Storm! Over here!
We were starting to get worried.
Lieutenant Paul Lytton. I've been assigned to you as an aide for the duration of the trip.
Lieutenant.
Why do I need an aide?
I think the army sees you as a non-renewable resource, Miss Storm.
I also speak Russian, Czech and Serbian, so hopefully I'll be of use to you during the symposium itself.
Your plane is this way.
It's not very big, is it?
No, but it is fast. We fly over the Pole, bear east and touch down at Petropavlovsk inside of nine hours.
Just ahead of one big, bad mother of a snowstorm, apparently.

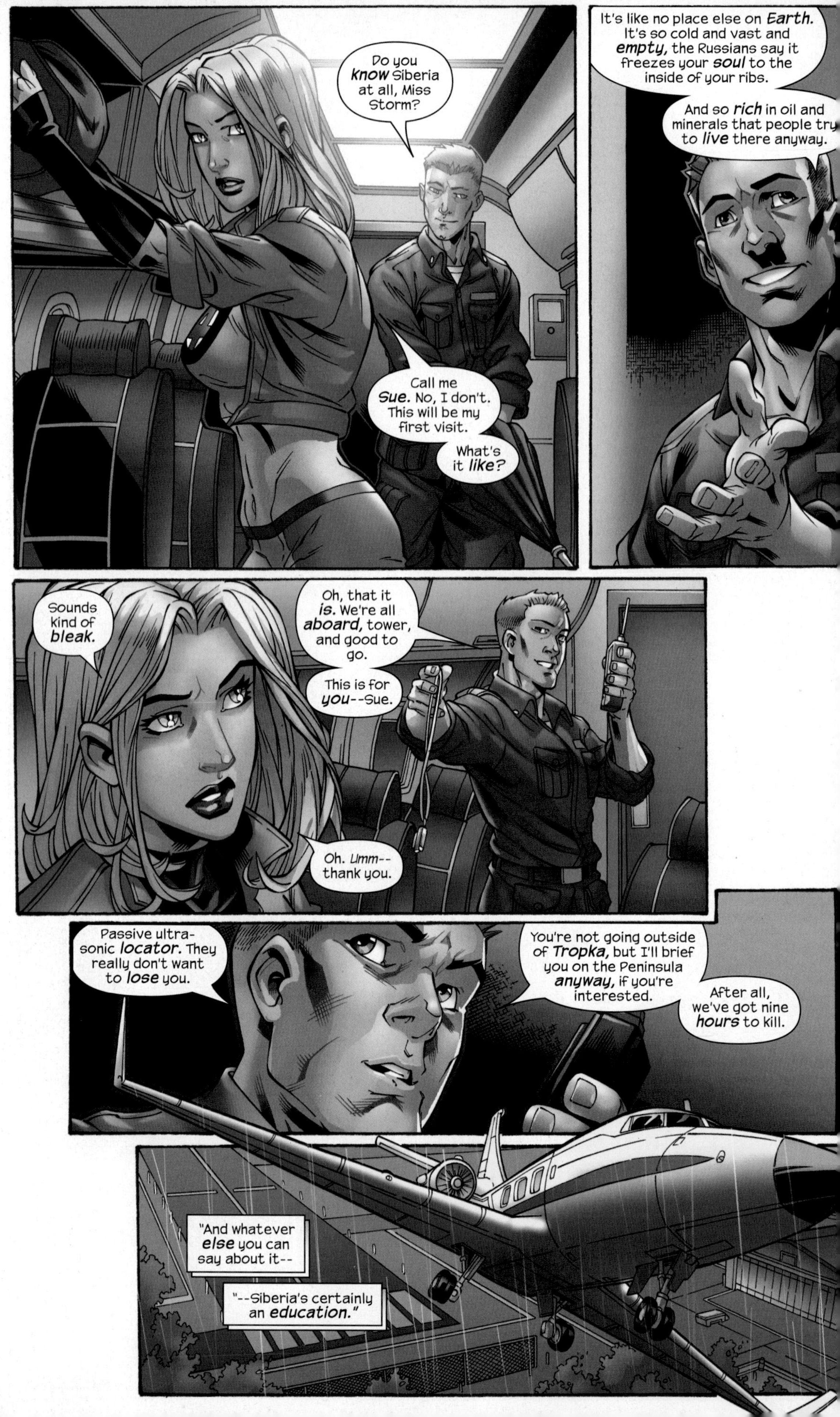
Do you know Siberia at all, Miss Storm?
Call me Sue. No, I don't. This will be my first visit.
What's it like?
It's like no place else on Earth. It's so cold and vast and empty, the Russians say it freezes your soul to the inside of your ribs.
And so rich in oil and minerals that people try to live there anyway.
Sounds kind of bleak.
Oh, that it is. We're all aboard, tower, and good to go.
This is for you--Sue.
Oh. Umm-- thank you.
Passive ultra-sonic locator. They really don't want to lose you.
You're not going outside of Tropka, but I'll brief you on the Peninsula anyway, if you're interested.
After all, we've got nine hours to kill.
"And whatever else you can say about it--
"--Siberia's certainly an education."

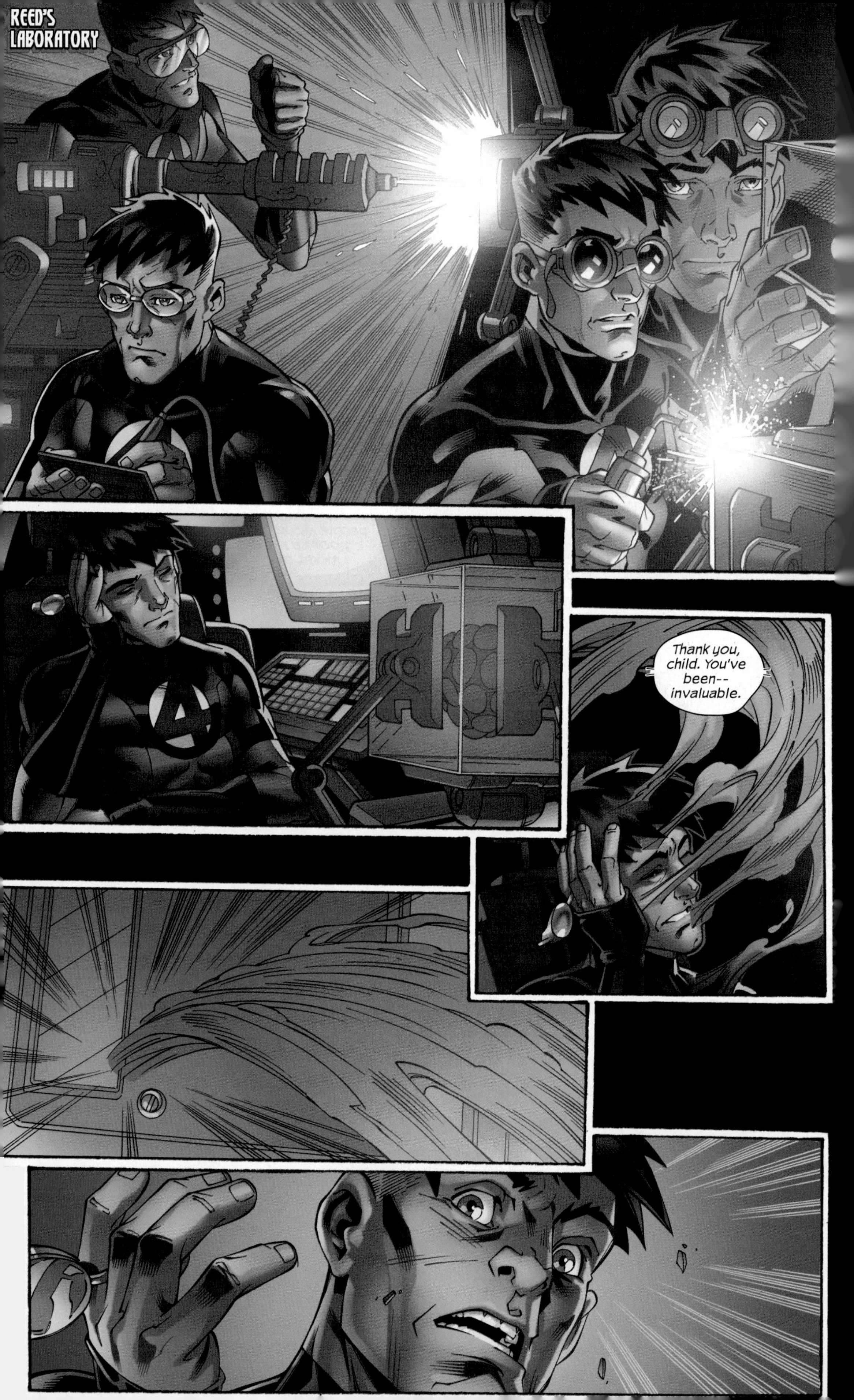
REED'S LABORATORY
Thank you, child. You've been-- invaluable.

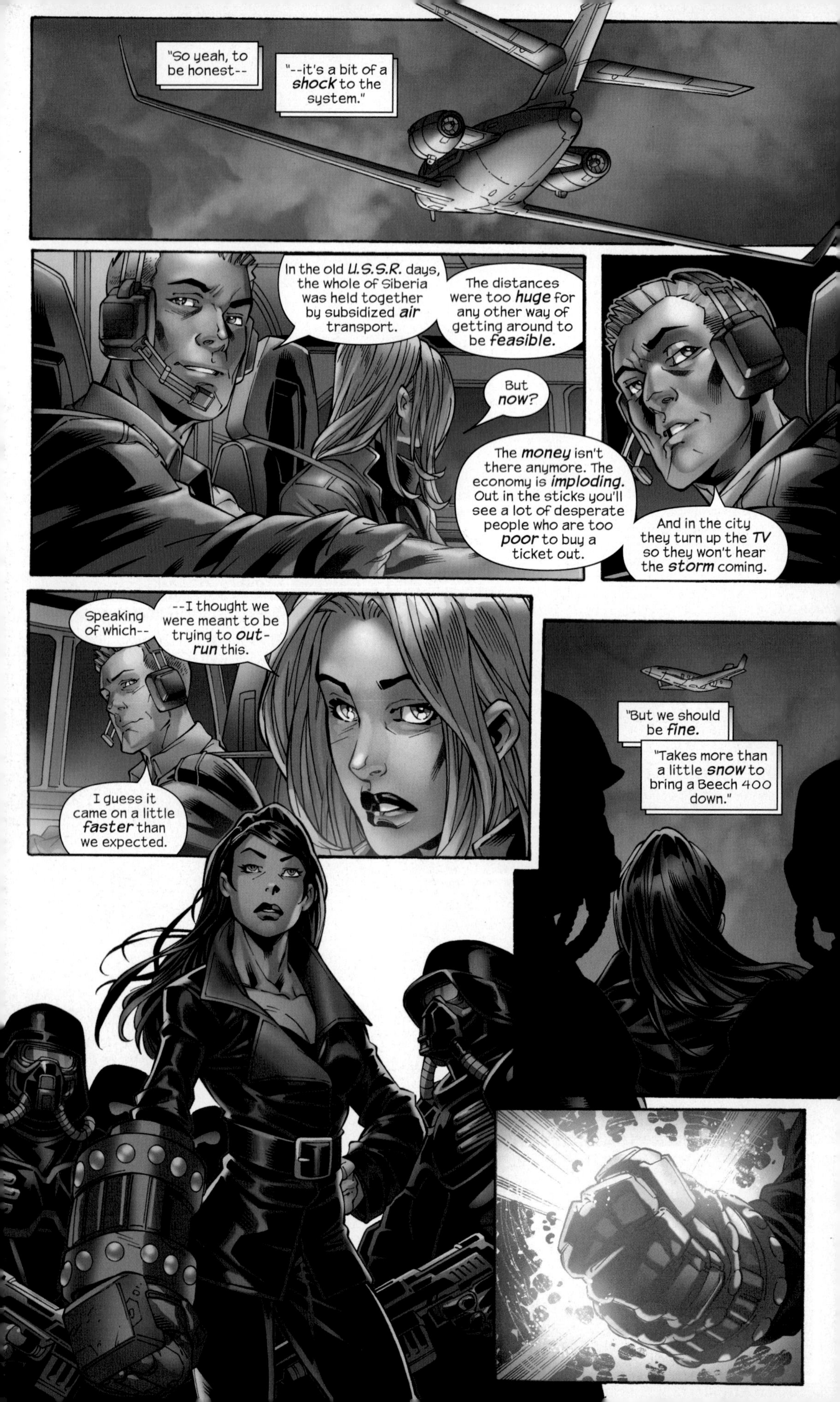
"So yeah, to be honest--
"--it's a bit of a *shock* to the system."
In the old *U.S.S.R.* days, the whole of Siberia was held together by subsidized *air* transport.
The distances were too *huge* for any other way of getting around to be *feasible.*
But *now?*
The *money* isn't there anymore. The economy is *imploding.* Out in the sticks you'll see a lot of desperate people who are too *poor* to buy a ticket out.
And in the city they turn up the *TV* so they won't hear the *storm* coming.
Speaking of which--
--I thought we were meant to be trying to *out-run* this.
I guess it came on a little *faster* than we expected.
"But we should be *fine.*
"Takes more than a little *snow* to bring a Beech 400 down."

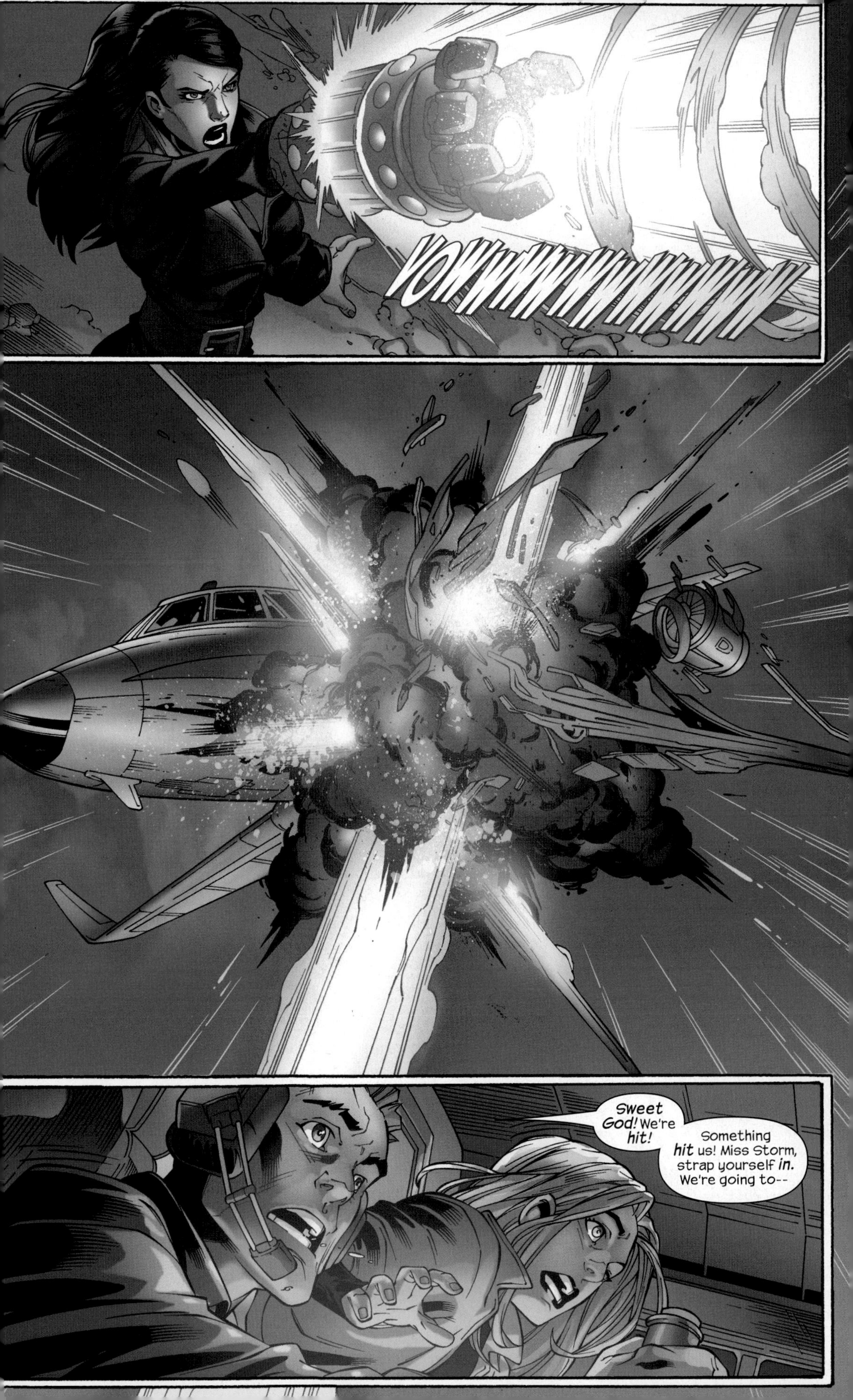
YOWWWWWWWWWWWWWWW
Sweet God! We're hit!
Something hit us! Miss Storm, strap yourself in. We're going to--

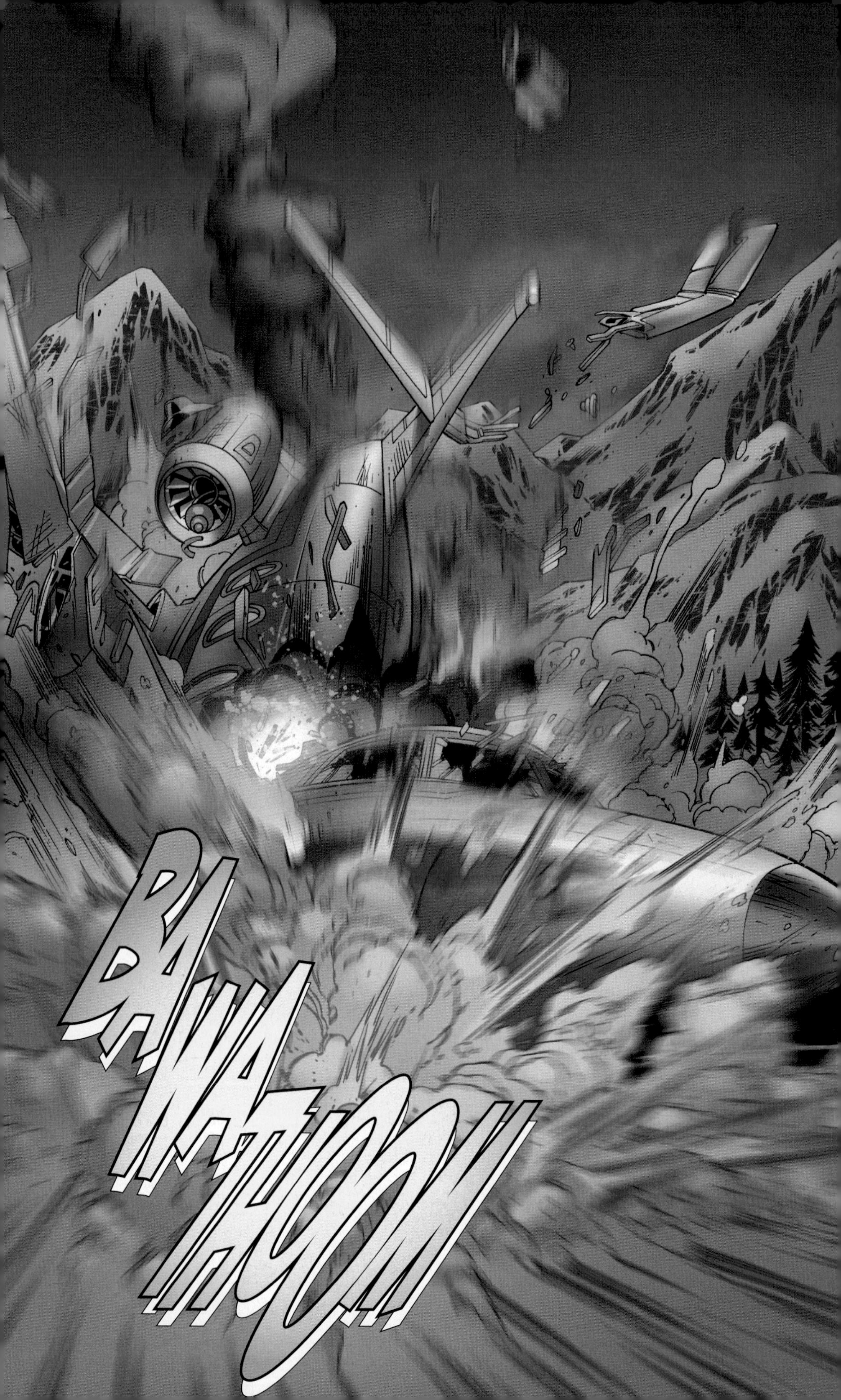
BWATHOOM

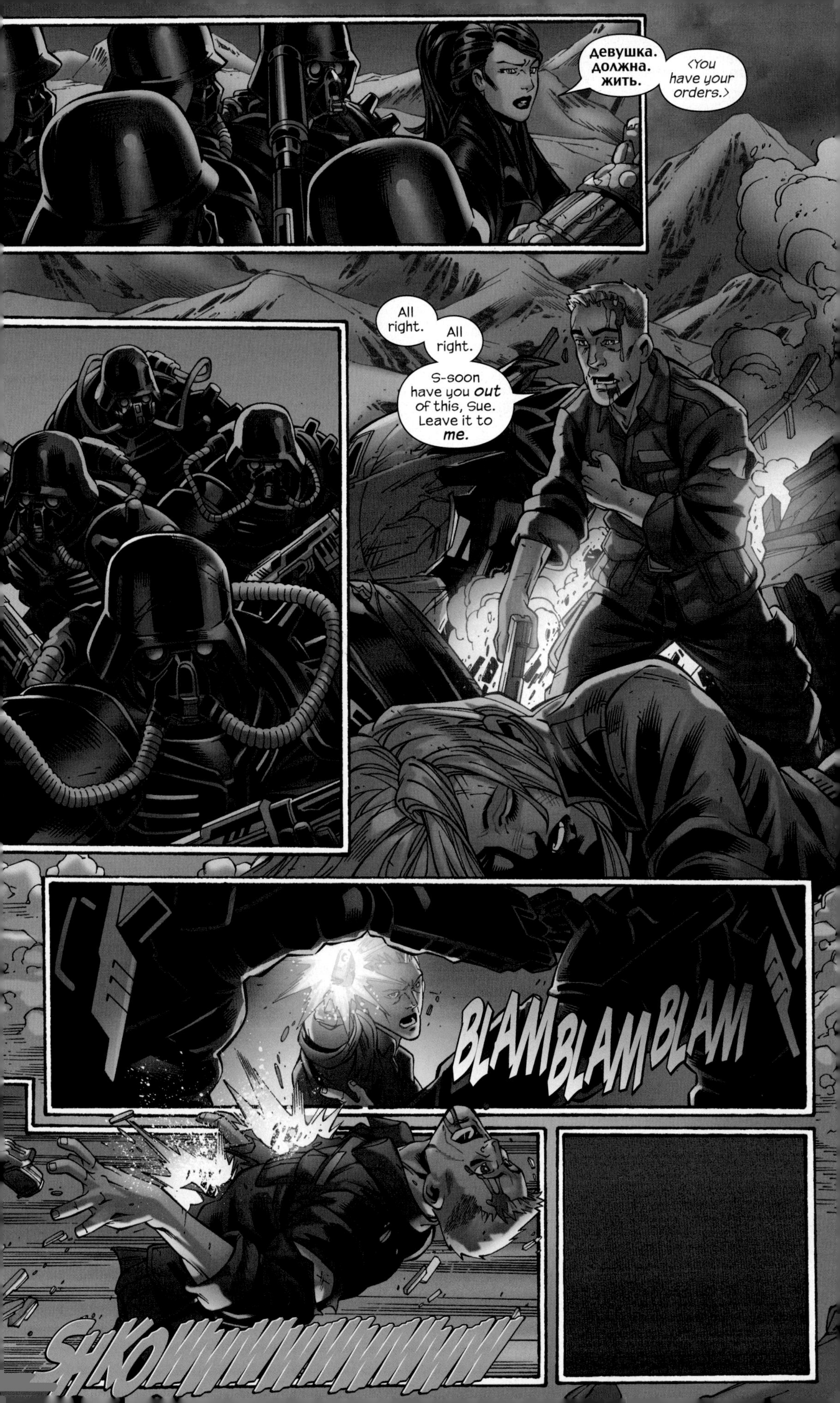
девушка.
должна.
жить.
<You have your orders.>
All right.
All right.
S-soon have you out of this, Sue. Leave it to me.
BLAMBLAMBLAM
SHKOWWWWWWWWWWW

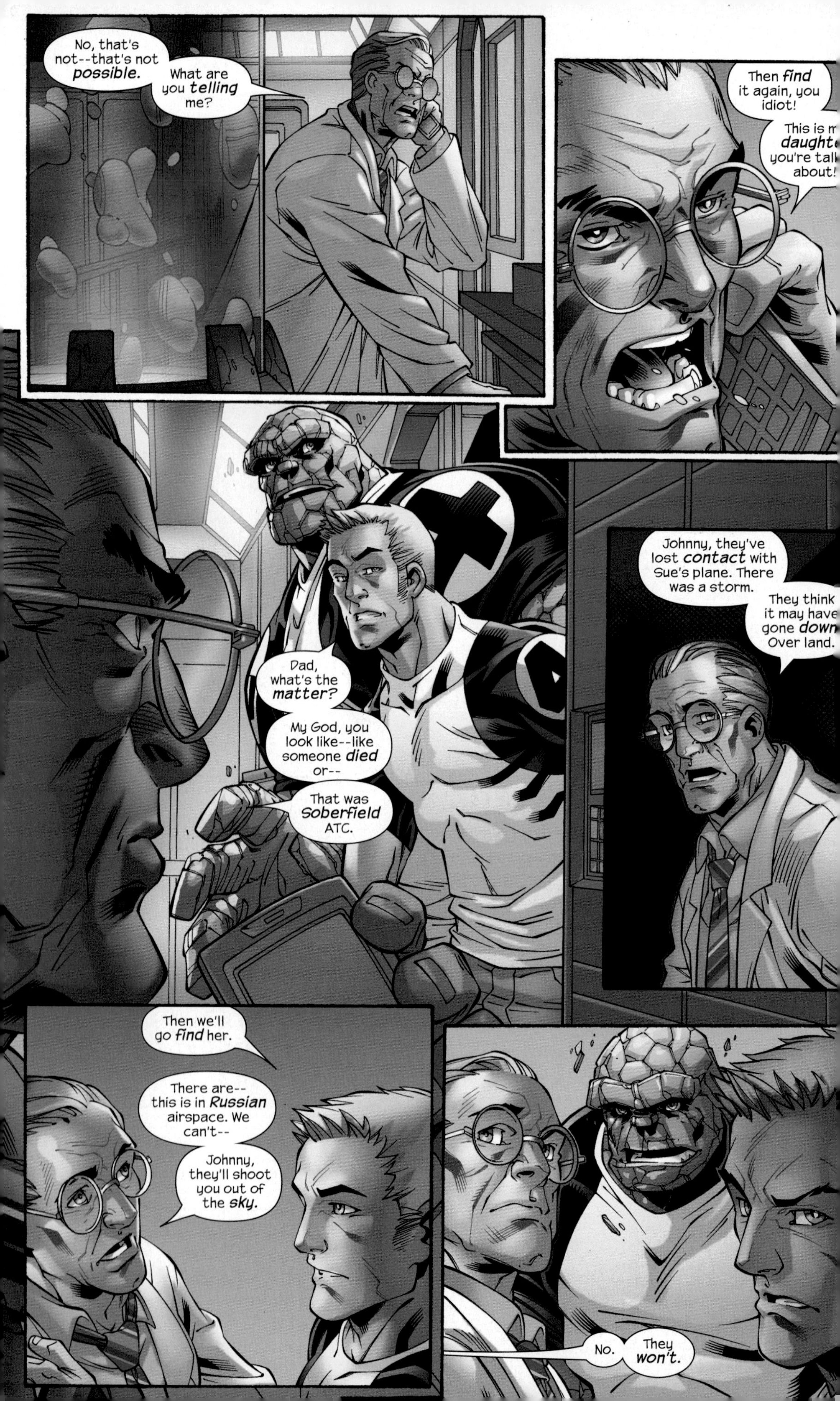
No, that's not--that's not possible.
What are you telling me?
Then find it again, you idiot!
This is m daught you're tal about!
Dad, what's the matter?
My God, you look like--like someone died or--
That was Soberfield ATC.
Johnny, they've lost contact with Sue's plane. There was a storm.
They think it may have gone down Over land.
Then we'll go find her.
There are-- this is in Russian airspace. We can't--
Johnny, they'll shoot you out of the sky.
No.
They won't.

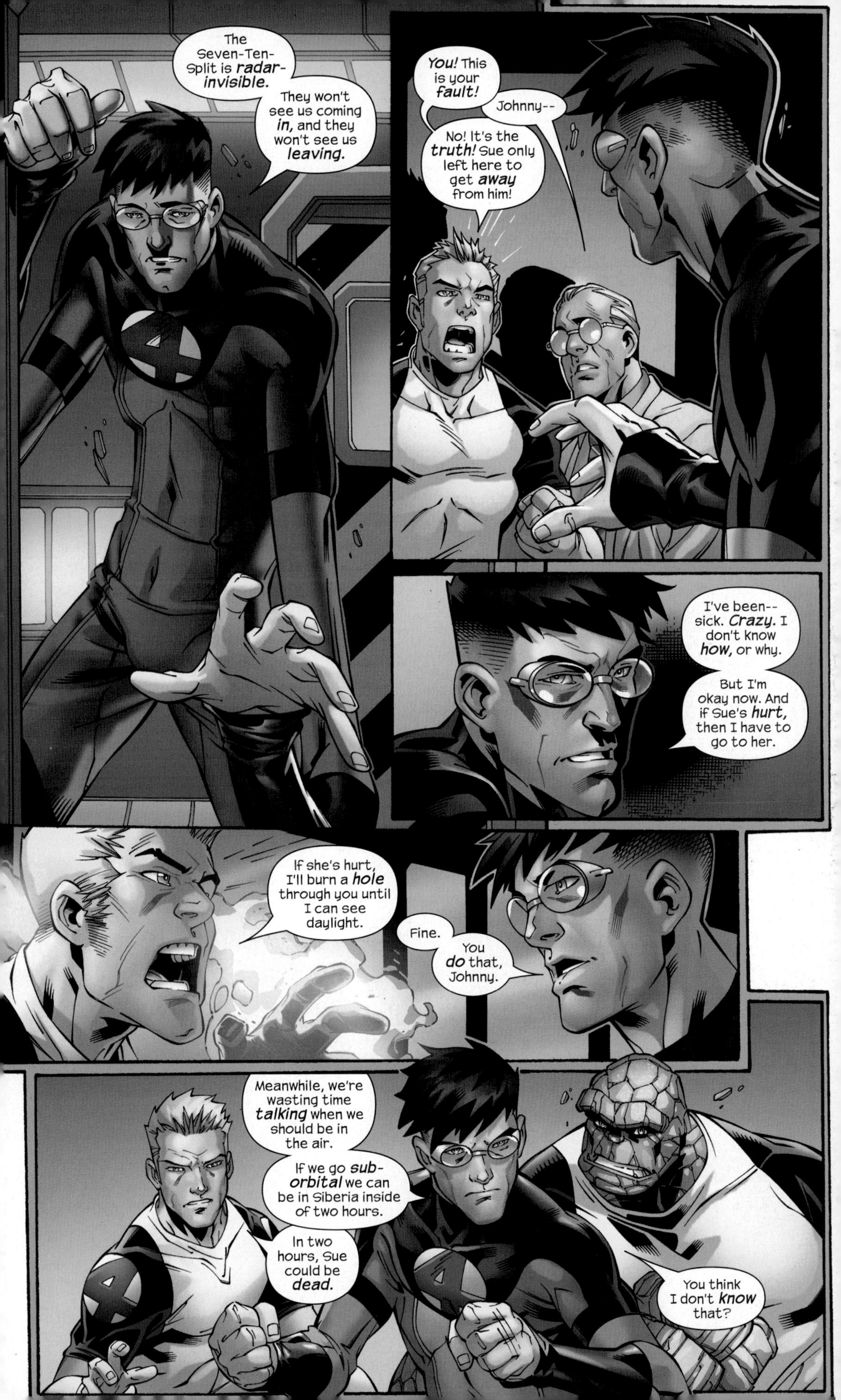

The Seven-Ten-Split is radar-invisible.
They won't see us coming in, and they won't see us leaving.
You! This is your fault!
Johnny--
No! It's the truth! Sue only left here to get away from him!
I've been--sick. Crazy. I don't know how, or why.
But I'm okay now. And if Sue's hurt, then I have to go to her.
If she's hurt, I'll burn a hole through you until I can see daylight.
Fine.
You do that, Johnny.
Meanwhile, we're wasting time talking when we should be in the air.
If we go sub-orbital we can be in Siberia inside of two hours.
In two hours, Sue could be dead.
You think I don't know that?

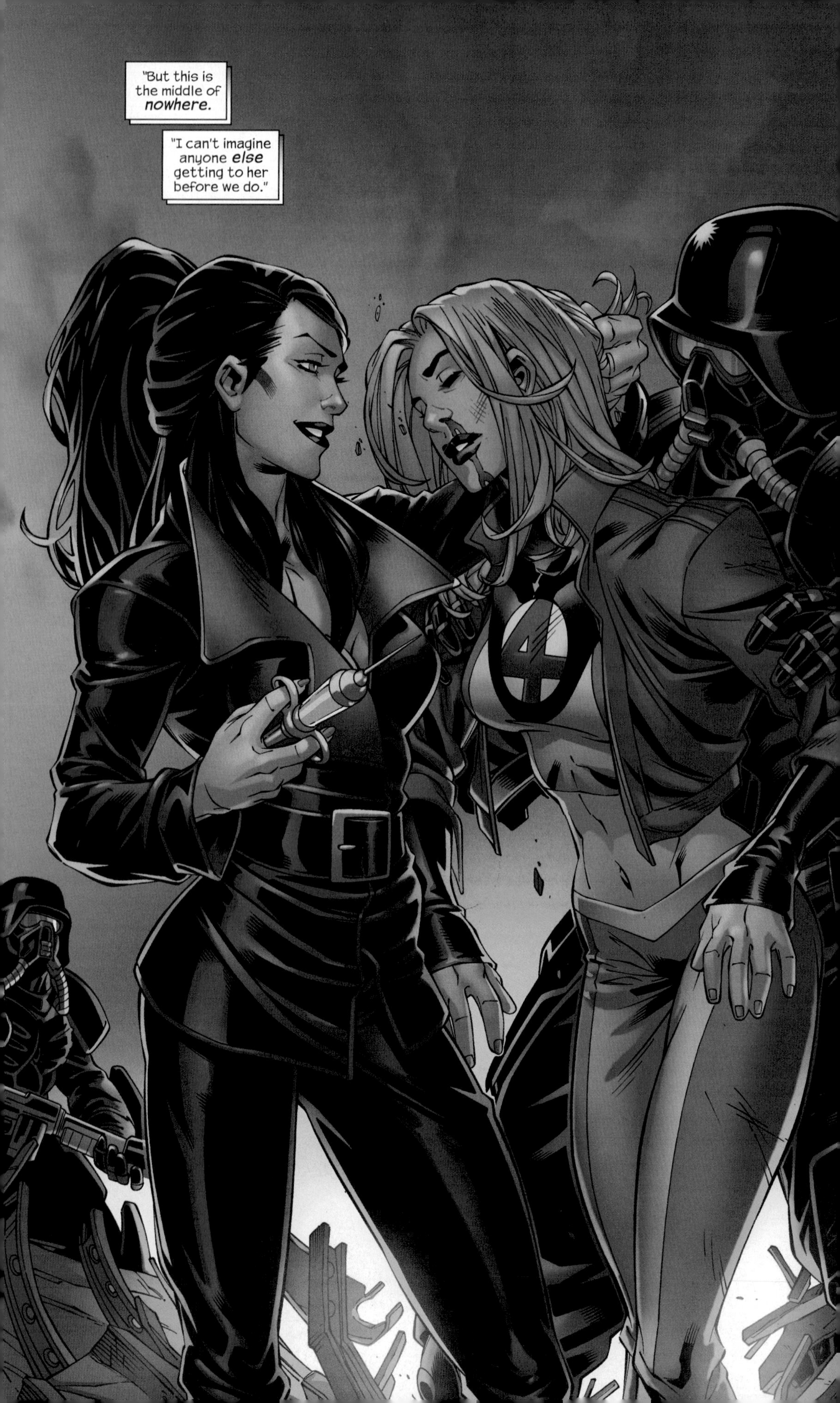
"But this is the middle of *nowhere.*
"I can't imagine anyone *else* getting to her before we do."

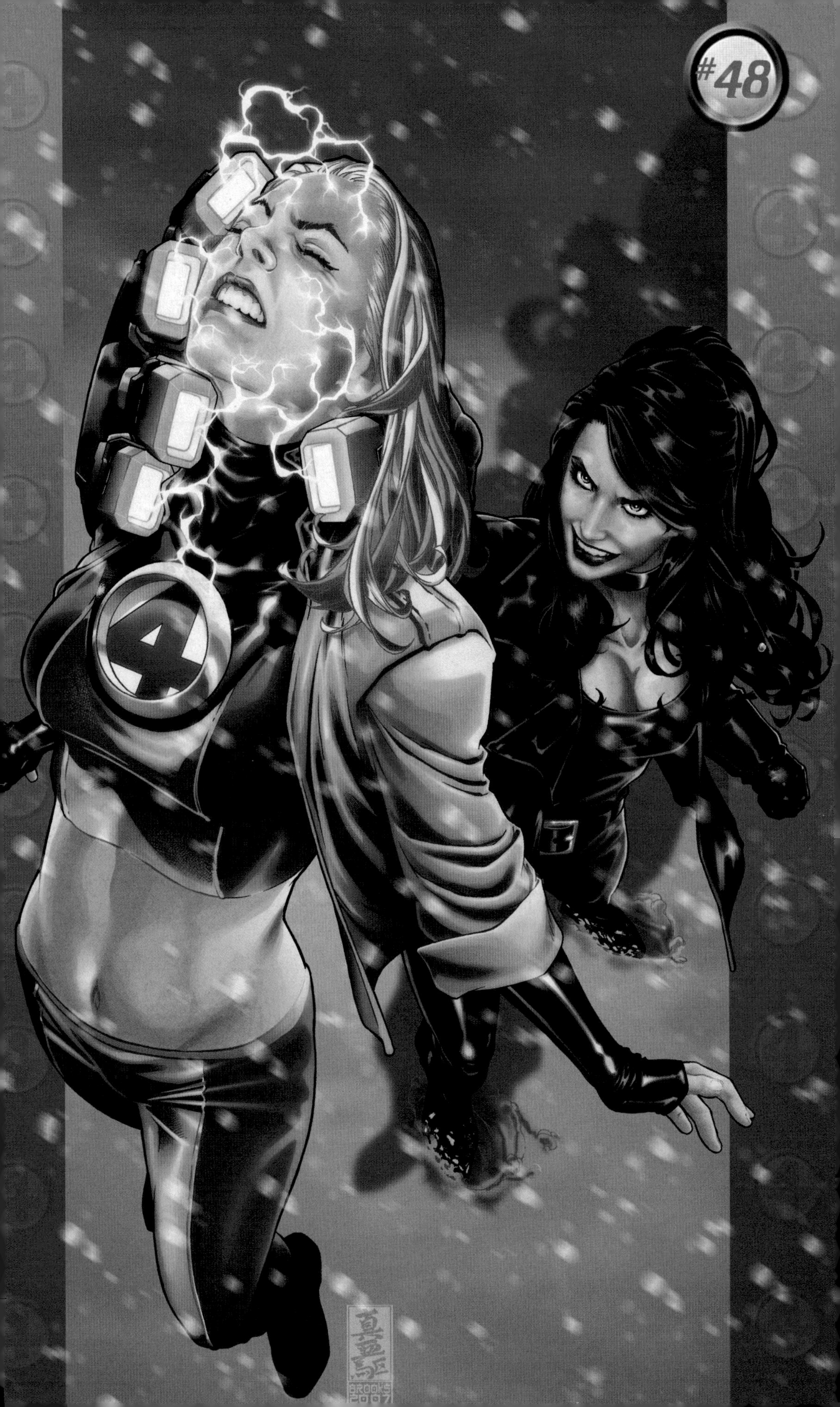
#48
BROOKS
2007

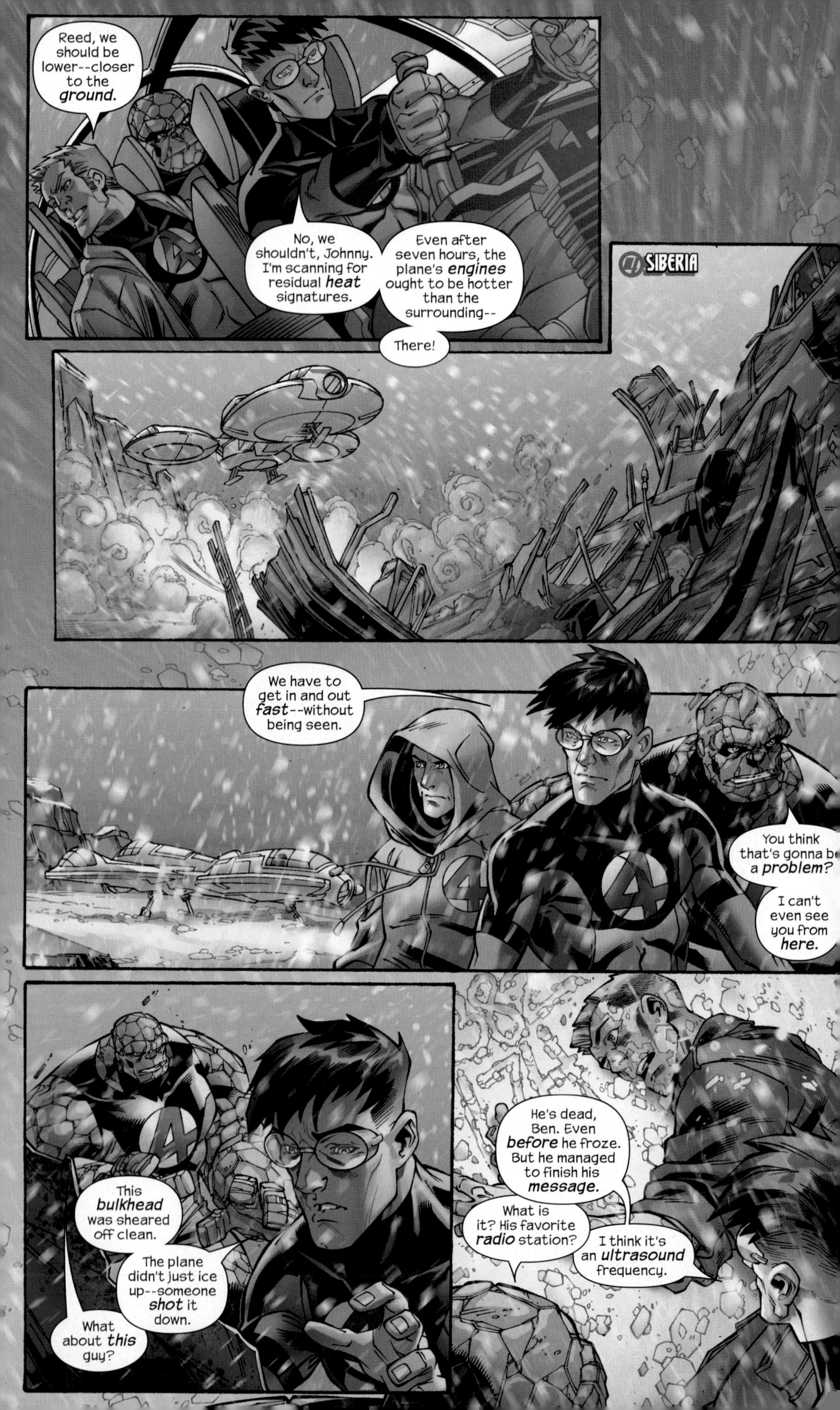
Reed, we should be lower--closer to the ground.
No, we shouldn't, Johnny. I'm scanning for residual heat signatures.
Even after seven hours, the plane's engines ought to be hotter than the surrounding--
There!
SIBERIA
We have to get in and out fast--without being seen.
You think that's gonna be a problem?
I can't even see you from here.
This bulkhead was sheared off clean.
The plane didn't just ice up--someone shot it down.
What about this guy?
He's dead, Ben. Even before he froze. But he managed to finish his message.
What is it? His favorite radio station?
I think it's an ultrasound frequency.

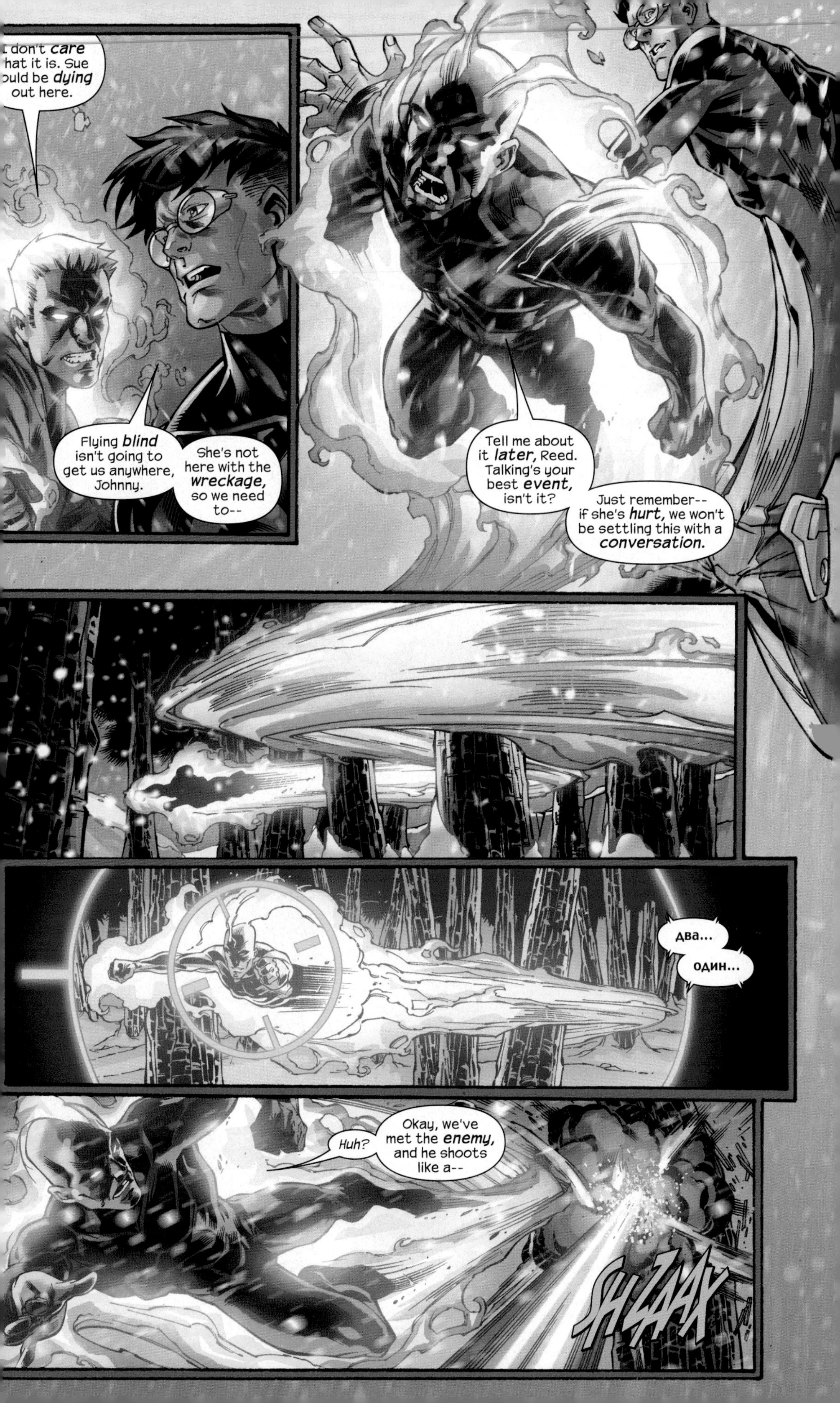

I don't care hat it is. Sue ould be dying out here.
Flying blind isn't going to get us anywhere, Johnny.
She's not here with the wreckage, so we need to--
Tell me about it later, Reed. Talking's your best event, isn't it?
Just remember-- if she's hurt, we won't be settling this with a conversation.
Два...
Один...
Huh?
Okay, we've met the enemy, and he shoots like a--
SHZAAX

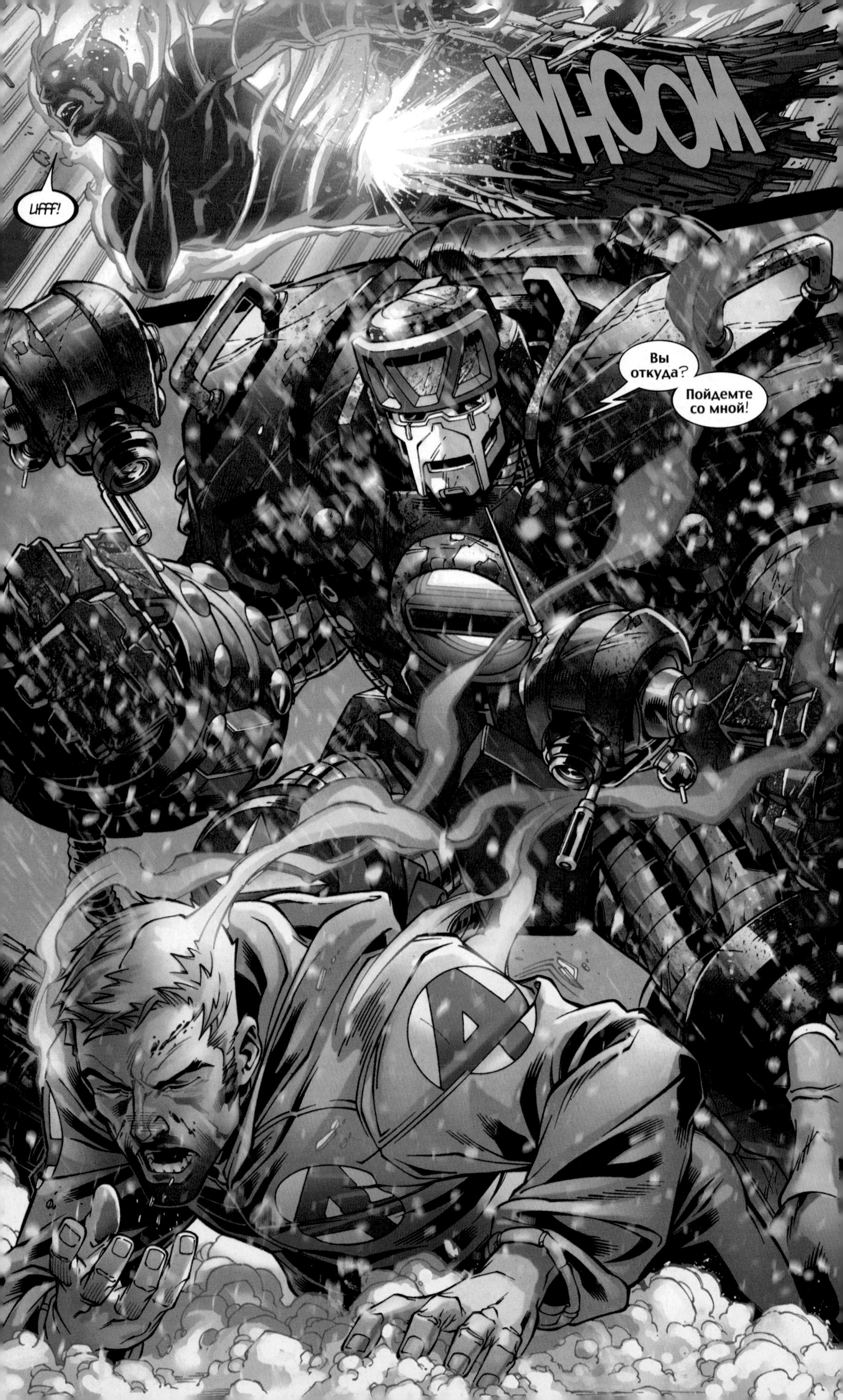
WHOOM
Цfff!
Вы откуда?
Пойдемте со мной!

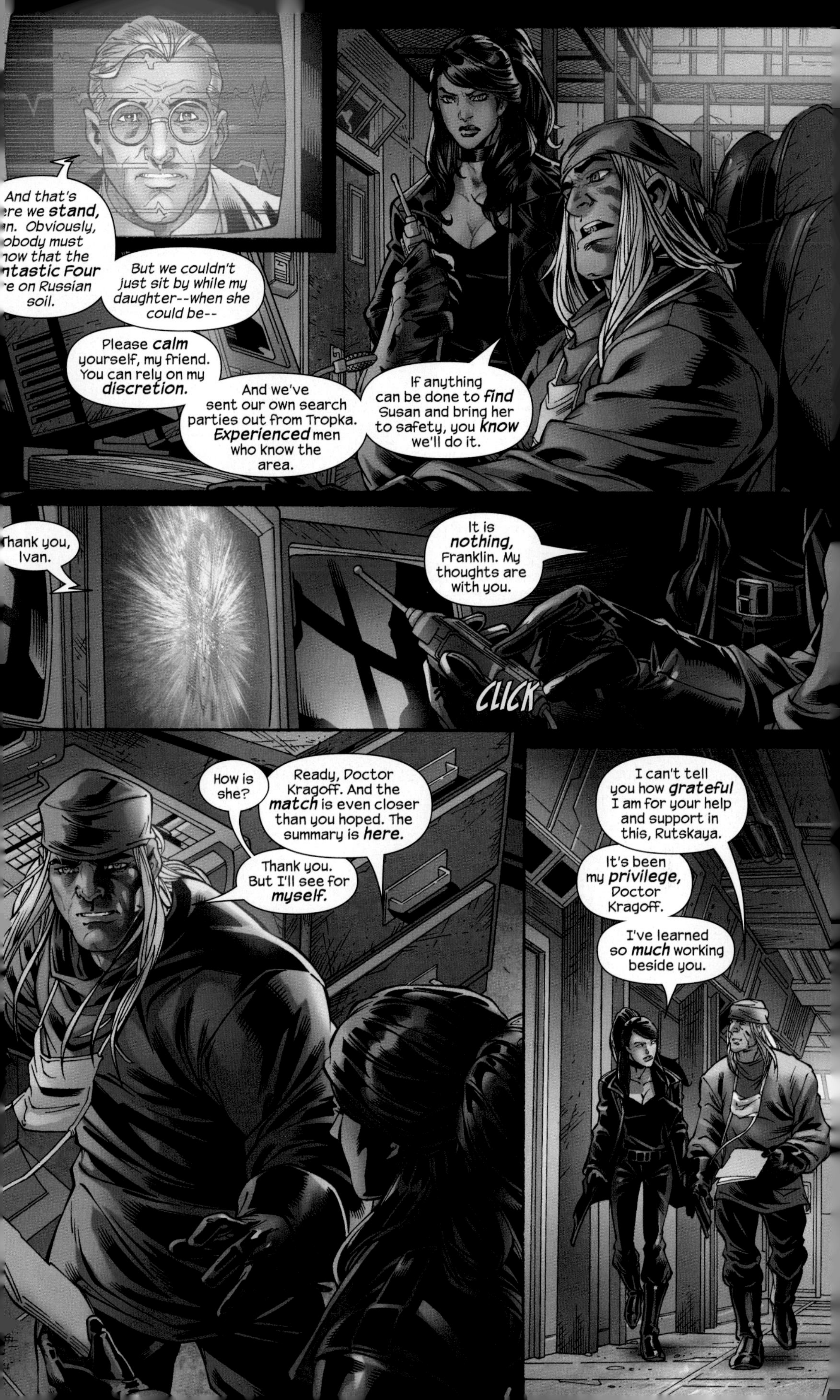
And that's
ere we stand,
n. Obviously,
obody must
now that the
ntastic Four
e on Russian
soil.
But we couldn't
just sit by while my
daughter--when she
could be--
Please calm
yourself, my friend.
You can rely on my
discretion.
And we've
sent our own search
parties out from Tropka.
Experienced men
who know the
area.
If anything
can be done to find
Susan and bring her
to safety, you know
we'll do it.
Thank you,
Ivan.
It is
nothing,
Franklin. My
thoughts are
with you.
CLICK
How is
she?
Ready, Doctor
Kragoff. And the
match is even closer
than you hoped. The
summary is here.
Thank you.
But I'll see for
myself.
I can't tell
you how grateful
I am for your help
and support in
this, Rutskaya.
It's been
my privilege,
Doctor
Kragoff.
I've learned
so much working
beside you.

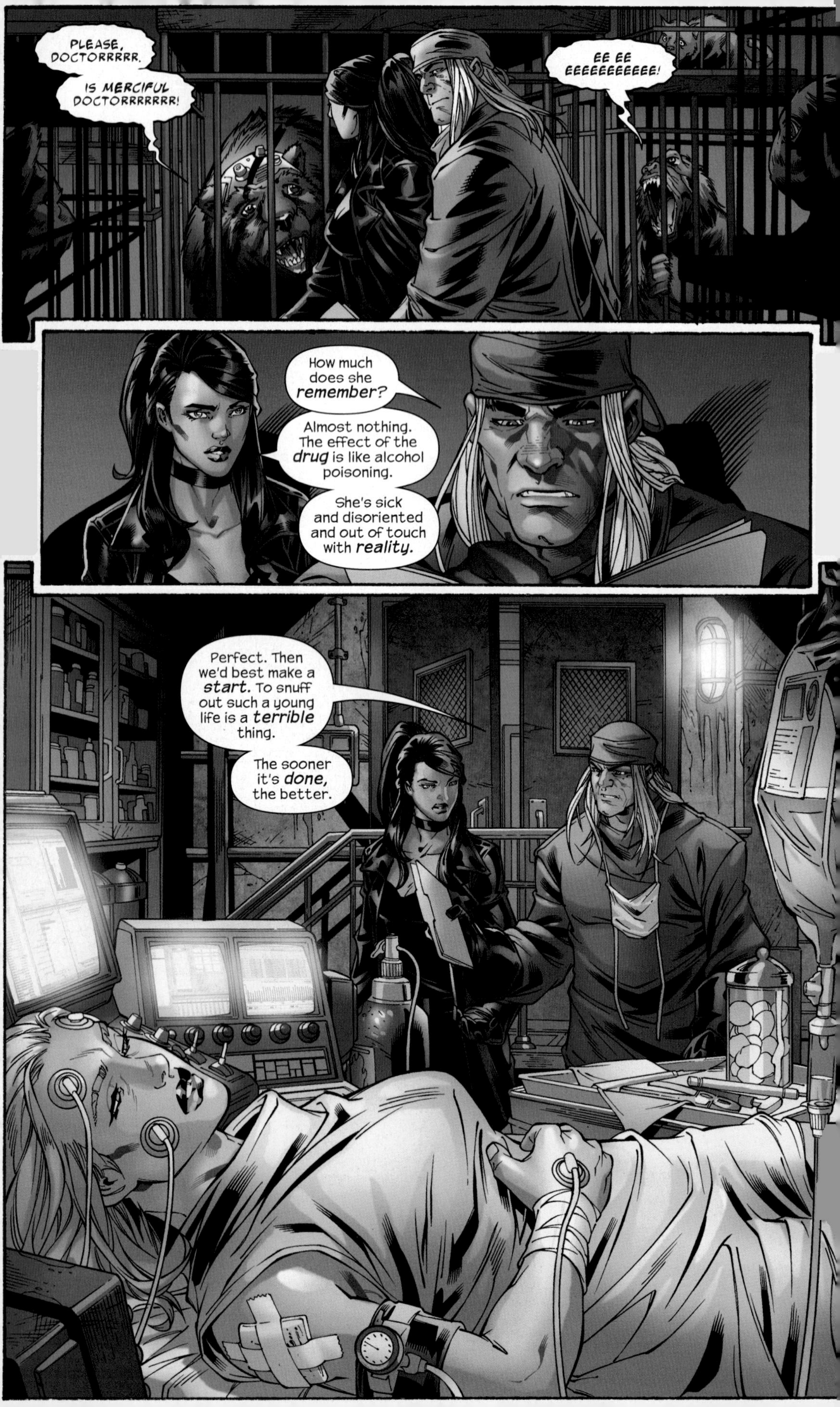
PLEASE, DOCTORRRRR.
IS MERCIFUL DOCTORRRRRRR!
EE EE EEEEEEEEEEE!
How much does she remember?
Almost nothing. The effect of the drug is like alcohol poisoning.
She's sick and disoriented and out of touch with reality.
Perfect. Then we'd best make a start. To snuff out such a young life is a terrible thing.
The sooner it's done, the better.

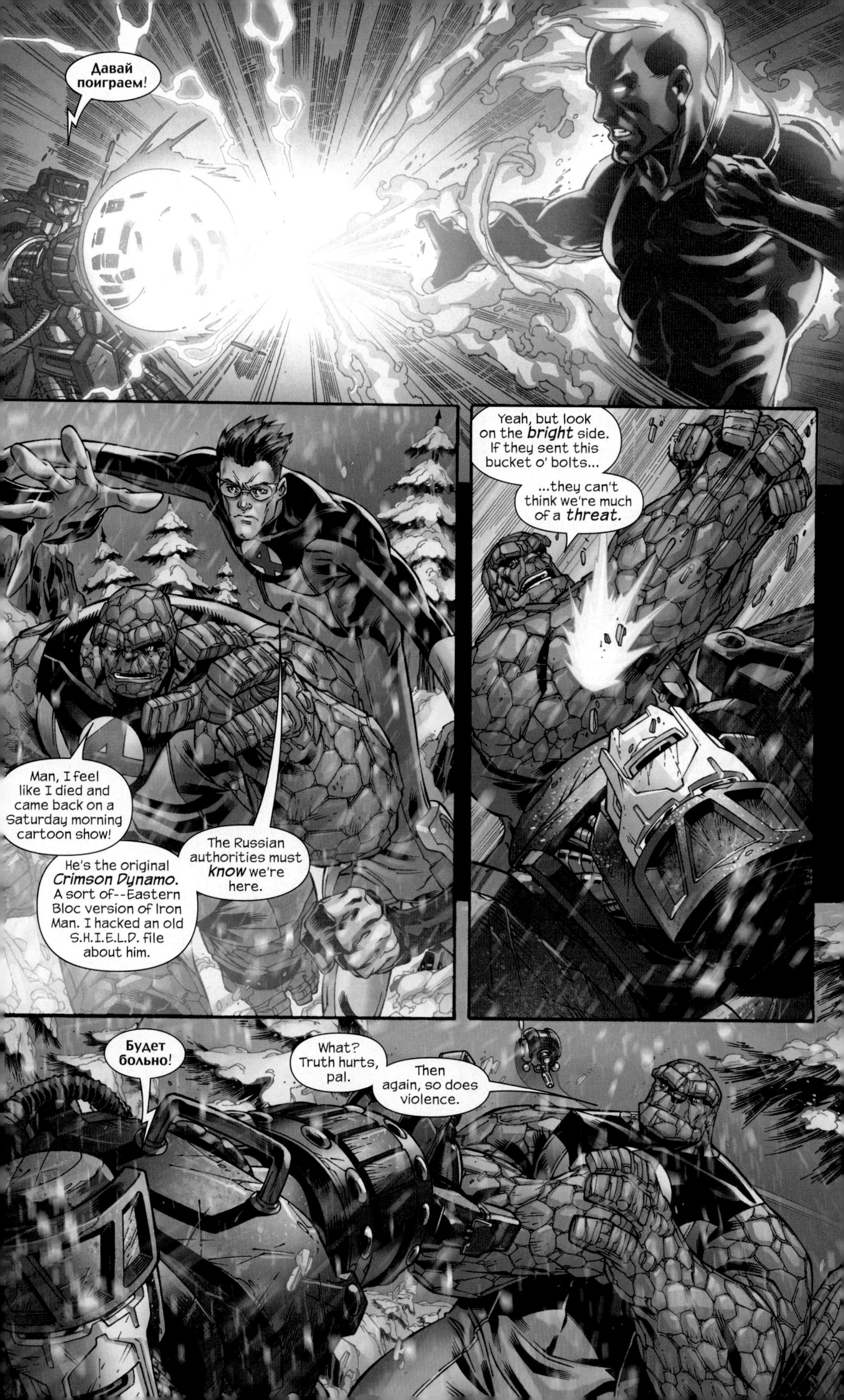
Давай поиграем!
Man, I feel like I died and came back on a Saturday morning cartoon show!
He's the original *Crimson Dynamo.* A sort of--Eastern Bloc version of Iron Man. I hacked an old S.H.I.E.L.D. file about him.
The Russian authorities must *know* we're here.
Yeah, but look on the *bright* side. If they sent this bucket o' bolts...
...they can't think we're much of a *threat.*
Будет больно!
What? Truth hurts, pal.
Then again, so does violence.

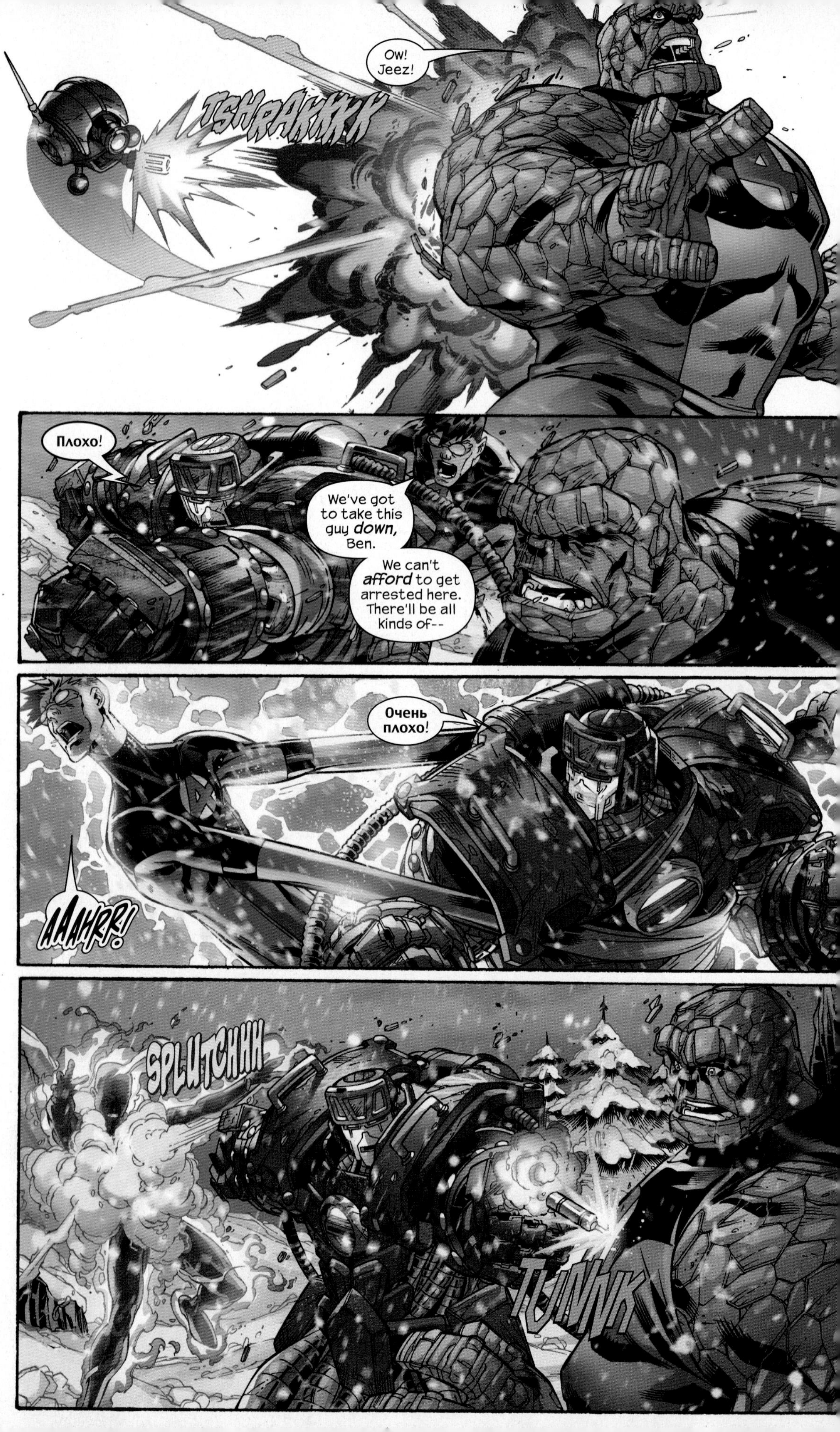

Ow! Jeez!
TSHRAKKKK
Плохо!
We've got to take this guy down, Ben.
We can't afford to get arrested here. There'll be all kinds of--
Очень плохо!
AAAHRR!
SPLUTCHHH
TUNNK

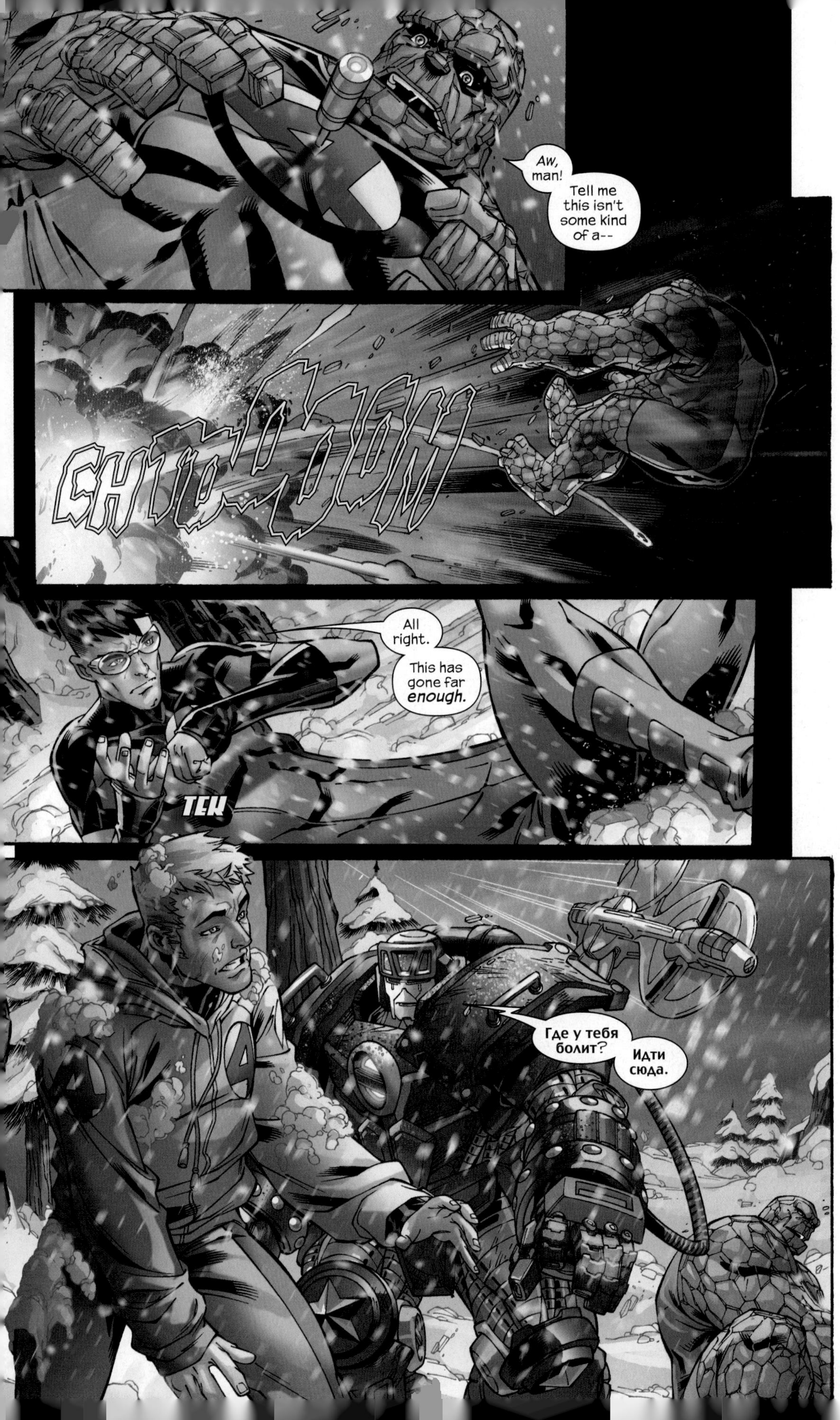

Aw, man!
Tell me this isn't some kind of a--
CHHOOOOM
All right.
This has gone far *enough.*
TEN
Где у тебя болит?
Идти сюда.

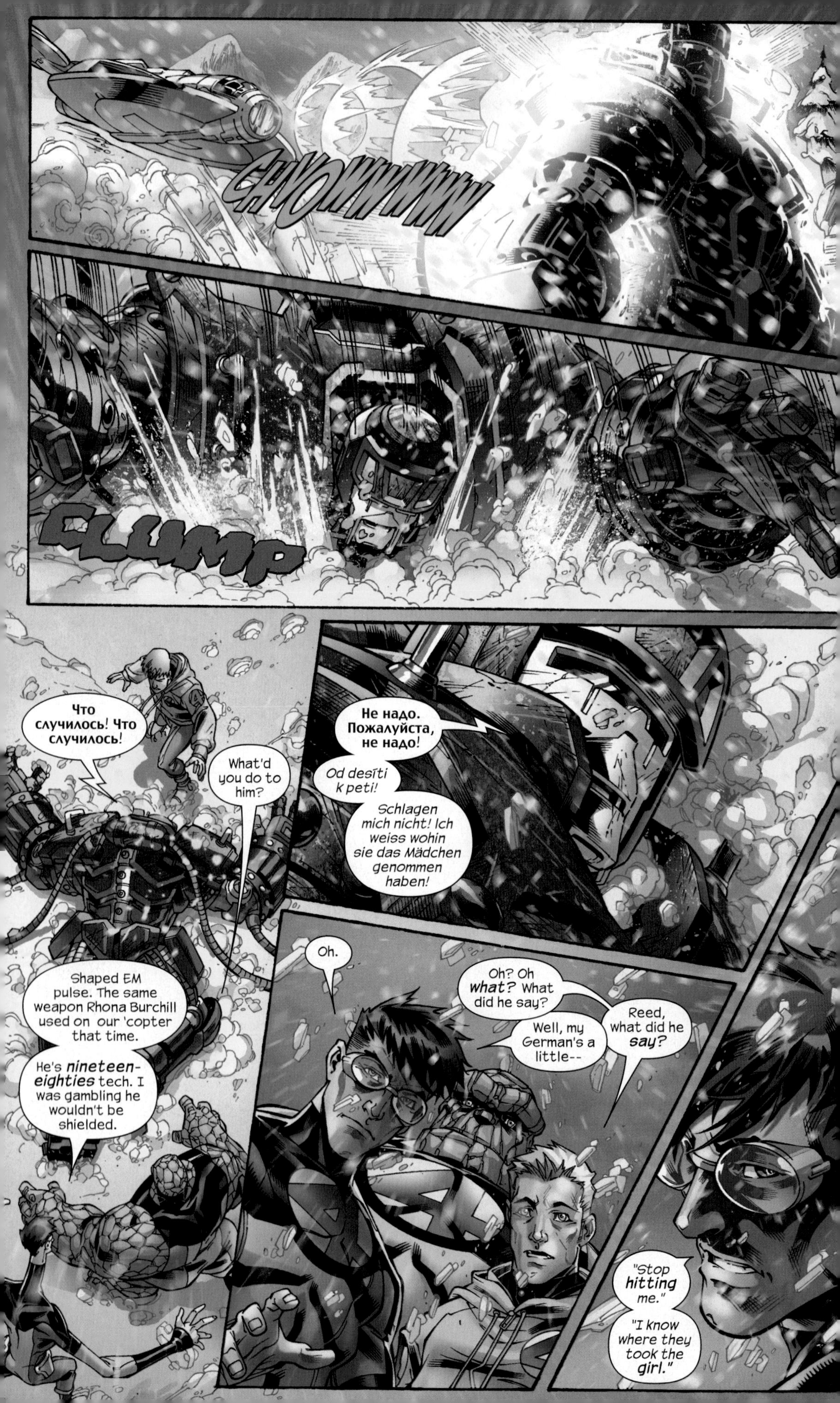

CHOOWWWWWWW
CLUMP
Что случилось! Что случилось!
What'd you do to him?
Не надо. Пожалуйста, не надо!
Od desíti k peti!
Schlagen mich nicht! Ich weiss wohin sie das Mädchen genommen haben!
Shaped EM pulse. The same weapon Rhona Burchill used on our 'copter that time.
He's *nineteen-eighties* tech. I was gambling he wouldn't be shielded.
Oh.
Oh? Oh *what?* What did he say?
Well, my German's a little--
Reed, what did he *say?*
"Stop *hitting* me."
"I know where they took the *girl.*"

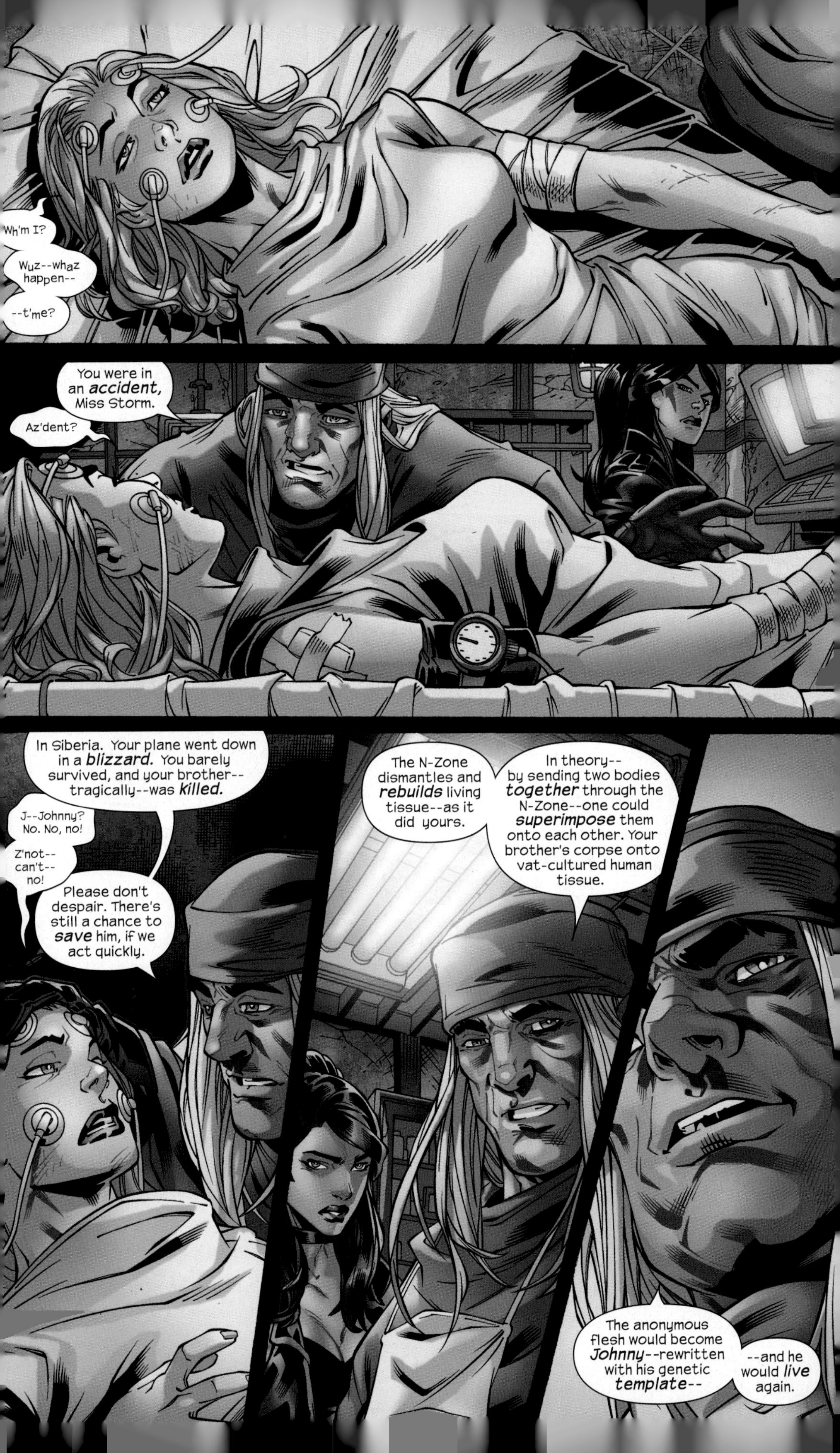
Wh'm I?
Wuz--whaz happen--
--t'me?
You were in an accident, Miss Storm.
Az'dent?
In Siberia. Your plane went down in a blizzard. You barely survived, and your brother--tragically--was killed.
J--Johnny? No. No, no!
Z'not--can't--no!
Please don't despair. There's still a chance to save him, if we act quickly.
The N-Zone dismantles and rebuilds living tissue--as it did yours.
In theory--by sending two bodies together through the N-Zone--one could superimpose them onto each other. Your brother's corpse onto vat-cultured human tissue.
The anonymous flesh would become Johnny--rewritten with his genetic template--
--and he would live again.

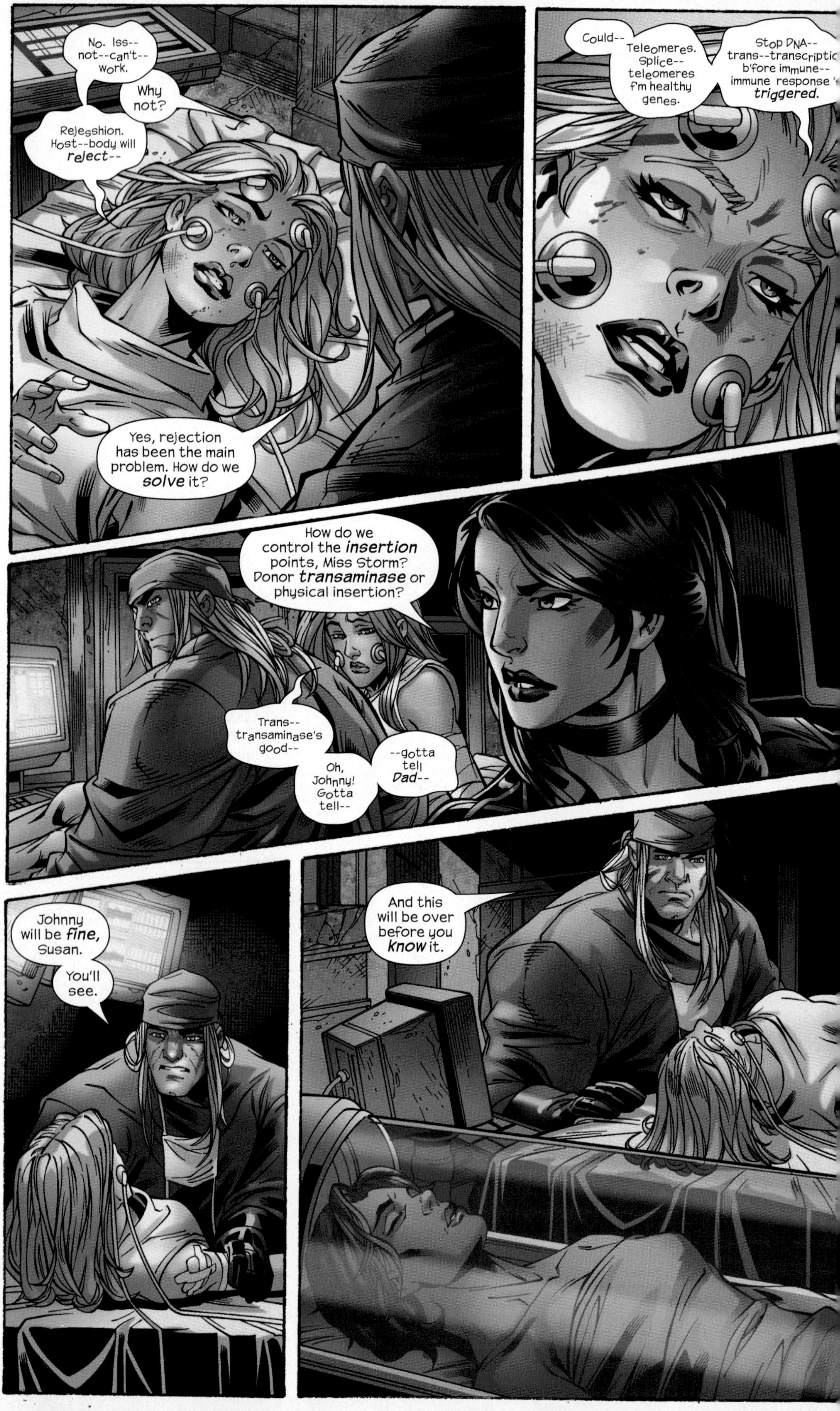
No. Iss--not--can't--work.
Why not?
Rejesshion. Host--body will *reject*--
Yes, rejection has been the main problem. How do we *solve* it?
Could--
Teleomeres. Splice--teleomeres f'm healthy genes.
Stop DNA--trans--transcriptio b'fore immune--immune response 's *triggered.*
How do we control the *insertion* points, Miss Storm? Donor *transaminase* or physical insertion?
Trans--transaminase's good--
Oh, Johnny! Gotta tell--
--gotta tell *Dad*--
Johnny will be *fine,* Susan.
You'll see.
And this will be over before you *know* it.

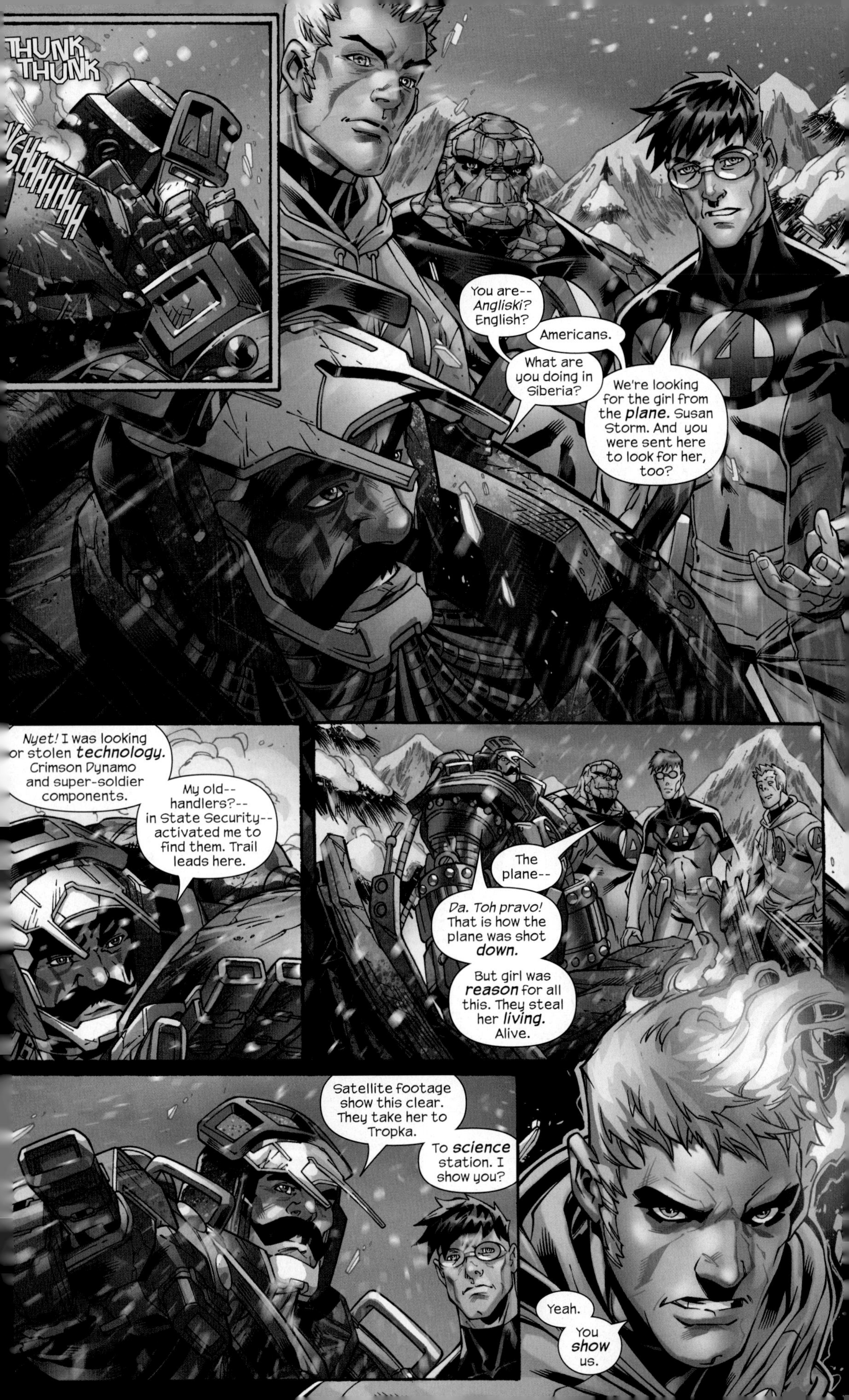
THUNK THUNK
SHHHHHHH
You are-- Angliski? English?
Americans.
What are you doing in Siberia?
We're looking for the girl from the plane. Susan Storm. And you were sent here to look for her, too?
Nyet! I was looking or stolen technology. Crimson Dynamo and super-soldier components.
My old-- handlers?-- in State Security-- activated me to find them. Trail leads here.
The plane--
Da. Toh pravo! That is how the plane was shot down.
But girl was reason for all this. They steal her living. Alive.
Satellite footage show this clear. They take her to Tropka.
To science station. I show you?
Yeah.
You show us.

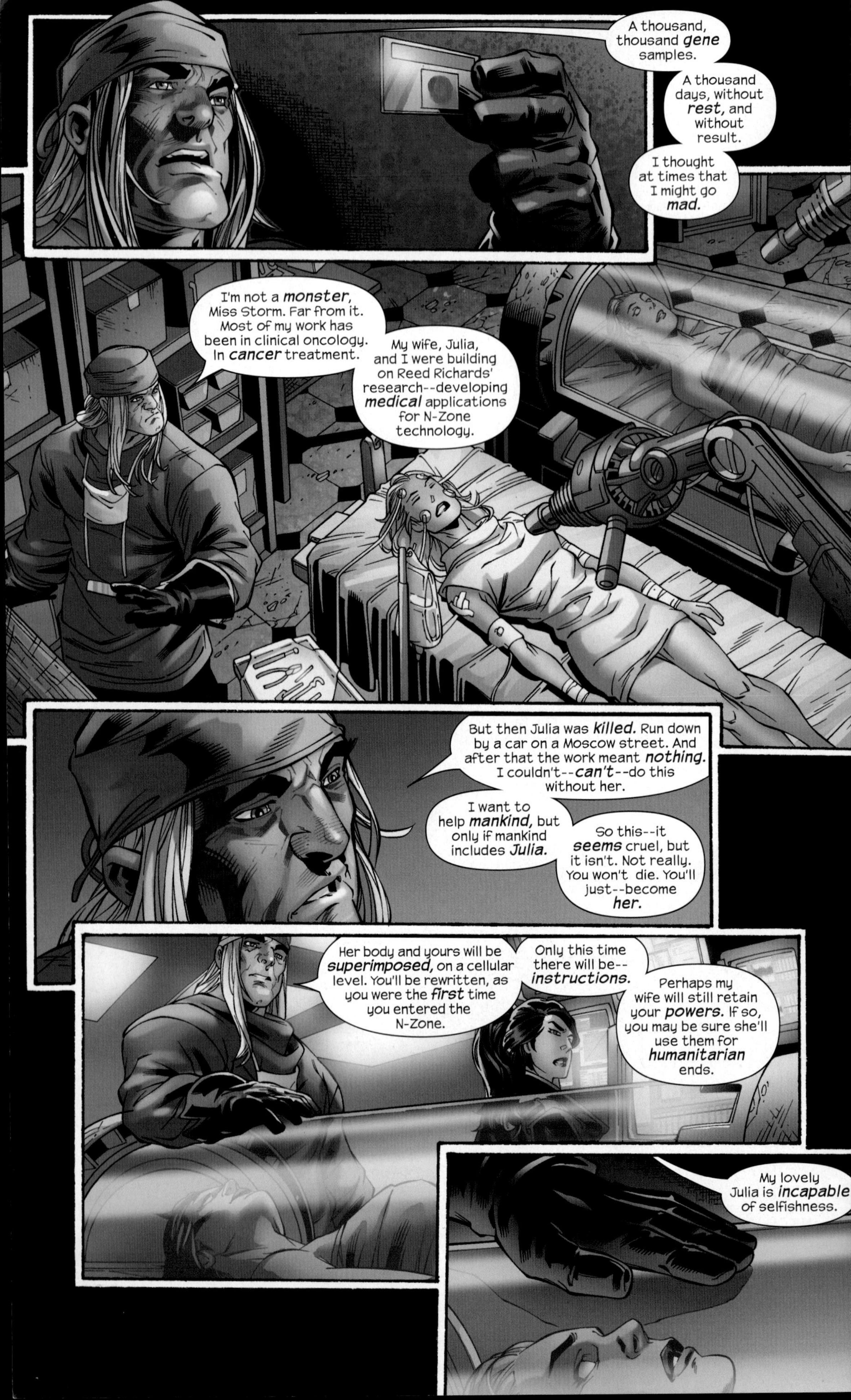
A thousand, thousand gene samples.
A thousand days, without rest, and without result.
I thought at times that I might go mad.
I'm not a monster, Miss Storm. Far from it. Most of my work has been in clinical oncology. In cancer treatment.
My wife, Julia, and I were building on Reed Richards' research--developing medical applications for N-Zone technology.
But then Julia was killed. Run down by a car on a Moscow street. And after that the work meant nothing. I couldn't--can't--do this without her.
I want to help mankind, but only if mankind includes Julia.
So this--it seems cruel, but it isn't. Not really. You won't die. You'll just--become her.
Her body and yours will be superimposed, on a cellular level. You'll be rewritten, as you were the first time you entered the N-Zone.
Only this time there will be--instructions.
Perhaps my wife will still retain your powers. If so, you may be sure she'll use them for humanitarian ends.
My lovely Julia is incapable of selfishness.

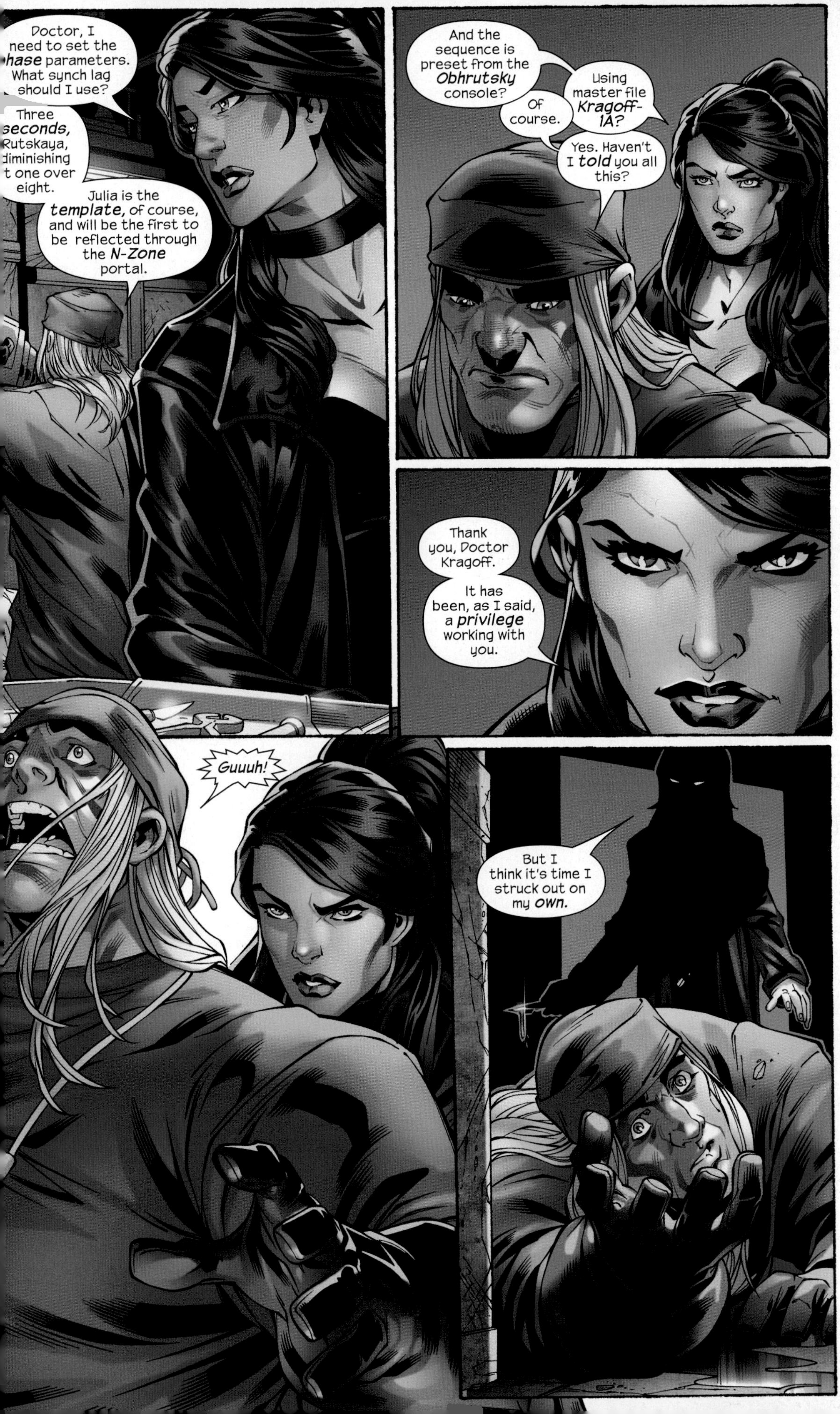

Doctor, I need to set the hase parameters. What synch lag should I use?
Three seconds, Rutskaya, diminishing t one over eight.
Julia is the template, of course, and will be the first to be reflected through the N-Zone portal.
And the sequence is preset from the Obhrutsky console?
Of course.
Using master file Kragoff-1A?
Yes. Haven't I told you all this?
Thank you, Doctor Kragoff.
It has been, as I said, a privilege working with you.
Guuuh!
But I think it's time I struck out on my own.

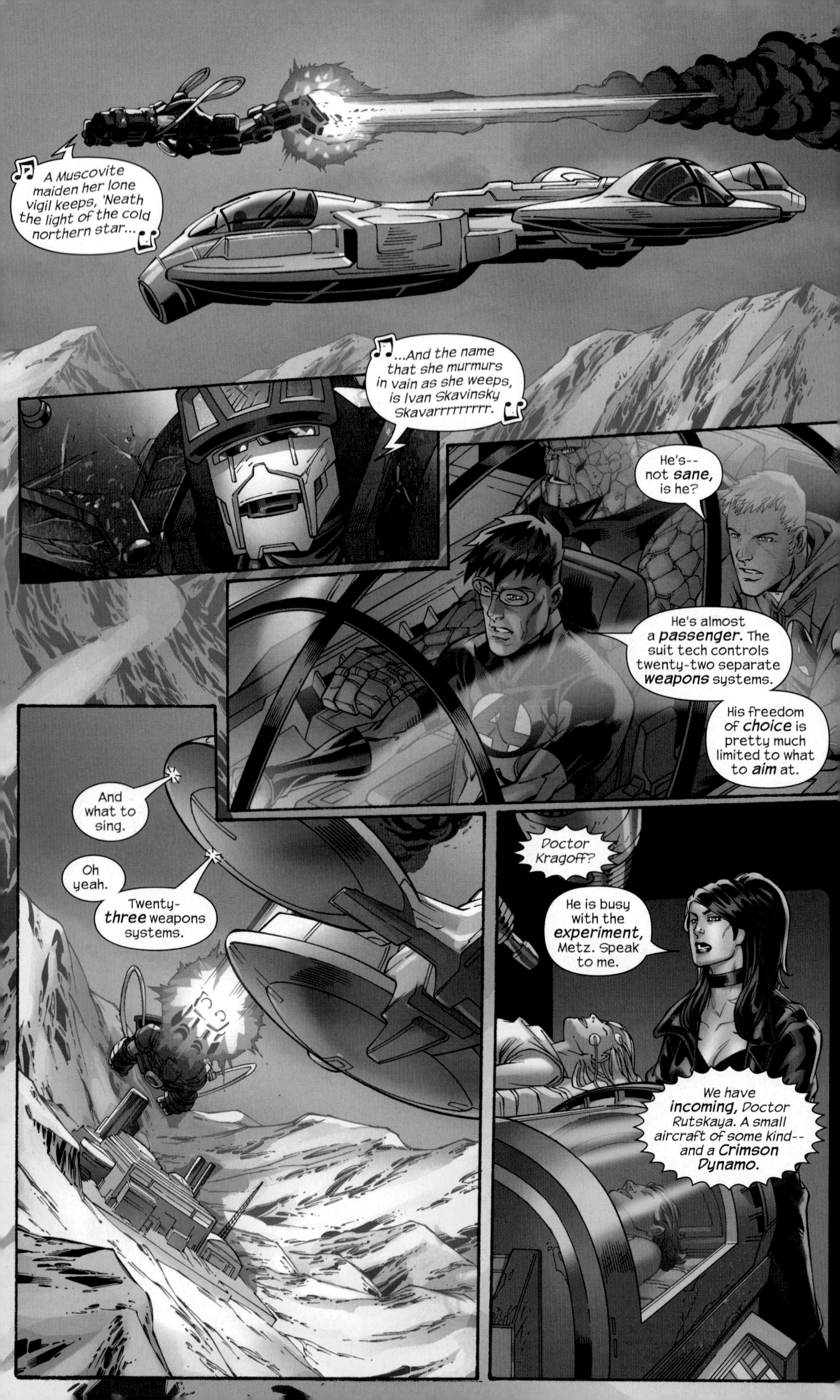
A Muscovite maiden her lone vigil keeps, 'Neath the light of the cold northern star...
...And the name that she murmurs in vain as she weeps, is Ivan Skavinsky Skavarrrrrrrrr.
He's-- not sane, is he?
He's almost a passenger. The suit tech controls twenty-two separate weapons systems.
His freedom of choice is pretty much limited to what to aim at.
And what to sing.
Oh yeah.
Twenty-three weapons systems.
Doctor Kragoff?
He is busy with the experiment, Metz. Speak to me.
We have incoming, Doctor Rutskaya. A small aircraft of some kind-- and a Crimson Dynamo.

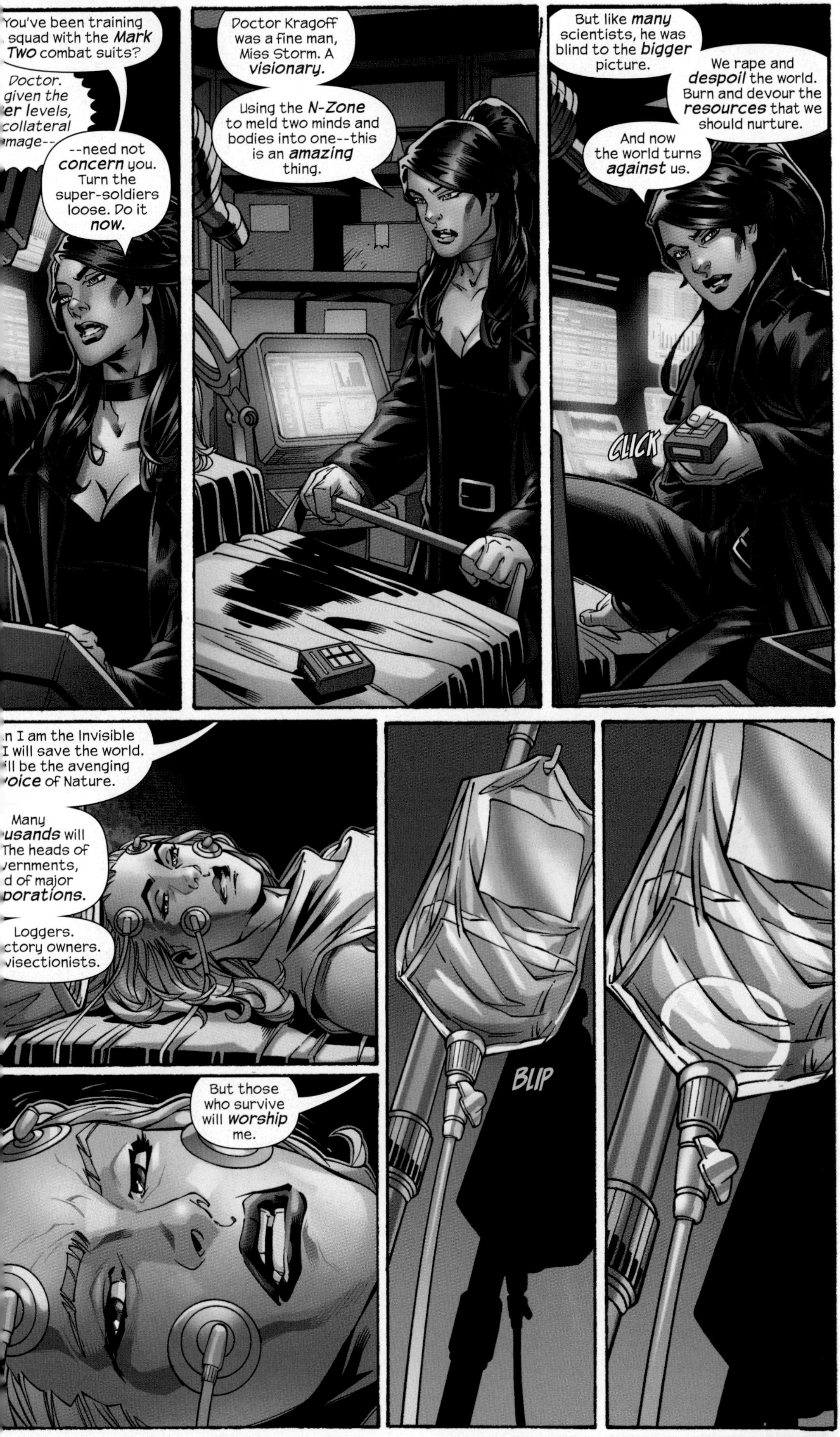

You've been training squad with the Mark Two combat suits?
Doctor. given the er levels, collateral mage--
--need not concern you. Turn the super-soldiers loose. Do it now.
Doctor Kragoff was a fine man, Miss Storm. A visionary.
Using the N-Zone to meld two minds and bodies into one--this is an amazing thing.
But like many scientists, he was blind to the bigger picture.
We rape and despoil the world. Burn and devour the resources that we should nurture.
And now the world turns against us.
CLICK
n I am the Invisible I will save the world. 'll be the avenging voice of Nature.
Many usands will The heads of vernments, d of major porations.
Loggers. ctory owners. visectionists.
But those who survive will worship me.
BLIP

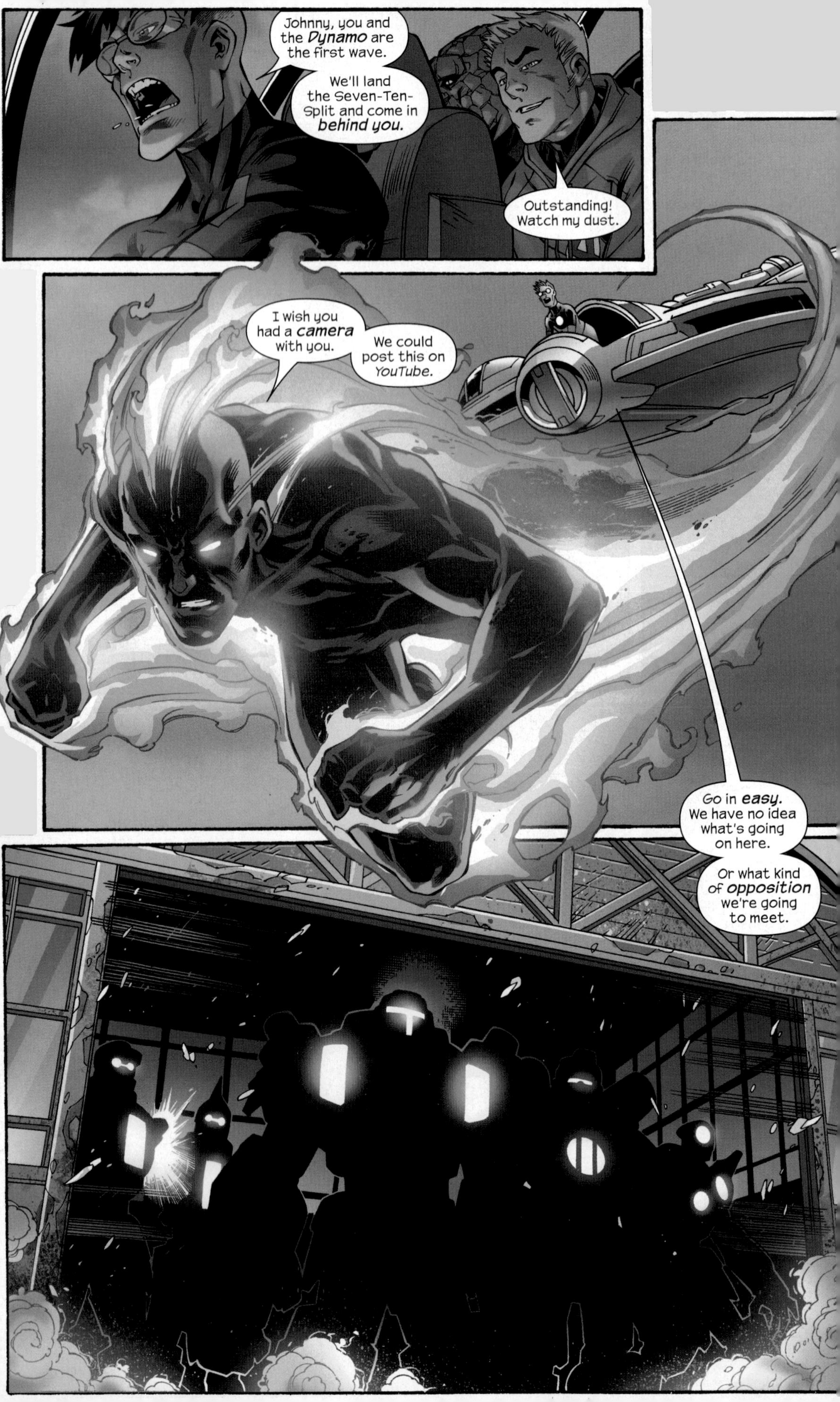
Johnny, you and the *Dynamo* are the first wave.
We'll land the Seven-Ten-Split and come in **behind you.**
Outstanding! Watch my dust.
I wish you had a **camera** with you.
We could post this on *YouTube.*
Go in **easy.** We have no idea what's going on here.
Or what kind of **opposition** we're going to meet.

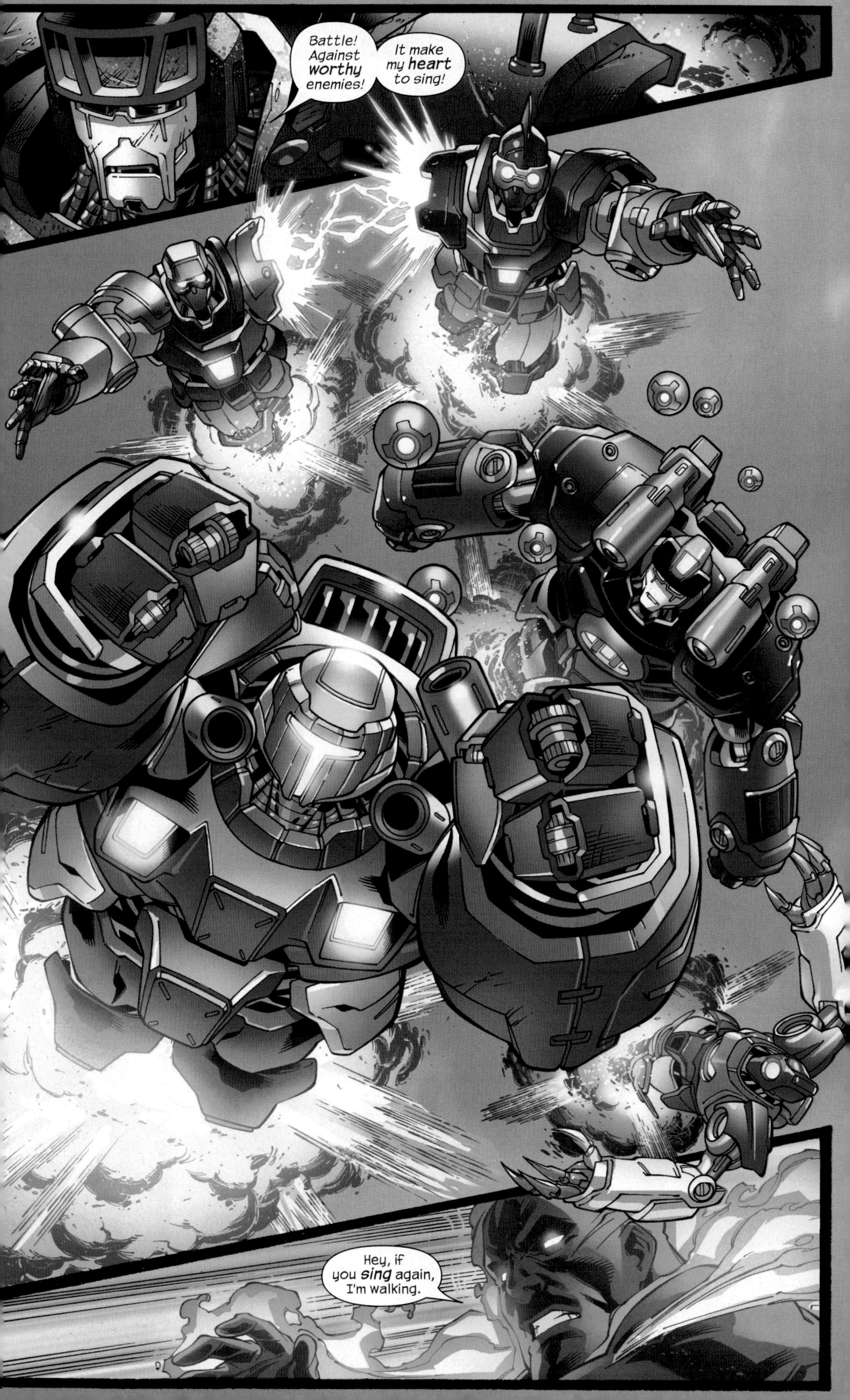
Battle! Against **worthy** enemies!
It make my **heart** to sing!
Hey, if you **sing** again, I'm walking.

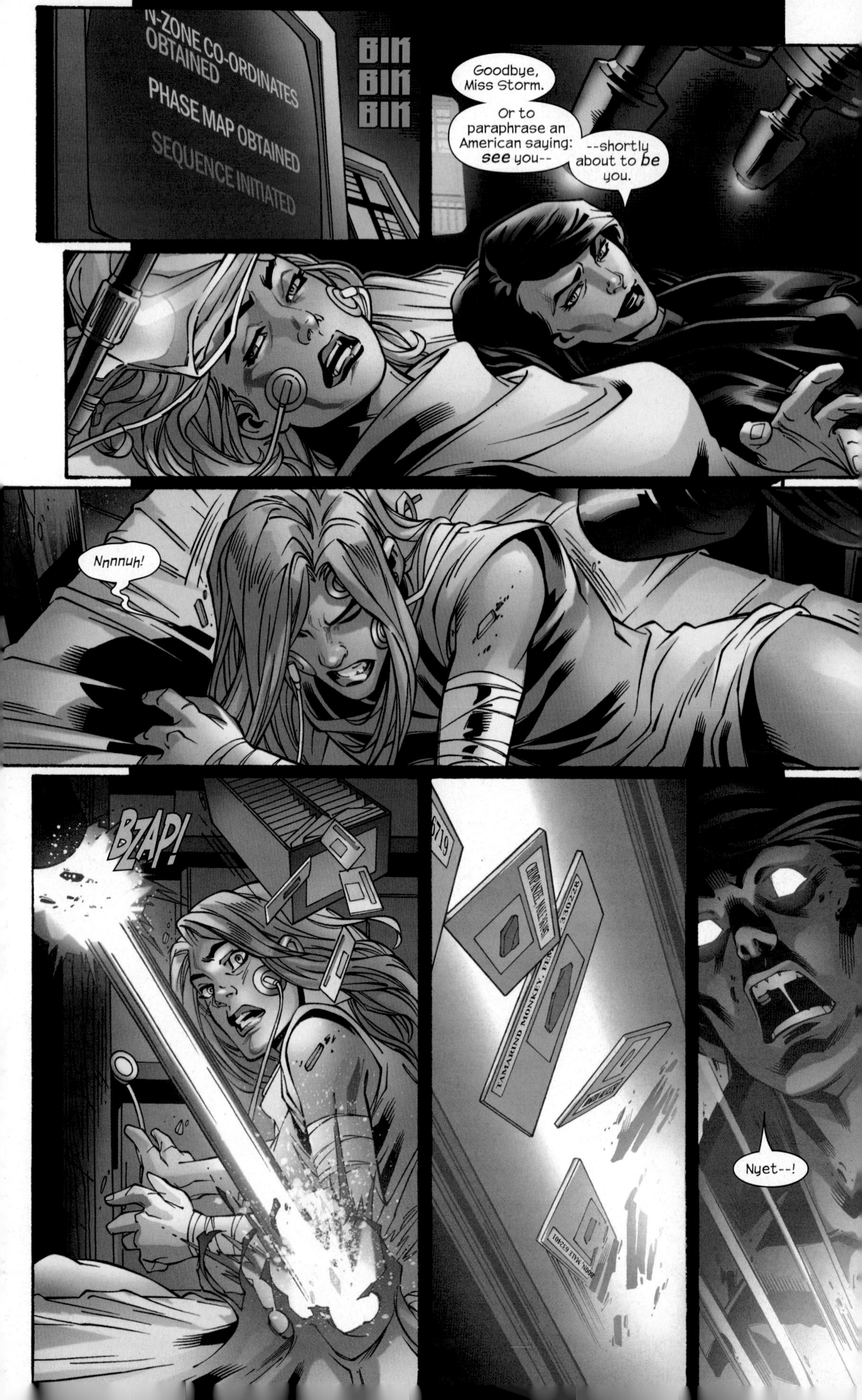
N-ZONE CO-ORDINATES OBTAINED
PHASE MAP OBTAINED
SEQUENCE INITIATED
BIK BIK BIK
Goodbye, Miss Storm.
Or to paraphrase an American saying: see you--
--shortly about to be you.
Nnnnuh!
BZAP!
TAMARIND MONKEY, FEM
Nyet--!

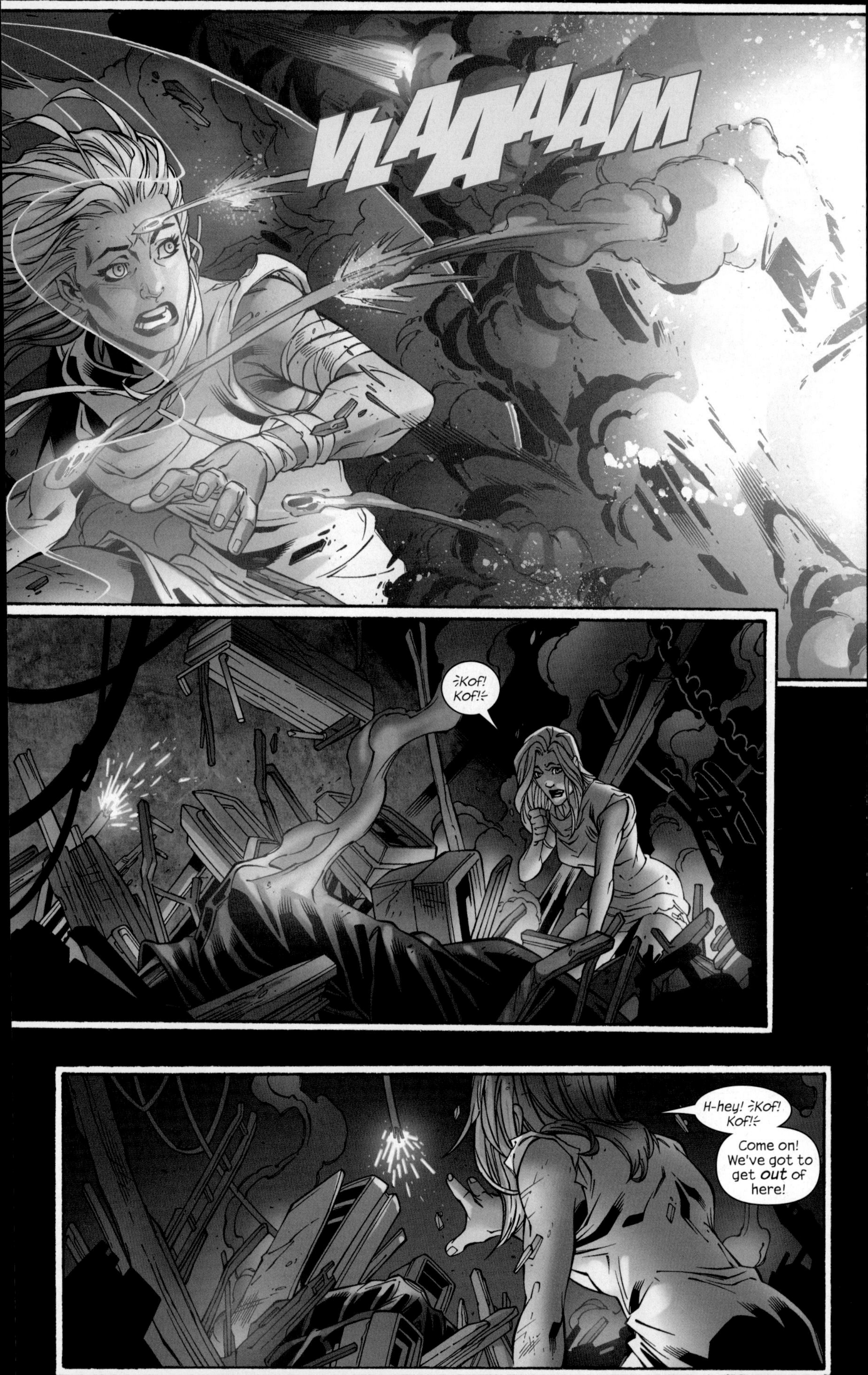
VLAAAAM
Kof! Kof!
H-hey! Kof! Kof!
Come on! We've got to get out of here!

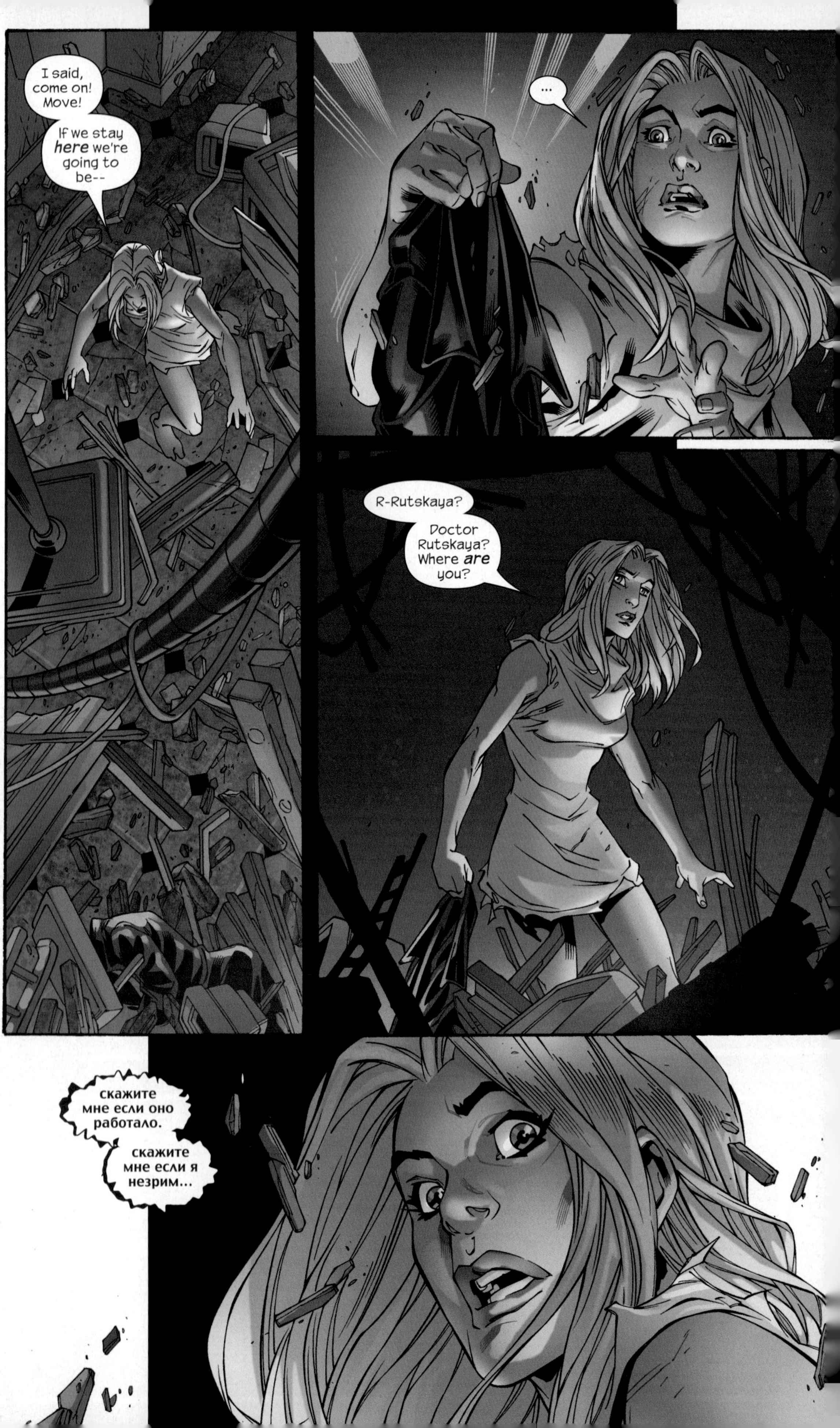
I said, come on! Move!
If we stay here we're going to be--
...
R-Rutskaya?
Doctor Rutskaya? Where are you?
скажите мне если оно работало.
скажите мне если я незрим...

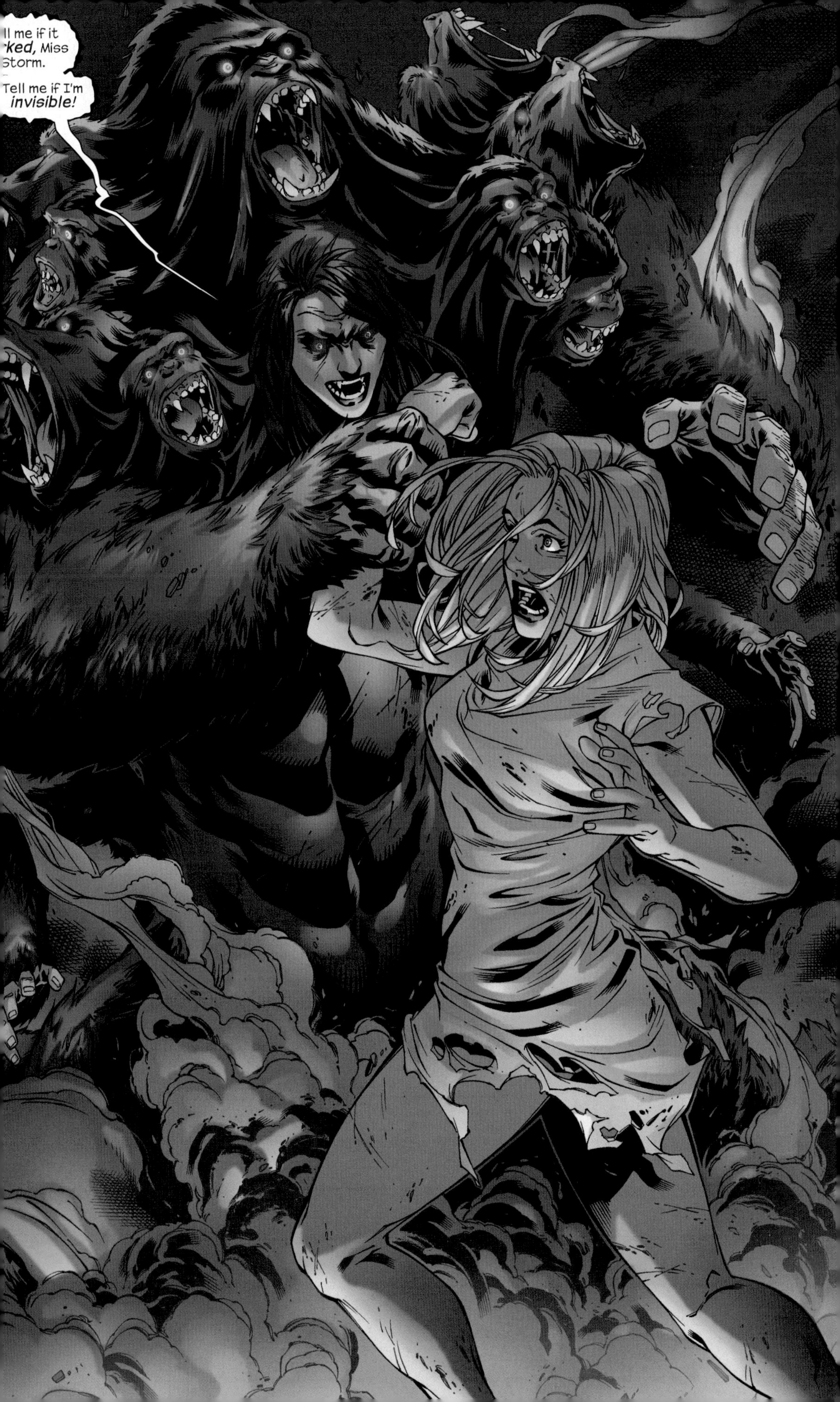
ll me if it
ked, Miss
Storm.
Tell me if I'm
invisible!

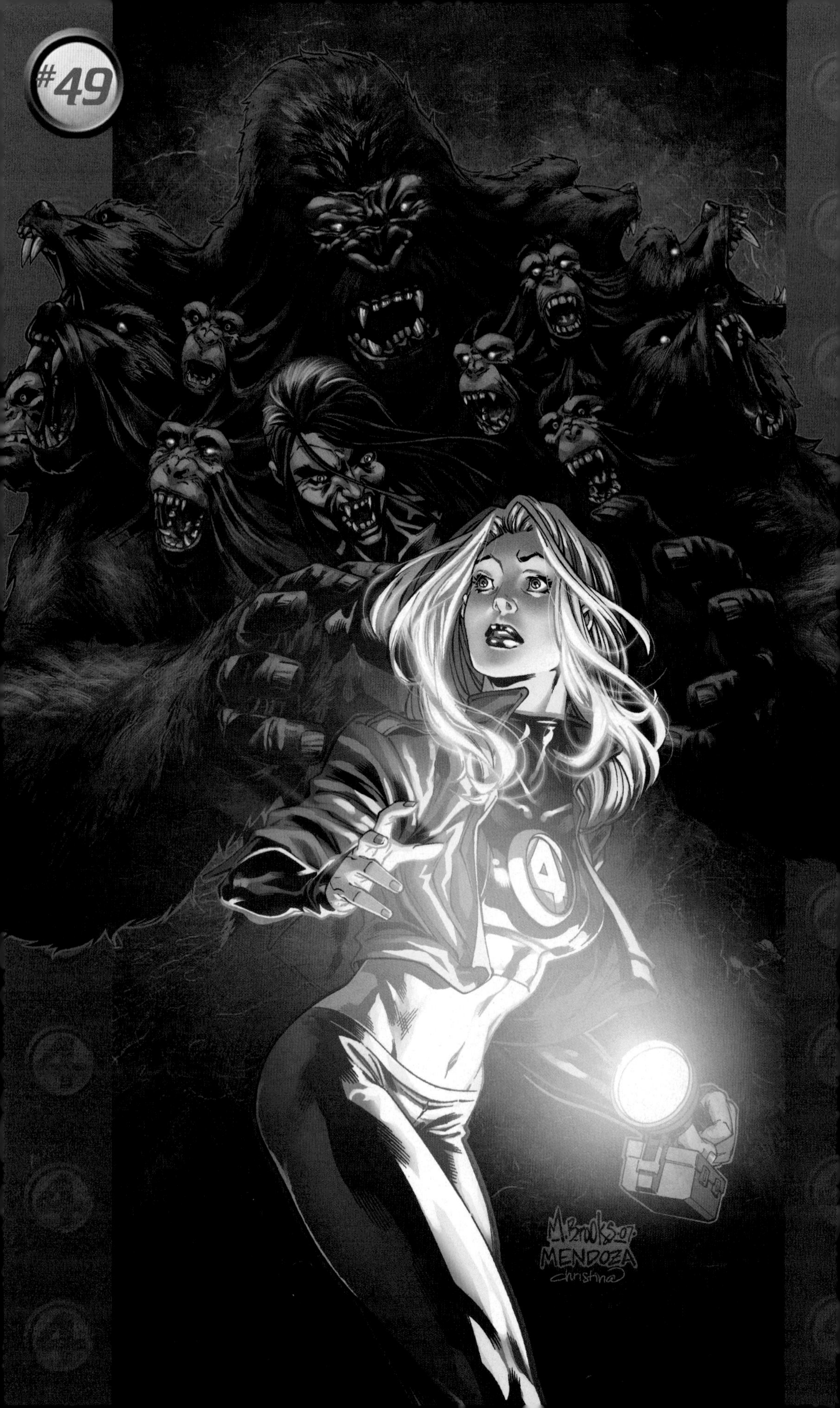
#49
M. Brooks 07
MENDOZA
christina

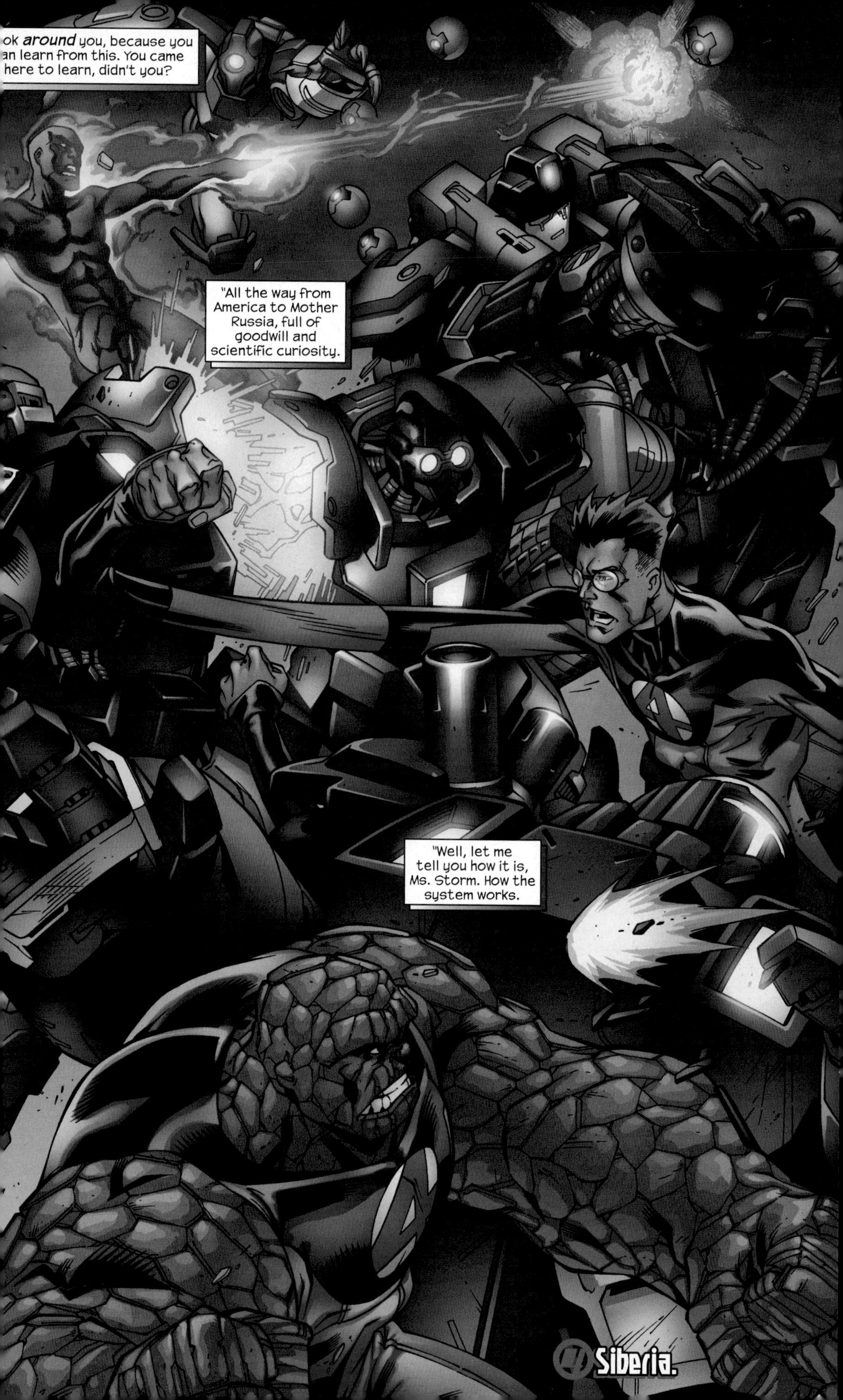
ok around you, because you an learn from this. You came here to learn, didn't you?
"All the way from America to Mother Russia, full of goodwill and scientific curiosity.
"Well, let me tell you how it is, Ms. Storm. How the system works.
Siberia.

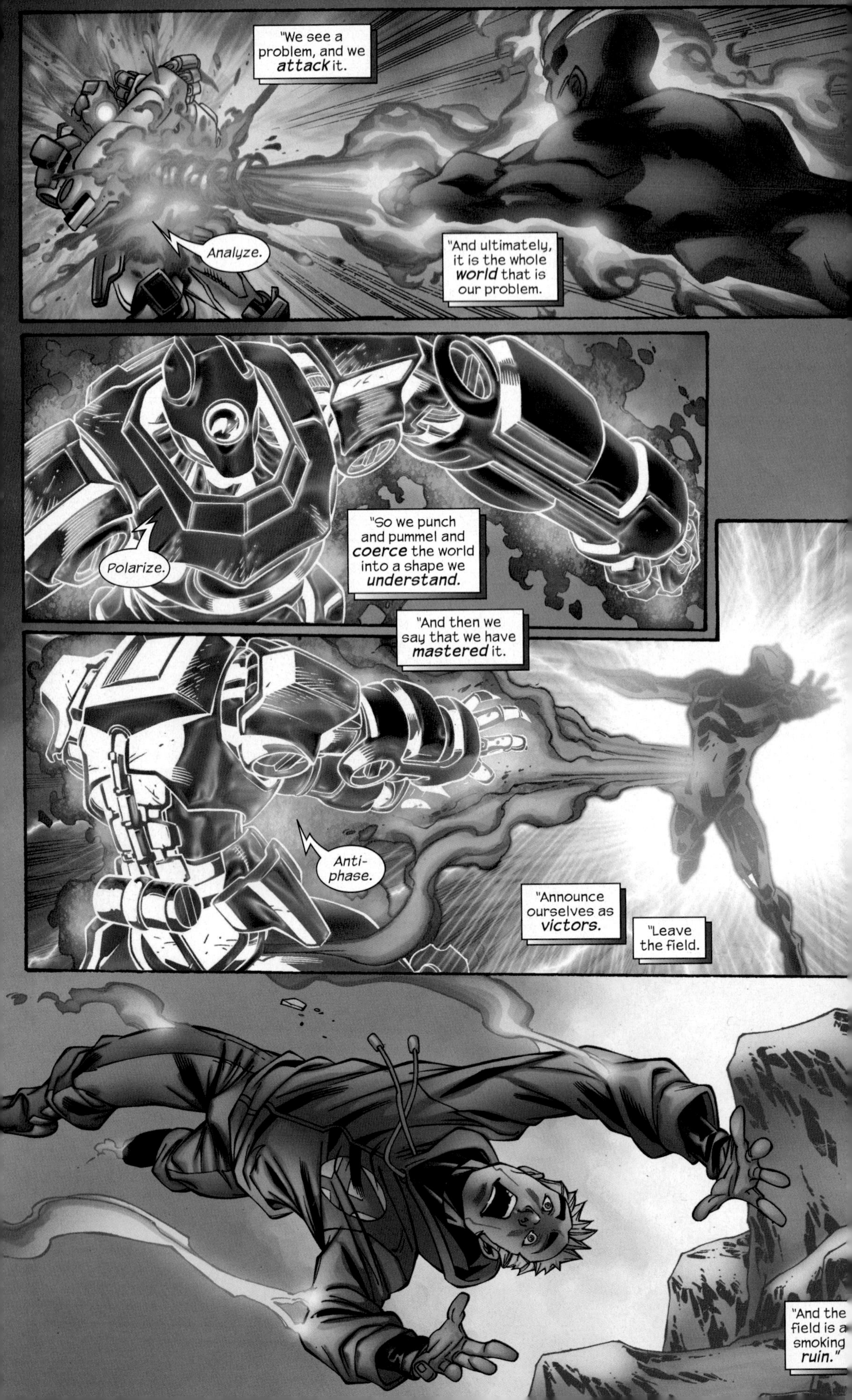
"We see a problem, and we *attack* it.
Analyze.
"And ultimately, it is the whole *world* that is our problem.
"So we punch and pummel and *coerce* the world into a shape we *understand*.
Polarize.
"And then we say that we have *mastered* it.
Anti-phase.
"Announce ourselves as *victors*.
"Leave the field.
"And the field is a smoking *ruin*."

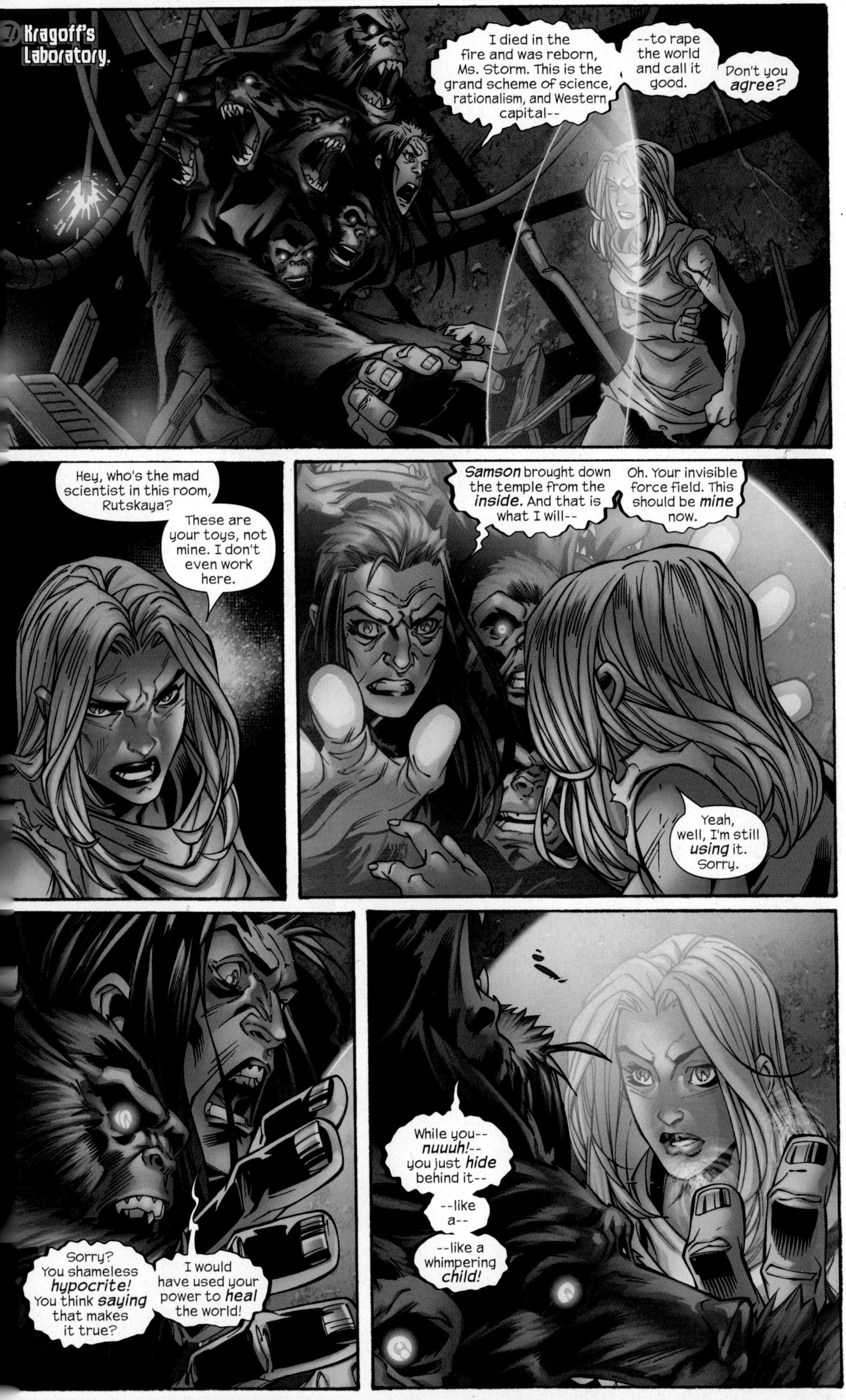
7 Kragoff's Laboratory.
I died in the fire and was reborn, Ms. Storm. This is the grand scheme of science, rationalism, and Western capital--
--to rape the world and call it good.
Don't you agree?
Hey, who's the mad scientist in this room, Rutskaya?
These are your toys, not mine. I don't even work here.
Samson brought down the temple from the inside. And that is what I will--
Oh. Your invisible force field. This should be mine now.
Yeah, well, I'm still using it. Sorry.
Sorry? You shameless hypocrite! You think saying that makes it true?
I would have used your power to heal the world!
While you-- nuuuh!-- you just hide behind it--
--like a--
--like a whimpering child!

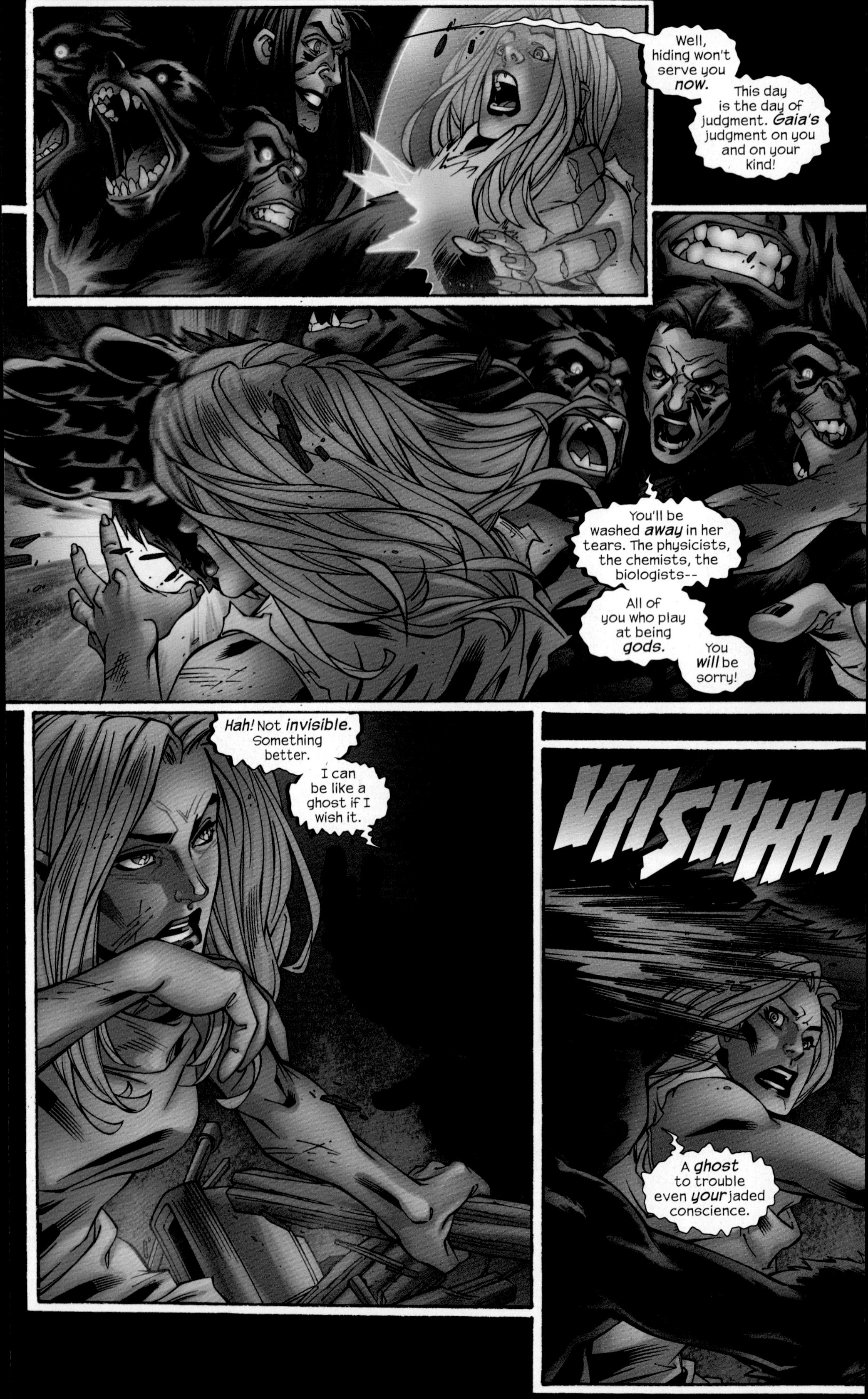
Well, hiding won't serve you *now.*
This day is the day of judgment. *Gaia's* judgment on you and on your kind!
You'll be washed *away* in her tears. The physicists, the chemists, the biologists--
All of you who play at being *gods.*
You *will* be sorry!
Hah! Not *invisible.* Something better.
I can be like a ghost if I wish it.
VIISHHH
A *ghost* to trouble even *your* jaded conscience.

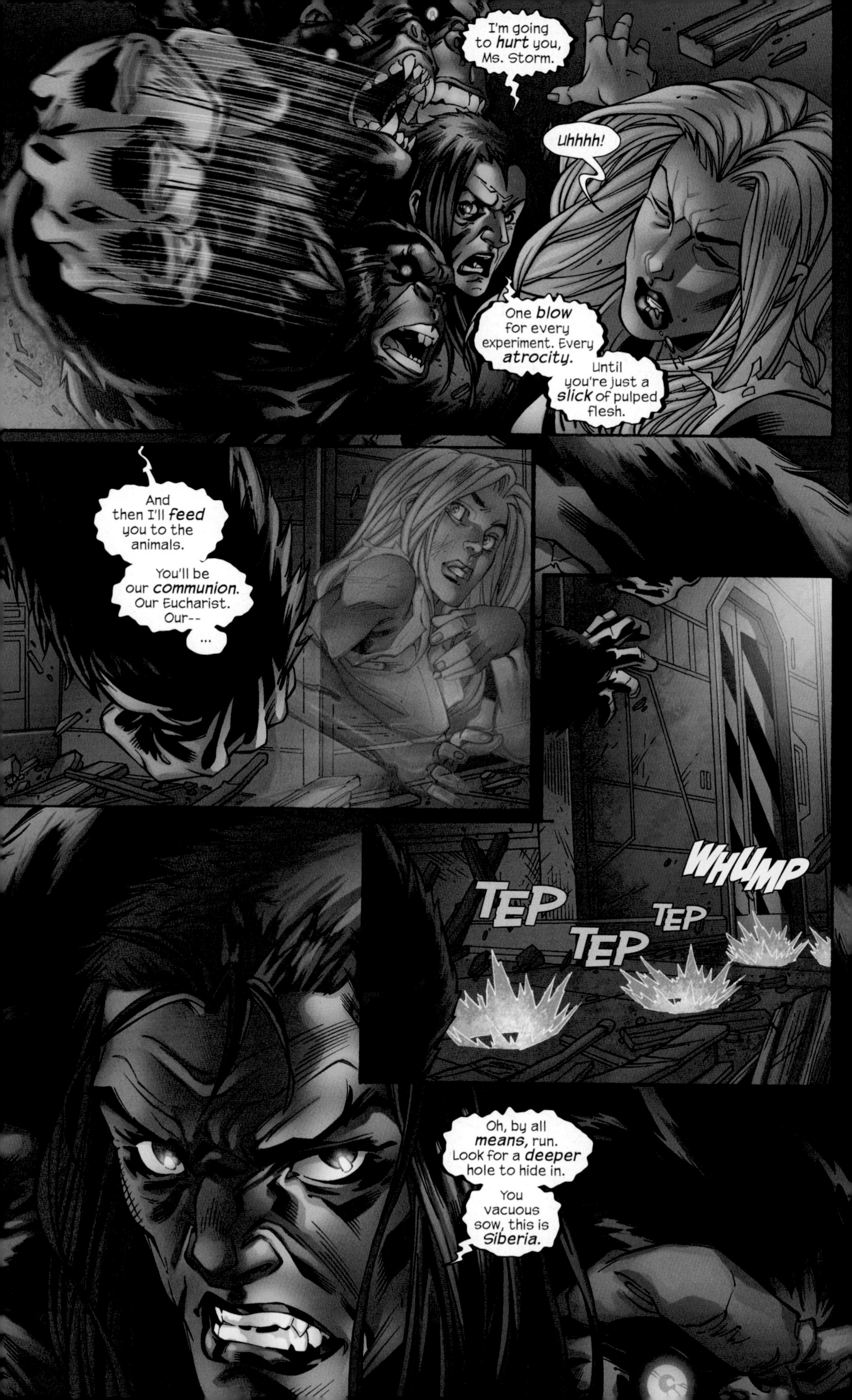
I'm going to hurt you, Ms. Storm.
Uhhhh!
One blow for every experiment. Every atrocity.
Until you're just a slick of pulped flesh.
And then I'll feed you to the animals.
You'll be our communion. Our Eucharist. Our--
...
WHUMP
TEP
TEP
TEP
Oh, by all means, run. Look for a deeper hole to hide in.
You vacuous sow, this is Siberia.

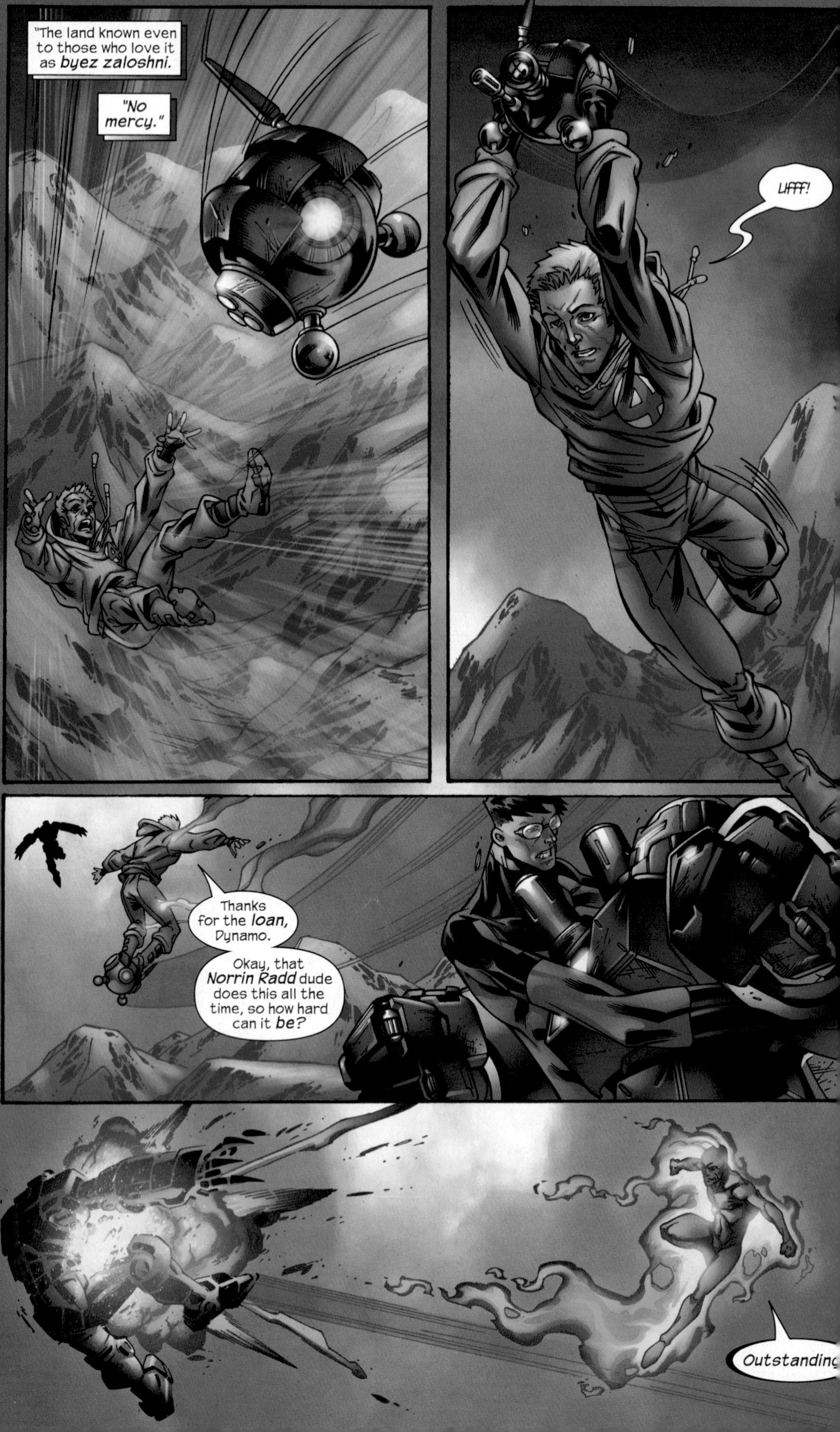
"The land known even to those who love it as *byez zaloshni.*
"No mercy."
UFFF!
Thanks for the *loan,* Dynamo.
Okay, that *Norrin Radd* dude does this all the time, so how hard can it *be?*
Outstanding

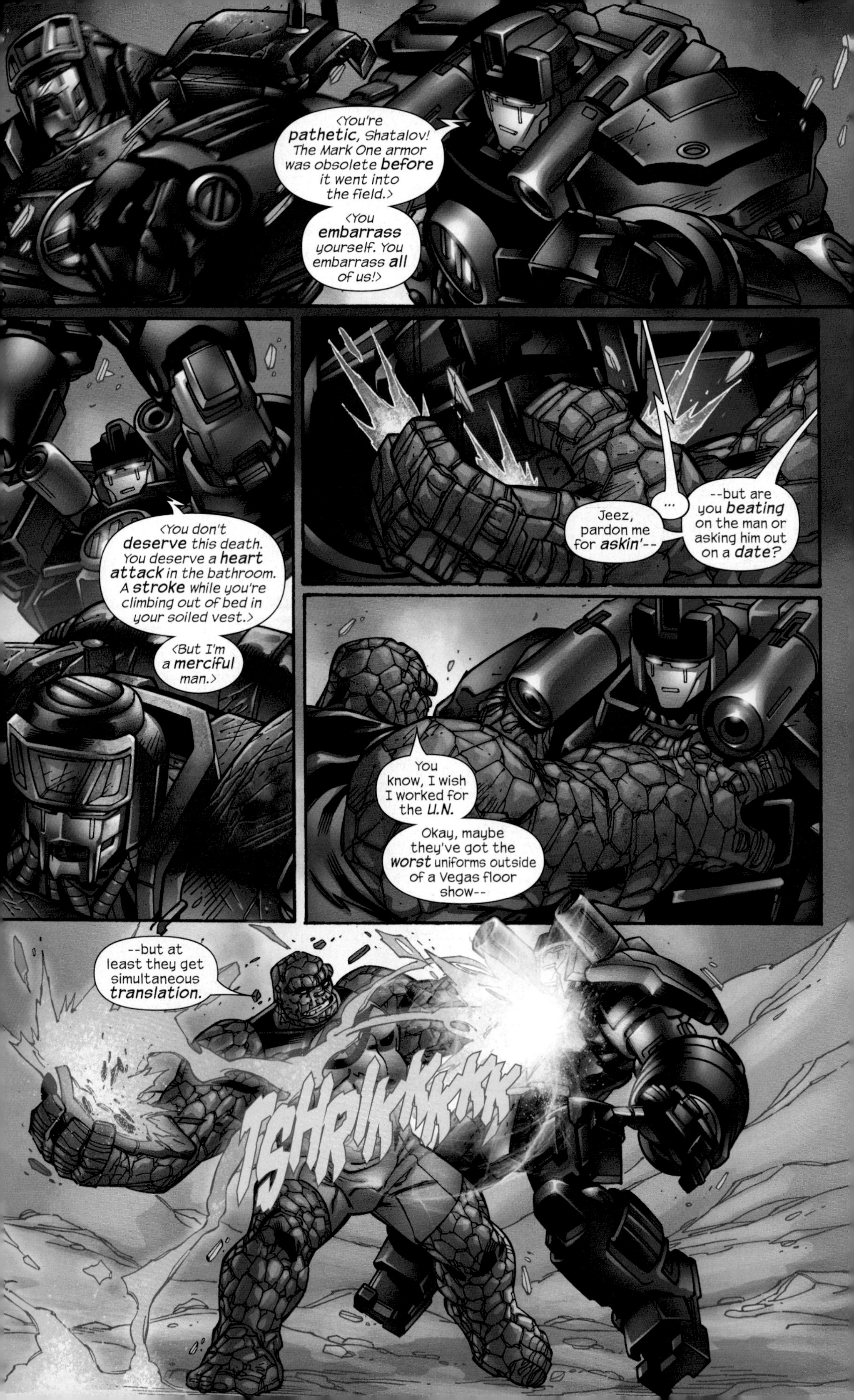

<You're pathetic, Shatalov! The Mark One armor was obsolete before it went into the field.>
<You embarrass yourself. You embarrass all of us!>
<You don't deserve this death. You deserve a heart attack in the bathroom. A stroke while you're climbing out of bed in your soiled vest.>
<But I'm a merciful man.>
...
Jeez, pardon me for askin'--
--but are you beating on the man or asking him out on a date?
You know, I wish I worked for the U.N.
Okay, maybe they've got the worst uniforms outside of a Vegas floor show--
--but at least they get simultaneous translation.
TSHRIKKKKK

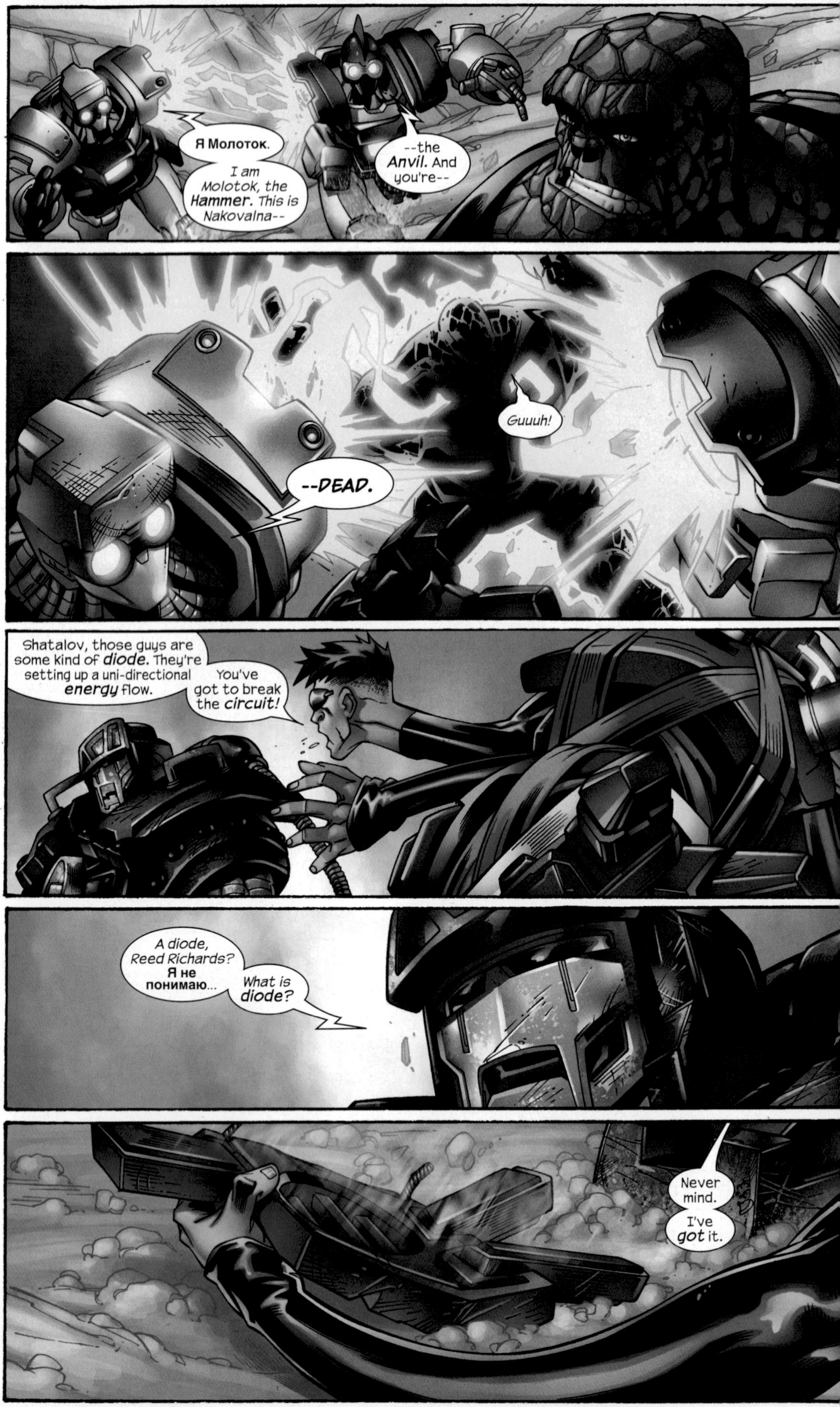
Я Молоток.
I am Molotok, the Hammer. This is Nakovalna--
--the Anvil. And you're--
Guuuh!
--DEAD.
Shatalov, those guys are some kind of diode. They're setting up a uni-directional energy flow.
You've got to break the circuit!
A diode, Reed Richards? Я не понимаю...
What is diode?
Never mind.
I've got it.

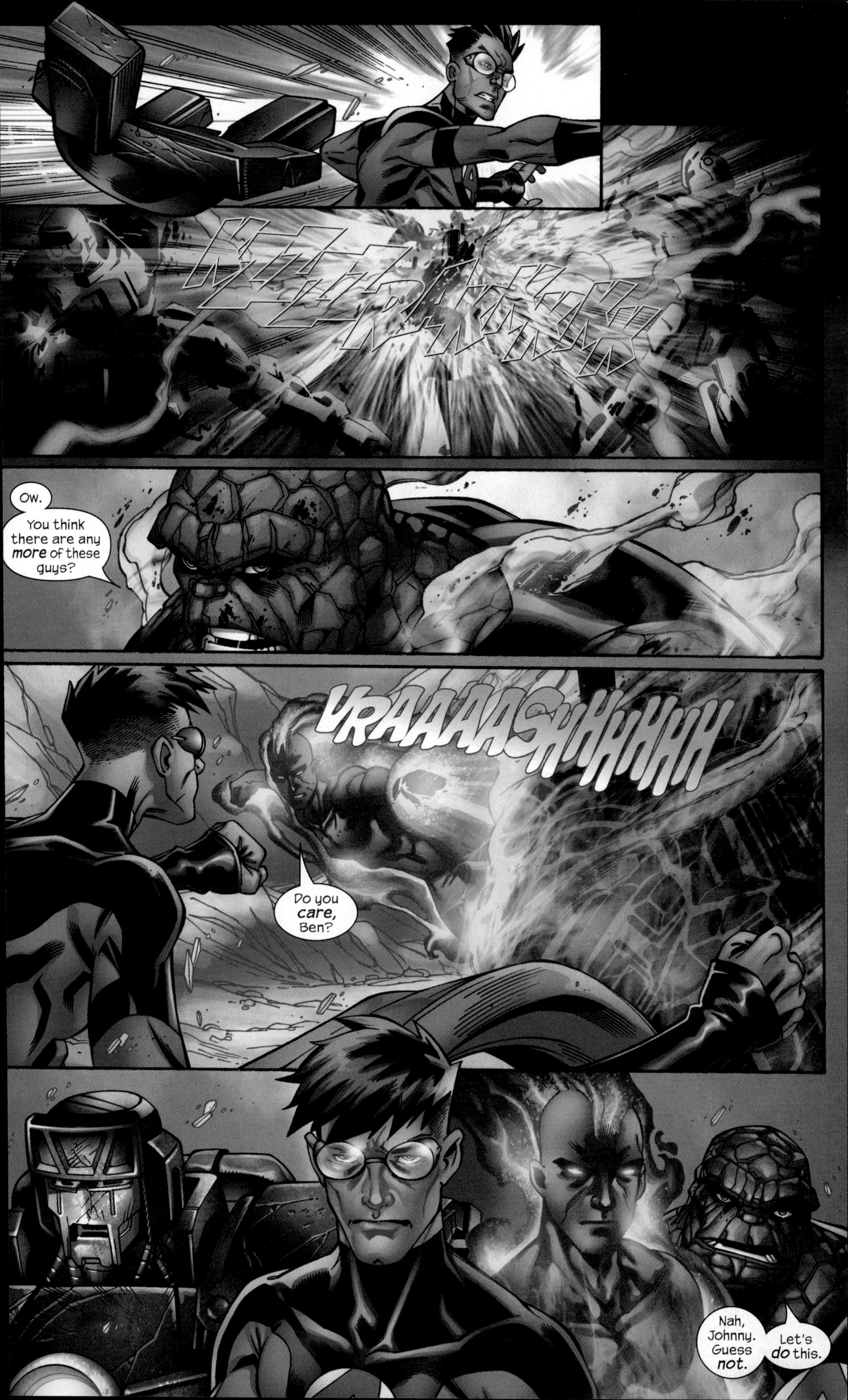
Ow.
You think there are any *more* of these guys?
VRAAAASHHHHHH
Do you *care,* Ben?
Nah, Johnny. Guess *not.*
Let's *do* this.

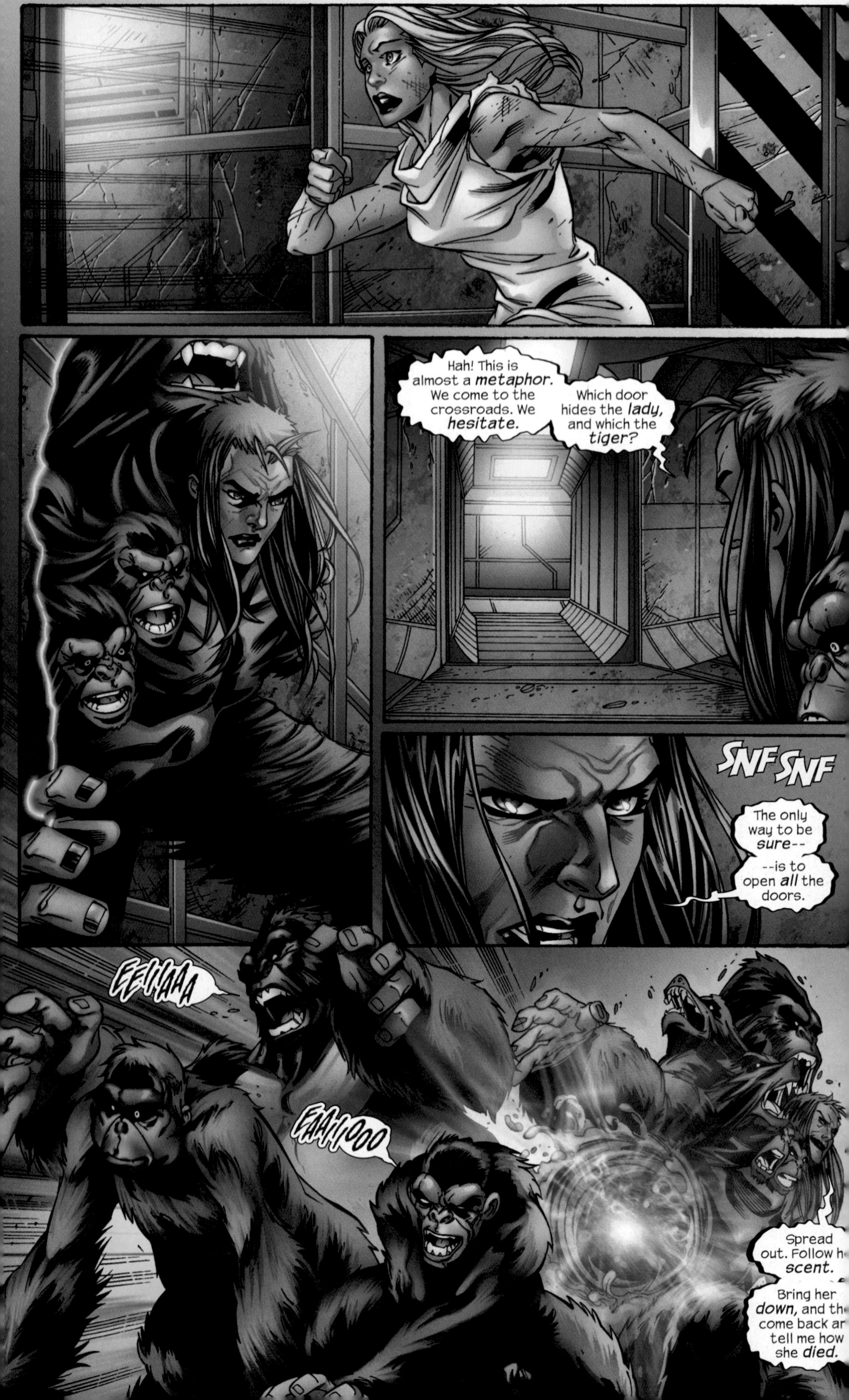
Hah! This is almost a *metaphor.* We come to the crossroads. We *hesitate.*
Which door hides the *lady,* and which the *tiger?*
SNF SNF
The only way to be *sure*--
--is to open *all* the doors.
EEIIAAA
EAAIIOOO
Spread out. Follow h *scent.*
Bring her *down,* and th come back ar tell me how she *died.*

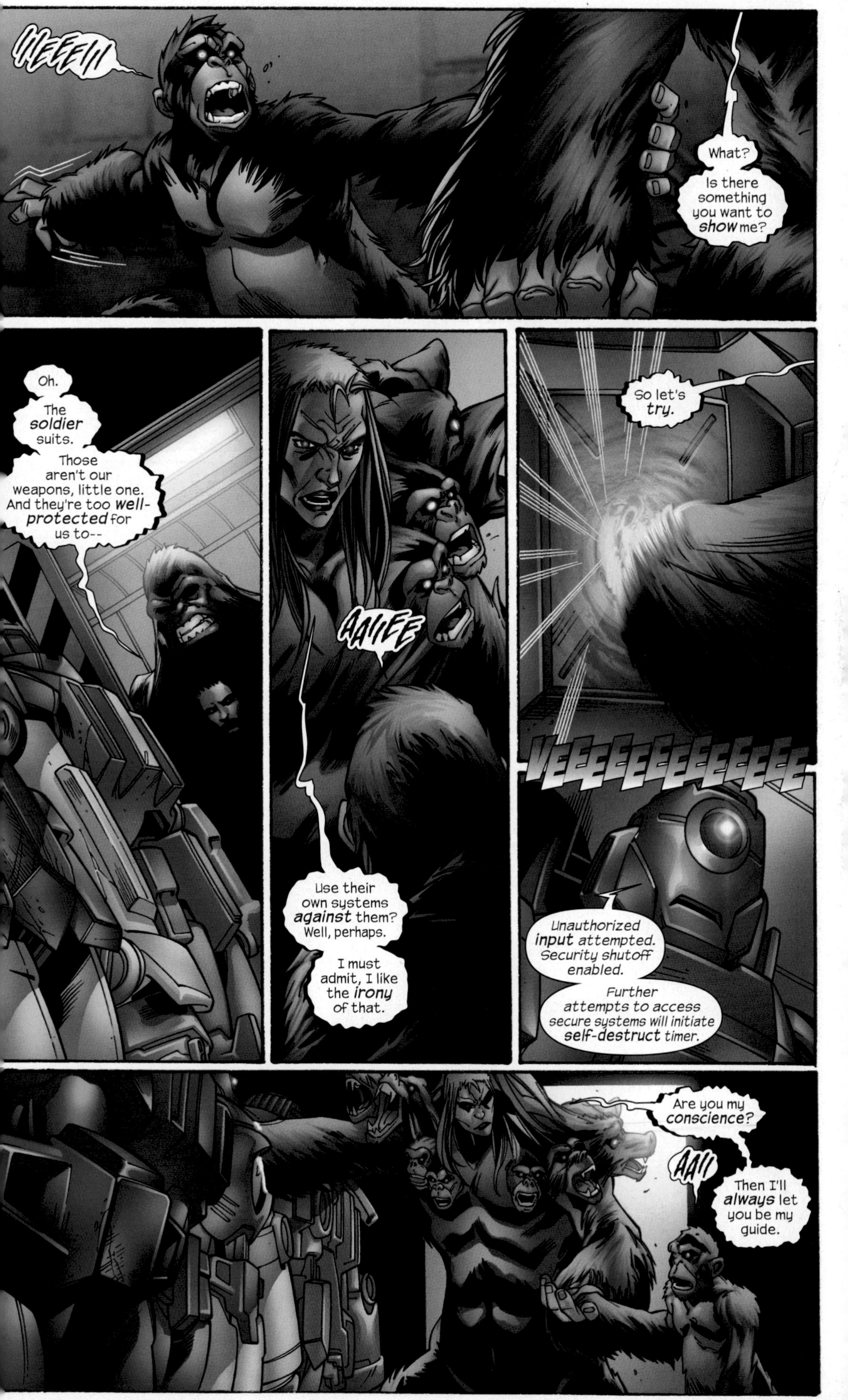
WEEEII
What? Is there something you want to show me?
Oh.
The soldier suits.
Those aren't our weapons, little one. And they're too well-protected for us to--
AAIIEE
Use their own systems against them? Well, perhaps.
I must admit, I like the irony of that.
So let's try.
VEEEEEEEEEEEEE
Unauthorized input attempted. Security shutoff enabled.
Further attempts to access secure systems will initiate self-destruct timer.
Are you my conscience?
AAII
Then I'll always let you be my guide.

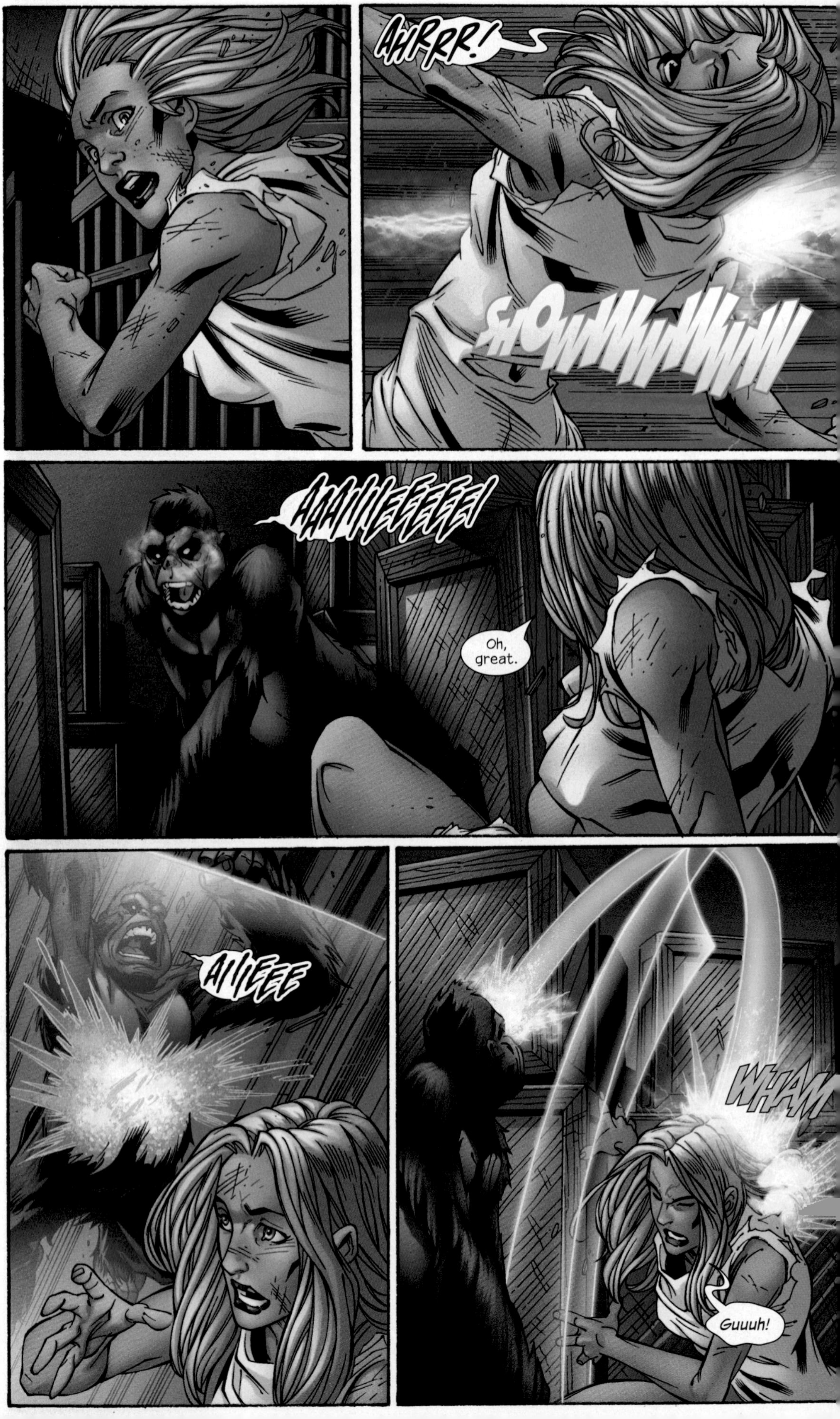
AHRRR!
SHOWWWWWWWWN
AAAIIIEEEEEE!
Oh, great.
AIIIEEE
WHAM
Guuuh!

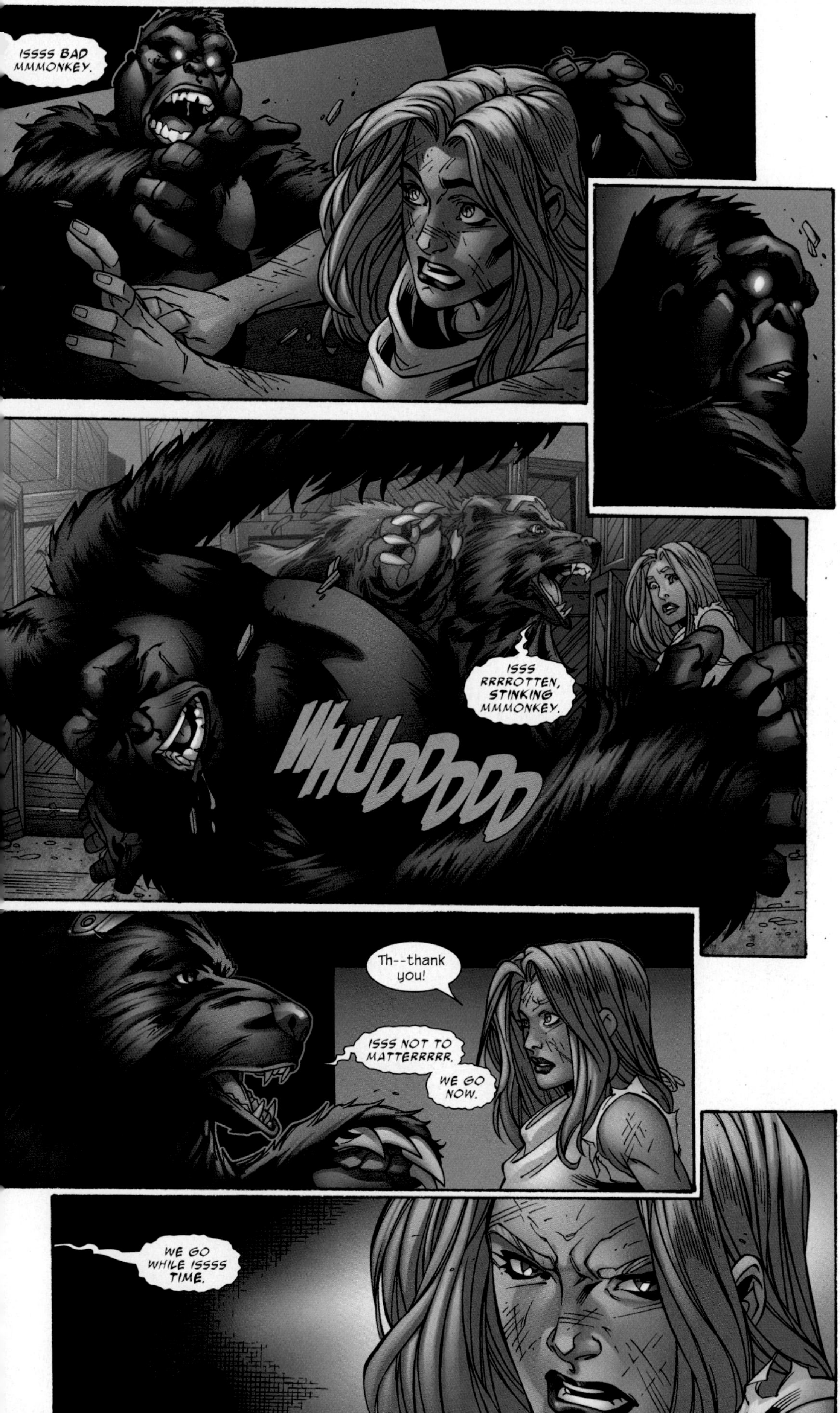
ISSSS BAD MMMONKEY.
ISSS RRRROTTEN, STINKING MMMONKEY.
WHUDDDDD
Th--thank you!
ISSS NOT TO MATTERRRRR.
WE GO NOW.
WE GO WHILE ISSSS TIME.

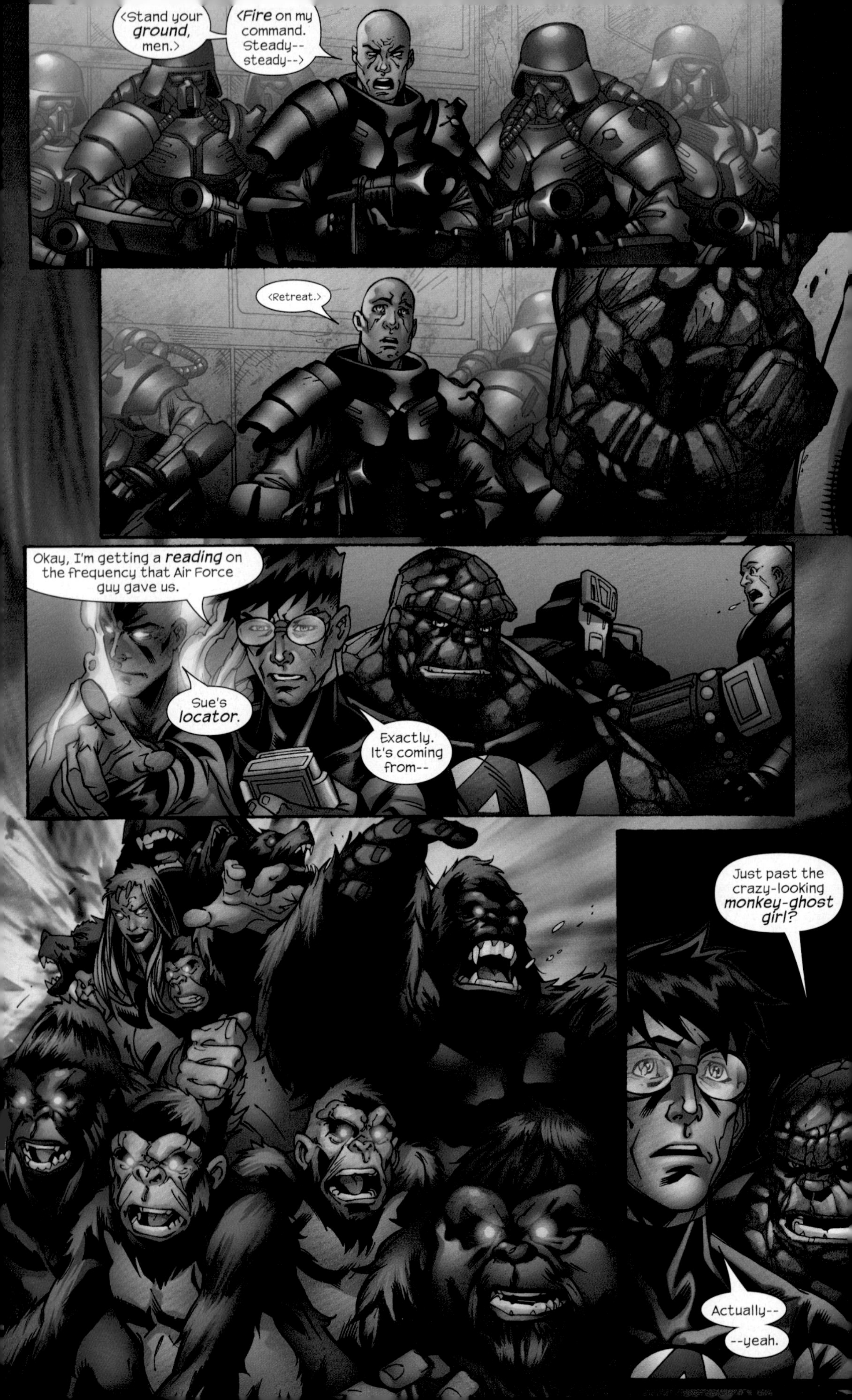

<Stand your *ground*, men.>
<*Fire* on my command. Steady-- steady-->
<Retreat.>
Okay, I'm getting a *reading* on the frequency that Air Force guy gave us.
Sue's *locator*.
Exactly. It's coming from--
Just past the crazy-looking *monkey-ghost girl*?
Actually--
--yeah.

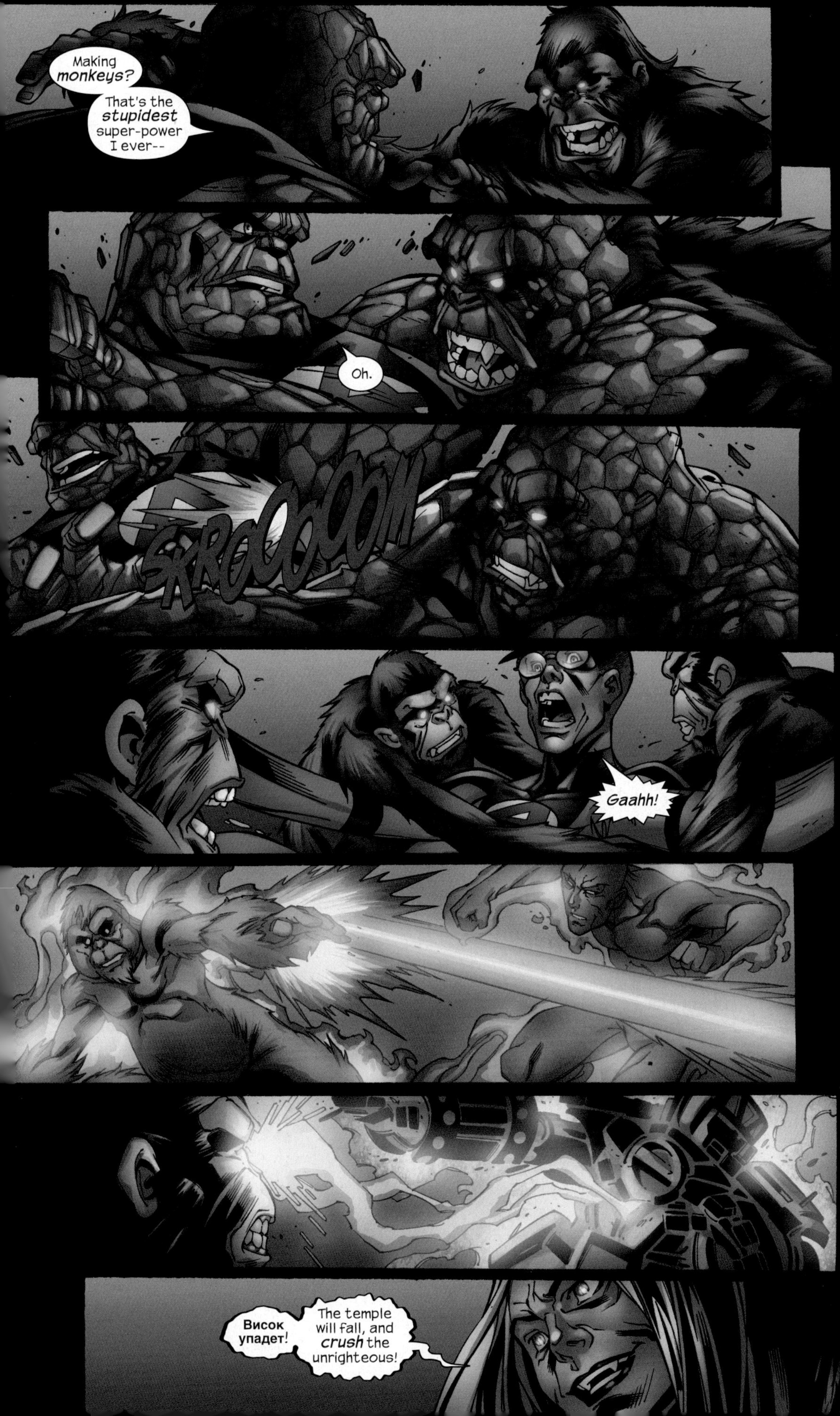
Making monkeys?
That's the stupidest super-power I ever--
Oh.
SKROOOOOM
Gaahh!
Висок упадет!
The temple will fall, and crush the unrighteous!

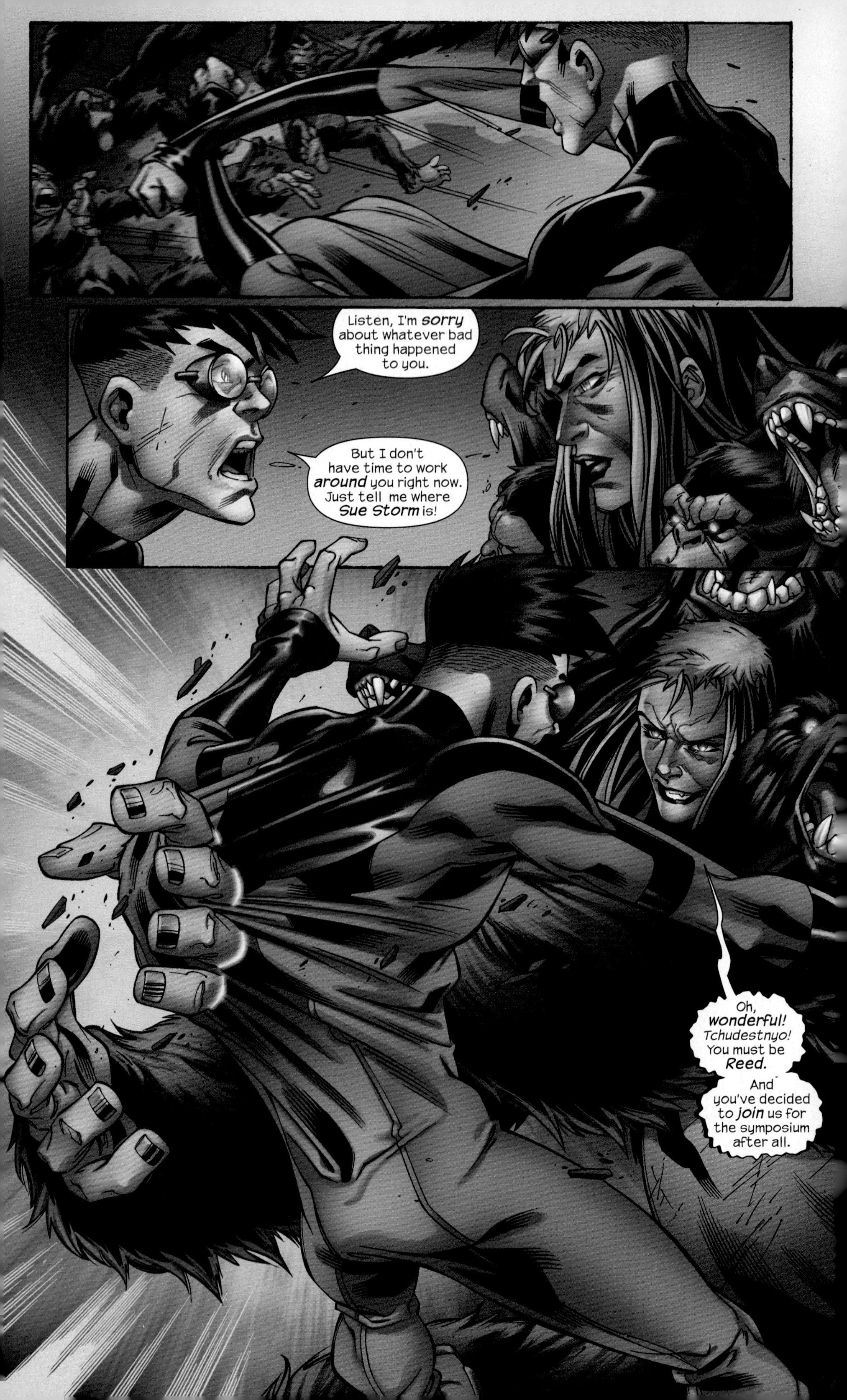
Listen, I'm sorry about whatever bad thing happened to you.
But I don't have time to work around you right now. Just tell me where Sue Storm is!
Oh, wonderful! Tchudestnyo! You must be Reed.
And you've decided to join us for the symposium after all.

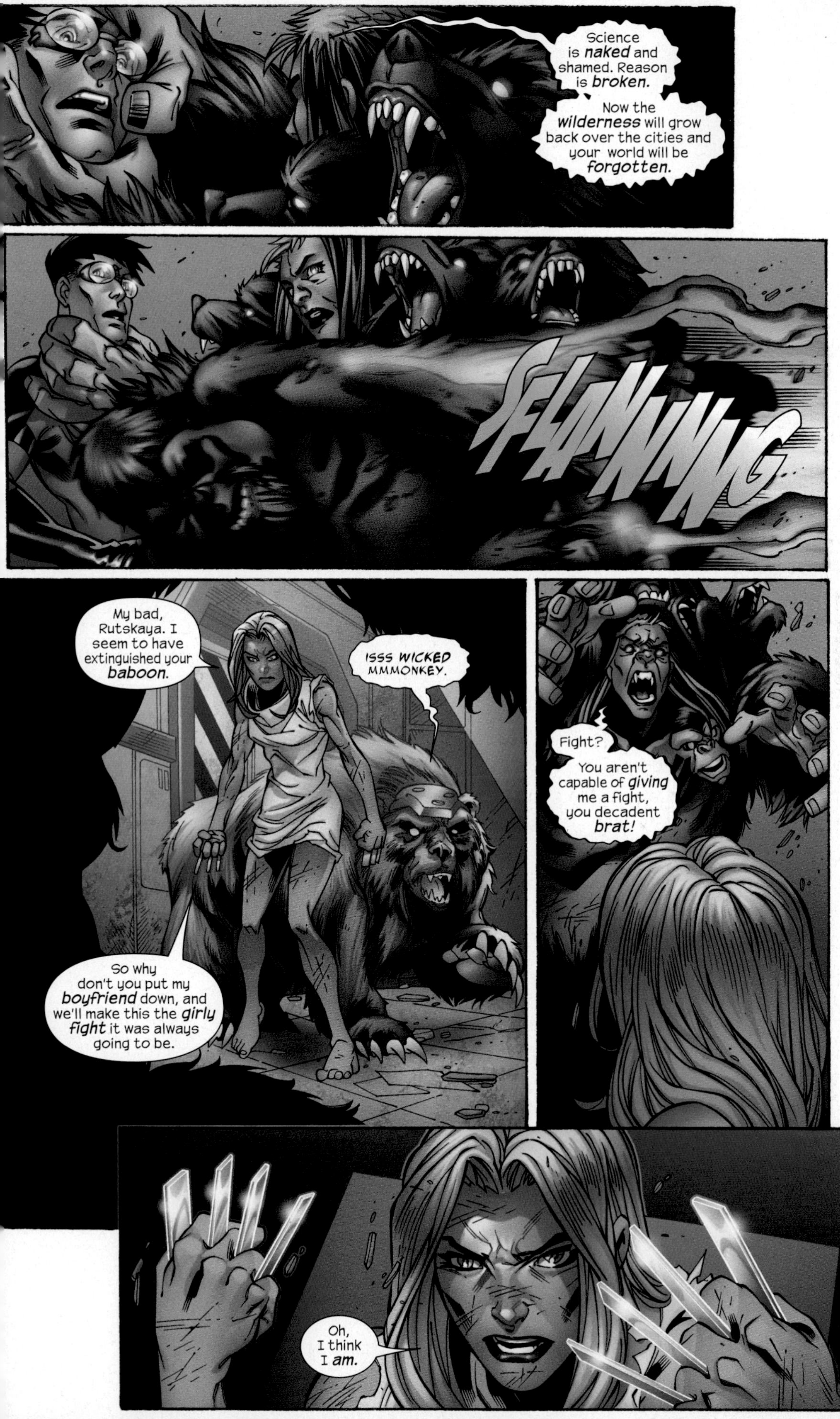
Science is naked and shamed. Reason is broken.
Now the wilderness will grow back over the cities and your world will be forgotten.
SHUNNNG
My bad, Rutskaya. I seem to have extinguished your baboon.
ISSS WICKED MMMONKEY.
So why don't you put my boyfriend down, and we'll make this the girly fight it was always going to be.
Fight?
You aren't capable of giving me a fight, you decadent brat!
Oh, I think I am.

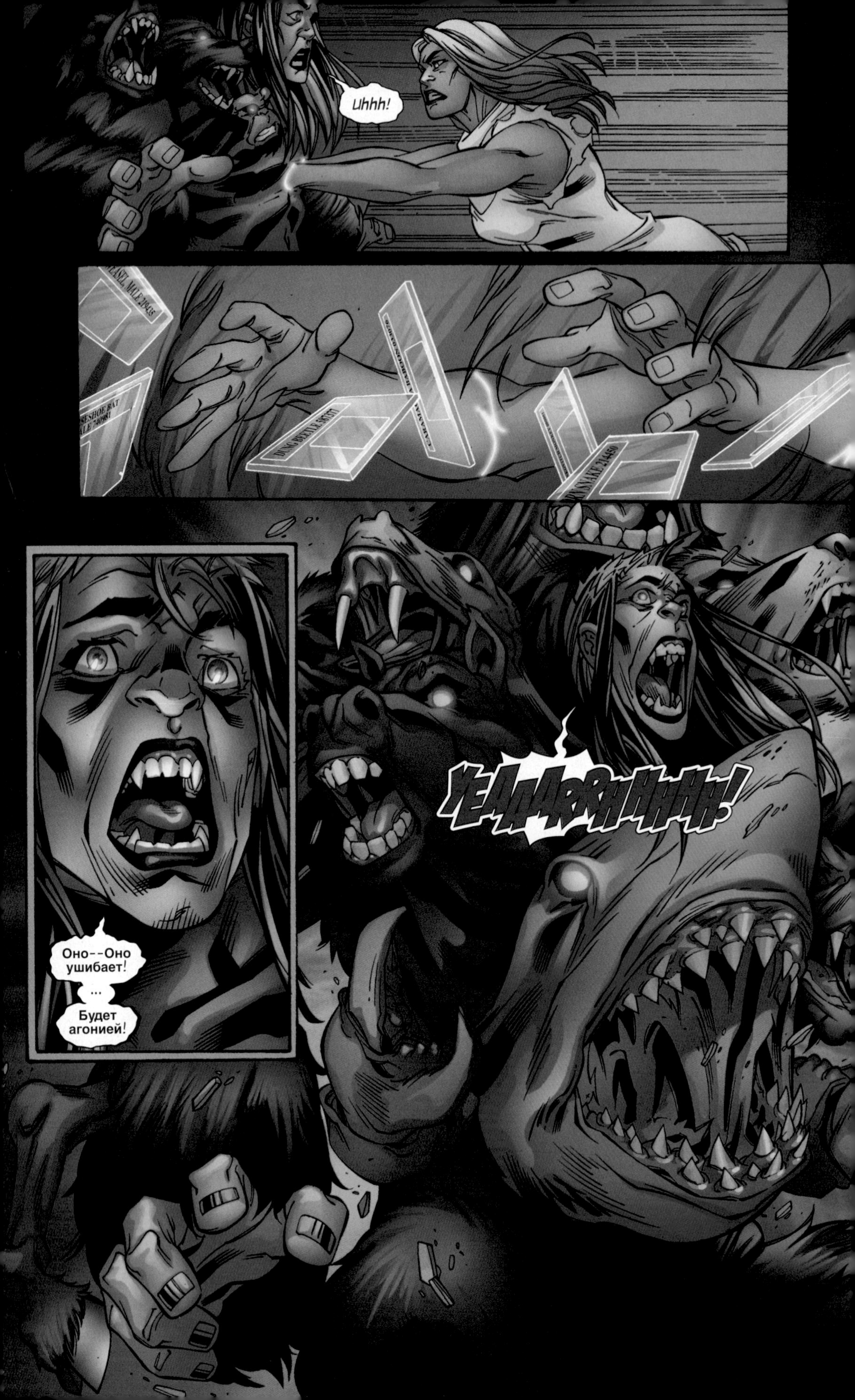
Uhhh!
DUNG BEETLE 585377
Оно--Оно ушибает!
...
Будет агонией!
YEAARHHHHH!

Wh-- what did you *do* to her?

Nothing. She's *unstable*.

I *got* that.

I mean-- morpho- genetically.

I just showed her a few more *options*.

And now she's having trouble sticking to a *decision*.

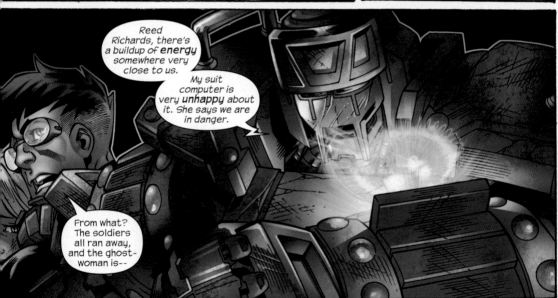

Reed Richards, there's a buildup of *energy* somewhere very close to us.

My suit computer is very *unhappy* about it. She says we are in danger.

From what? The soldiers all ran away, and the ghost-woman is--

The *suits!* The suits have a *nuclear power* source.

Shatalov, what's the *setting* on the timer? When they self-destruct, how *long* do they take to--

VEEEEEEEEEEEEEE

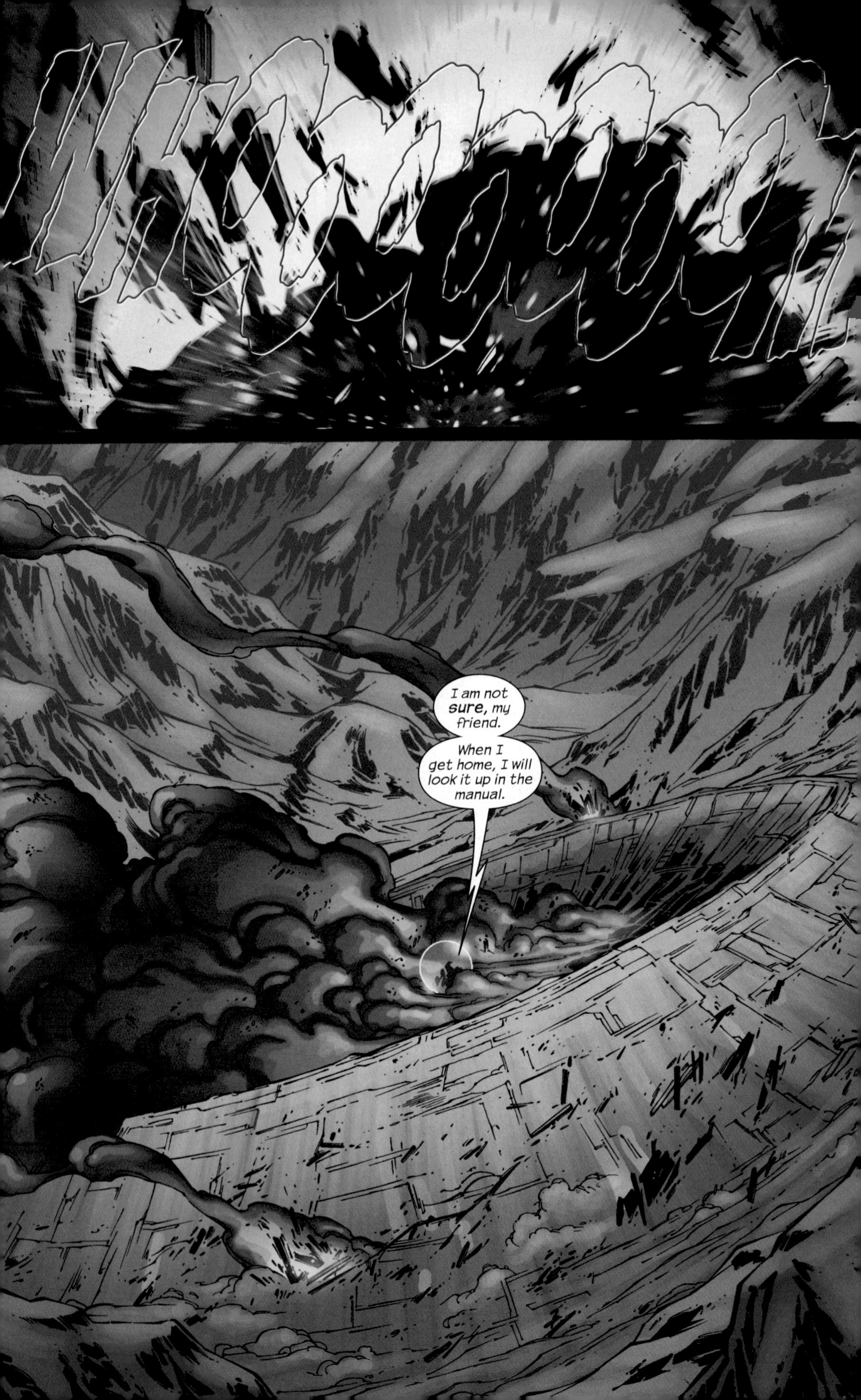

I am not **sure,** my friend.
When I get home, I will look it up in the manual.

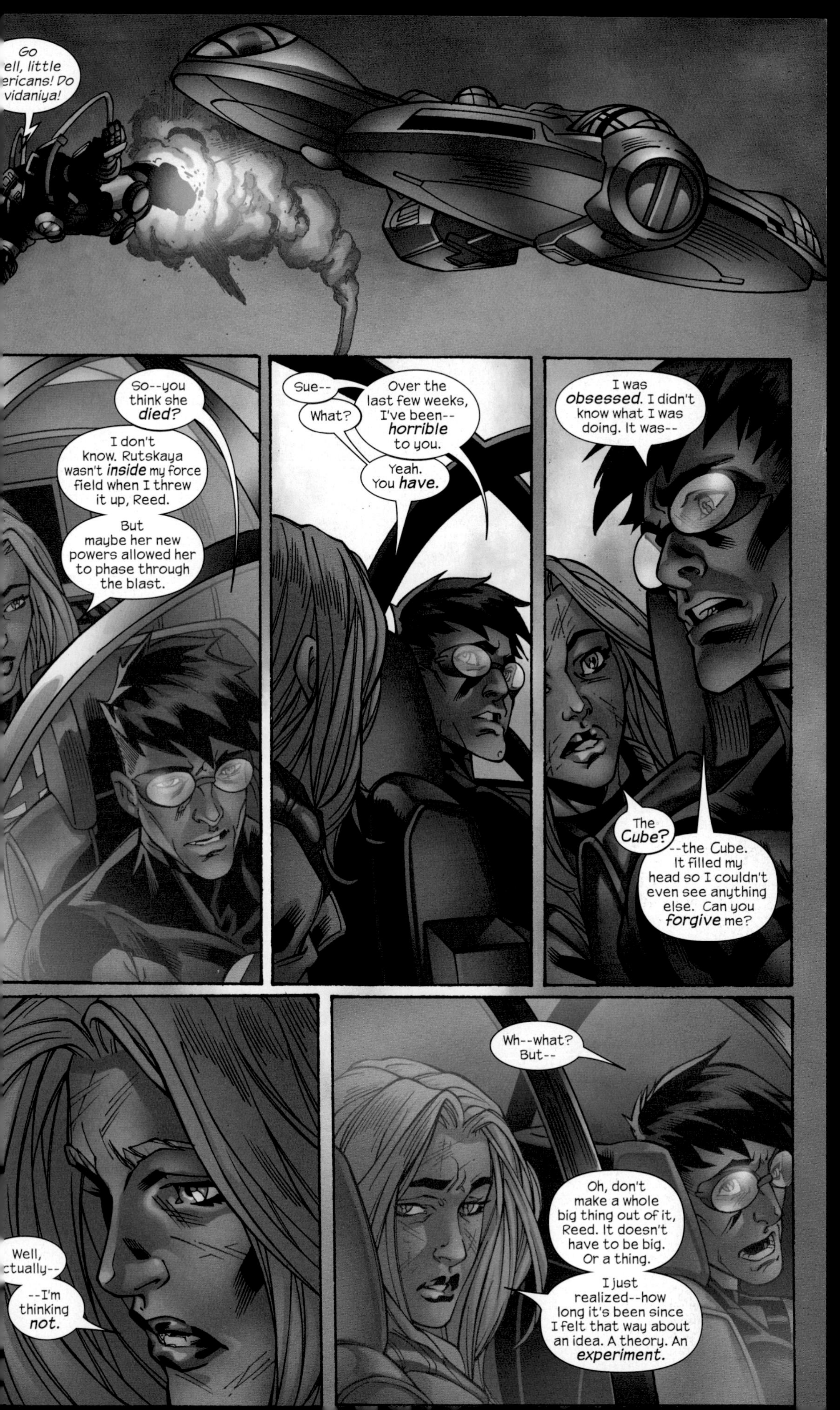

Go
ell, little
ericans! Do
vidaniya!
So--you think she *died?*
I don't know. Rutskaya wasn't *inside* my force field when I threw it up, Reed.
But maybe her new powers allowed her to phase through the blast.
Sue--
What?
Over the last few weeks, I've been-- *horrible* to you.
Yeah. You *have.*
I was *obsessed.* I didn't know what I was doing. It was--
The *Cube?*
--the Cube. It filled my head so I couldn't even see anything else. Can you *forgive* me?
Well,
ctually--
--I'm thinking *not.*
Wh--what? But--
Oh, don't make a whole big thing out of it, Reed. It doesn't have to be big. Or a thing.
I just realized--how long it's been since I felt that way about an idea. A theory. An *experiment.*

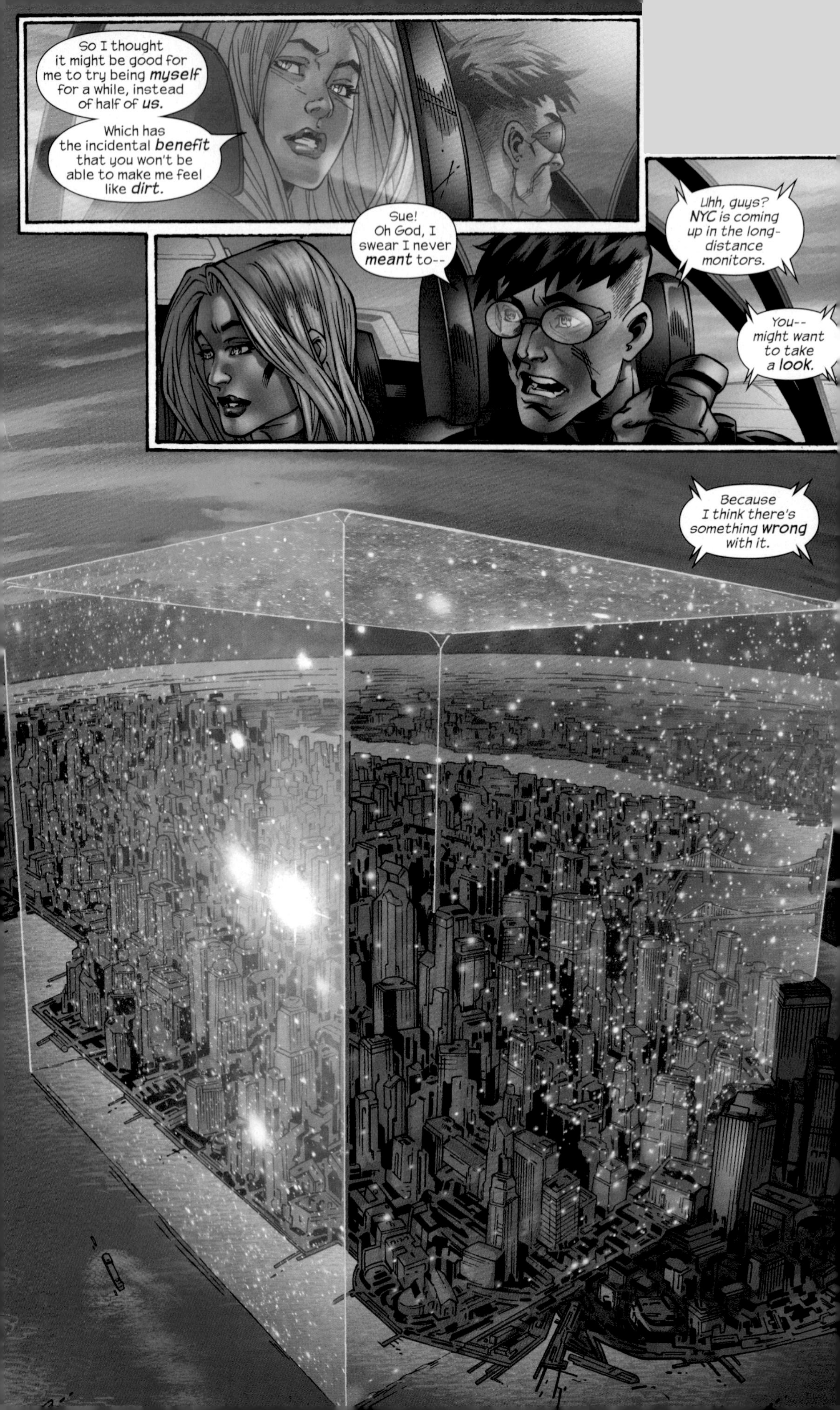
So I thought it might be good for me to try being *myself* for a while, instead of half of *us.*
Which has the incidental *benefit* that you won't be able to make me feel like *dirt.*
Sue! Oh God, I swear I never *meant* to--
Uhh, guys? *NYC* is coming up in the long-distance monitors.
You--might want to take a *look.*
Because I think there's something *wrong* with it.

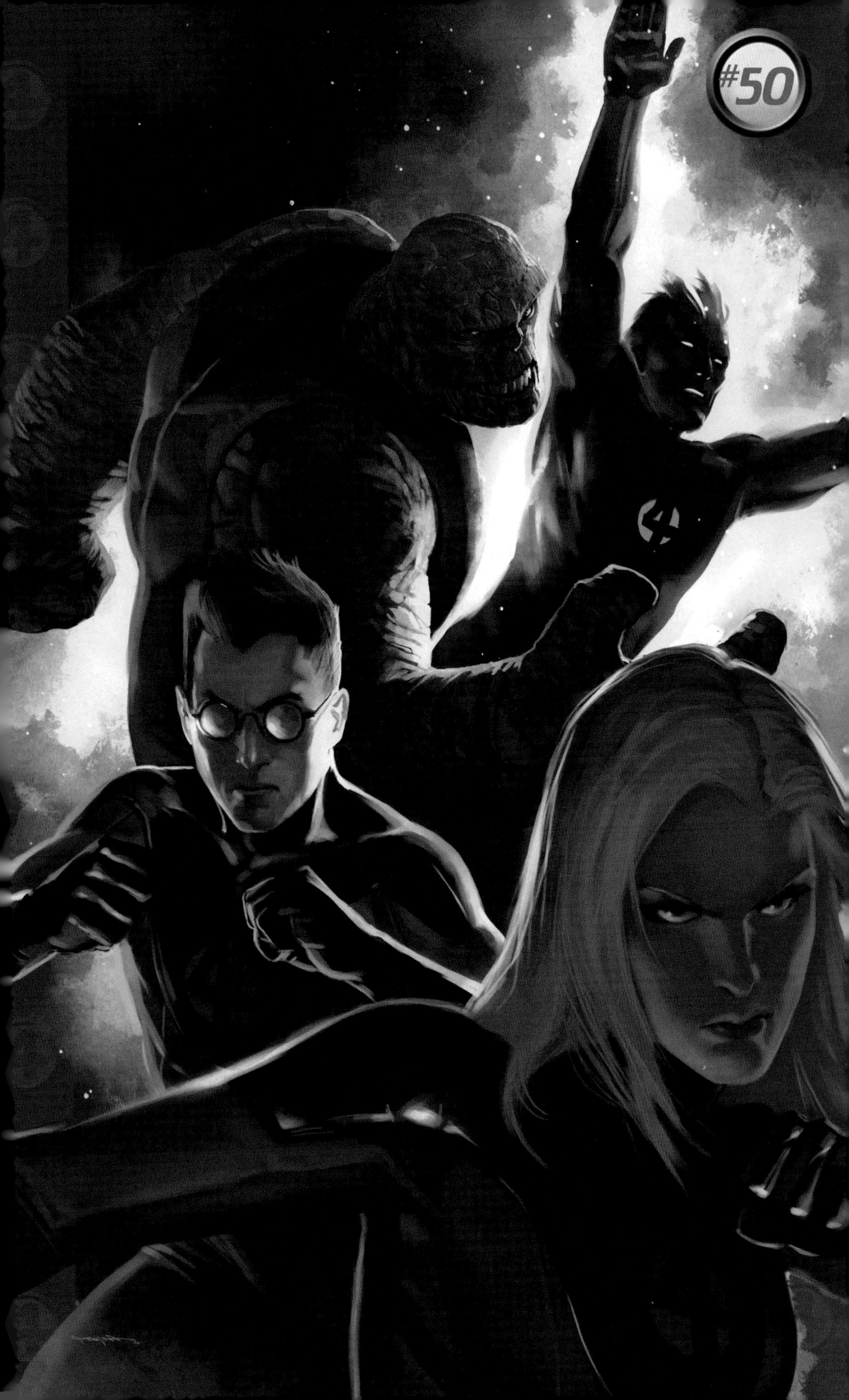
#50

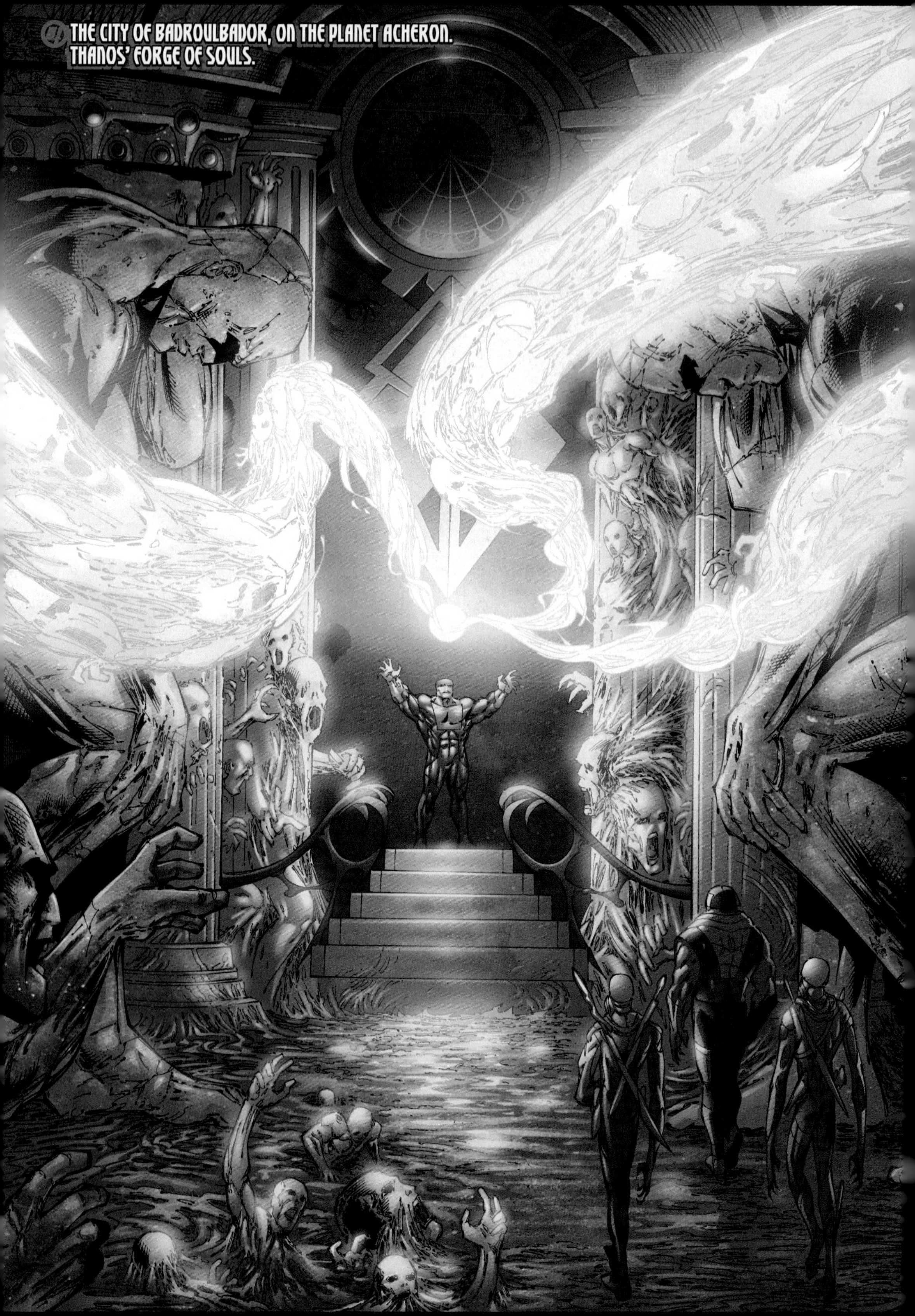
THE CITY OF BADROULBADOR, ON THE PLANET ACHERON.
THANOS' FORGE OF SOULS.

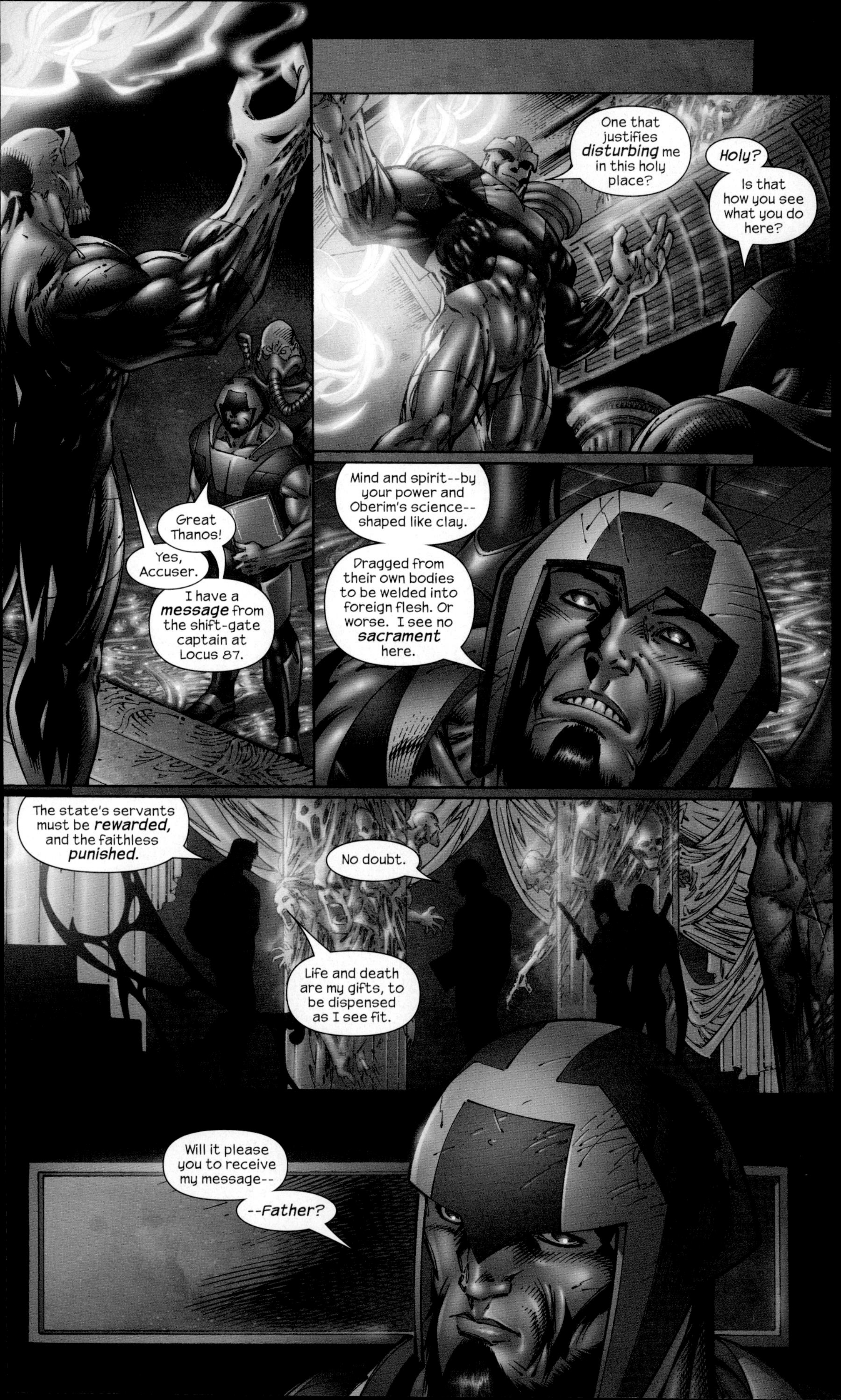
One that justifies disturbing me in this holy place?
Holy?
Is that how you see what you do here?
Great Thanos!
Yes, Accuser.
I have a message from the shift-gate captain at Locus 87.
Mind and spirit--by your power and Oberim's science--shaped like clay.
Dragged from their own bodies to be welded into foreign flesh. Or worse. I see no sacrament here.
The state's servants must be rewarded, and the faithless punished.
No doubt.
Life and death are my gifts, to be dispensed as I see fit.
Will it please you to receive my message--
--Father?

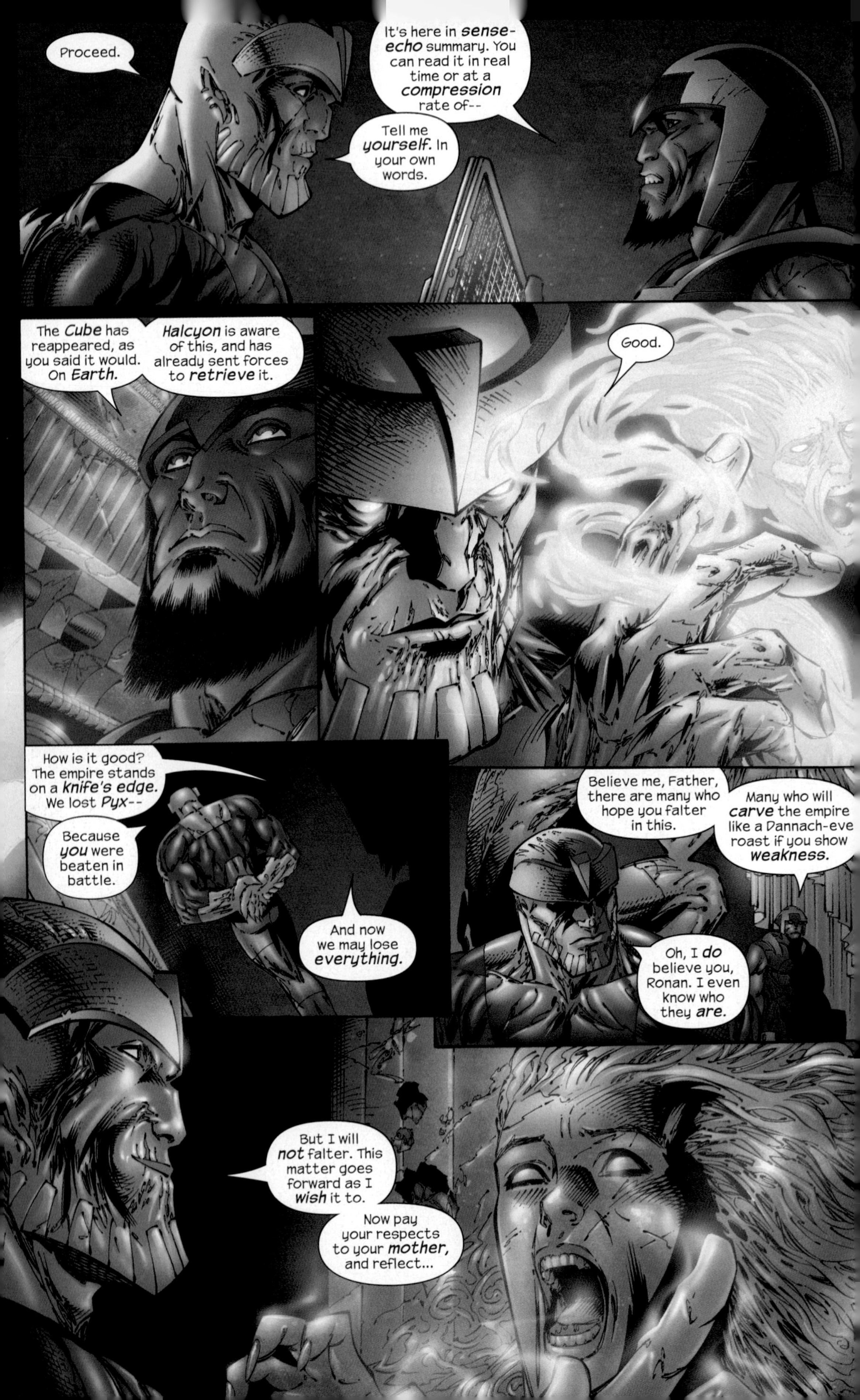
Proceed.
It's here in sense-echo summary. You can read it in real time or at a compression rate of--
Tell me yourself. In your own words.
The Cube has reappeared, as you said it would. On Earth.
Halcyon is aware of this, and has already sent forces to retrieve it.
Good.
How is it good? The empire stands on a knife's edge. We lost Pyx--
Because you were beaten in battle.
And now we may lose everything.
Believe me, Father, there are many who hope you falter in this.
Many who will carve the empire like a Dannach-eve roast if you show weakness.
Oh, I do believe you, Ronan. I even know who they are.
But I will not falter. This matter goes forward as I wish it to.
Now pay your respects to your mother, and reflect...

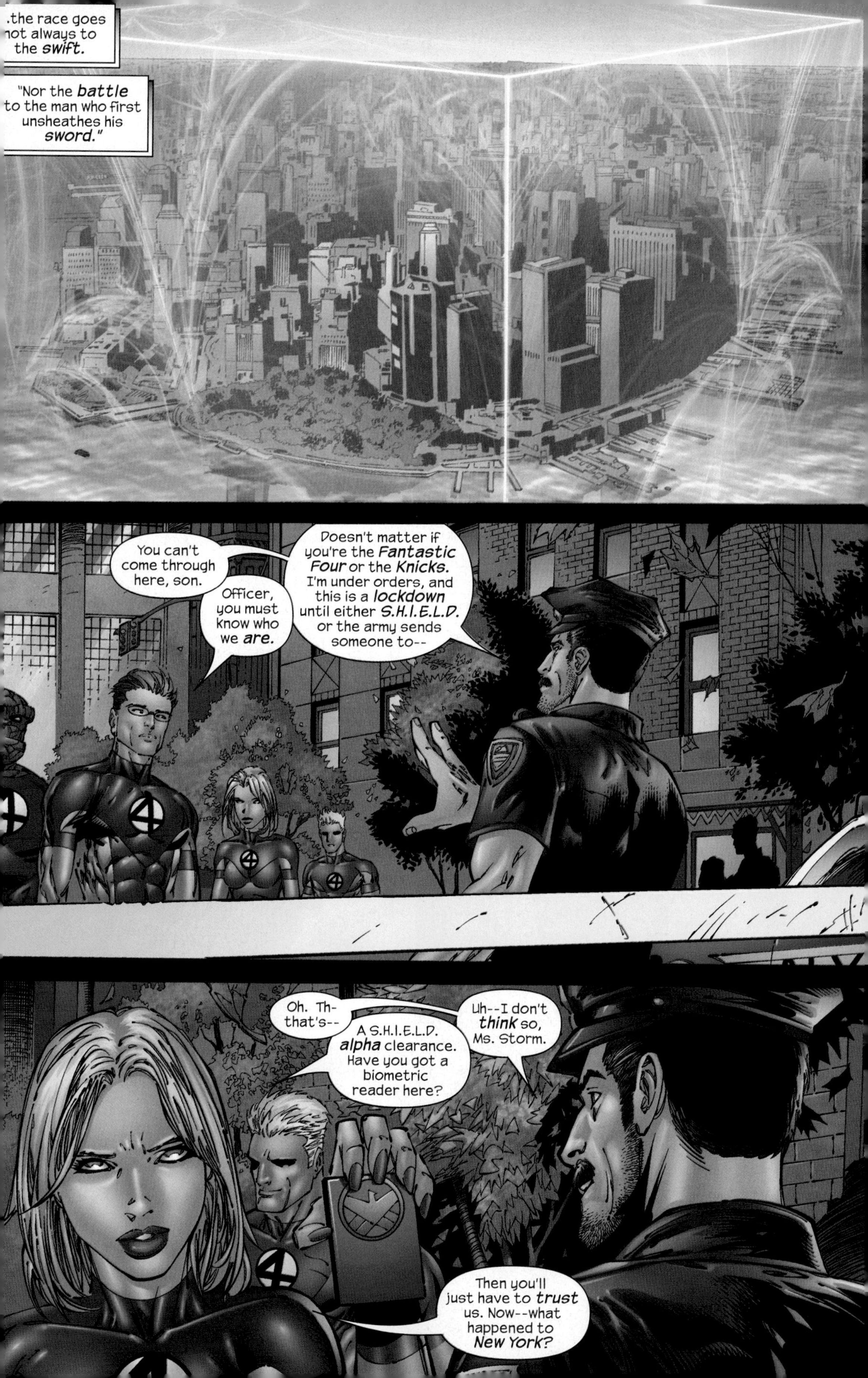
.the race goes not always to the *swift.*
"Nor the *battle* to the man who first unsheathes his *sword.*"
You can't come through here, son.
Officer, you must know who we *are.*
Doesn't matter if you're the *Fantastic Four* or the *Knicks.* I'm under orders, and this is a *lockdown* until either *S.H.I.E.L.D.* or the army sends someone to--
Oh. Th-that's--
A S.H.I.E.L.D. *alpha* clearance. Have you got a biometric reader here?
Uh--I don't *think* so, Ms. Storm.
Then you'll just have to *trust* us. Now--what happened to *New York?*

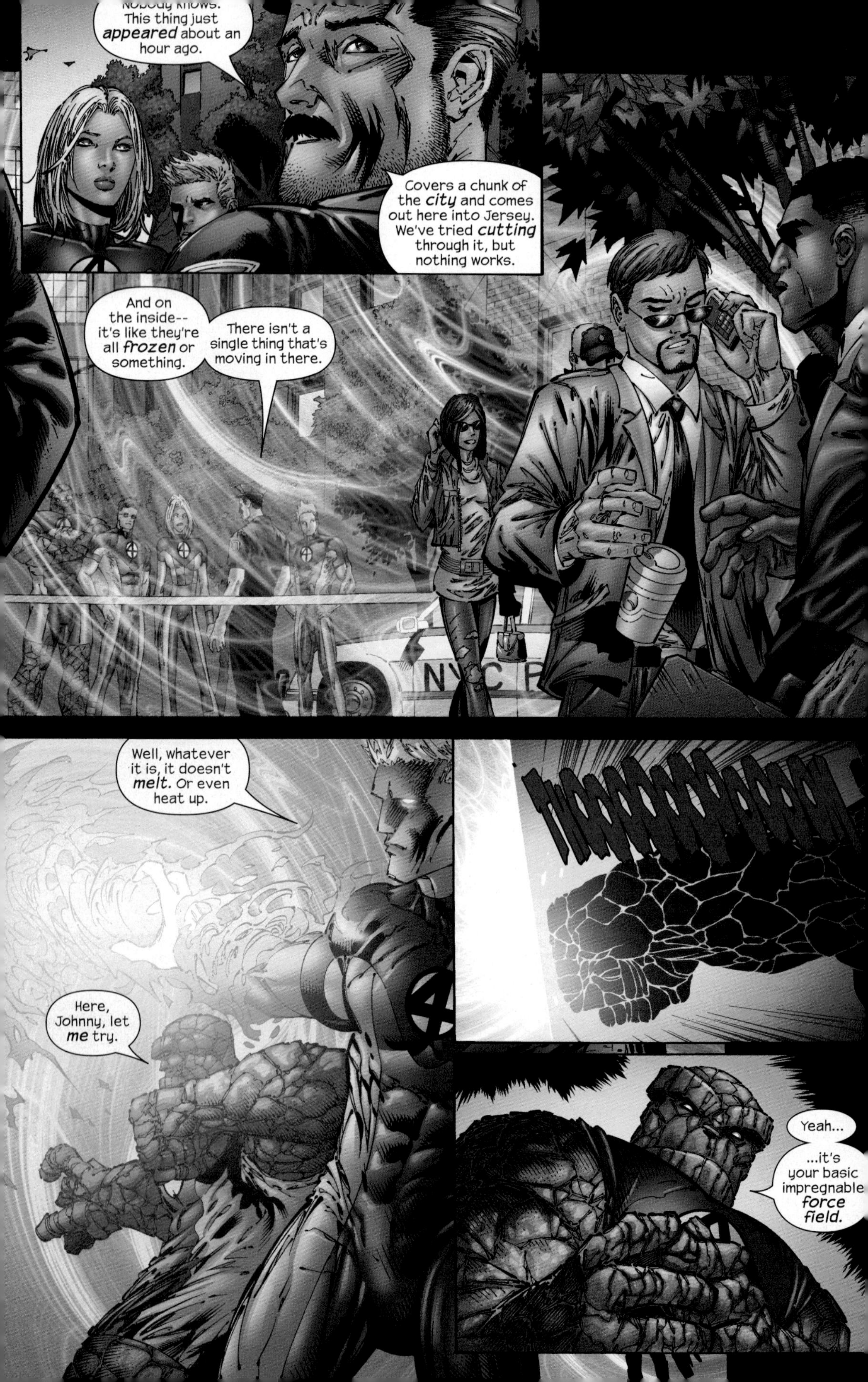
This thing just appeared about an hour ago.
Covers a chunk of the city and comes out here into Jersey. We've tried cutting through it, but nothing works.
And on the inside--it's like they're all frozen or something.
There isn't a single thing that's moving in there.
Well, whatever it is, it doesn't melt. Or even heat up.
Here, Johnny, let me try.
Yeah...
...it's your basic impregnable force field.

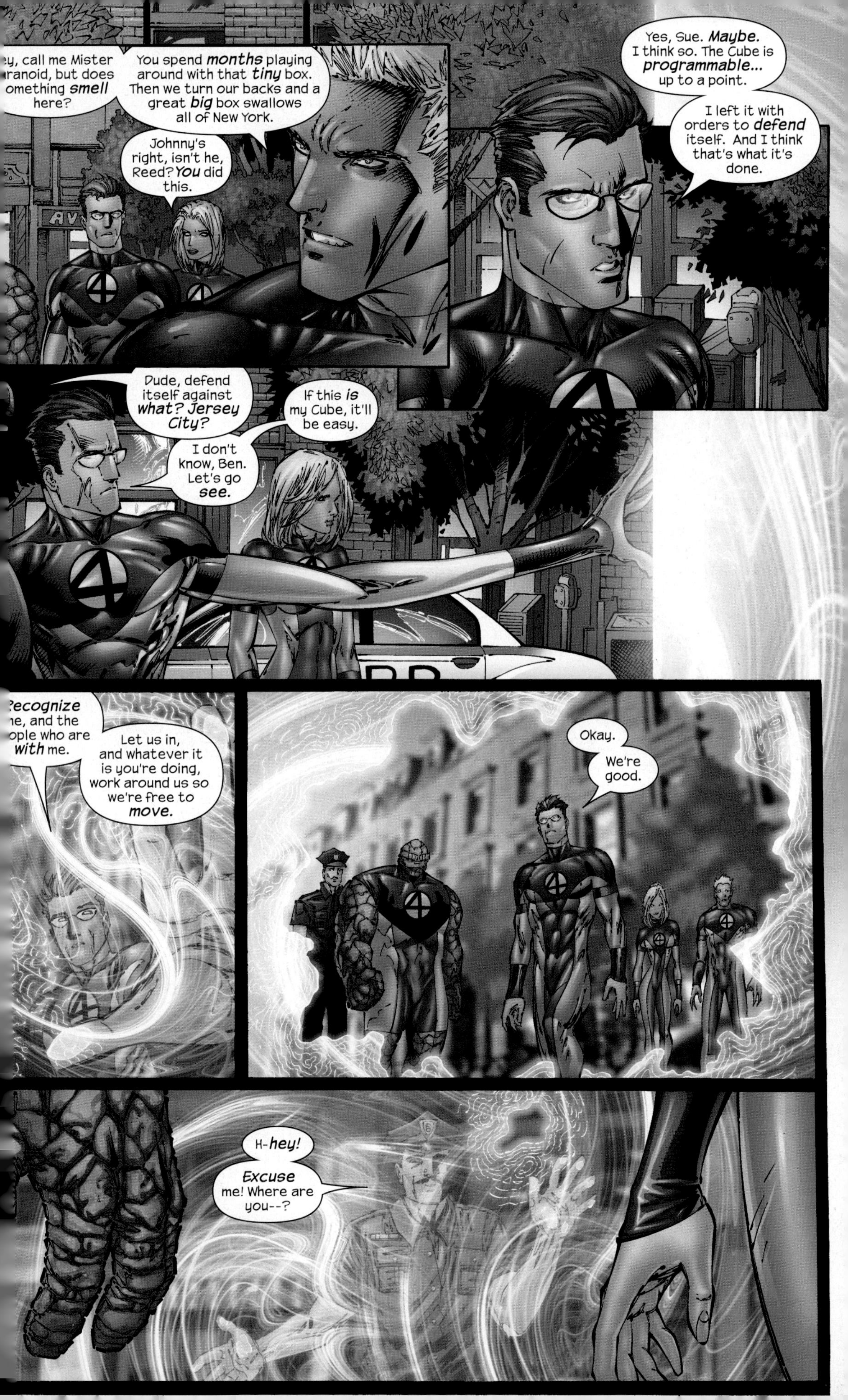

ey, call me Mister
aranoid, but does
omething *smell*
here?
You spend **months** playing around with that *tiny* box. Then we turn our backs and a great *big* box swallows all of New York.
Johnny's right, isn't he, Reed? *You* did this.
Yes, Sue. *Maybe.* I think so. The Cube is ***programmable...*** up to a point.
I left it with orders to ***defend*** itself. And I think that's what it's done.
Dude, defend itself against ***what? Jersey City?***
I don't know, Ben. Let's go ***see.***
If this ***is*** my Cube, it'll be easy.
ecognize
e, and the
ople who are
with me.
Let us in, and whatever it is you're doing, work around us so we're free to ***move.***
Okay.
We're good.
H-***hey!***
Excuse me! Where are you--?

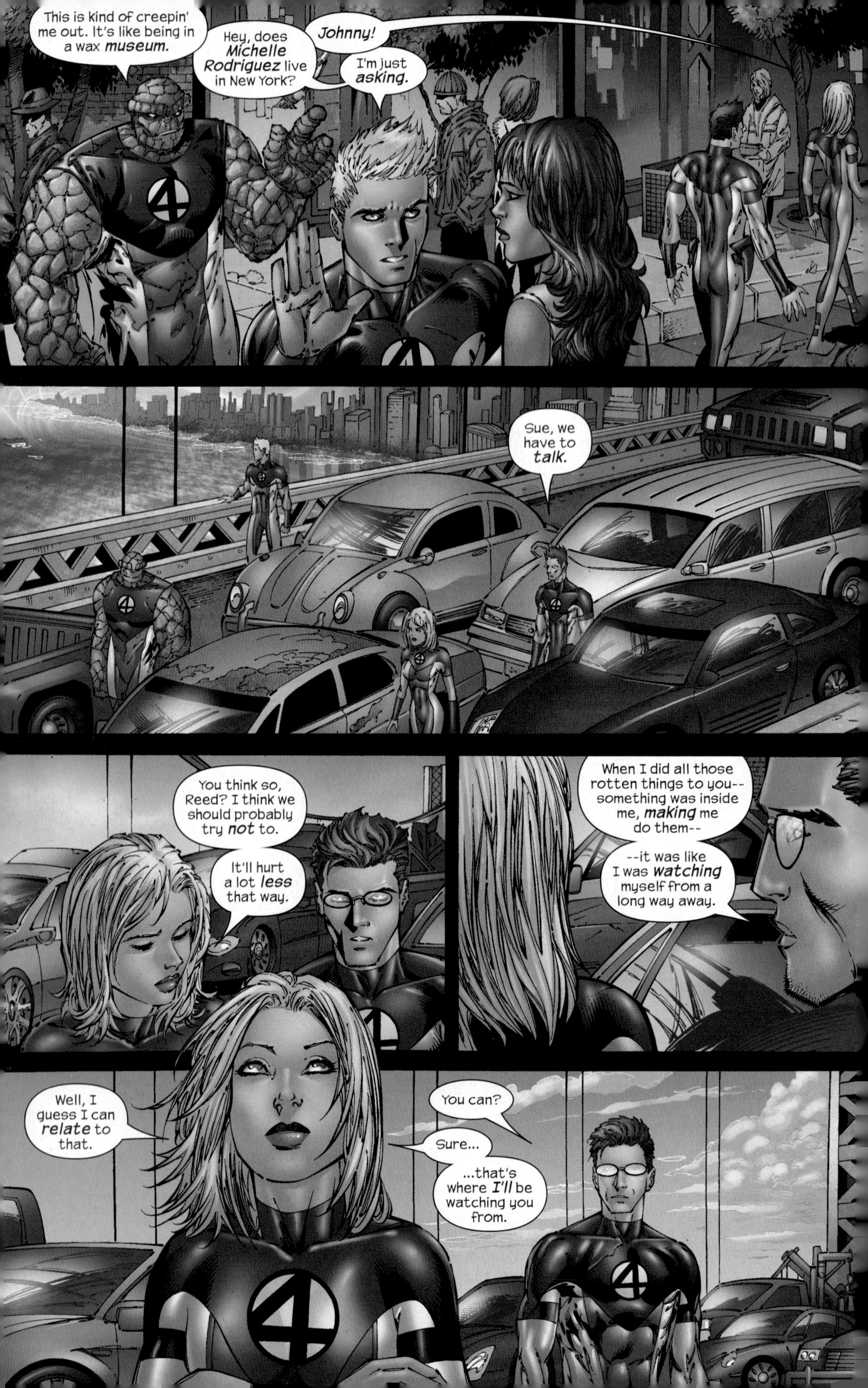
This is kind of creepin' me out. It's like being in a wax museum.
Hey, does Michelle Rodriguez live in New York?
Johnny!
I'm just asking.
Sue, we have to talk.
You think so, Reed? I think we should probably try not to.
It'll hurt a lot less that way.
When I did all those rotten things to you-- something was inside me, making me do them--
--it was like I was watching myself from a long way away.
Well, I guess I can relate to that.
You can?
Sure...
...that's where I'll be watching you from.

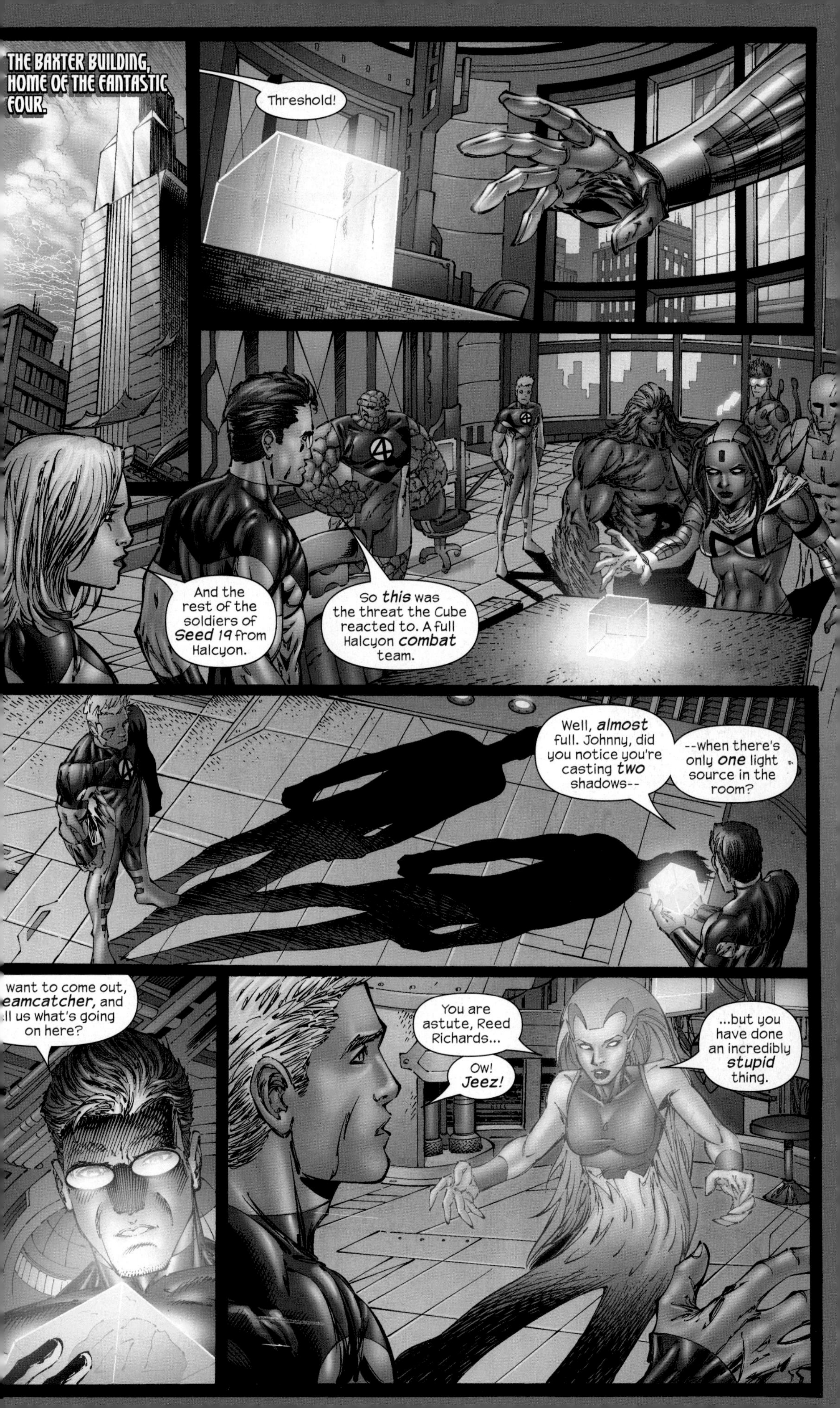

THE BAXTER BUILDING, HOME OF THE FANTASTIC FOUR.
Threshold!
And the rest of the soldiers of Seed 19 from Halcyon.
So this was the threat the Cube reacted to. A full Halcyon combat team.
Well, almost full. Johnny, did you notice you're casting two shadows--
--when there's only one light source in the room?
want to come out, eamcatcher, and ll us what's going on here?
You are astute, Reed Richards...
Ow! Jeez!
...but you have done an incredibly stupid thing.

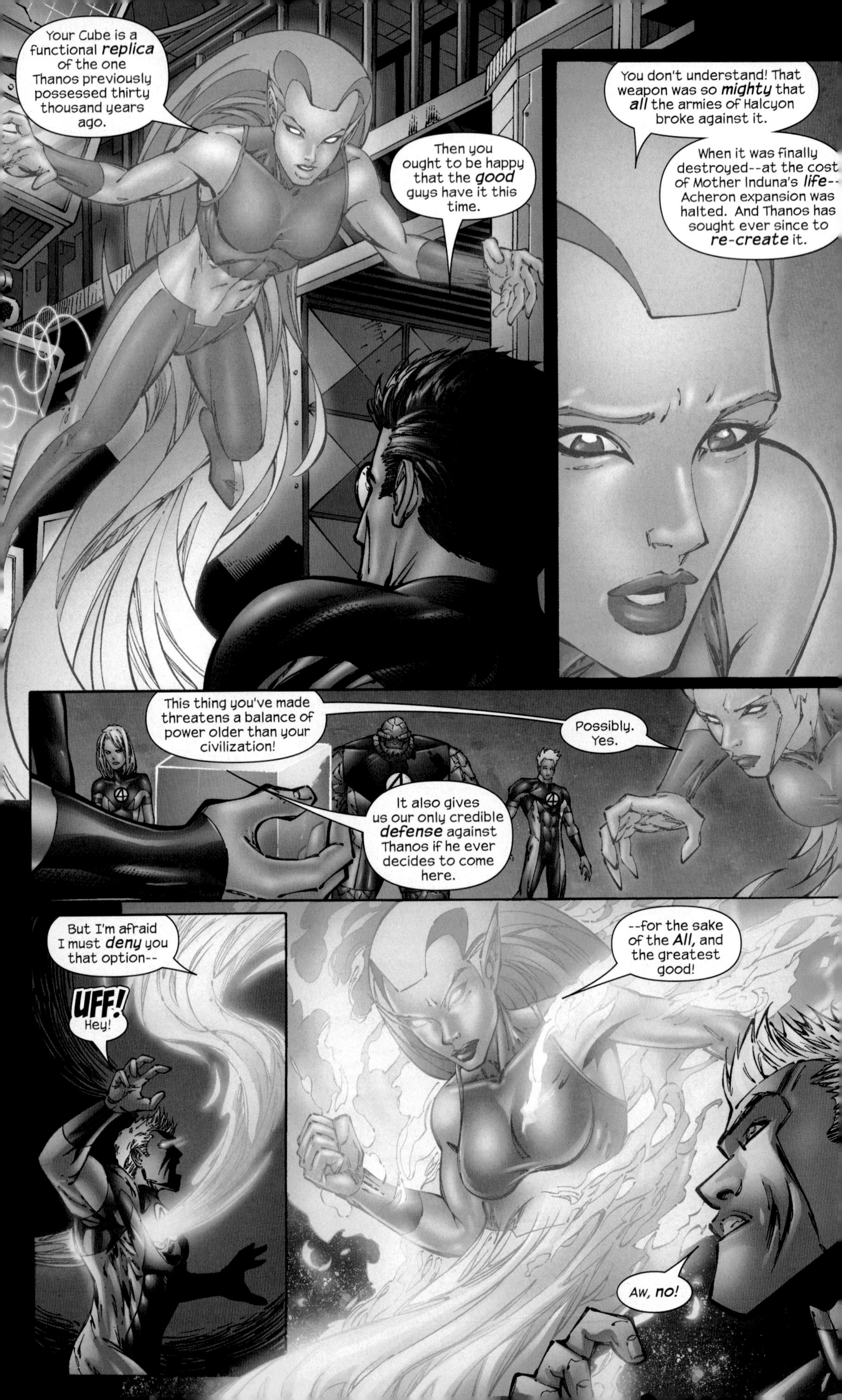
Your Cube is a functional replica of the one Thanos previously possessed thirty thousand years ago.
Then you ought to be happy that the good guys have it this time.
You don't understand! That weapon was so mighty that all the armies of Halcyon broke against it.
When it was finally destroyed--at the cost of Mother Induna's life--Acheron expansion was halted. And Thanos has sought ever since to re-create it.
This thing you've made threatens a balance of power older than your civilization!
Possibly. Yes.
It also gives us our only credible defense against Thanos if he ever decides to come here.
But I'm afraid I must deny you that option--
UFF!
Hey!
--for the sake of the All, and the greatest good!
Aw, no!

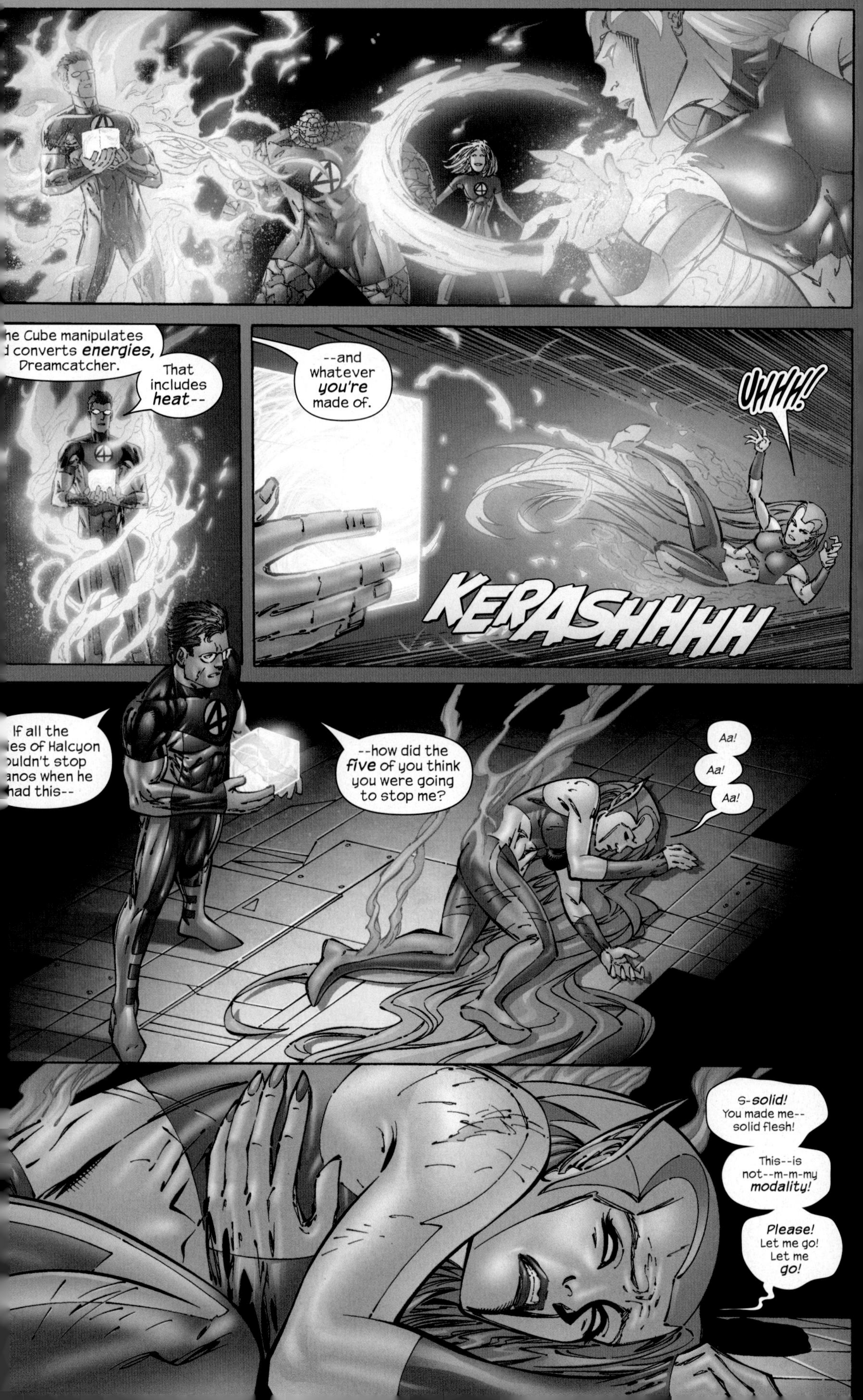

he Cube manipulates
d converts energies,
Dreamcatcher.
That includes heat--
--and whatever you're made of.
UHHH!
KERASHHHH
If all the
ies of Halcyon
ouldn't stop
anos when he
had this--
--how did the five of you think you were going to stop me?
Aa!
Aa!
Aa!
S-solid! You made me-- solid flesh!
This--is not--m-m-my modality!
Please! Let me go! Let me go!

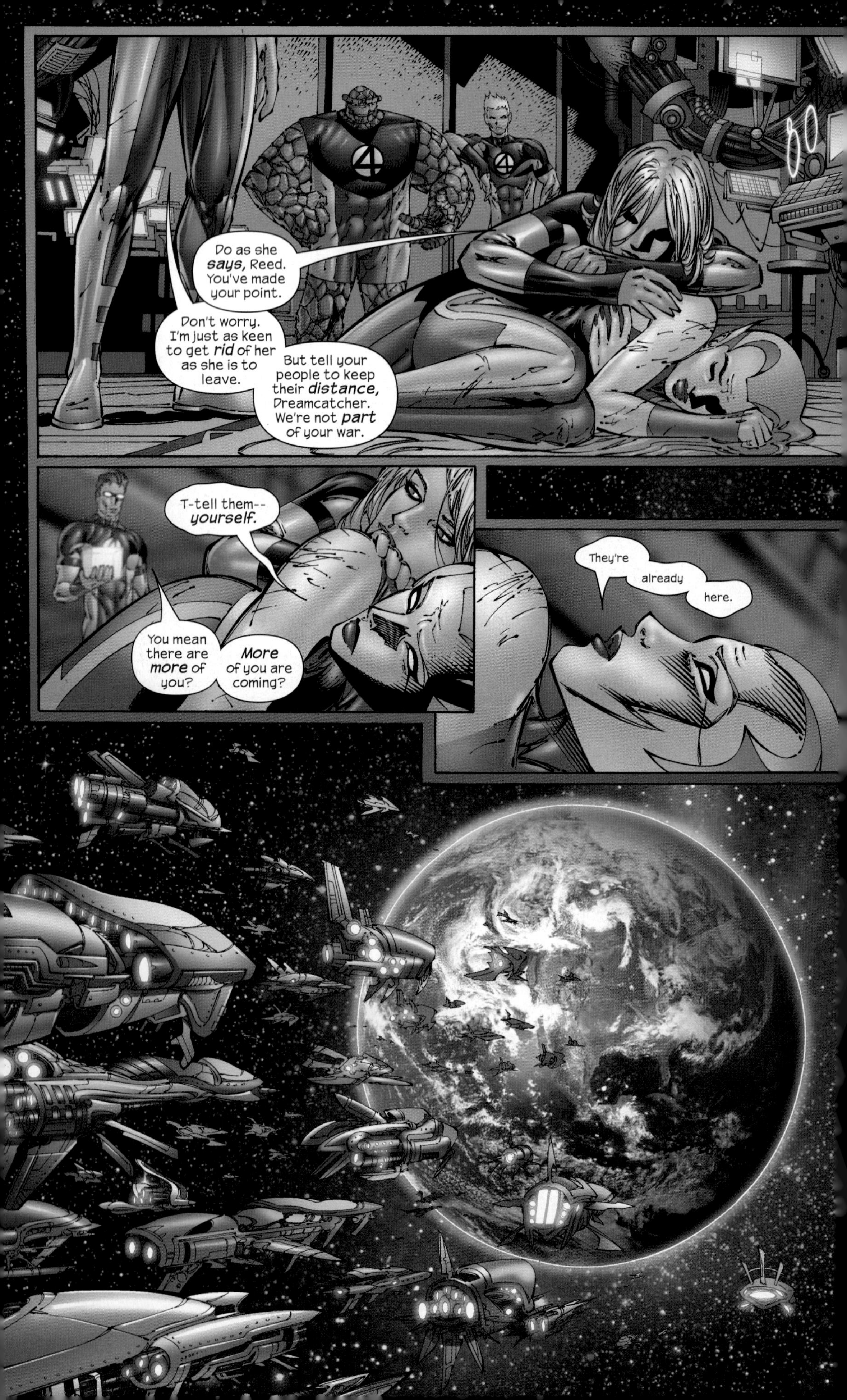
Do as she says, Reed. You've made your point.
Don't worry. I'm just as keen to get rid of her as she is to leave.
But tell your people to keep their distance, Dreamcatcher. We're not part of your war.
T-tell them-- yourself.
You mean there are more of you?
More of you are coming?
They're already here.

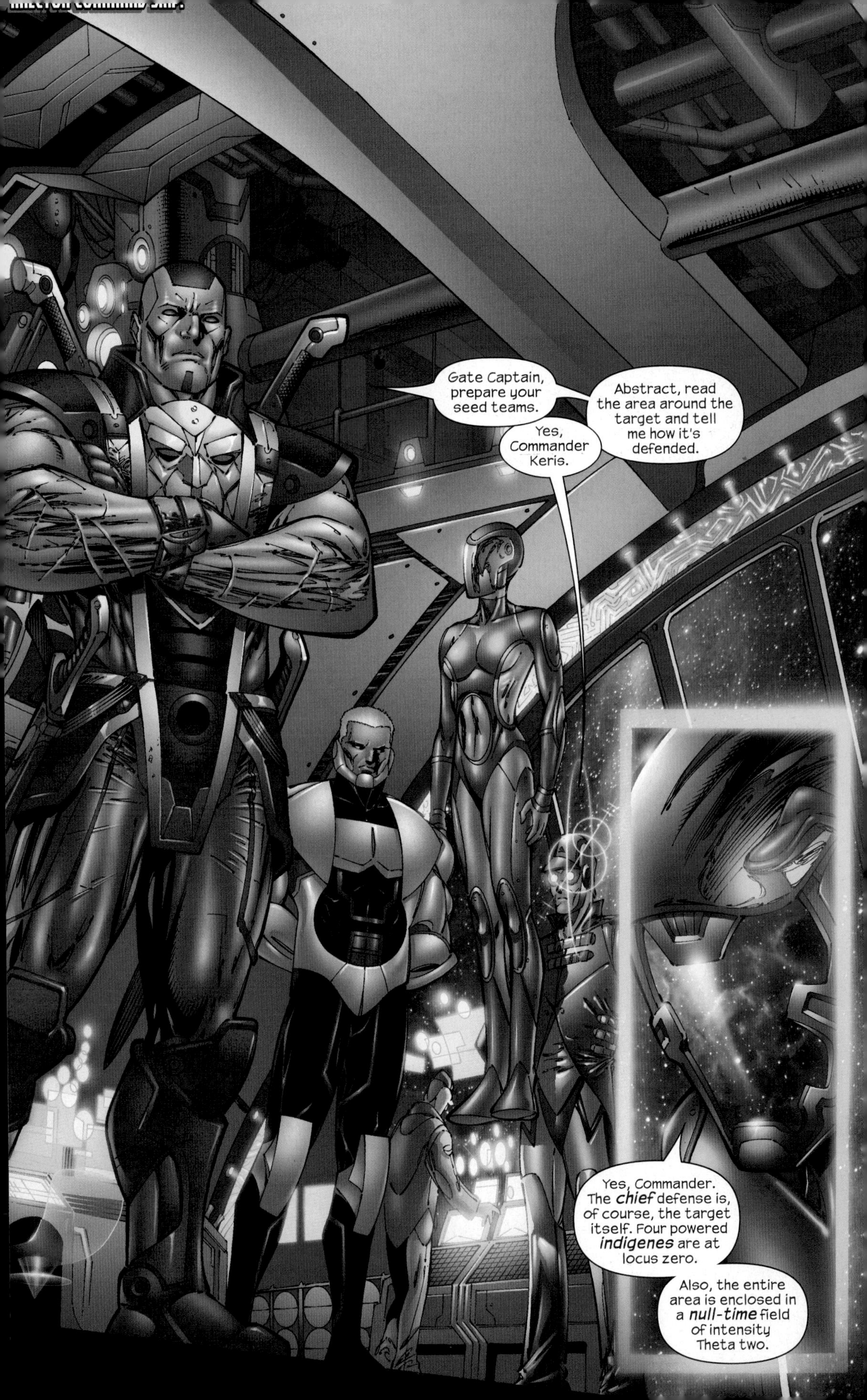
Gate Captain, prepare your seed teams.
Abstract, read the area around the target and tell me how it's defended.
Yes, Commander Keris.
Yes, Commander. The *chief* defense is, of course, the target itself. Four powered *indigenes* are at locus zero.
Also, the entire area is enclosed in a *null-time* field of intensity Theta two.

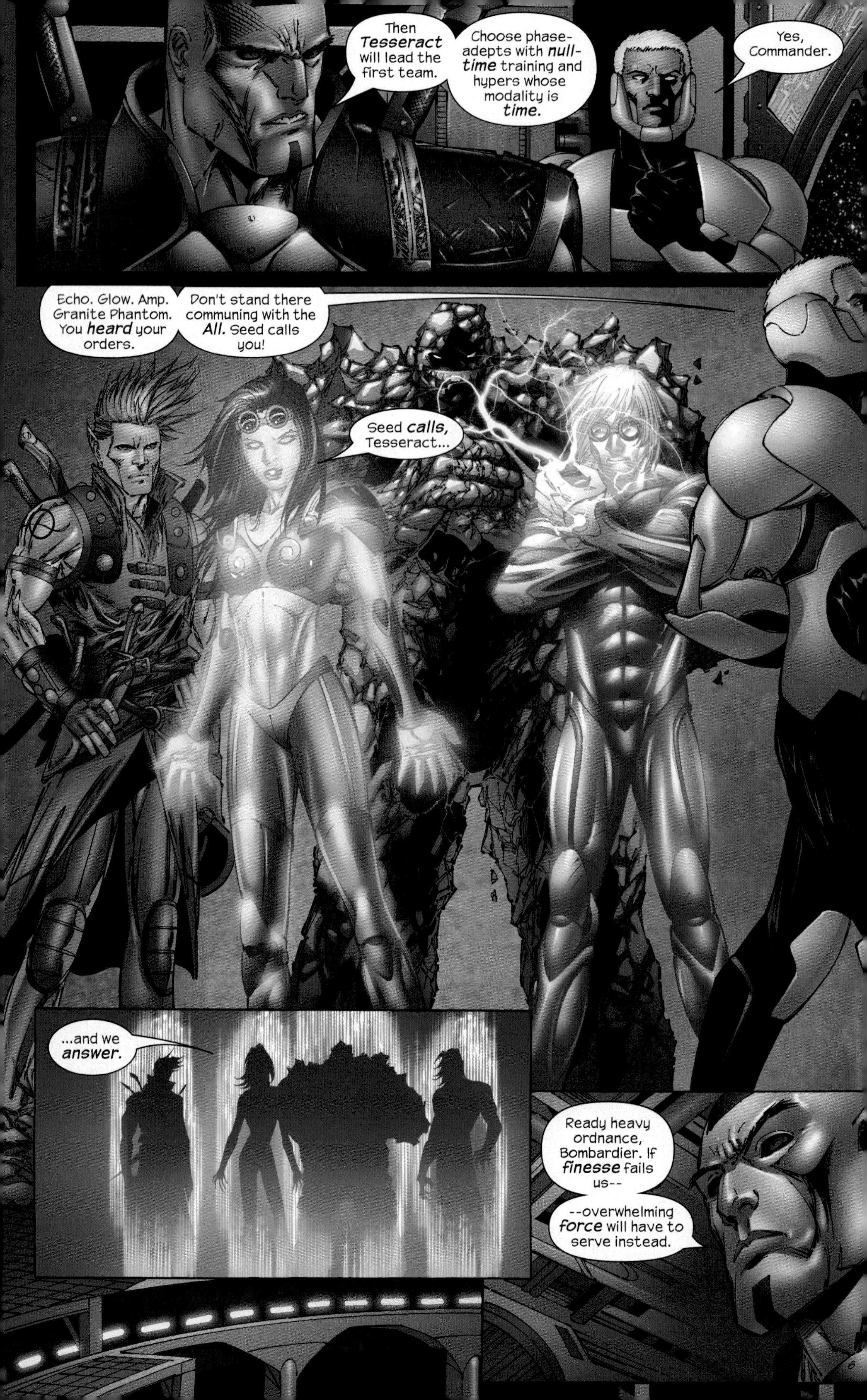

Then Tesseract will lead the first team.
Choose phase-adepts with null-time training and hypers whose modality is time.
Yes, Commander.
Echo. Glow. Amp. Granite Phantom. You heard your orders.
Don't stand there communing with the All. Seed calls you!
Seed calls, Tesseract...
...and we answer.
Ready heavy ordnance, Bombardier. If finesse fails us--
--overwhelming force will have to serve instead.

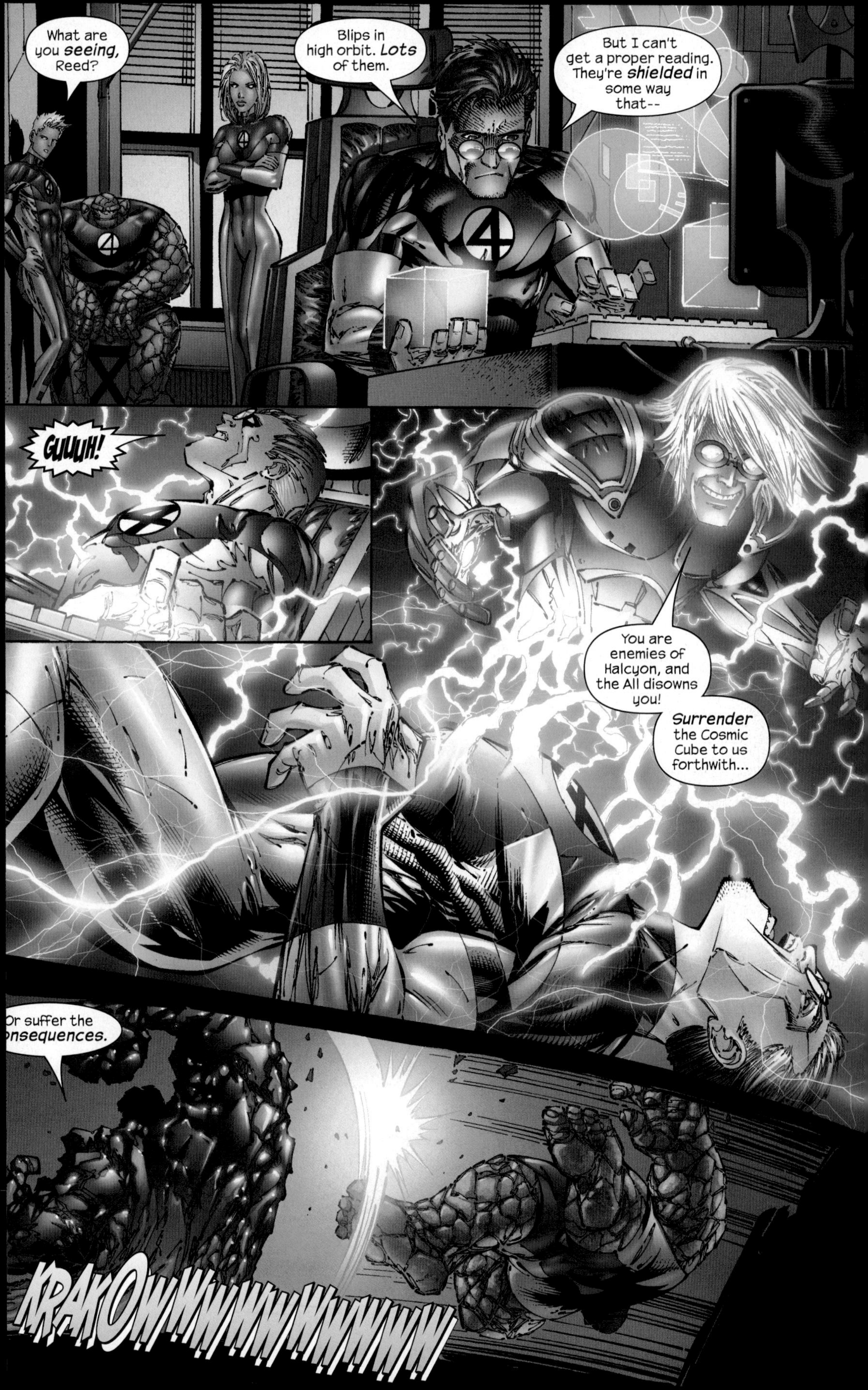
What are you *seeing,* Reed?
Blips in high orbit. *Lots* of them.
But I can't get a proper reading. They're *shielded* in some way that--
GUUUH!
You are enemies of Halcyon, and the All disowns you!
Surrender the Cosmic Cube to us forthwith...
Or suffer the *onsequences.*
KRAKOWWWWWWWWWWWW

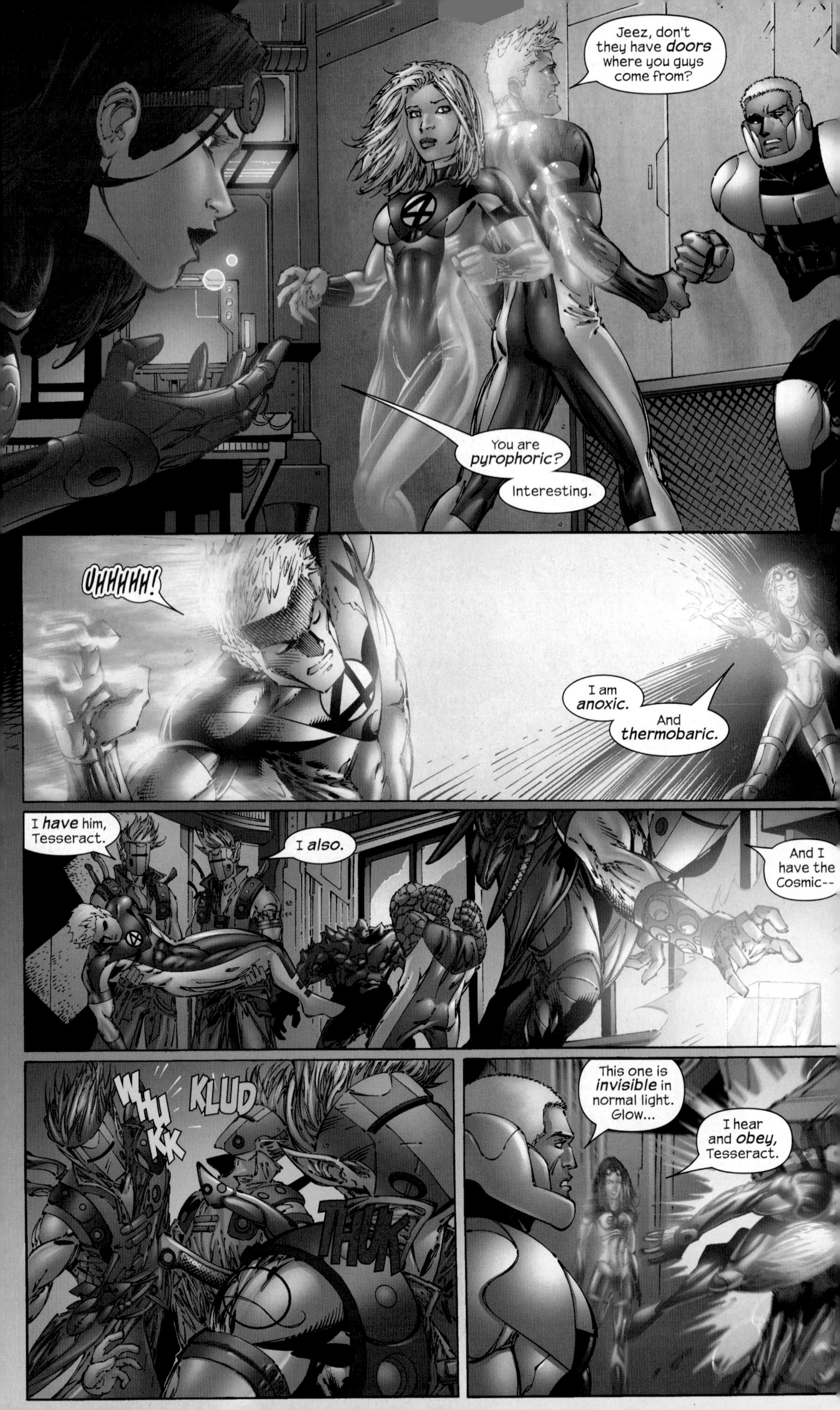
Jeez, don't they have doors where you guys come from?
You are pyrophoric?
Interesting.
OHHHHH!
I am anoxic.
And thermobaric.
I have him, Tesseract.
I also.
And I have the Cosmic--
WHUKK
KLUD
THUK
This one is invisible in normal light. Glow...
I hear and obey, Tesseract.

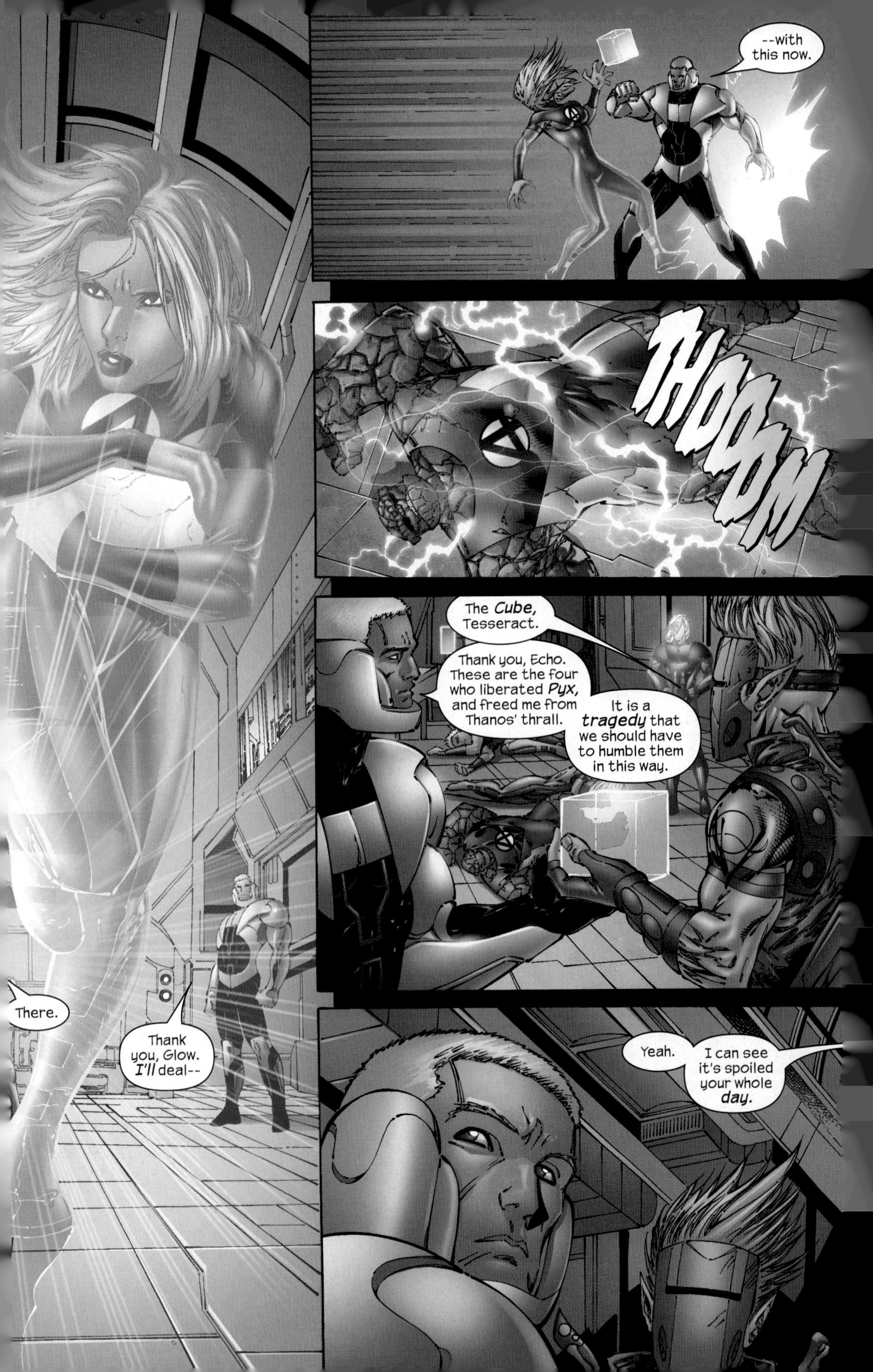
--with
this now.
THOOOOM
The Cube,
Tesseract.
Thank you, Echo.
These are the four
who liberated Pyx,
and freed me from
Thanos' thrall.
It is a
tragedy that
we should have
to humble them
in this way.
There.
Thank
you, Glow.
I'll deal--
Yeah.
I can see
it's spoiled
your whole
day.

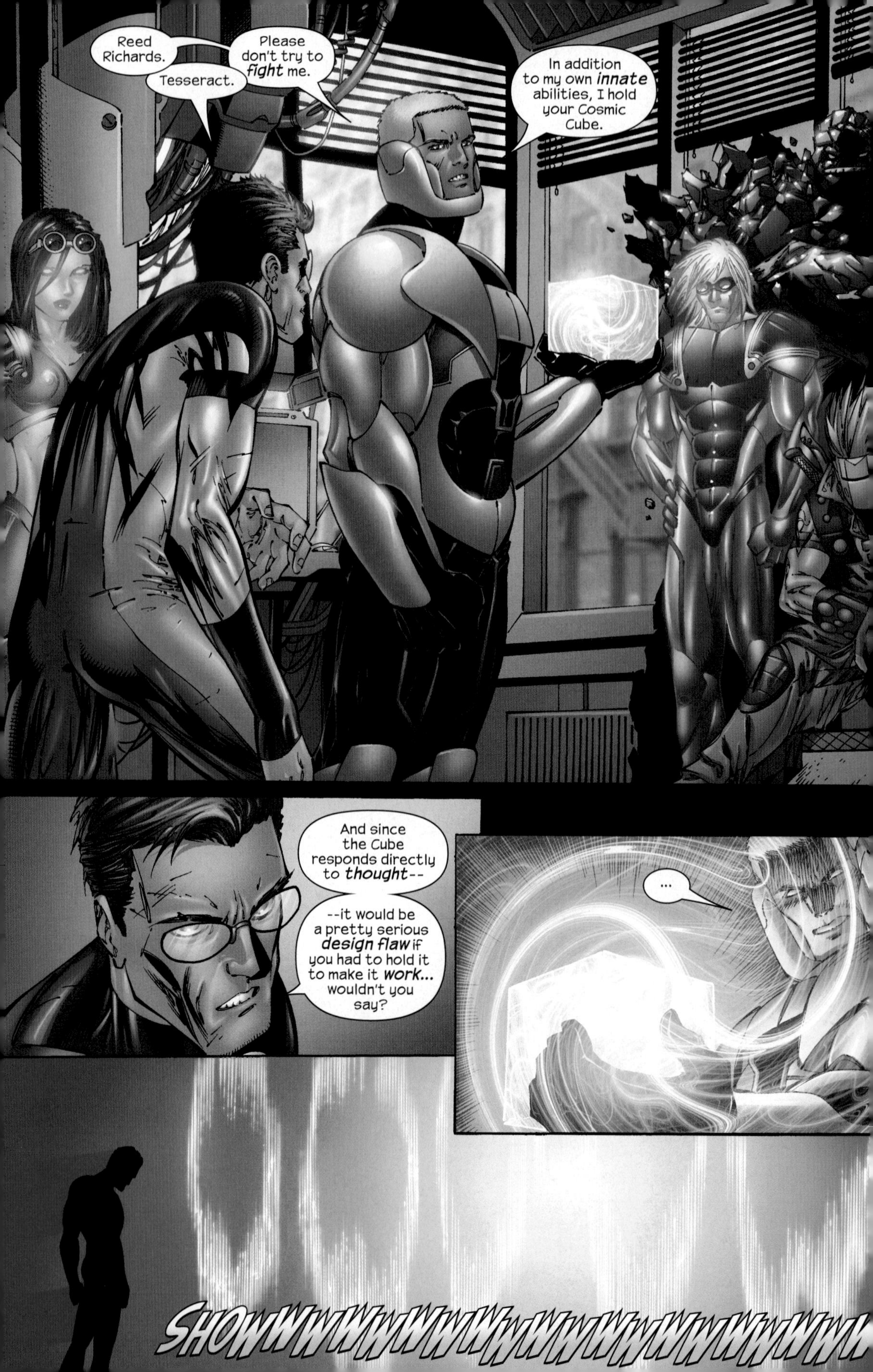
Reed Richards.
Tesseract.
Please don't try to fight me.
In addition to my own innate abilities, I hold your Cosmic Cube.
And since the Cube responds directly to thought--
--it would be a pretty serious design flaw if you had to hold it to make it work... wouldn't you say?
...
SHOWWWWWWWWWWWWWWWWWWWWWWWWWWWWWWW

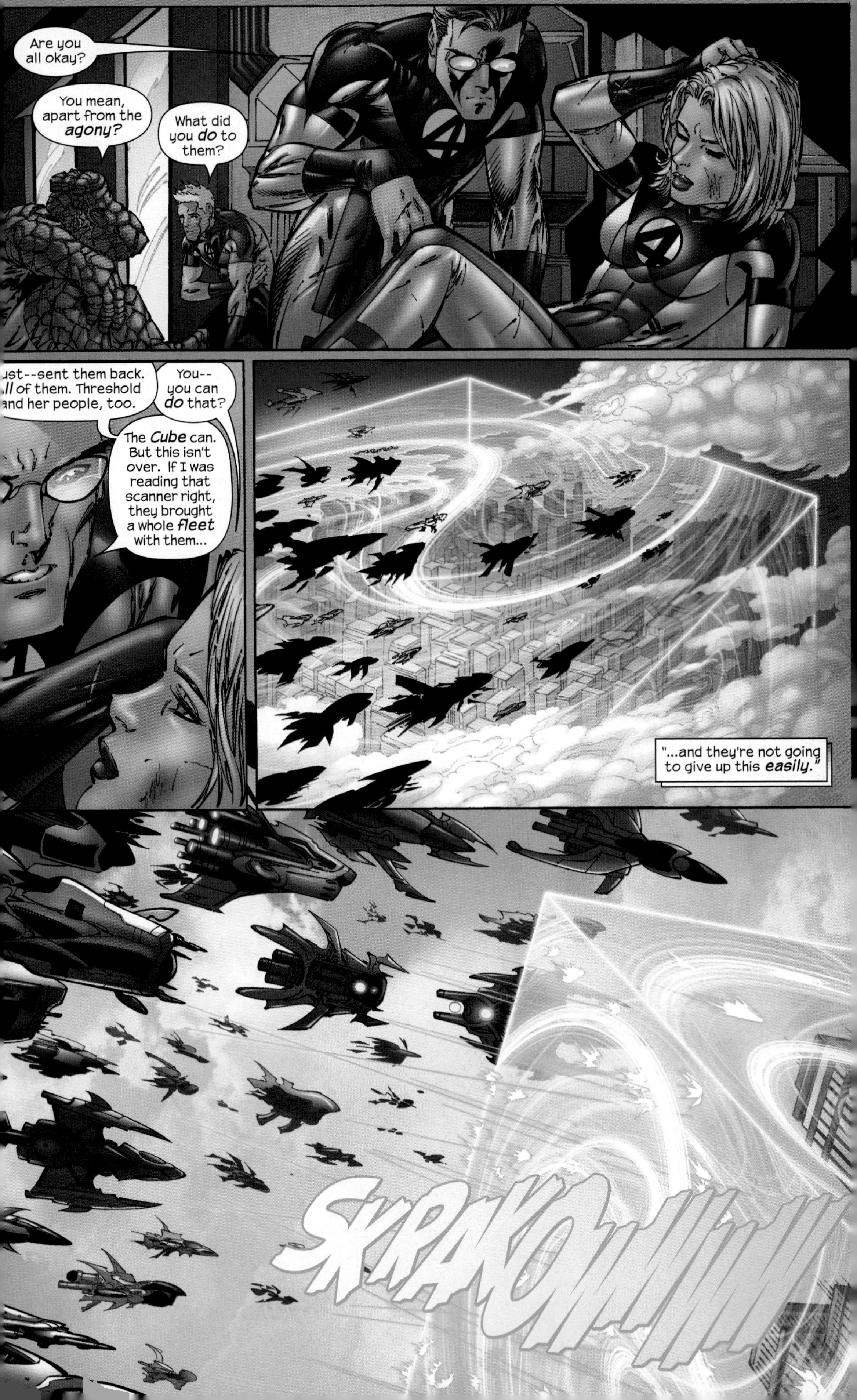
Are you all okay?
You mean, apart from the *agony?*
What did you *do* to them?
ust--sent them back. ll of them. Threshold and her people, too.
You-- you can *do* that?
The *Cube* can. But this isn't over. If I was reading that scanner right, they brought a whole *fleet* with them...
"...and they're not going to give up this *easily.*"
SKRAKOWWWWW

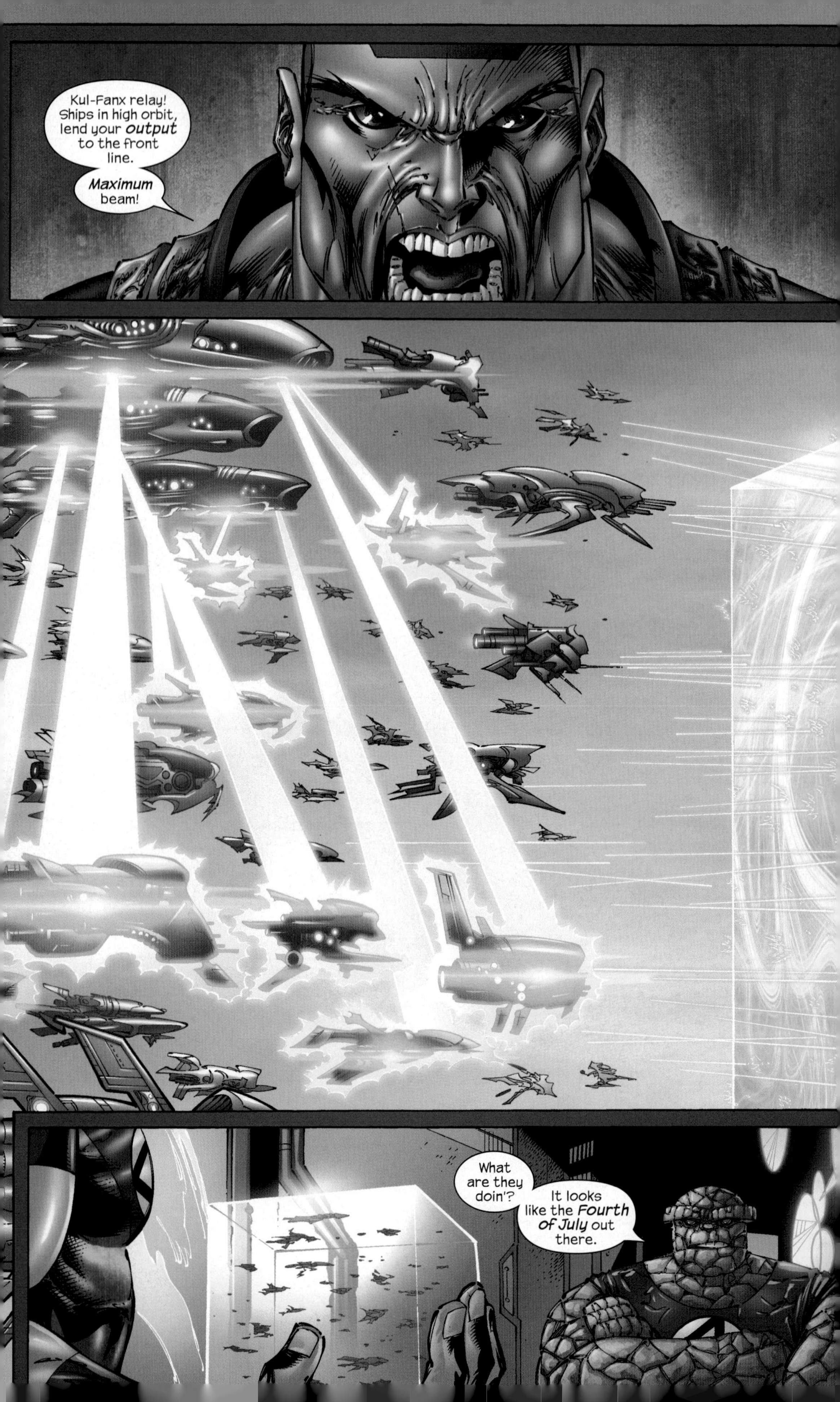
Kul-Fanx relay! Ships in high orbit, lend your *output* to the front line.
Maximum beam!
What are they doin'?
It looks like the *Fourth of July* out there.

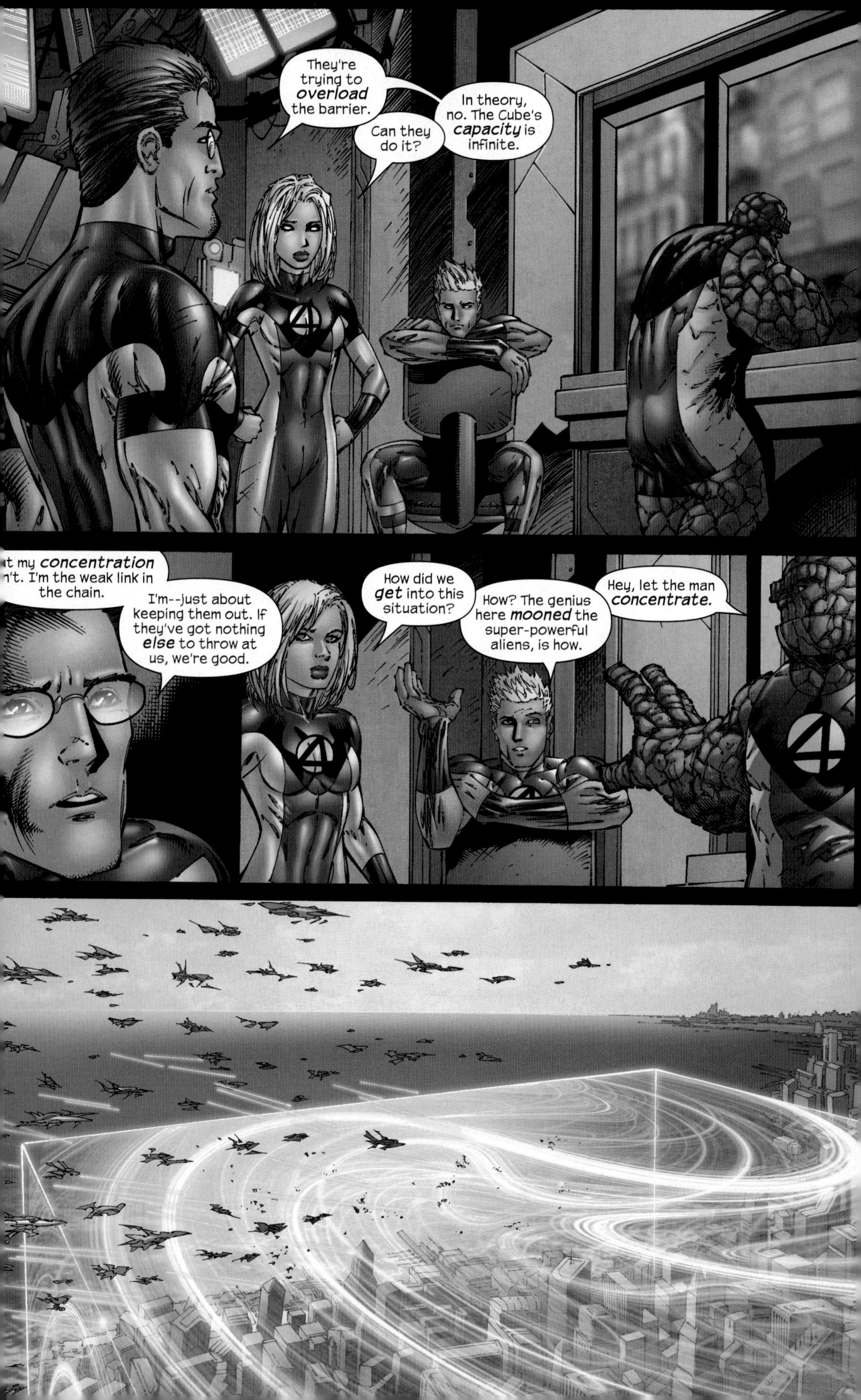
They're trying to overload the barrier.
Can they do it?
In theory, no. The Cube's capacity is infinite.
...t my concentration ...n't. I'm the weak link in the chain.
I'm--just about keeping them out. If they've got nothing else to throw at us, we're good.
How did we get into this situation?
How? The genius here mooned the super-powerful aliens, is how.
Hey, let the man concentrate.

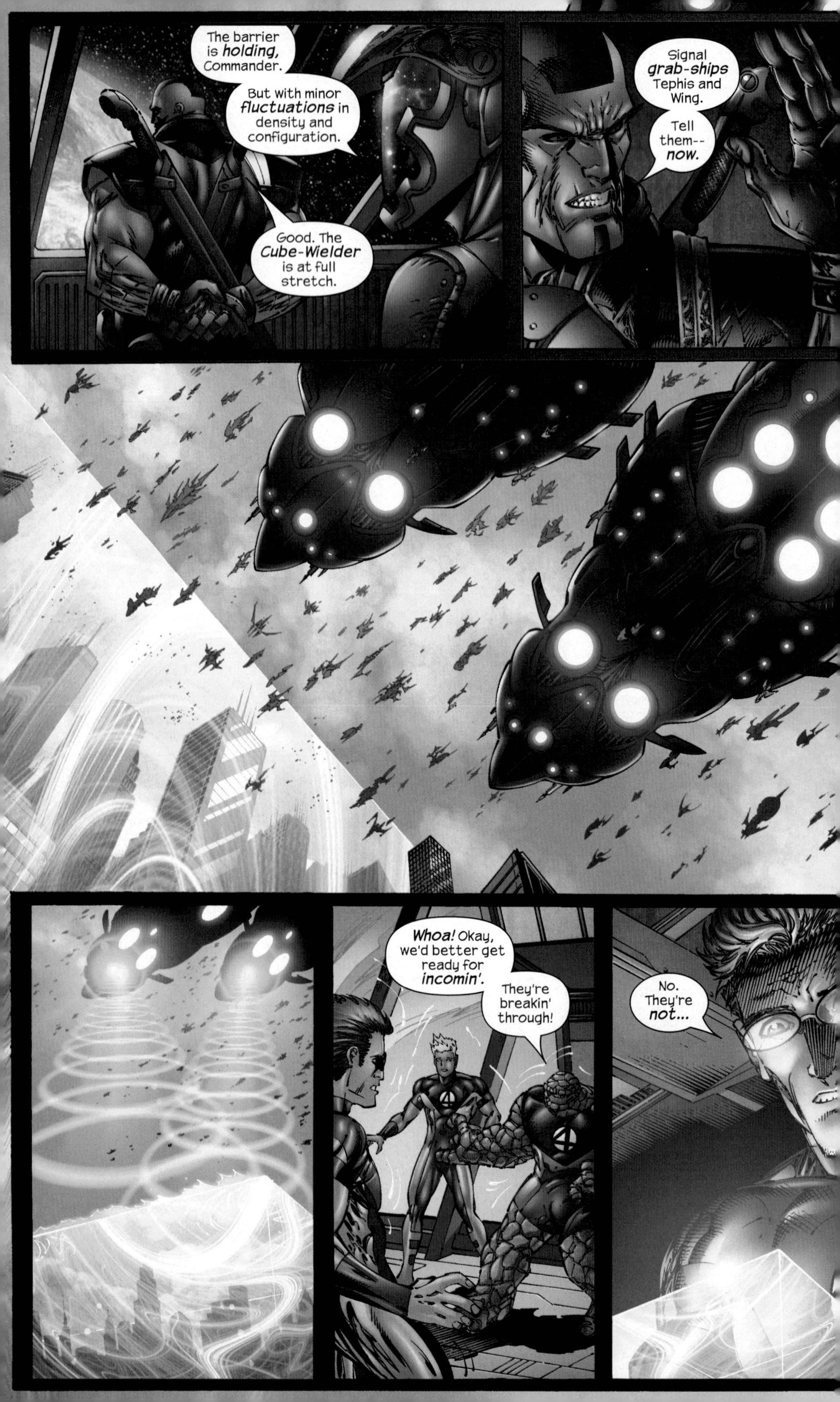
The barrier is holding, Commander.
But with minor fluctuations in density and configuration.
Good. The Cube-Wielder is at full stretch.
Signal grab-ships Tephis and Wing.
Tell them-- now.
Whoa! Okay, we'd better get ready for incomin'.
They're breakin' through!
No. They're not...

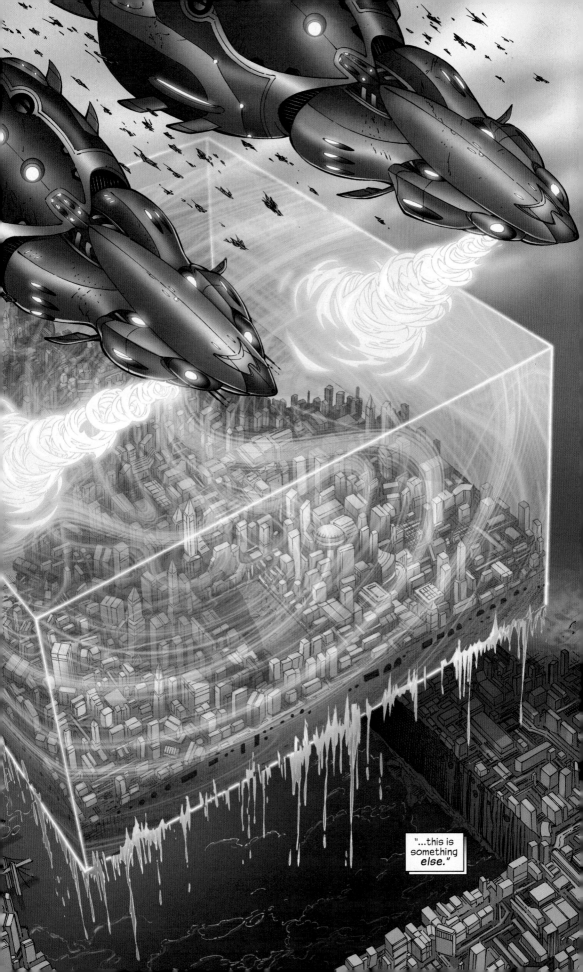

"...this is something *else.*"

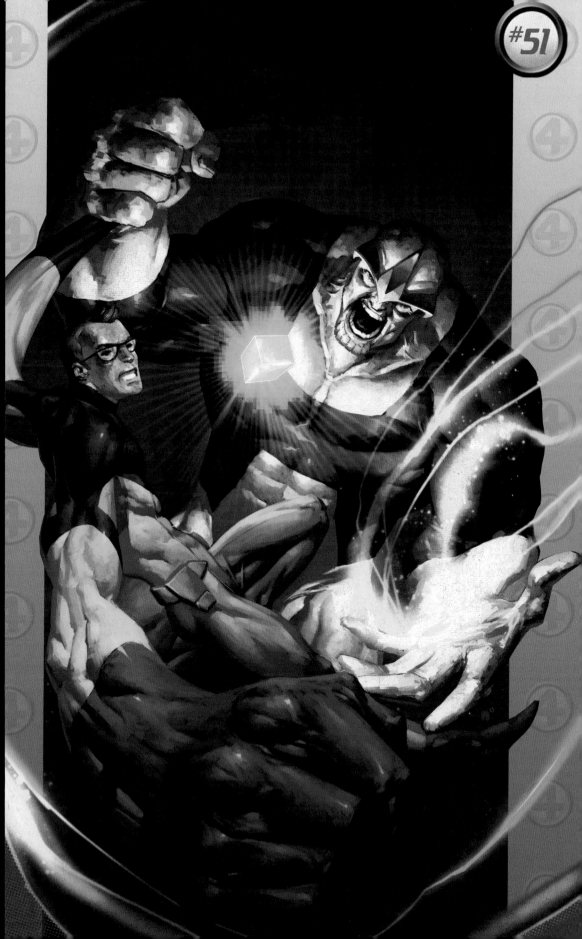

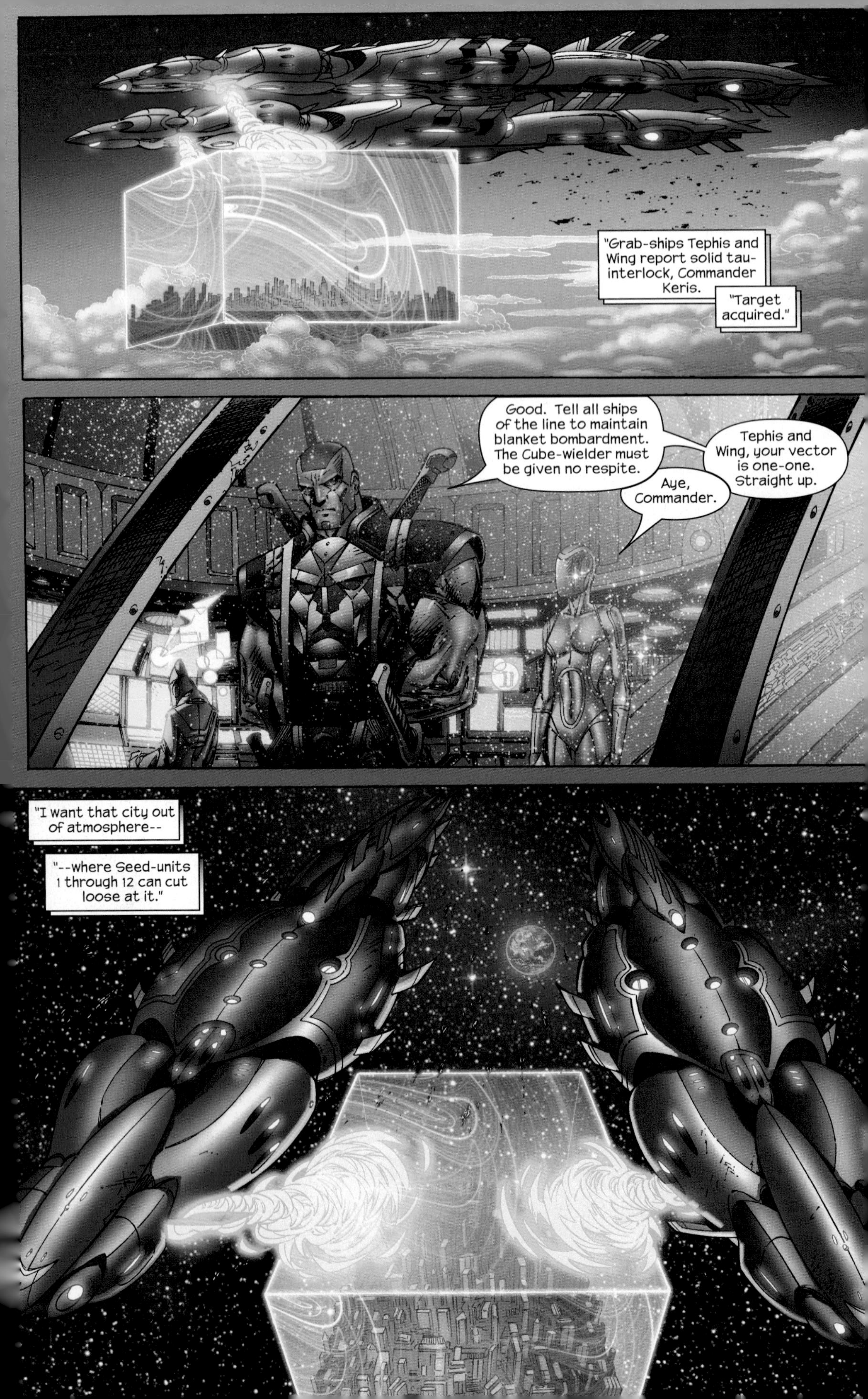
"Grab-ships Tephis and Wing report solid tau-interlock, Commander Keris.
"Target acquired."
Good. Tell all ships of the line to maintain blanket bombardment. The Cube-wielder must be given no respite.
Tephis and Wing, your vector is one-one. Straight up.
Aye, Commander.
"I want that city out of atmosphere--
"--where Seed-units 1 through 12 can cut loose at it."

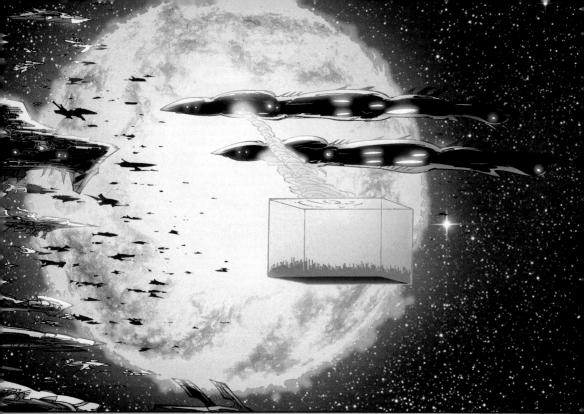

Clear of *atmosphere*, commander.

Tell the grab-ships to *withdraw*.

Mauler of Seed 1, *Nightmare* of Seed 4, *Gehenna* of Seed 12, scramble on my--

Commander!

e got two physical ips and two *psi- spikes*. Big.

heorize o Acheron *ywhales*, nmanned.

"They were hiding in the *sun*--

"--and they're right on *top* of us."

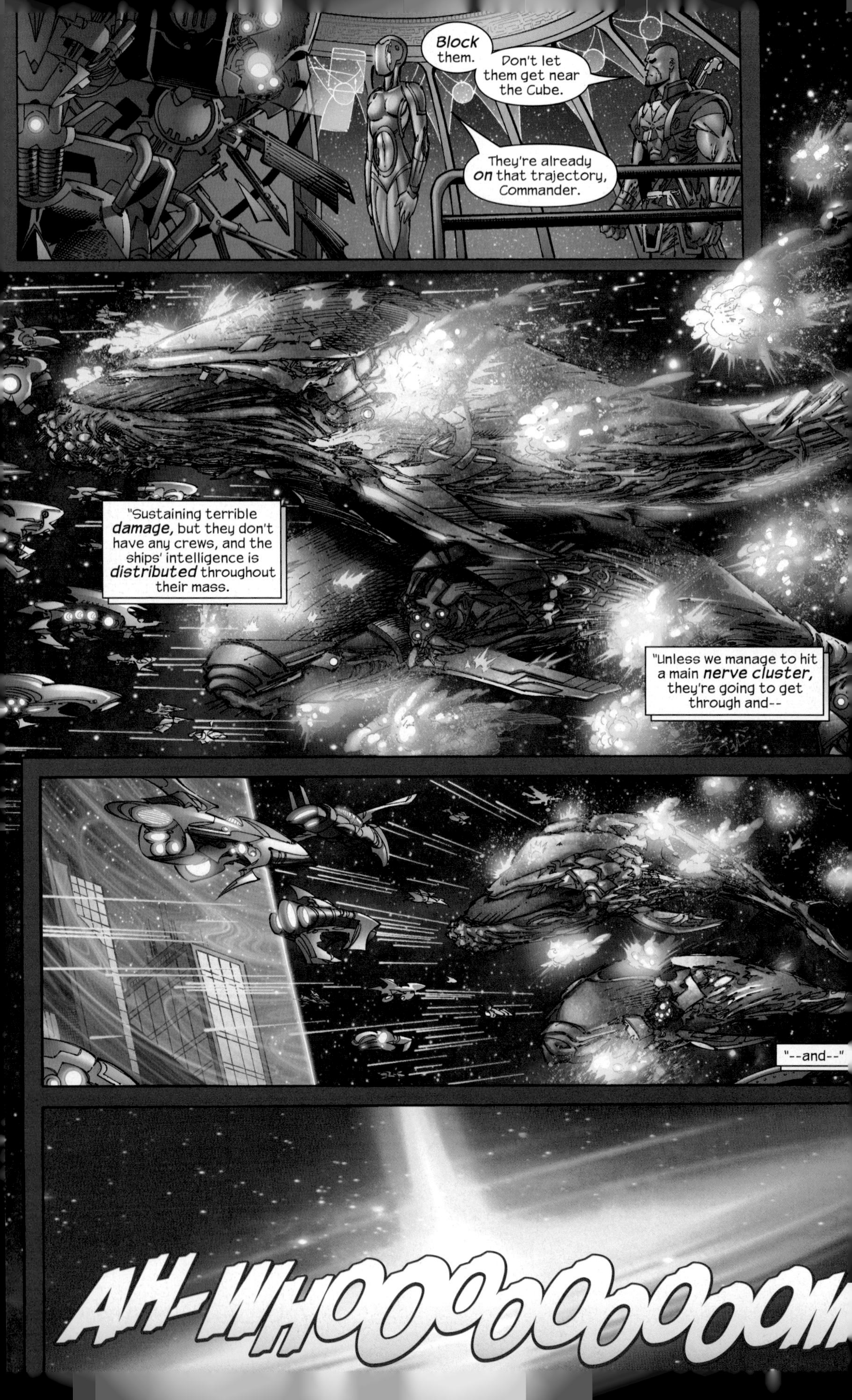
Block them.
Don't let them get near the Cube.
They're already on that trajectory, Commander.
"Sustaining terrible damage, but they don't have any crews, and the ships' intelligence is distributed throughout their mass.
"Unless we manage to hit a main nerve cluster, they're going to get through and--
"--and--"
AH-WHOOOOOOOOOOM

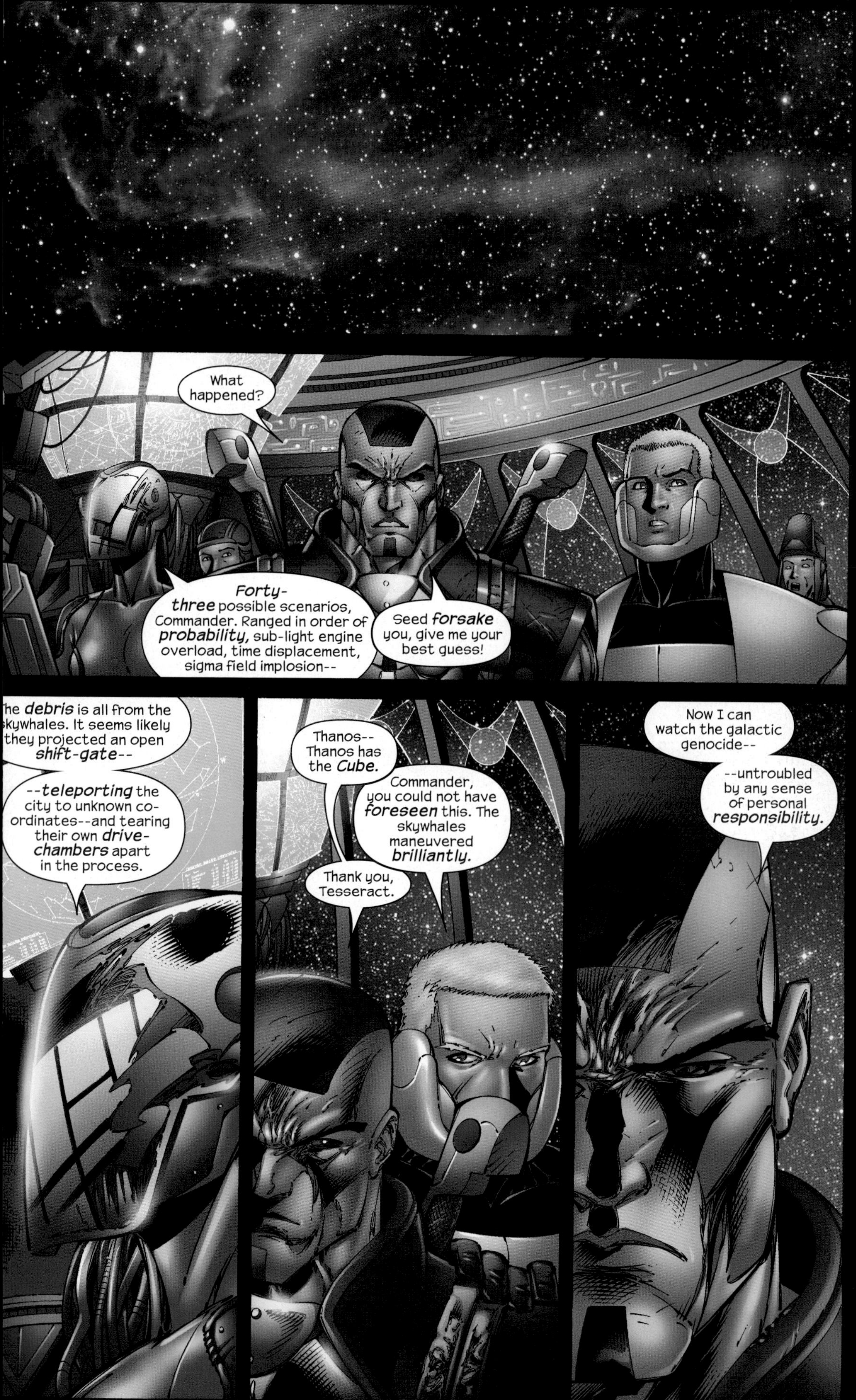
What happened?
Forty-three possible scenarios, Commander. Ranged in order of probability, sub-light engine overload, time displacement, sigma field implosion--
Seed forsake you, give me your best guess!
The debris is all from the skywhales. It seems likely they projected an open shift-gate--
--teleporting the city to unknown co-ordinates--and tearing their own drive-chambers apart in the process.
Thanos--Thanos has the Cube.
Commander, you could not have foreseen this. The skywhales maneuvered brilliantly.
Thank you, Tesseract.
Now I can watch the galactic genocide--
--untroubled by any sense of personal responsibility.

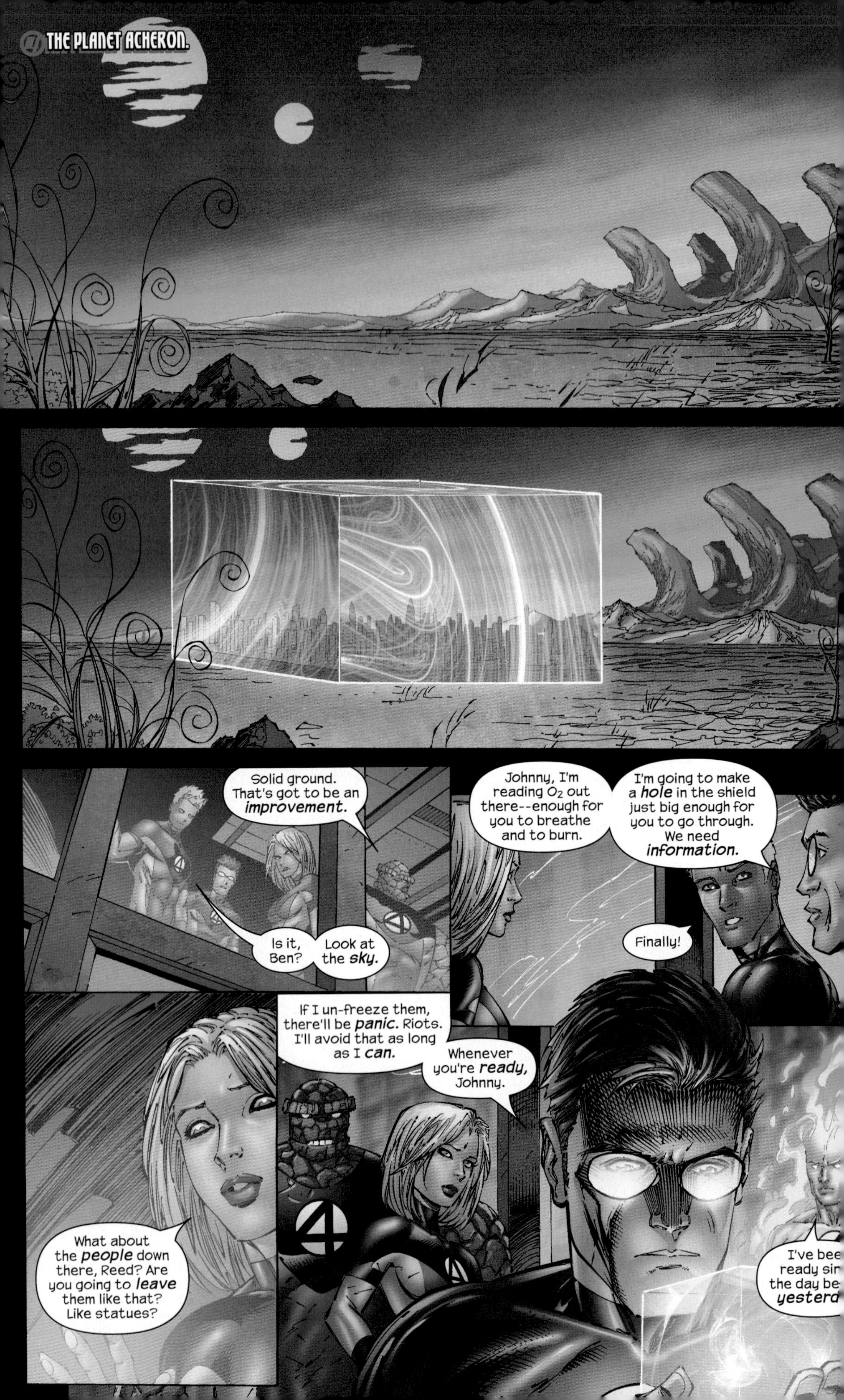

THE PLANET ACHERON.
Solid ground. That's got to be an *improvement.*
Is it, Ben?
Look at the *sky.*
Johnny, I'm reading O_2 out there--enough for you to breathe and to burn.
I'm going to make a *hole* in the shield just big enough for you to go through. We need *information.*
Finally!
What about the *people* down there, Reed? Are you going to *leave* them like that? Like statues?
If I un-freeze them, there'll be *panic.* Riots. I'll avoid that as long as I *can.*
Whenever you're *ready,* Johnny.

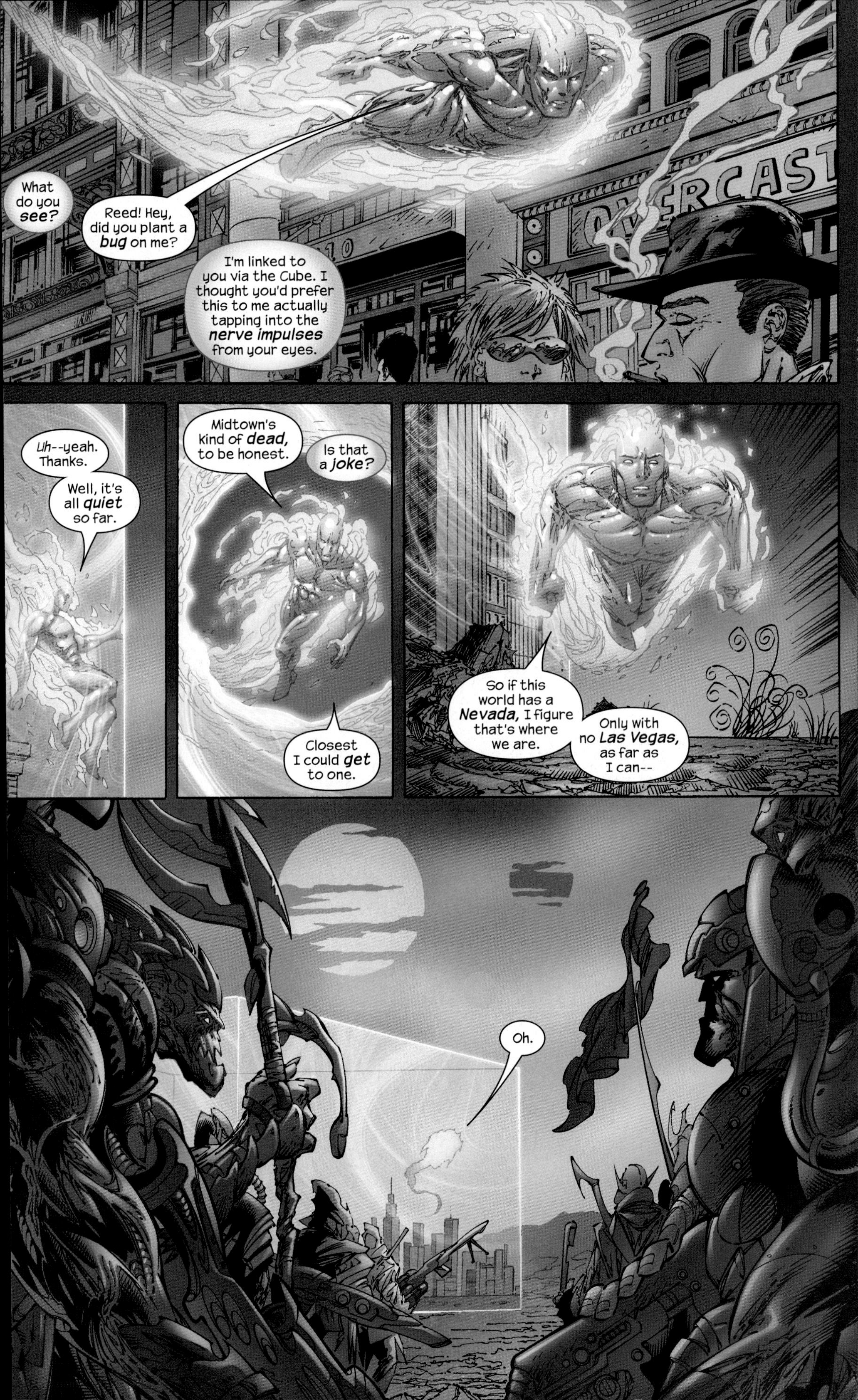
OVERCAST
What do you **see?**
Reed! Hey, did you plant a **bug** on me?
I'm linked to you via the Cube. I thought you'd prefer this to me actually tapping into the **nerve impulses** from your eyes.
Uh--yeah. Thanks.
Well, it's all **quiet** so far.
Midtown's kind of **dead,** to be honest.
Is that a **joke?**
Closest I could **get** to one.
So if this world has a **Nevada,** I figure that's where we are.
Only with no **Las Vegas,** as far as I can--
Oh.

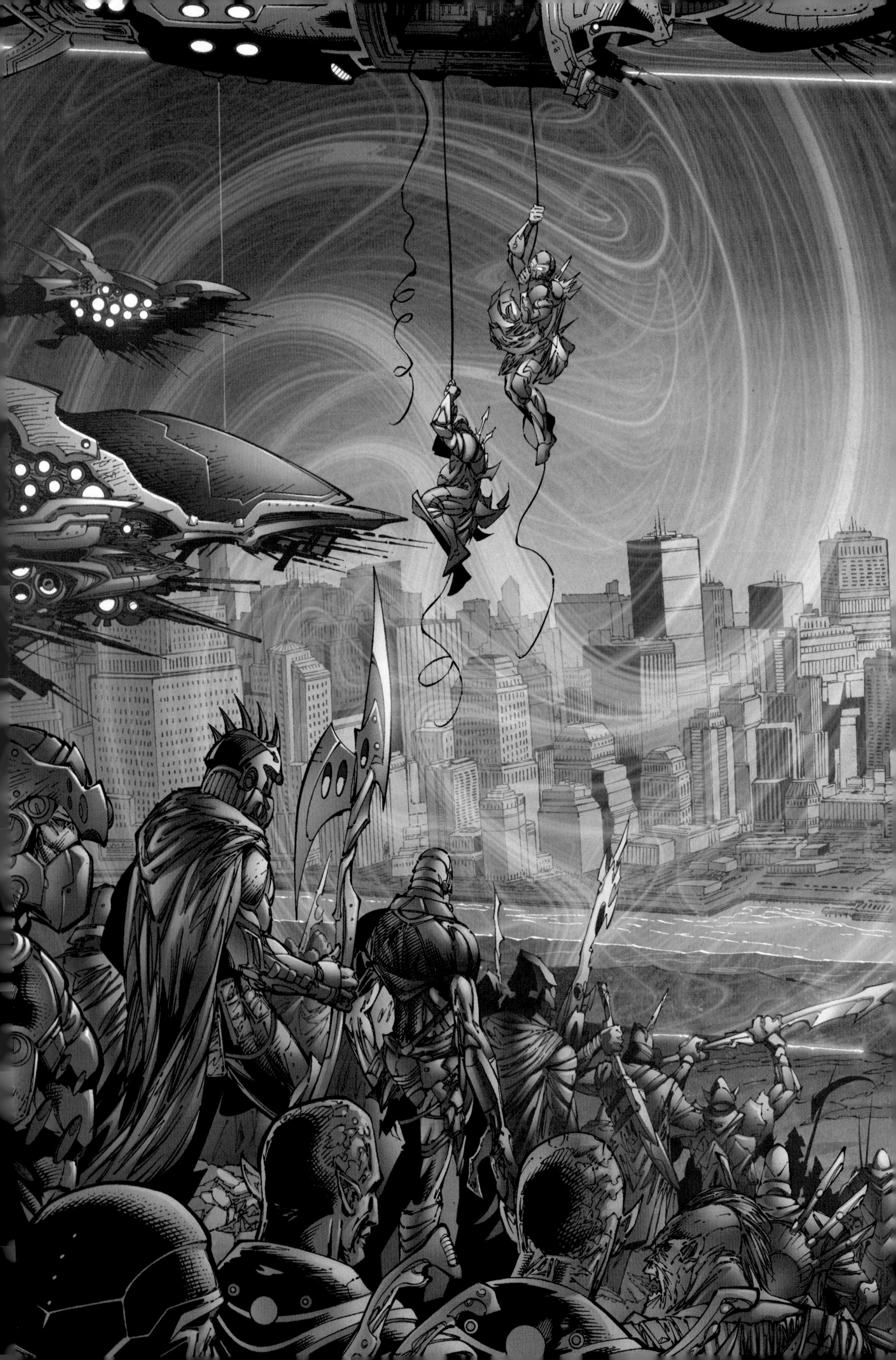

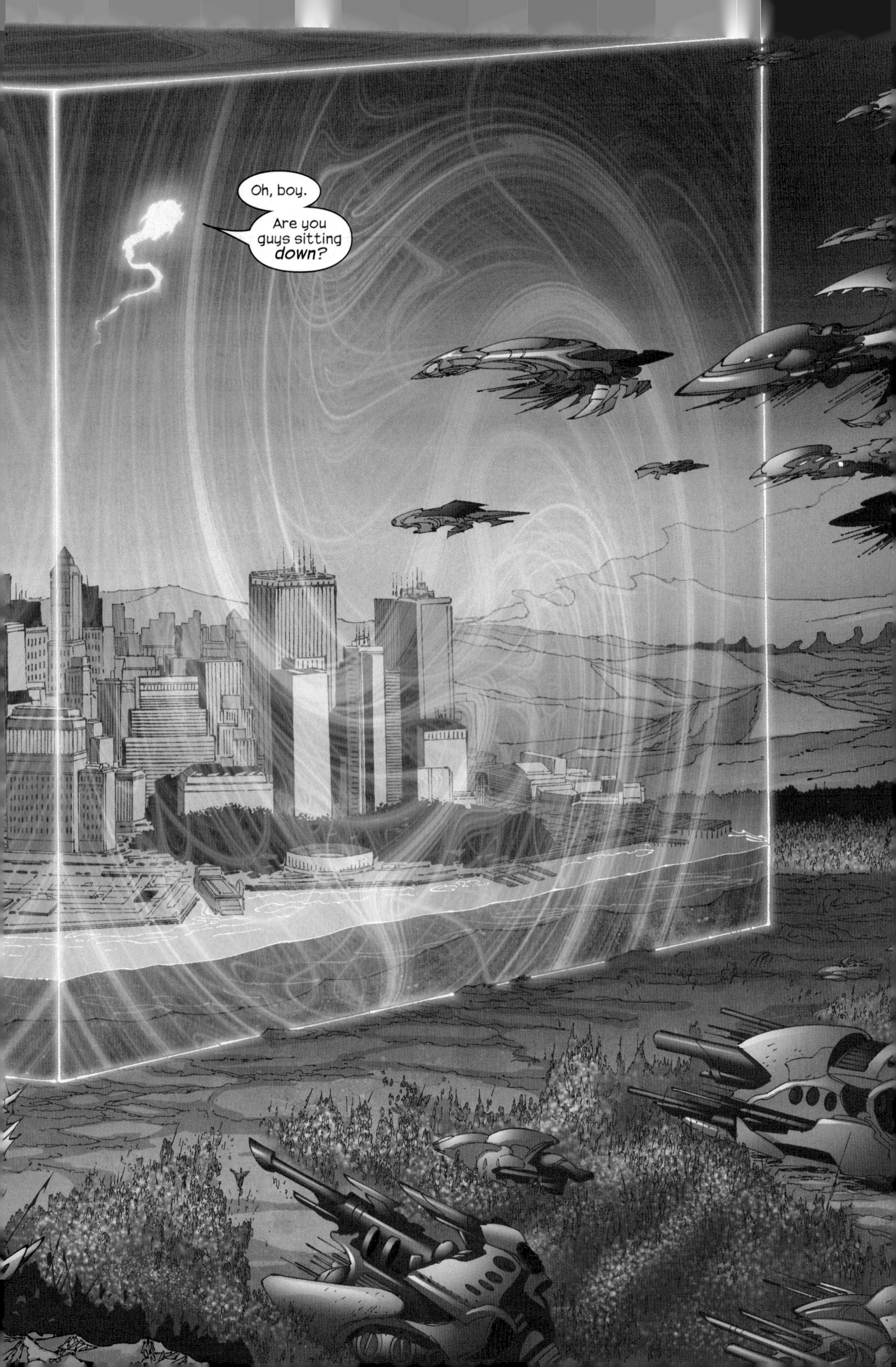
Oh, boy.
Are you guys sitting *down*?

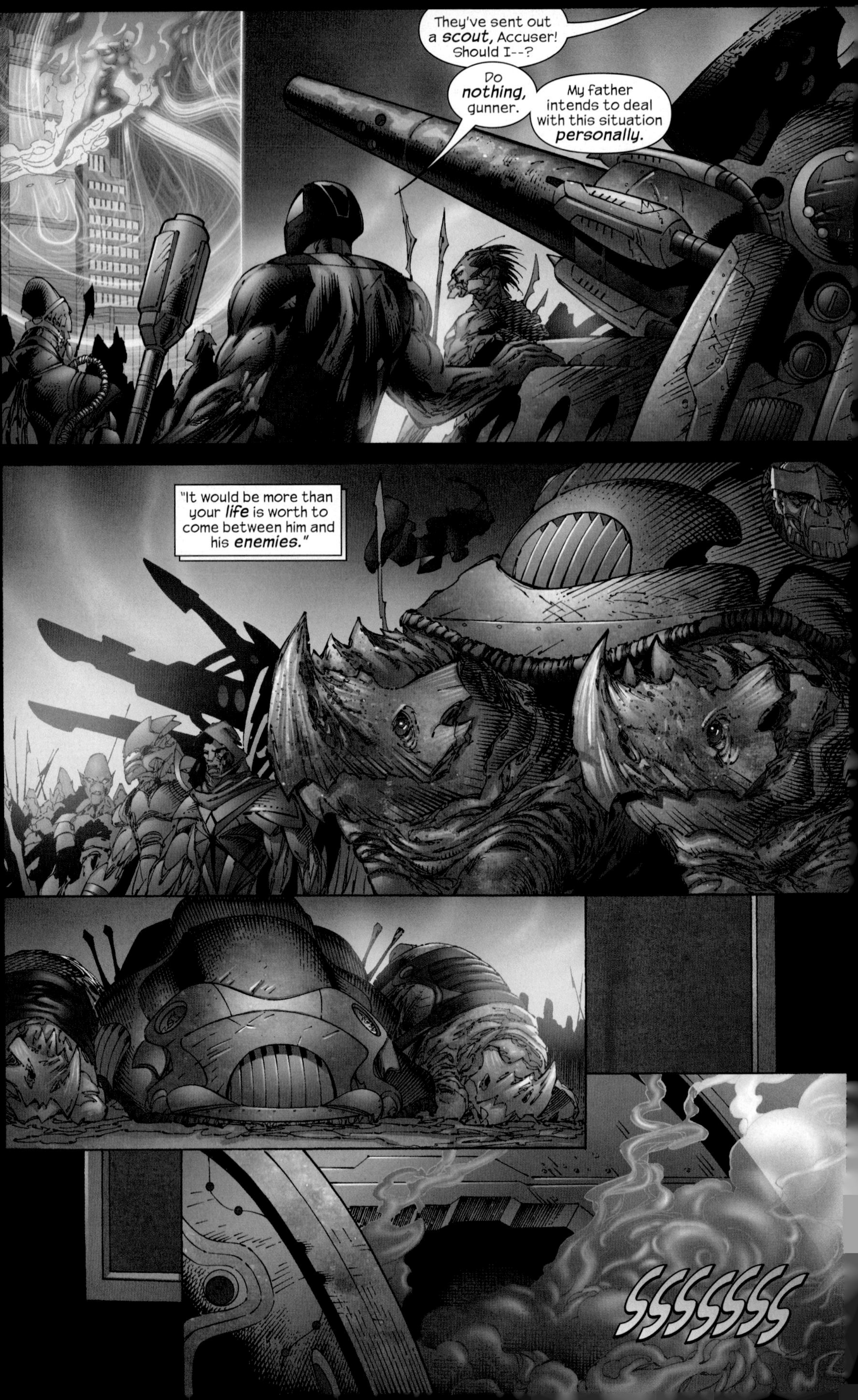
They've sent out a *scout,* Accuser! Should I--?
Do *nothing,* gunner.
My father intends to deal with this situation *personally.*
"It would be more than your *life* is worth to come between him and his *enemies.*"
SSSSSSS

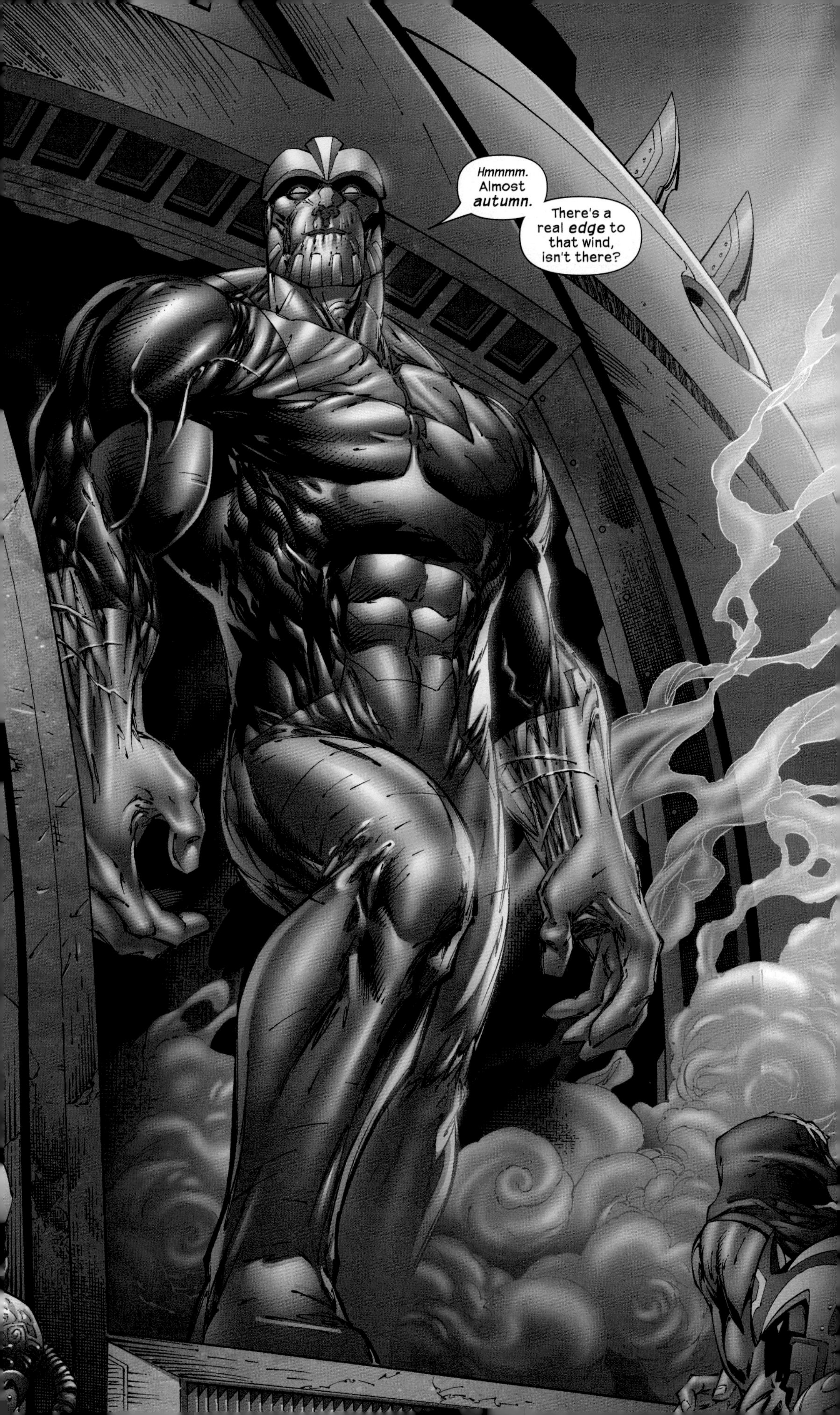
Hmmmm. Almost *autumn*.
There's a real *edge* to that wind, isn't there?

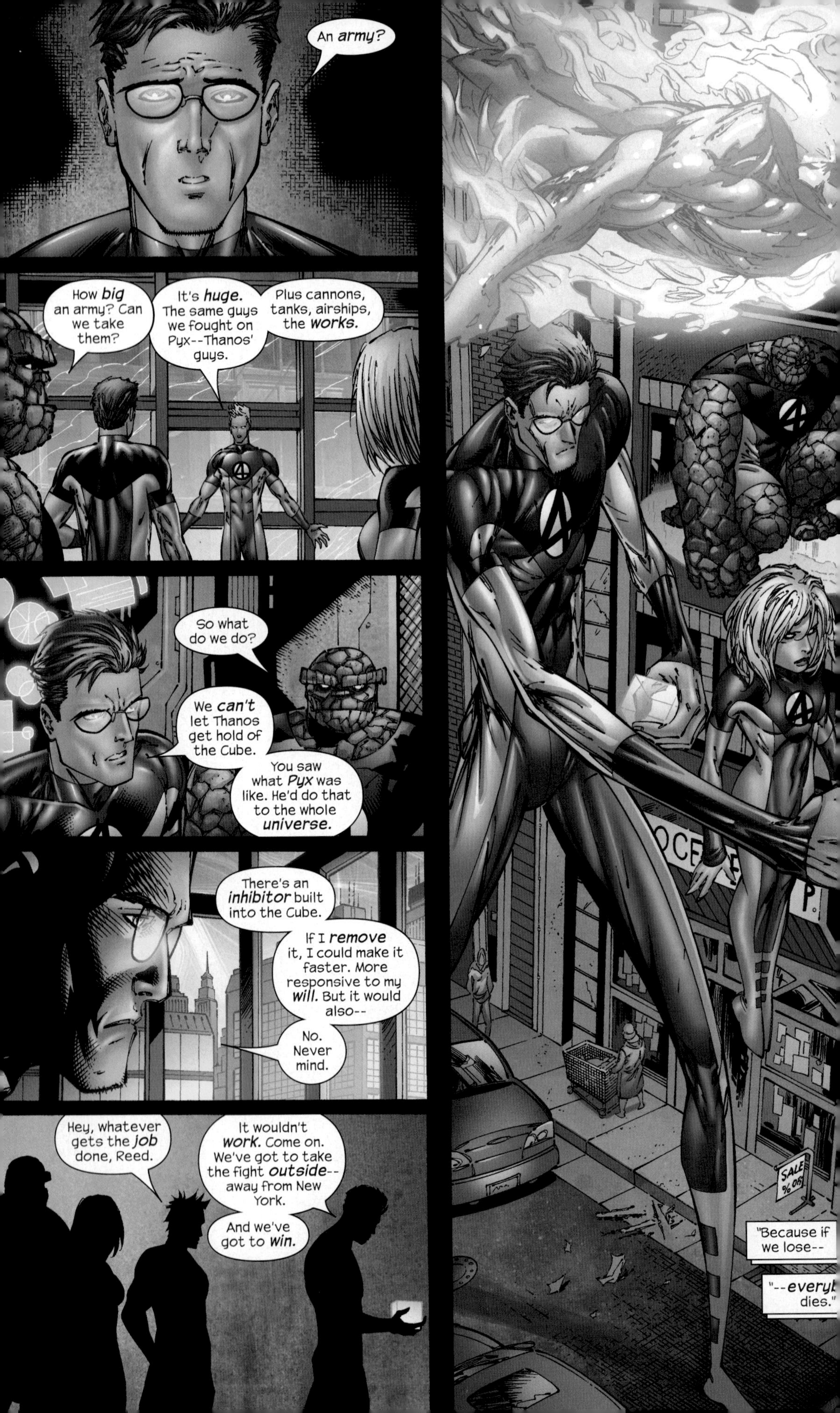
An *army?*
How *big* an army? Can we take them?
It's *huge.* The same guys we fought on Pyx--Thanos' guys.
Plus cannons, tanks, airships, the *works.*
So what do we do?
We *can't* let Thanos get hold of the Cube.
You saw what *Pyx* was like. He'd do that to the whole *universe.*
There's an *inhibitor* built into the Cube.
If I *remove* it, I could make it faster. More responsive to my *will.* But it would also--
No. Never mind.
Hey, whatever gets the *job* done, Reed.
It wouldn't *work.* Come on. We've got to take the fight *outside*-- away from New York.
And we've got to *win.*
SALE
"Because if we lose--
"--*everyt* dies."

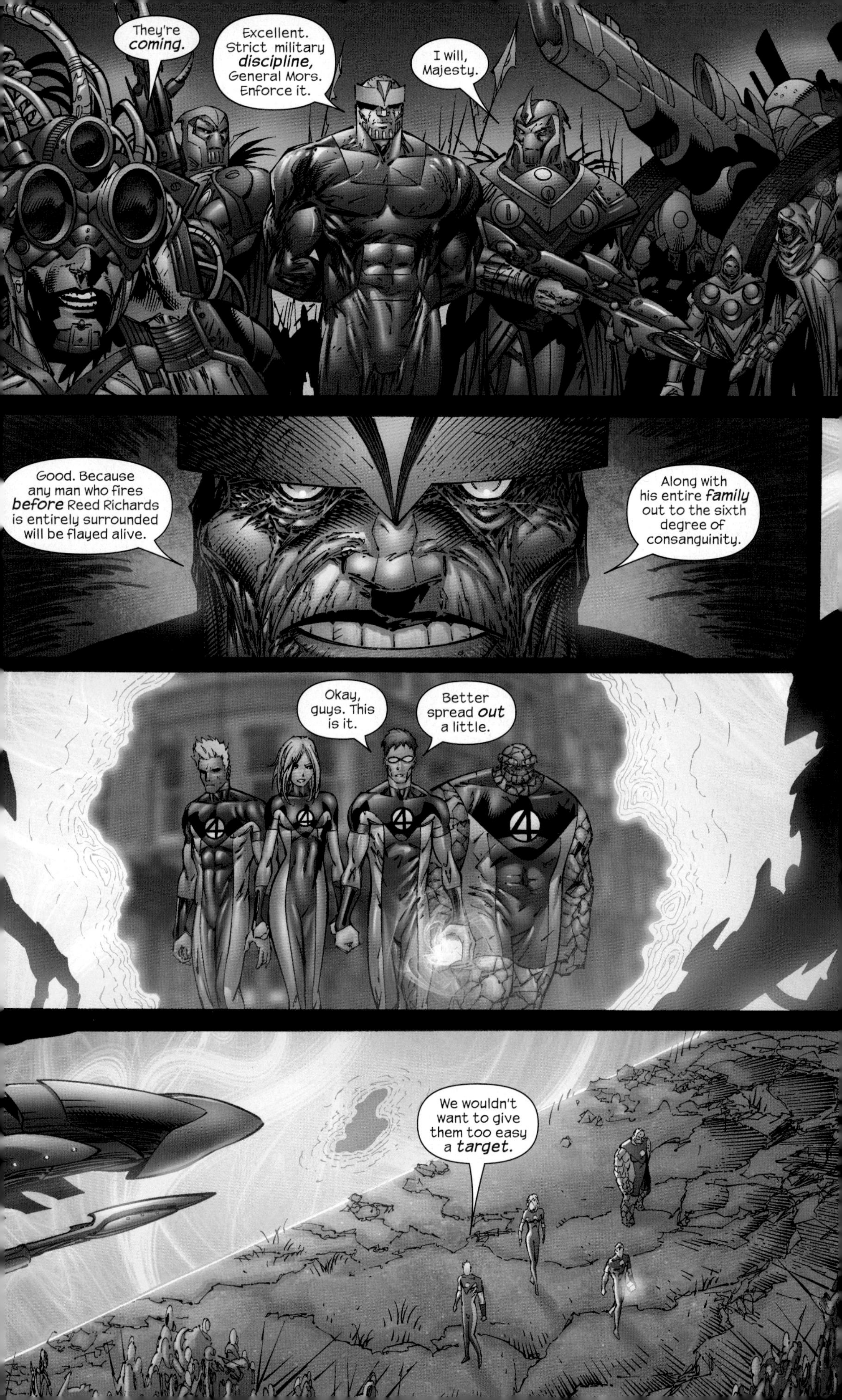
They're *coming.*
Excellent. Strict military *discipline,* General Mors. Enforce it.
I will, Majesty.
Good. Because any man who fires *before* Reed Richards is entirely surrounded will be flayed alive.
Along with his entire *family* out to the sixth degree of consanguinity.
Okay, guys. This is it.
Better spread *out* a little.
We wouldn't want to give them too easy a *target.*

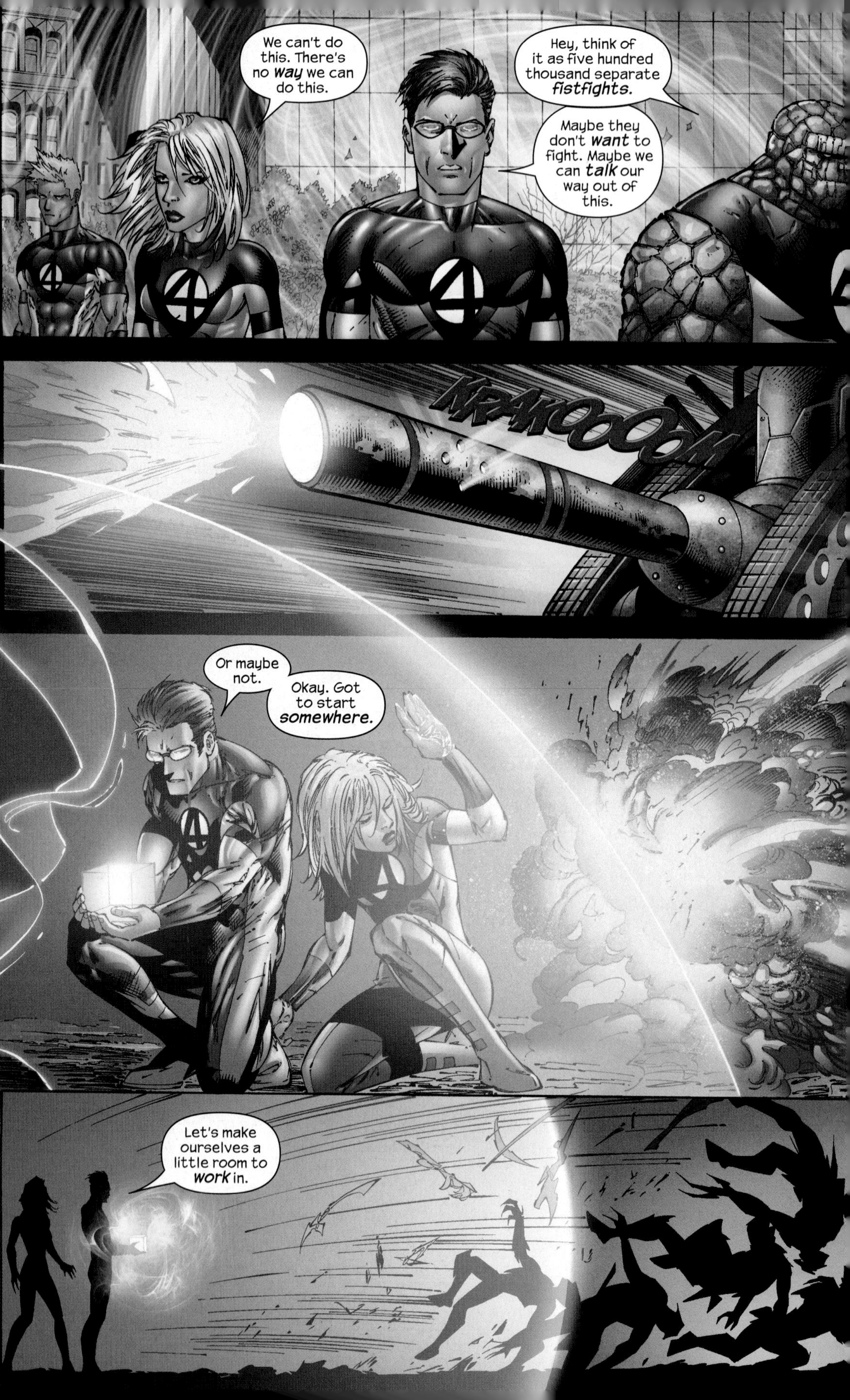

We can't do this. There's no way we can do this.
Hey, think of it as five hundred thousand separate fistfights.
Maybe they don't want to fight. Maybe we can talk our way out of this.
KRAKOOOOOM
Or maybe not.
Okay. Got to start somewhere.
Let's make ourselves a little room to work in.

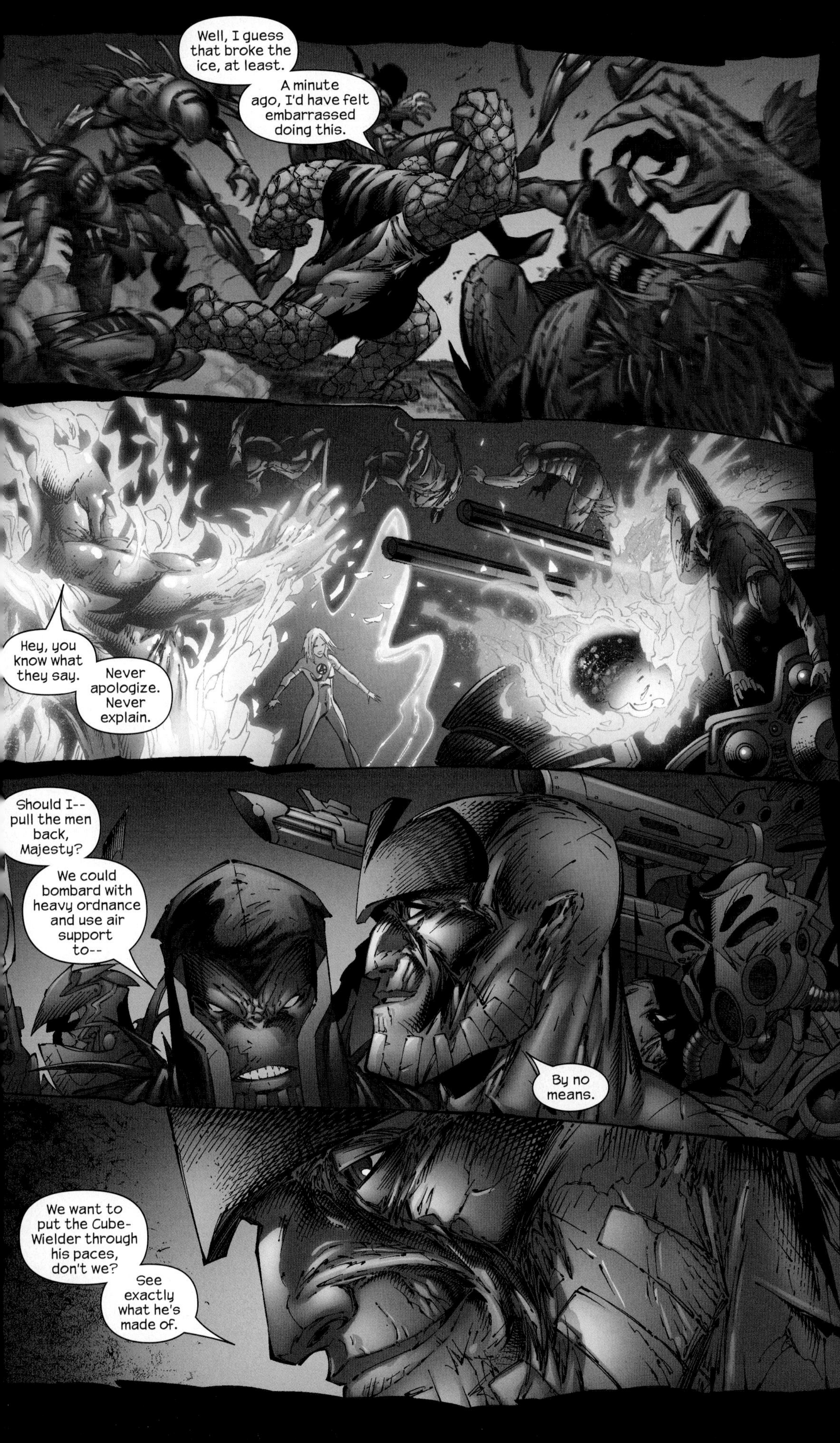

Well, I guess that broke the ice, at least.
A minute ago, I'd have felt embarrassed doing this.
Hey, you know what they say.
Never apologize. Never explain.
Should I-- pull the men back, Majesty?
We could bombard with heavy ordnance and use air support to--
By no means.
We want to put the Cube-Wielder through his paces, don't we?
See exactly what he's made of.

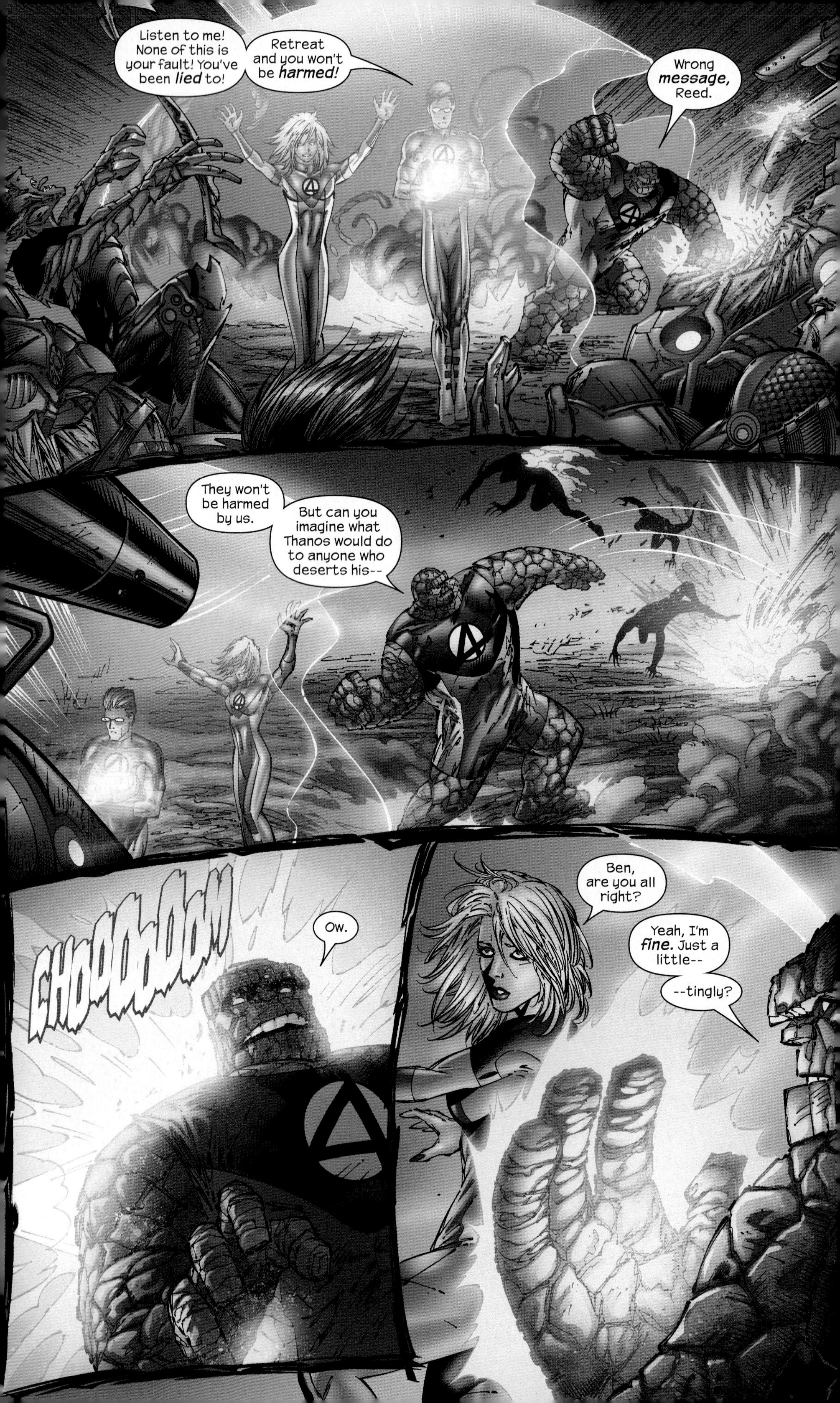
Listen to me! None of this is your fault! You've been *lied* to!
Retreat and you won't be ***harmed!***
Wrong ***message,*** Reed.
They won't be harmed by us.
But can you imagine what Thanos would do to anyone who deserts his--
CHOOOOOM
Ow.
Ben, are you all right?
Yeah, I'm ***fine.*** Just a little--
--tingly?

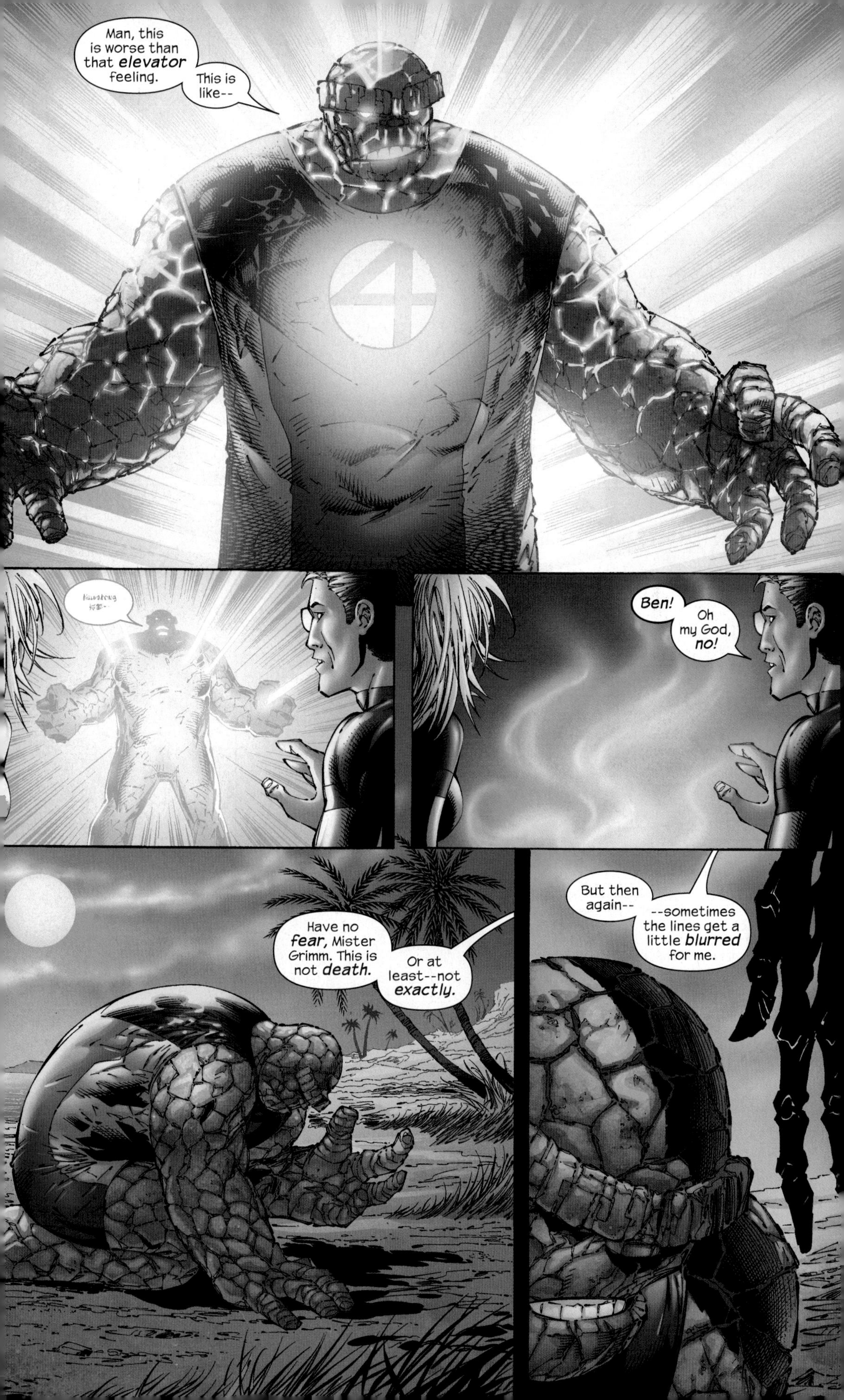

Man, this is worse than that *elevator* feeling.
This is like--
Ben!
Oh my God, *no!*
Have no *fear,* Mister Grimm. This is not *death.*
Or at least--not *exactly.*
But then again--
--sometimes the lines get a little *blurred* for me.

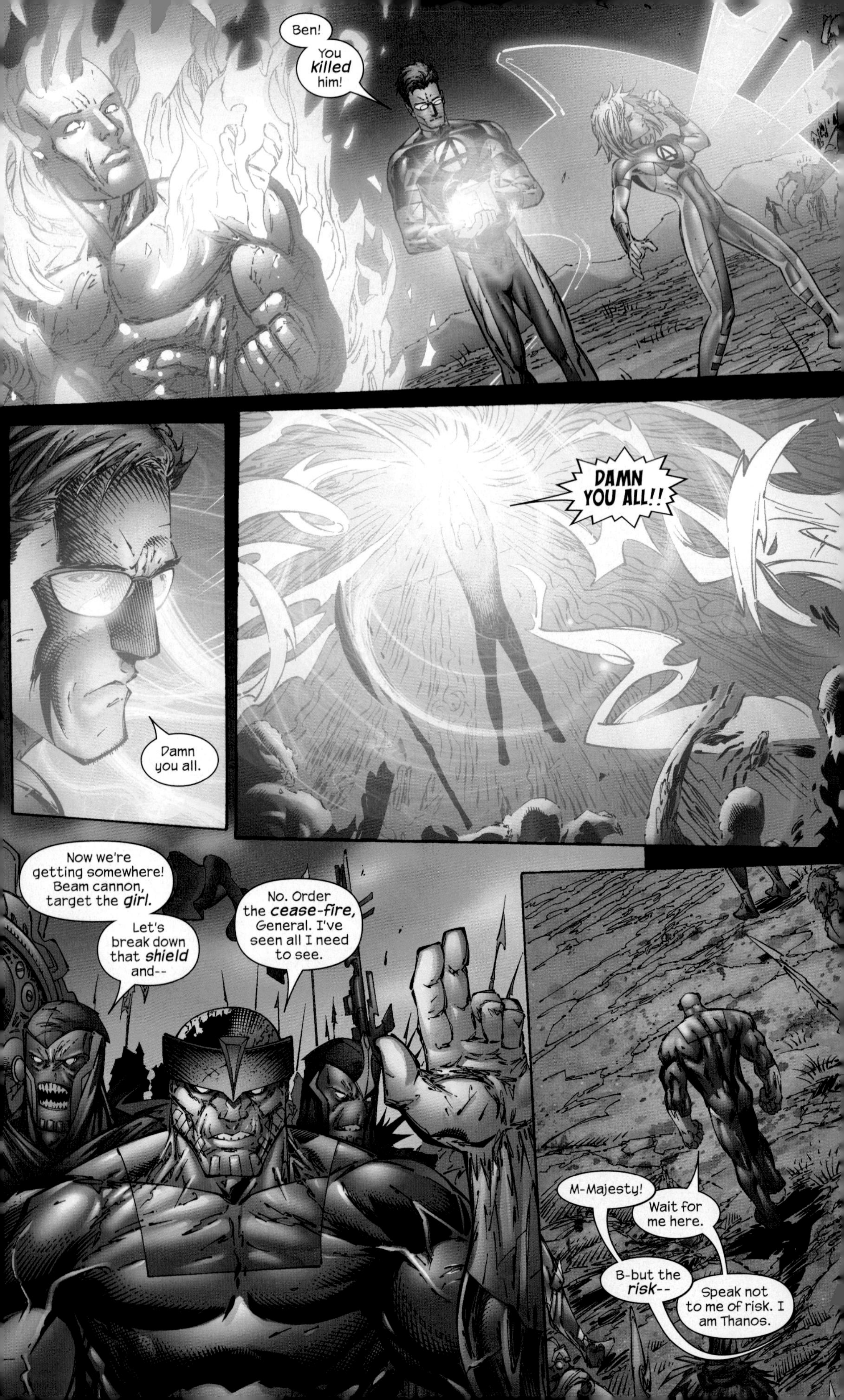
Ben!
You killed him!
Damn you all.
DAMN YOU ALL!!
Now we're getting somewhere! Beam cannon, target the girl.
Let's break down that shield and--
No. Order the cease-fire, General. I've seen all I need to see.
M-Majesty!
Wait for me here.
B-but the risk--
Speak not to me of risk. I am Thanos.

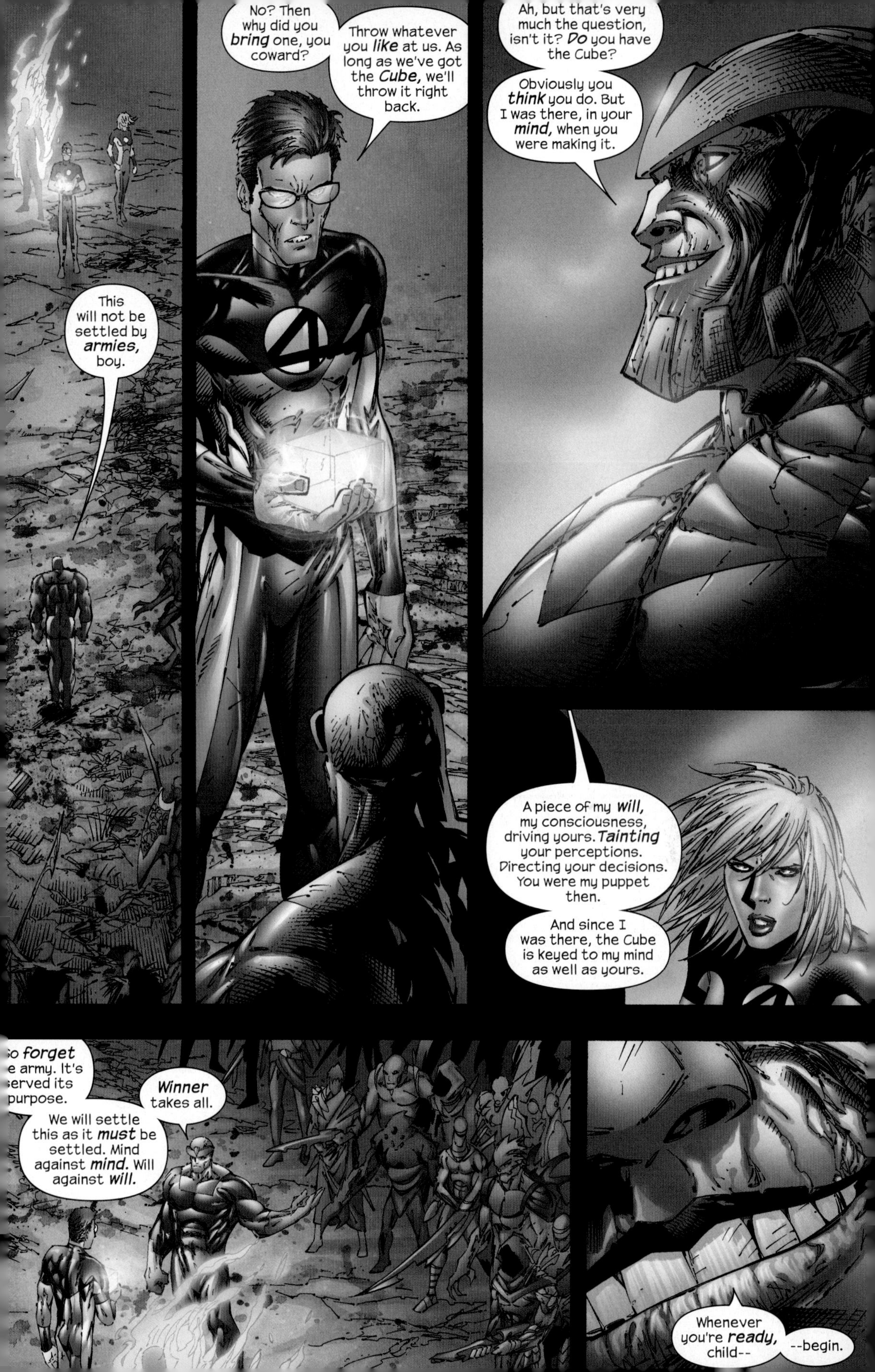
No? Then why did you bring one, you coward?
This will not be settled by armies, boy.
Throw whatever you like at us. As long as we've got the Cube, we'll throw it right back.
Ah, but that's very much the question, isn't it? Do you have the Cube?
Obviously you think you do. But I was there, in your mind, when you were making it.
A piece of my will, my consciousness, driving yours. Tainting your perceptions. Directing your decisions. You were my puppet then.
And since I was there, the Cube is keyed to my mind as well as yours.
So forget the army. It's served its purpose.
We will settle this as it must be settled. Mind against mind. Will against will.
Winner takes all.
Whenever you're ready, child--
--begin.

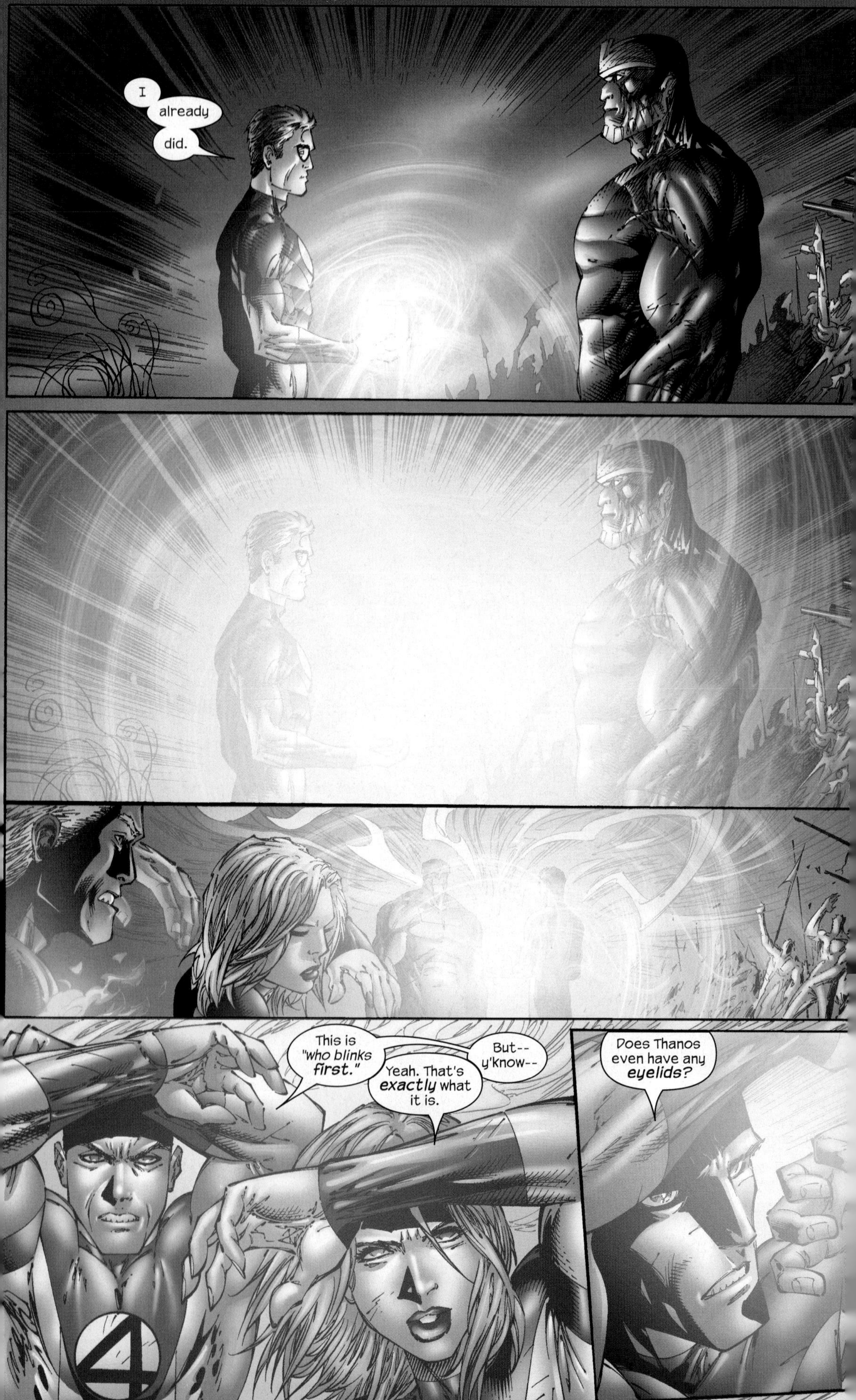
I already did.
This is "who blinks first."
But-- y'know--
Yeah. That's exactly what it is.
Does Thanos even have any eyelids?

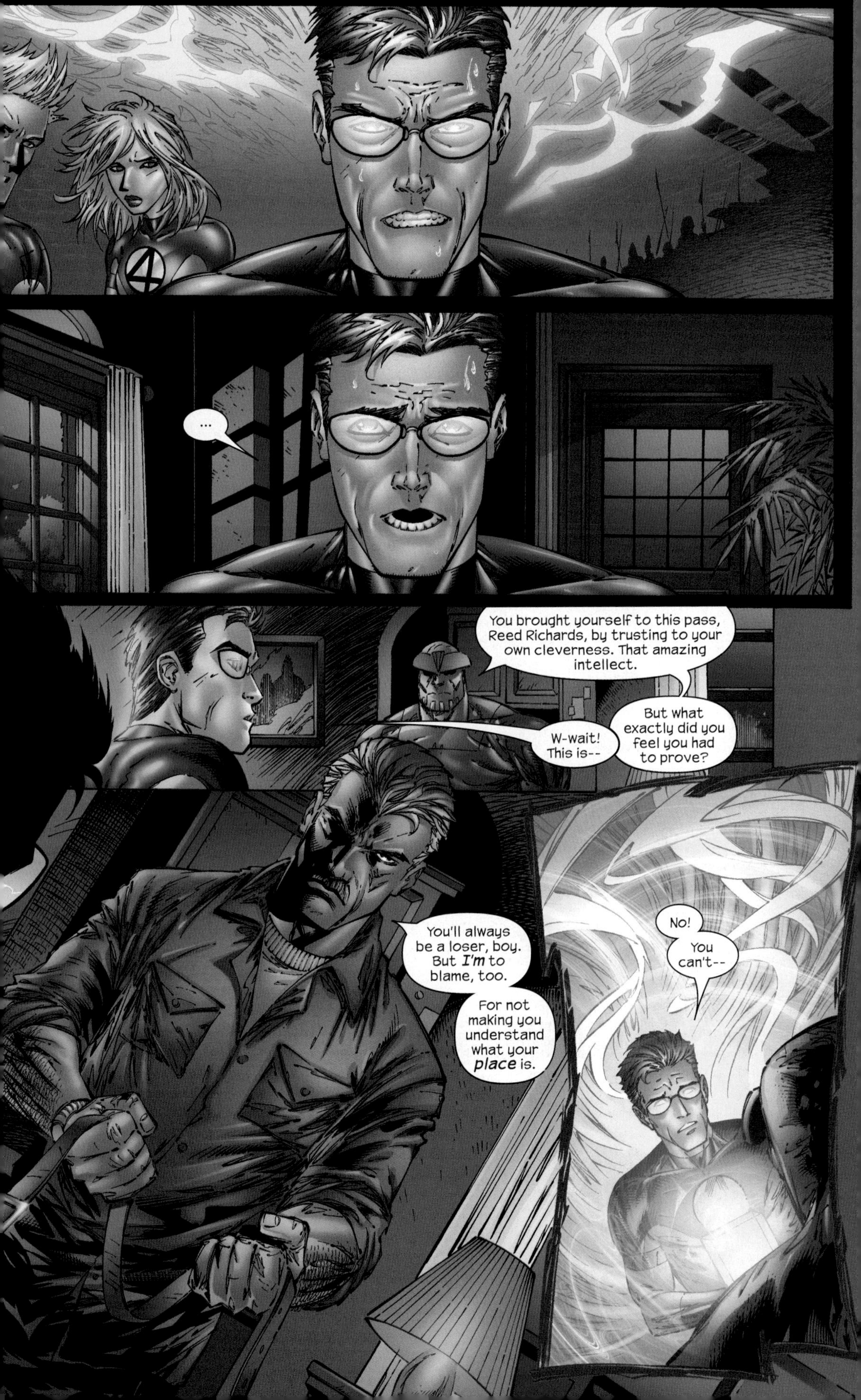
...
You brought yourself to this pass, Reed Richards, by trusting to your own cleverness. That amazing intellect.
But what exactly did you feel you had to prove?
W-wait! This is--
You'll always be a loser, boy. But *I'm* to blame, too.
For not making you understand what your *place* is.
No!
You can't--

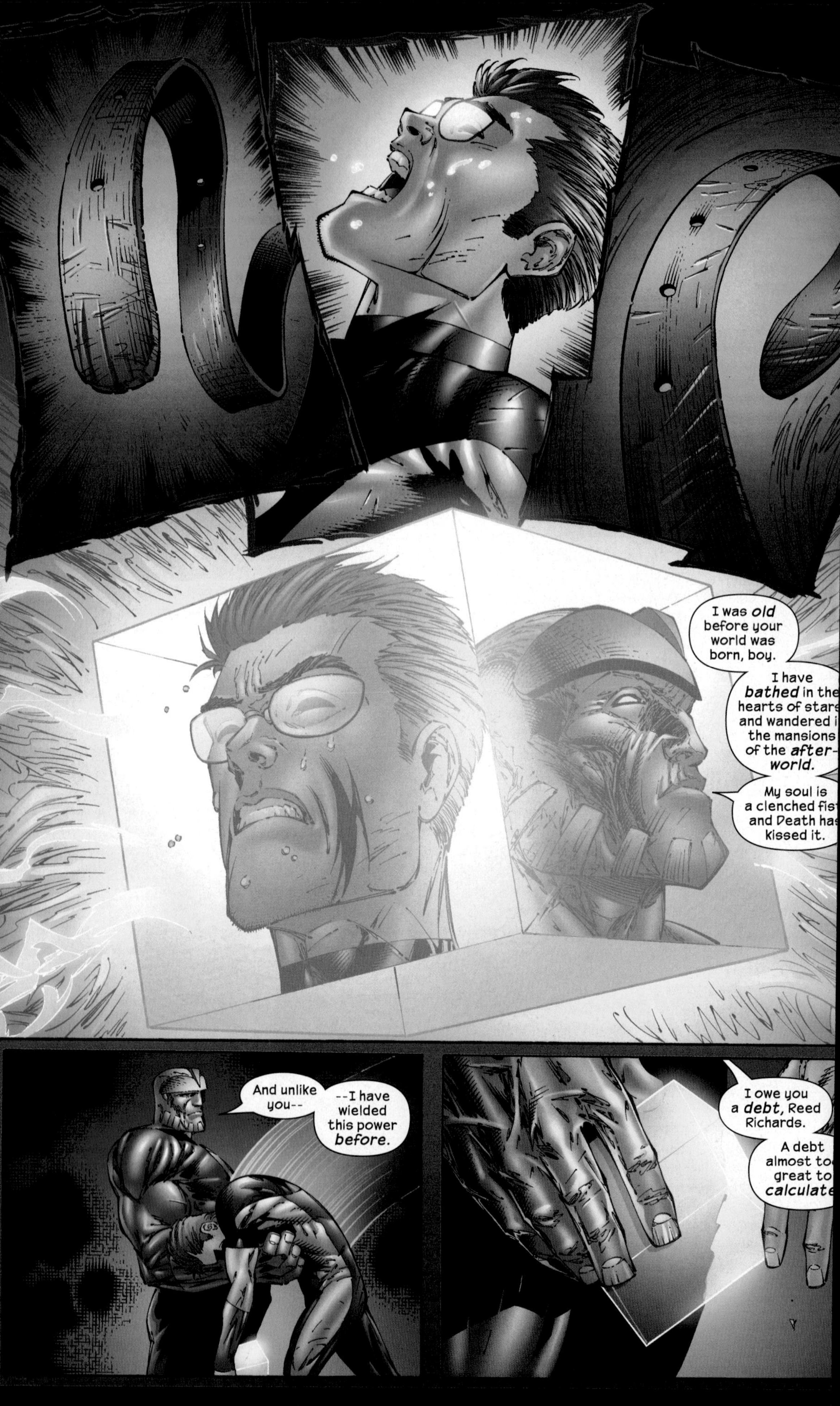

I was *old* before your world was born, boy.
I have *bathed* in the hearts of stars and wandered in the mansions of the *after-world.*
My soul is a clenched fist and Death has kissed it.
And unlike you--
--I have wielded this power *before.*
I owe you a *debt,* Reed Richards.
A debt almost too great to *calculate*

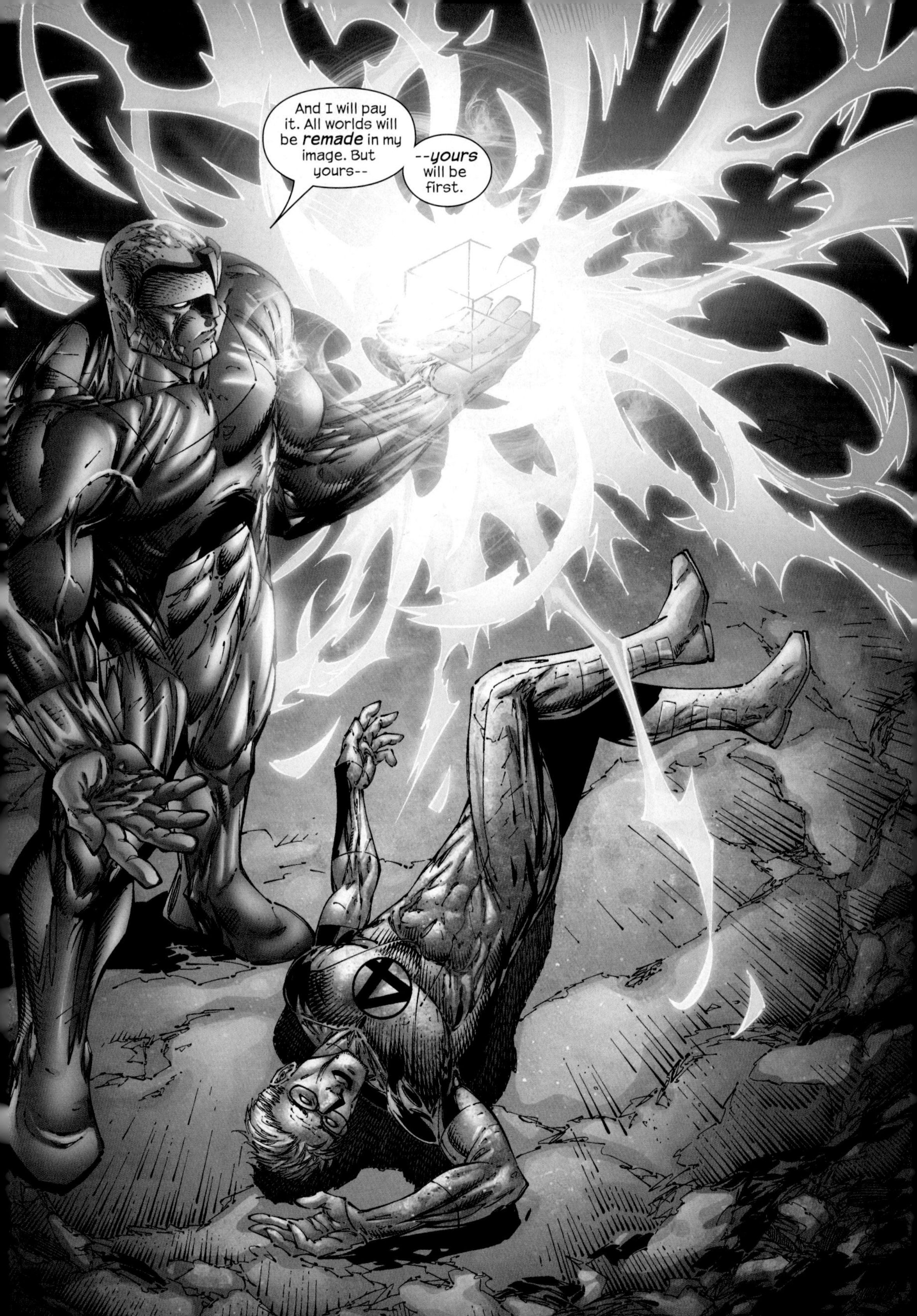
And I will pay it. All worlds will be *remade* in my image. But yours--
--*yours* will be first.

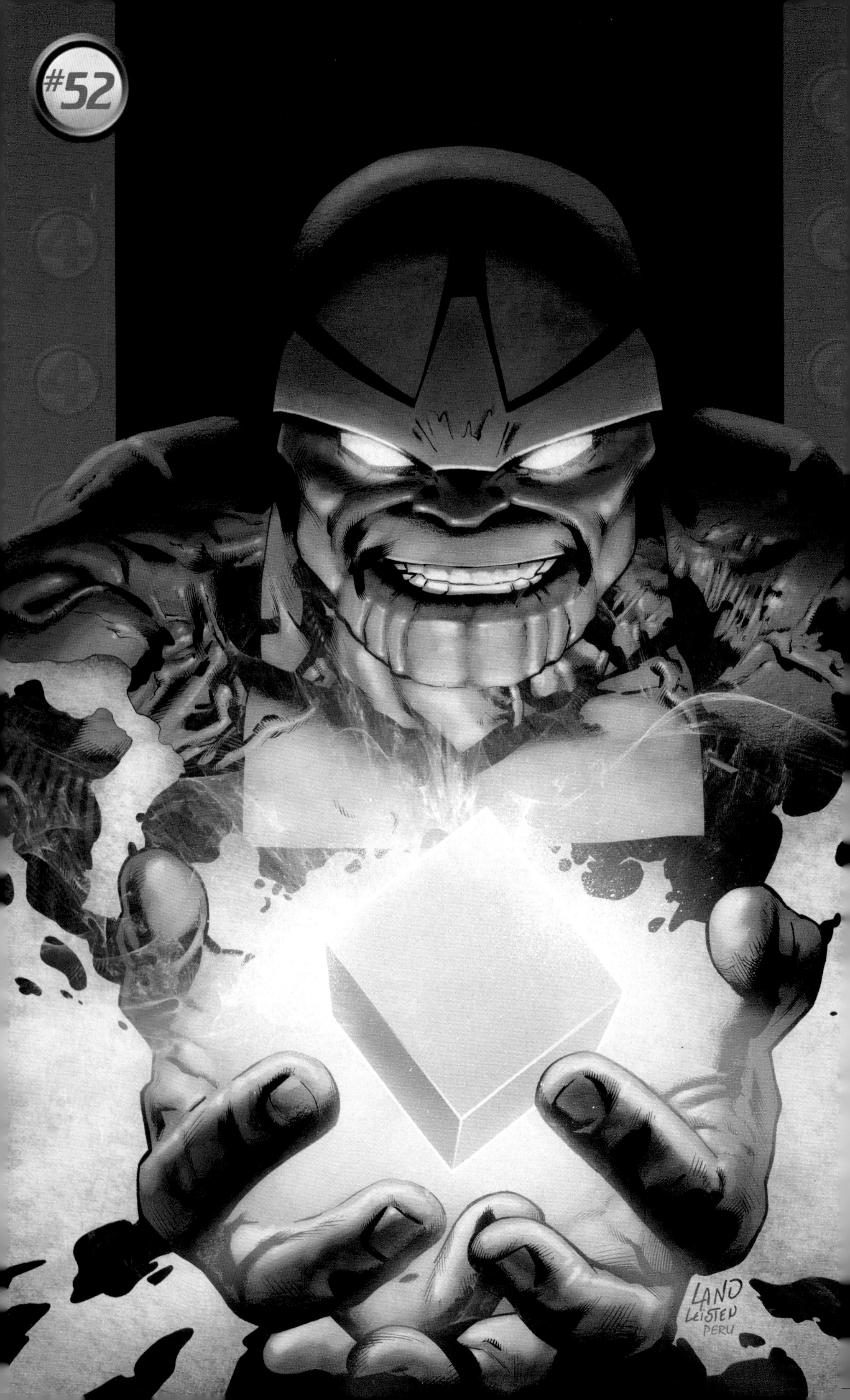
#52
LAND
LEISTEN
PERU

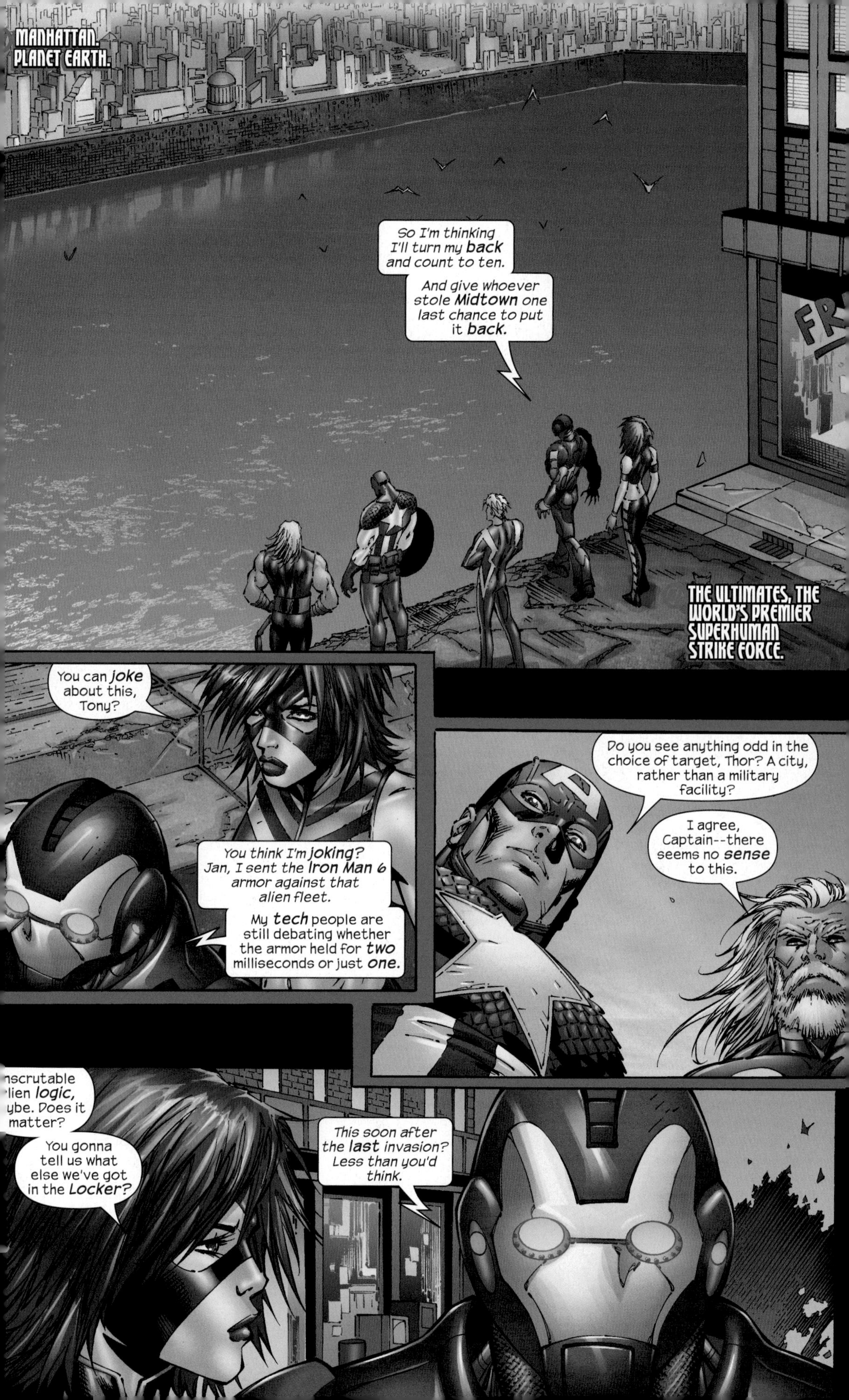
MANHATTAN.
PLANET EARTH.
So I'm thinking I'll turn my back and count to ten.
And give whoever stole Midtown one last chance to put it back.
FR
THE ULTIMATES, THE WORLD'S PREMIER SUPERHUMAN STRIKE FORCE.
You can joke about this, Tony?
You think I'm joking? Jan, I sent the Iron Man 6 armor against that alien fleet.
My tech people are still debating whether the armor held for two milliseconds or just one.
Do you see anything odd in the choice of target, Thor? A city, rather than a military facility?
I agree, Captain--there seems no sense to this.
nscrutable lien logic, ybe. Does it matter?
You gonna tell us what else we've got in the Locker?
This soon after the last invasion? Less than you'd think.

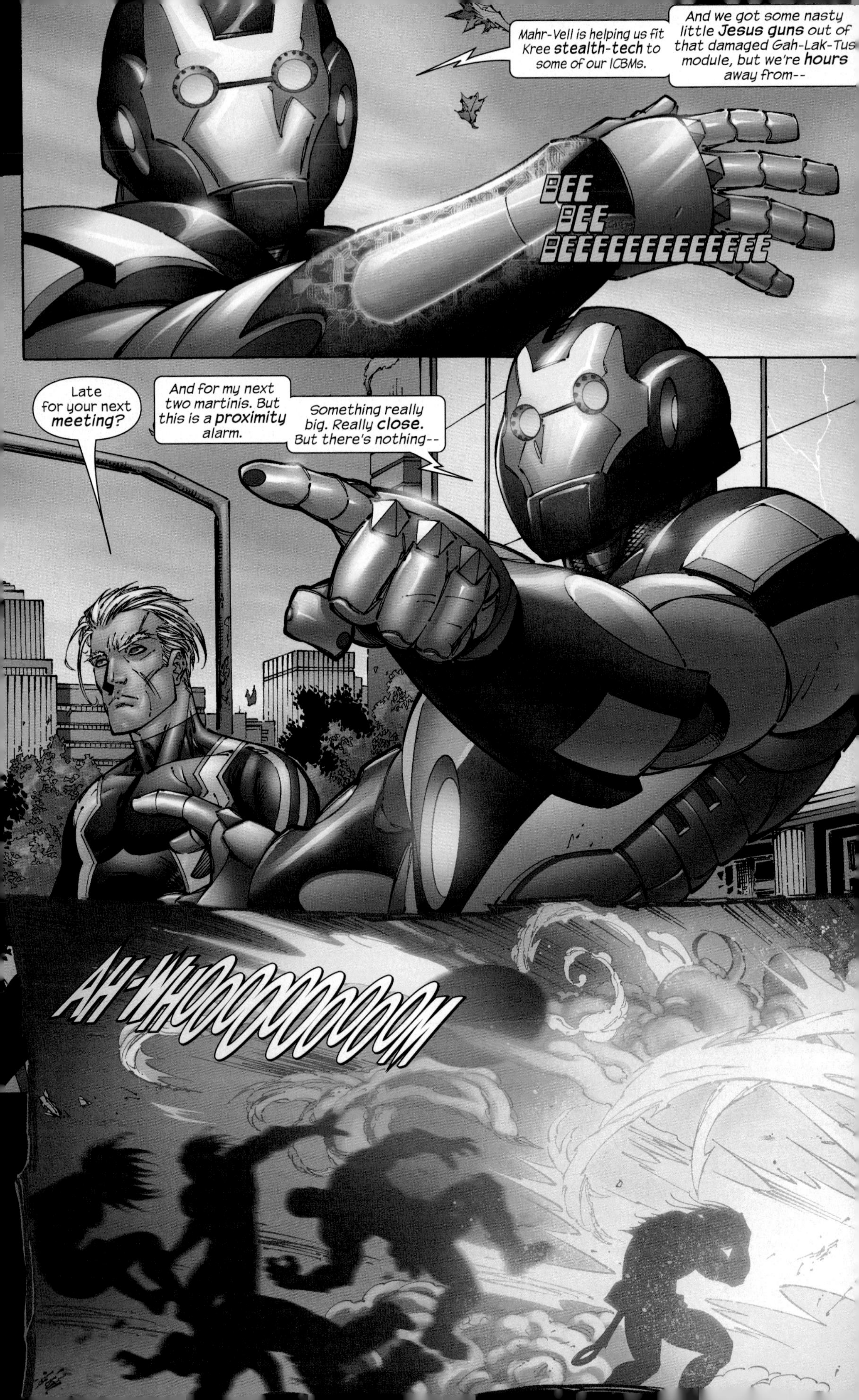
Mahr-Vell is helping us fit Kree **stealth-tech** to some of our ICBMs.
And we got some nasty little **Jesus guns** out of that damaged Gah-Lak-Tus module, but we're **hours** away from--
BEE
BEE
BEEEEEEEEEEEEEE
Late for your next **meeting?**
And for my next two martinis. But this is a **proximity** alarm.
Something really big. Really **close.** But there's nothing--
AH-WHOOOOOOOOOM

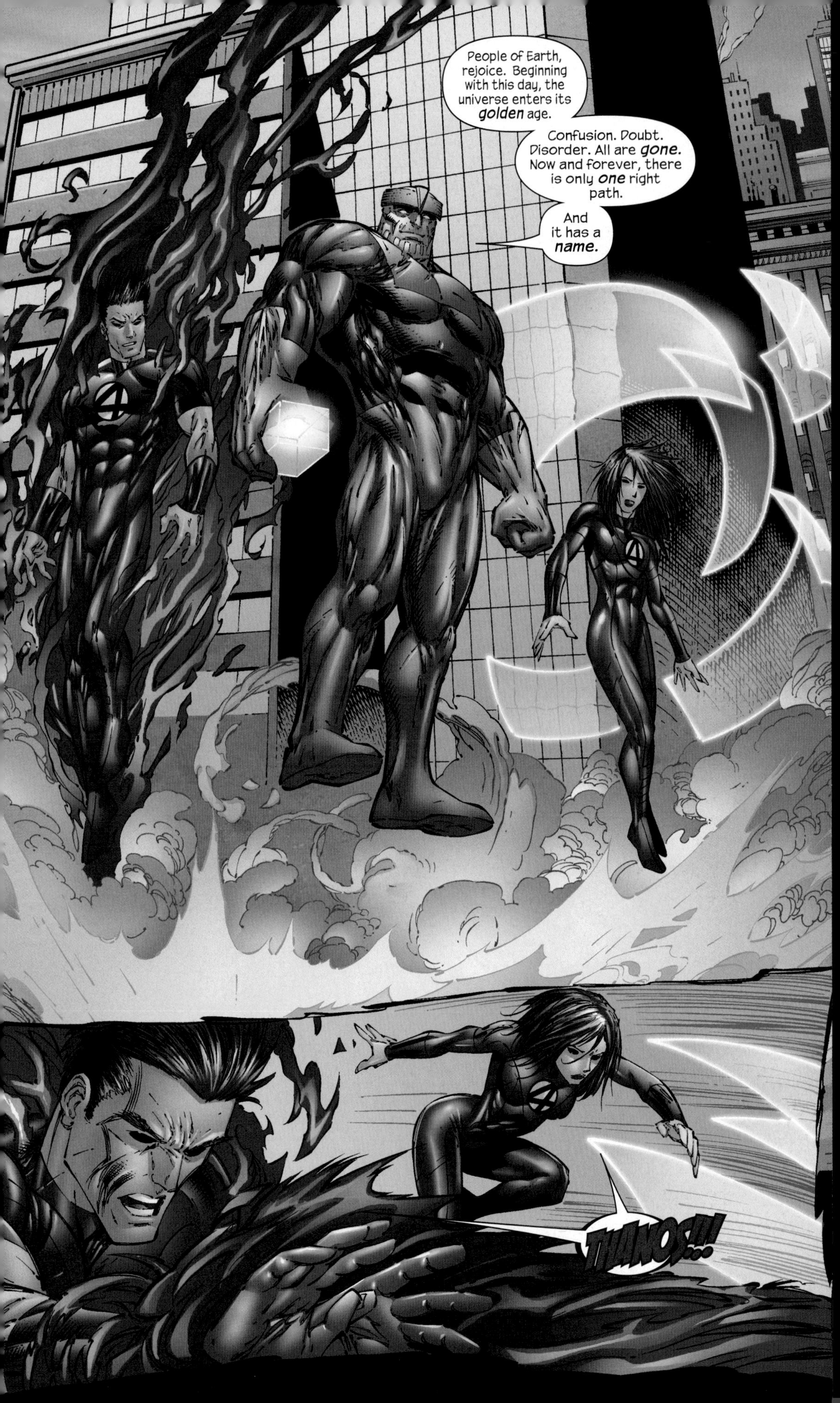
People of Earth, rejoice. Beginning with this day, the universe enters its golden age.
Confusion. Doubt. Disorder. All are gone. Now and forever, there is only one right path.
And it has a name.
THANOS!!!

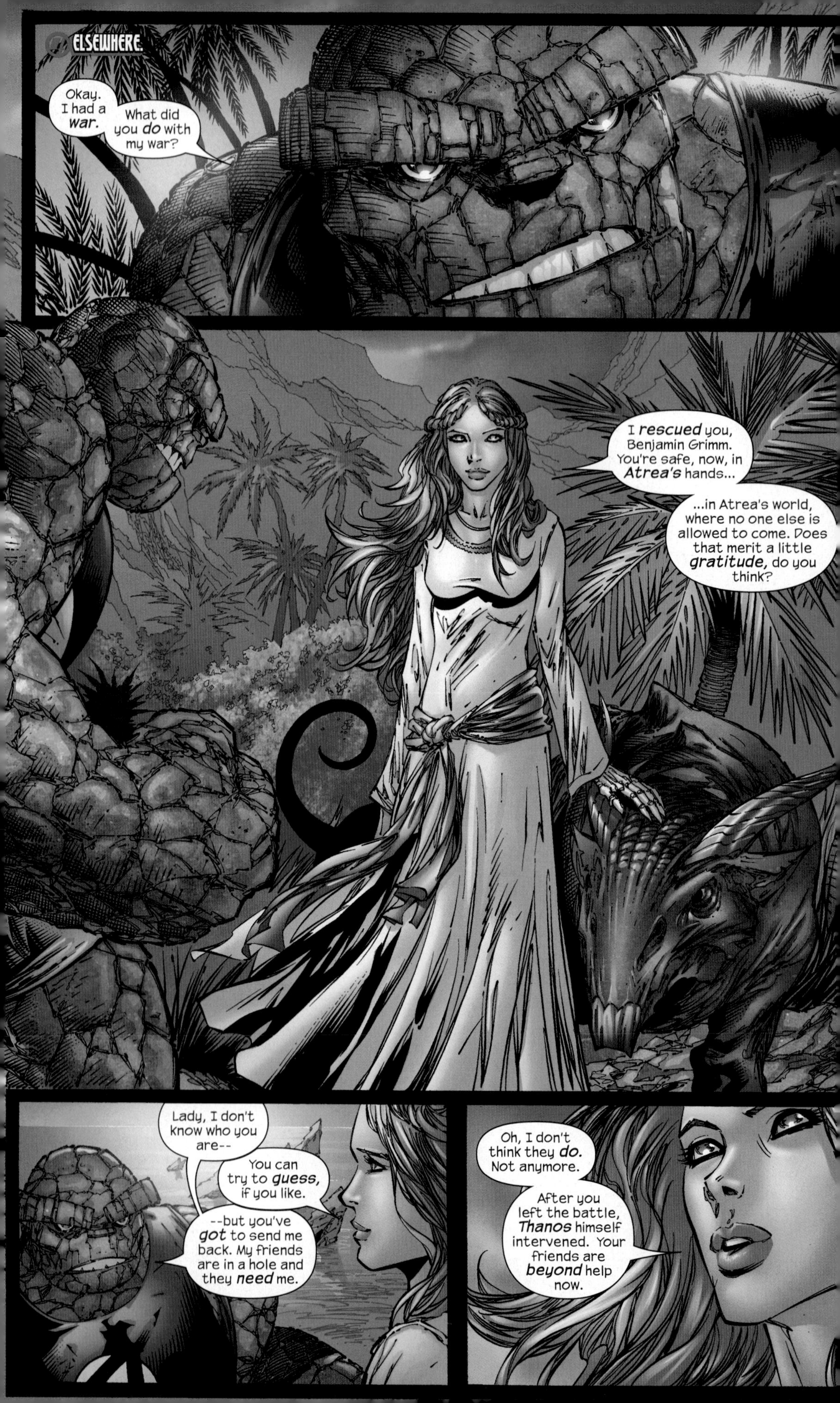

ELSEWHERE.
Okay. I had a war.
What did you do with my war?
I rescued you, Benjamin Grimm. You're safe, now, in Atrea's hands...
...in Atrea's world, where no one else is allowed to come. Does that merit a little gratitude, do you think?
Lady, I don't know who you are--
You can try to guess, if you like.
--but you've got to send me back. My friends are in a hole and they need me.
Oh, I don't think they do. Not anymore.
After you left the battle, Thanos himself intervened. Your friends are beyond help now.

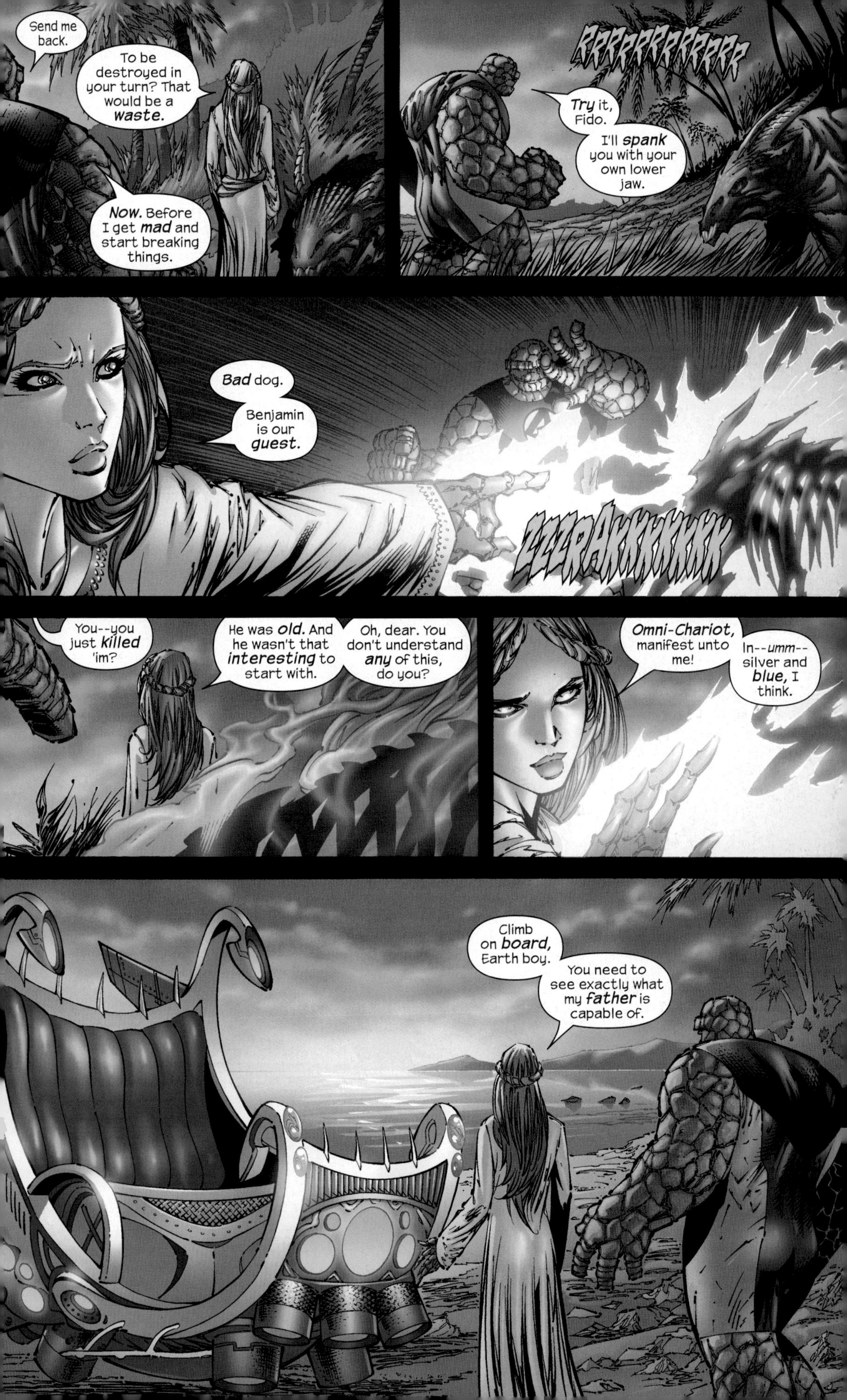
Send me back.
To be destroyed in your turn? That would be a waste.
Now. Before I get mad and start breaking things.
RRRRRRRRRRRR
Try it, Fido.
I'll spank you with your own lower jaw.
Bad dog.
Benjamin is our guest.
ZZZRAKKKKKKK
You--you just killed 'im?
He was old. And he wasn't that interesting to start with.
Oh, dear. You don't understand any of this, do you?
Omni-Chariot, manifest unto me!
In--umm--silver and blue, I think.
Climb on board, Earth boy.
You need to see exactly what my father is capable of.

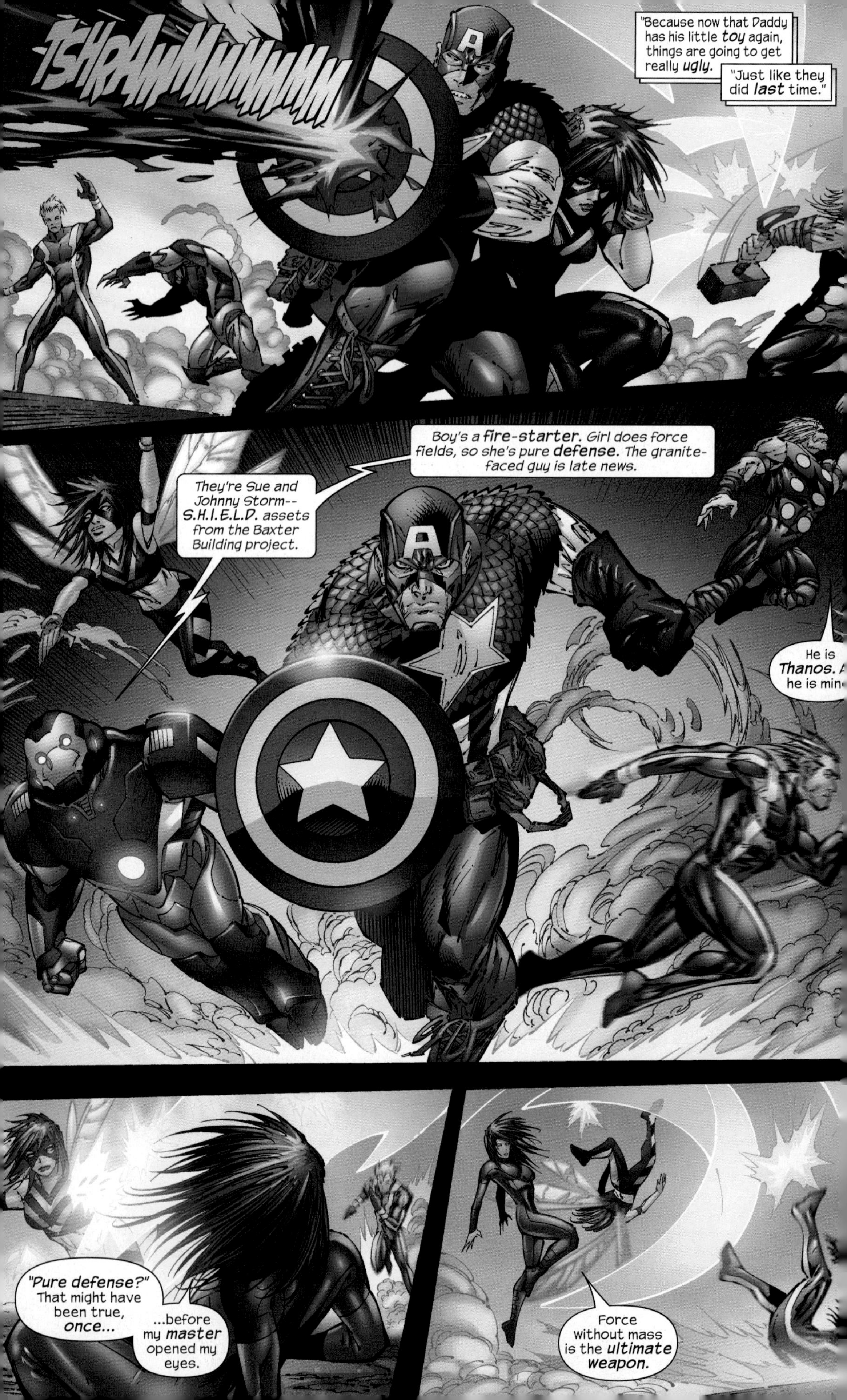

TSHRAAMMMMMMMM
"Because now that Daddy has his little toy again, things are going to get really ugly.
"Just like they did last time."
They're Sue and Johnny Storm-- S.H.I.E.L.D. assets from the Baxter Building project.
Boy's a fire-starter. Girl does force fields, so she's pure defense. The granite-faced guy is late news.
"Pure defense?" That might have been true, once...
...before my master opened my eyes.
Force without mass is the ultimate weapon.

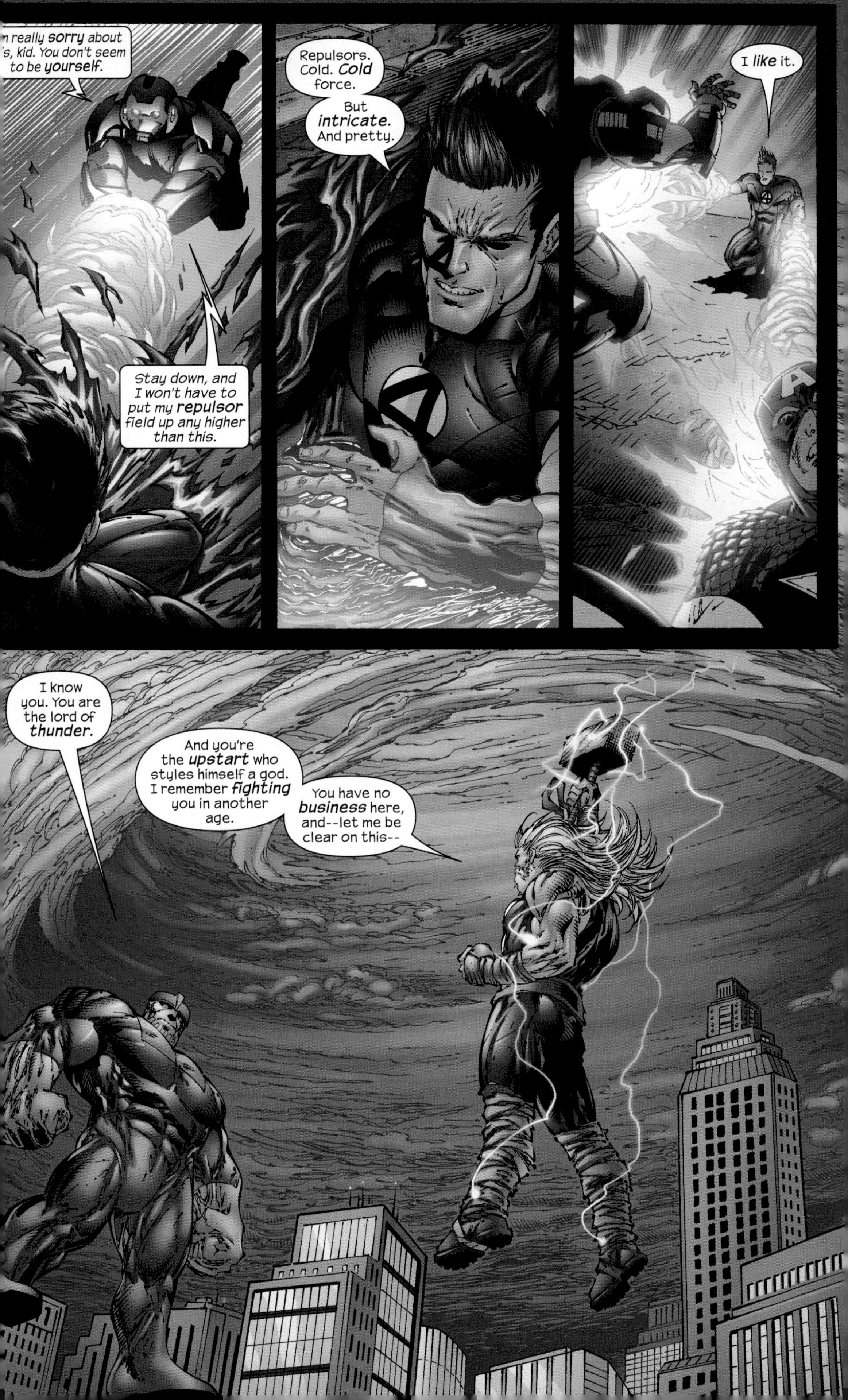

...n really sorry about ...s, kid. You don't seem to be yourself.
Stay down, and I won't have to put my repulsor field up any higher than this.
Repulsors. Cold. Cold force.
But intricate. And pretty.
I like it.
I know you. You are the lord of thunder.
And you're the upstart who styles himself a god. I remember fighting you in another age.
You have no business here, and--let me be clear on this--

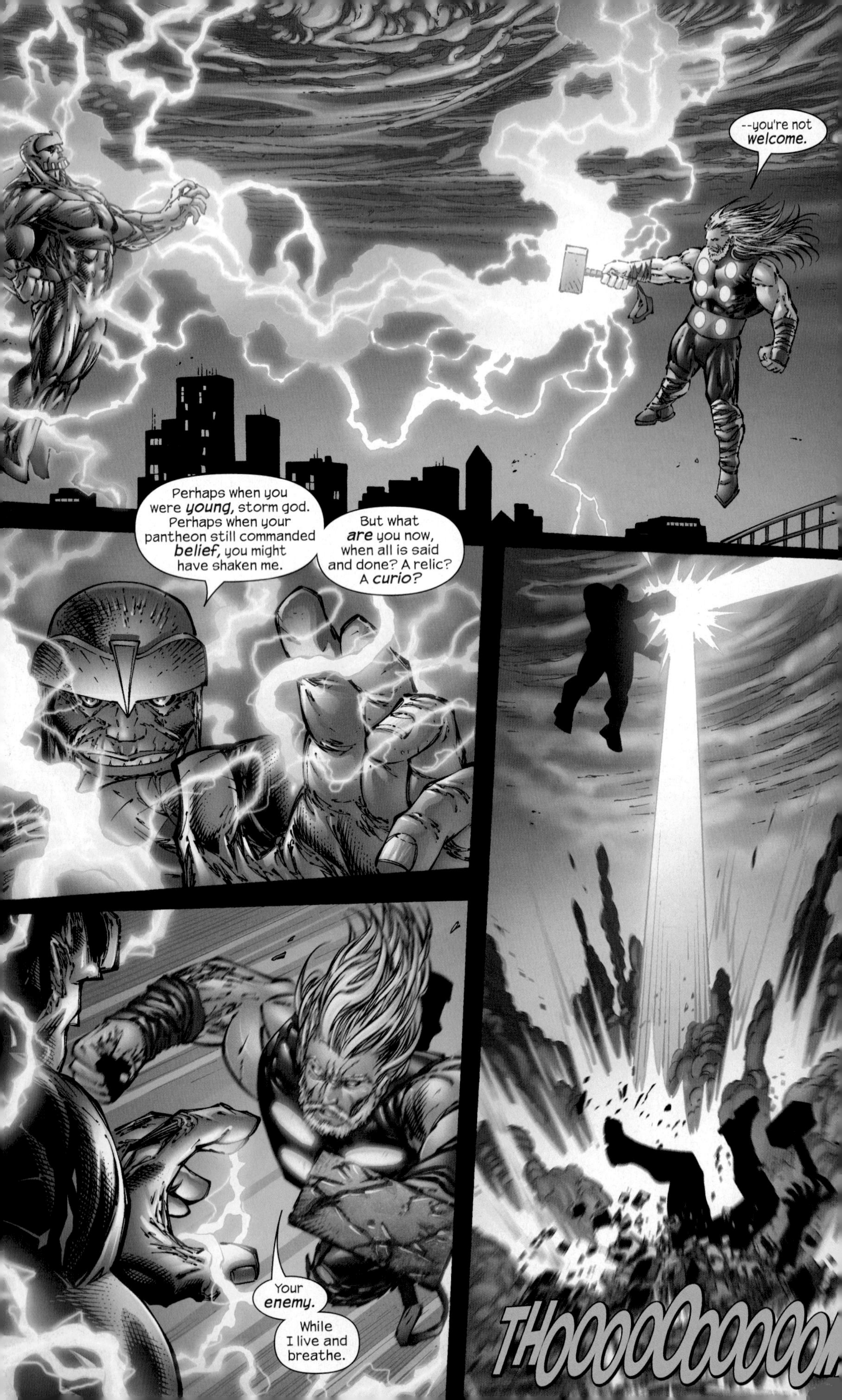
--you're not welcome.
Perhaps when you were young, storm god. Perhaps when your pantheon still commanded belief, you might have shaken me.
But what are you now, when all is said and done? A relic? A curio?
Your enemy.
While I live and breathe.
THOOOOOOOOOOM

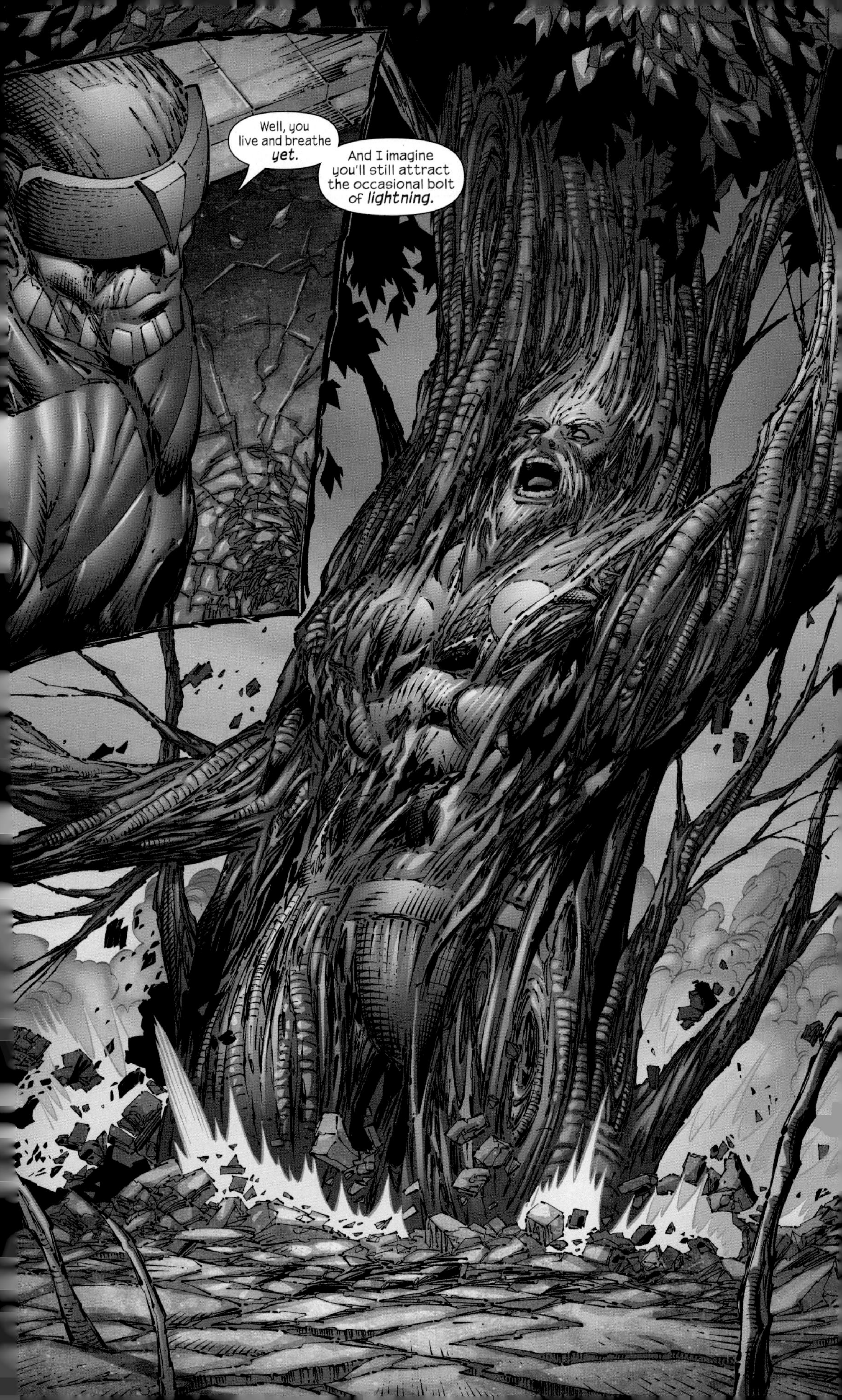
Well, you live and breathe *yet.*
And I imagine you'll still attract the occasional bolt of *lightning.*

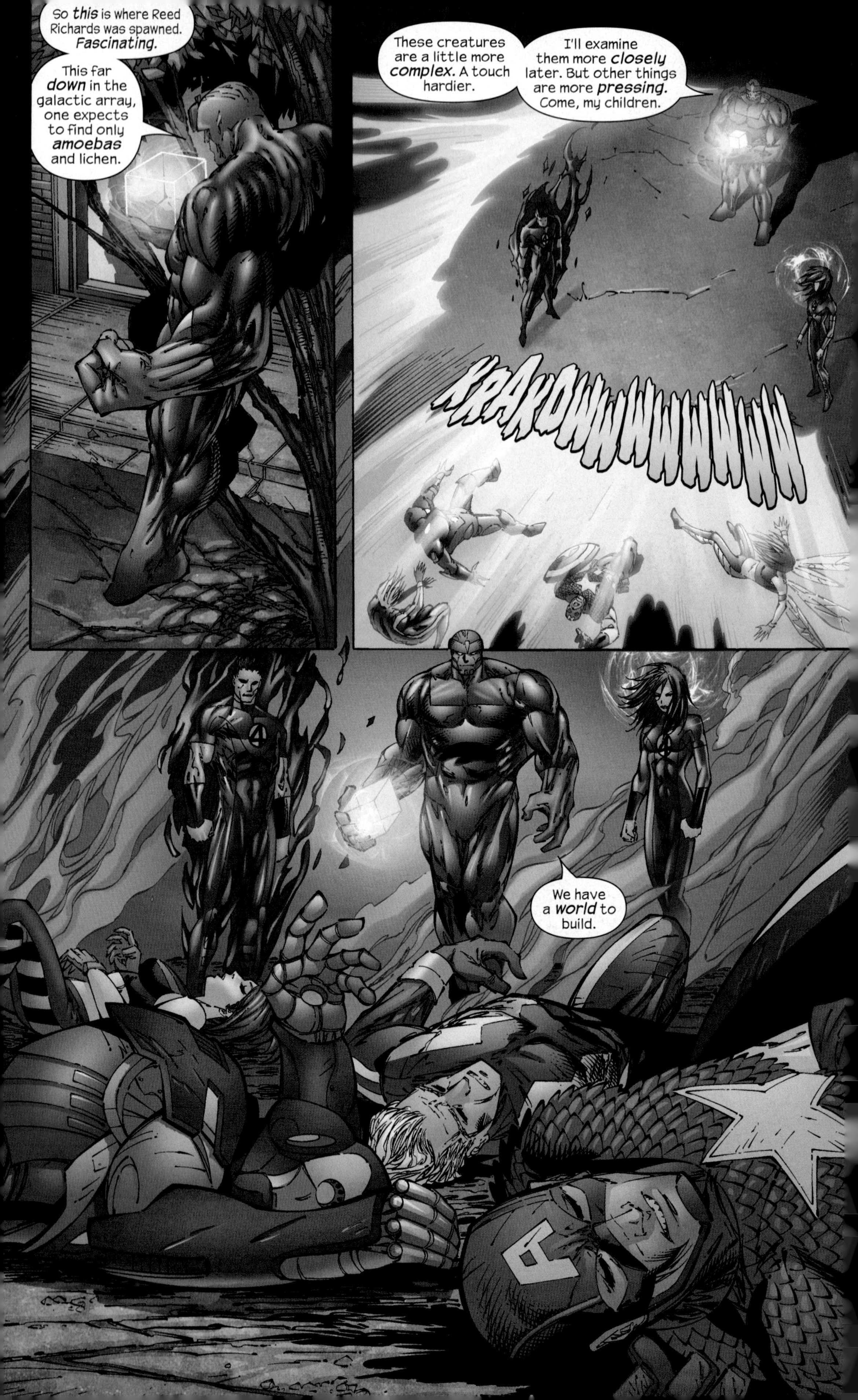
So this is where Reed Richards was spawned. Fascinating.
This far down in the galactic array, one expects to find only amoebas and lichen.
These creatures are a little more complex. A touch hardier.
I'll examine them more closely later. But other things are more pressing. Come, my children.
KRAKOWWWWWWWWW
We have a world to build.

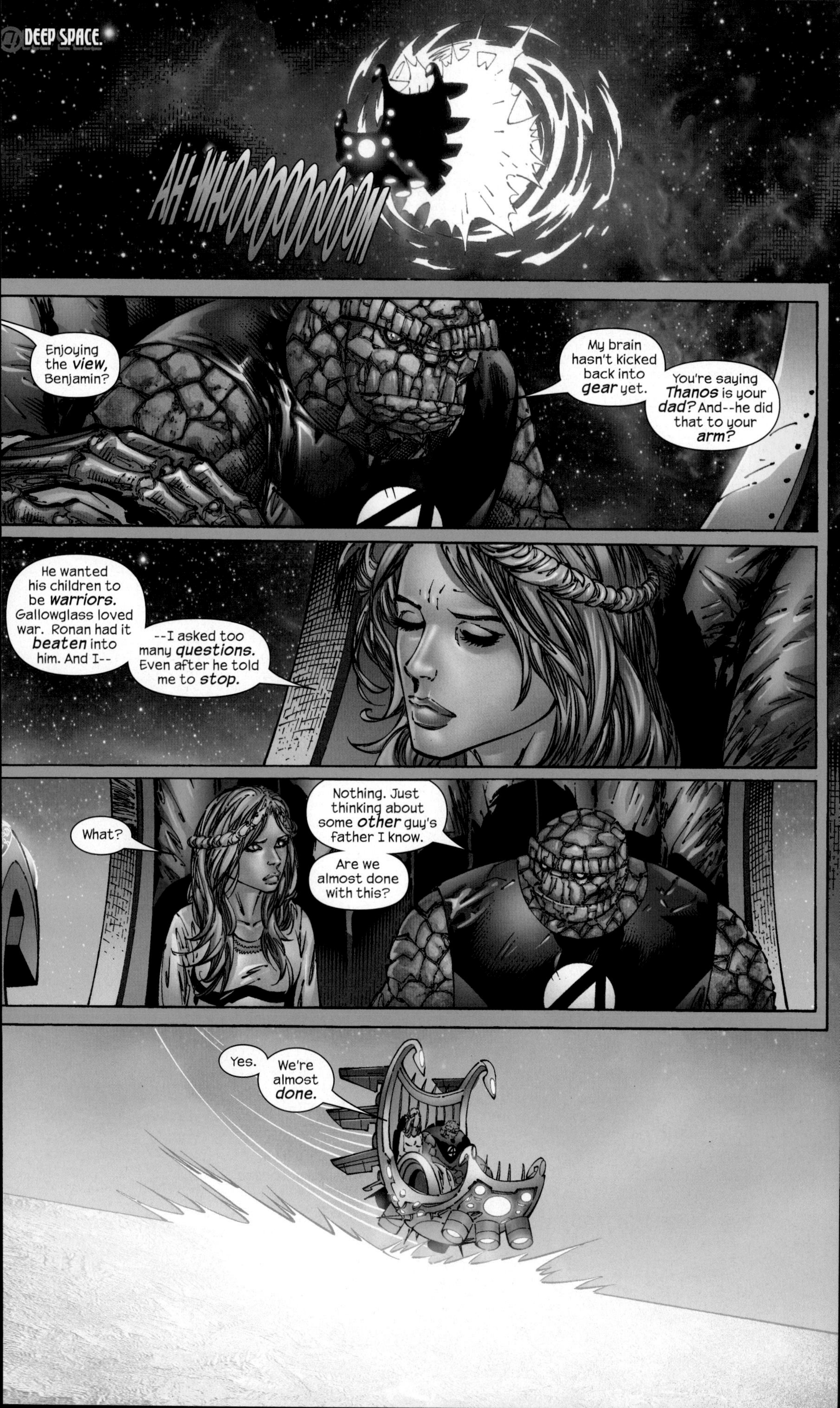
DEEP SPACE.
AH-WHOOOOOOOOOOM
Enjoying the view, Benjamin?
My brain hasn't kicked back into gear yet.
You're saying Thanos is your dad? And--he did that to your arm?
He wanted his children to be warriors. Gallowglass loved war. Ronan had it beaten into him. And I--
--I asked too many questions. Even after he told me to stop.
What?
Nothing. Just thinking about some other guy's father I know.
Are we almost done with this?
Yes.
We're almost done.

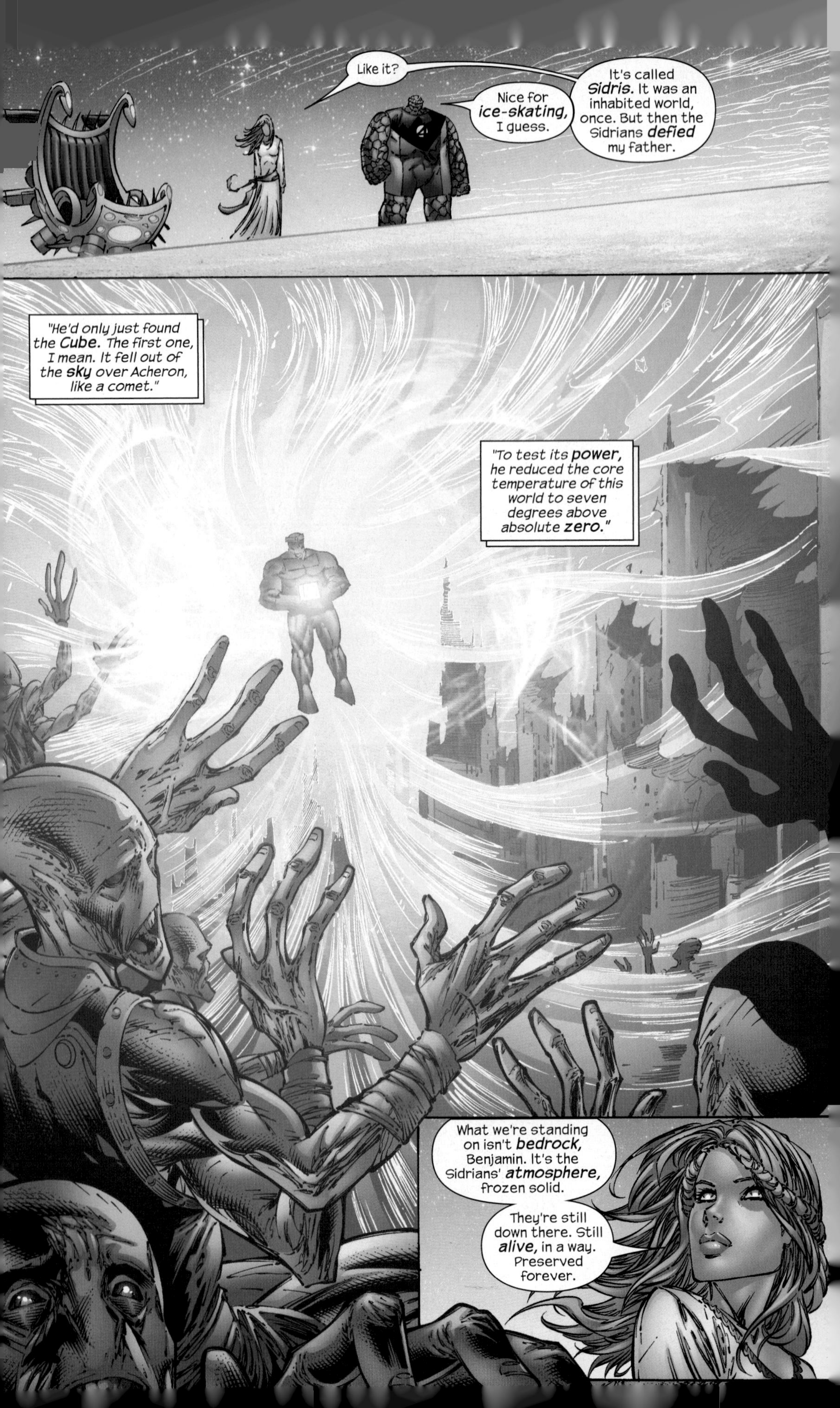
Like it?
Nice for *ice-skating,* I guess.
It's called *Sidris.* It was an inhabited world, once. But then the Sidrians *defied* my father.
"He'd only just found the *Cube.* The first one, I mean. It fell out of the *sky* over Acheron, like a comet."
"To test its *power,* he reduced the core temperature of this world to seven degrees above absolute *zero.*"
What we're standing on isn't *bedrock,* Benjamin. It's the Sidrians' *atmosphere,* frozen solid.
They're still down there. Still *alive,* in a way. Preserved forever.

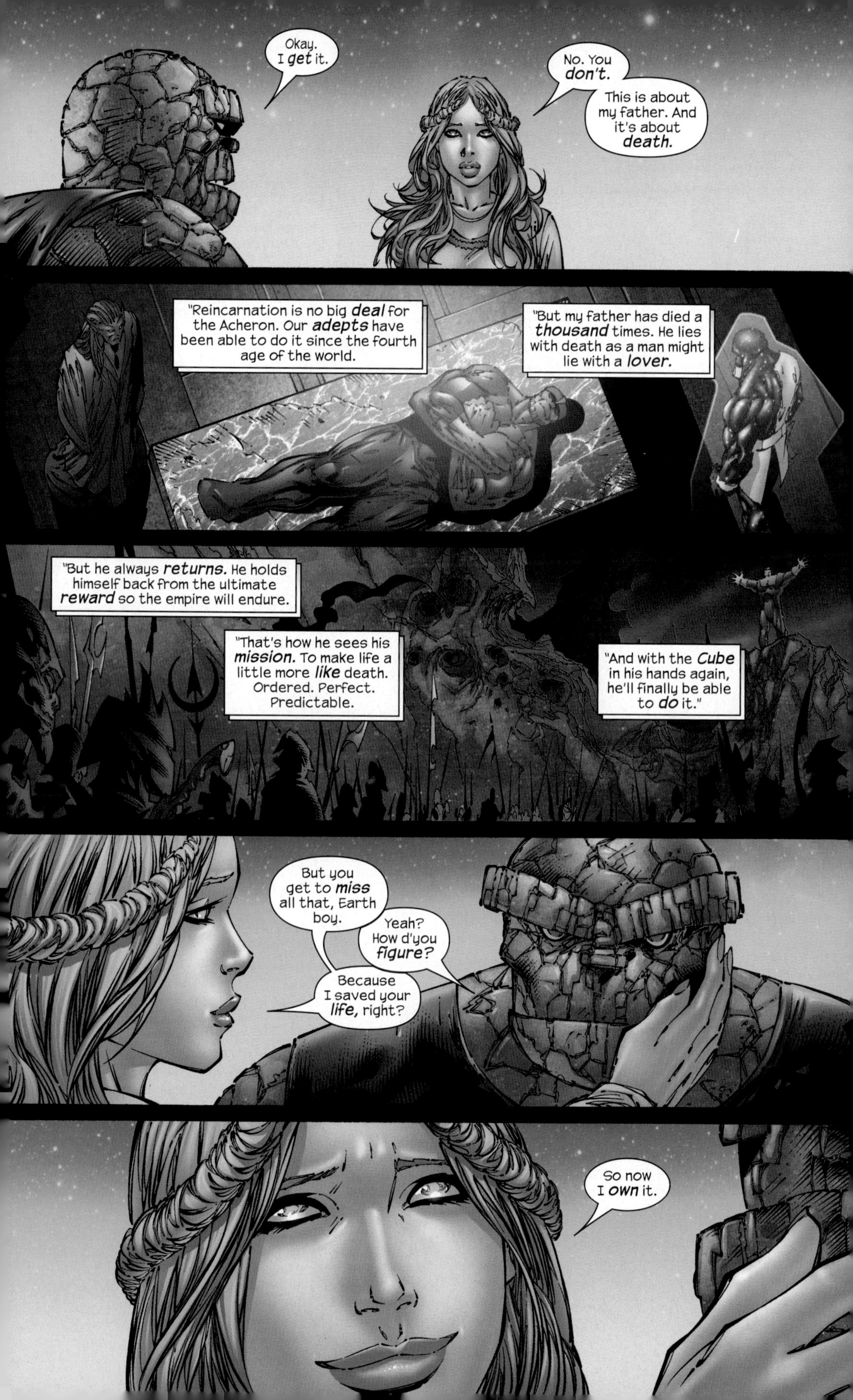

Okay. I get it.
No. You don't.
This is about my father. And it's about death.
"Reincarnation is no big deal for the Acheron. Our adepts have been able to do it since the fourth age of the world.
"But my father has died a thousand times. He lies with death as a man might lie with a lover.
"But he always returns. He holds himself back from the ultimate reward so the empire will endure.
"That's how he sees his mission. To make life a little more like death. Ordered. Perfect. Predictable.
"And with the Cube in his hands again, he'll finally be able to do it."
But you get to miss all that, Earth boy.
Yeah? How d'you figure?
Because I saved your life, right?
So now I own it.

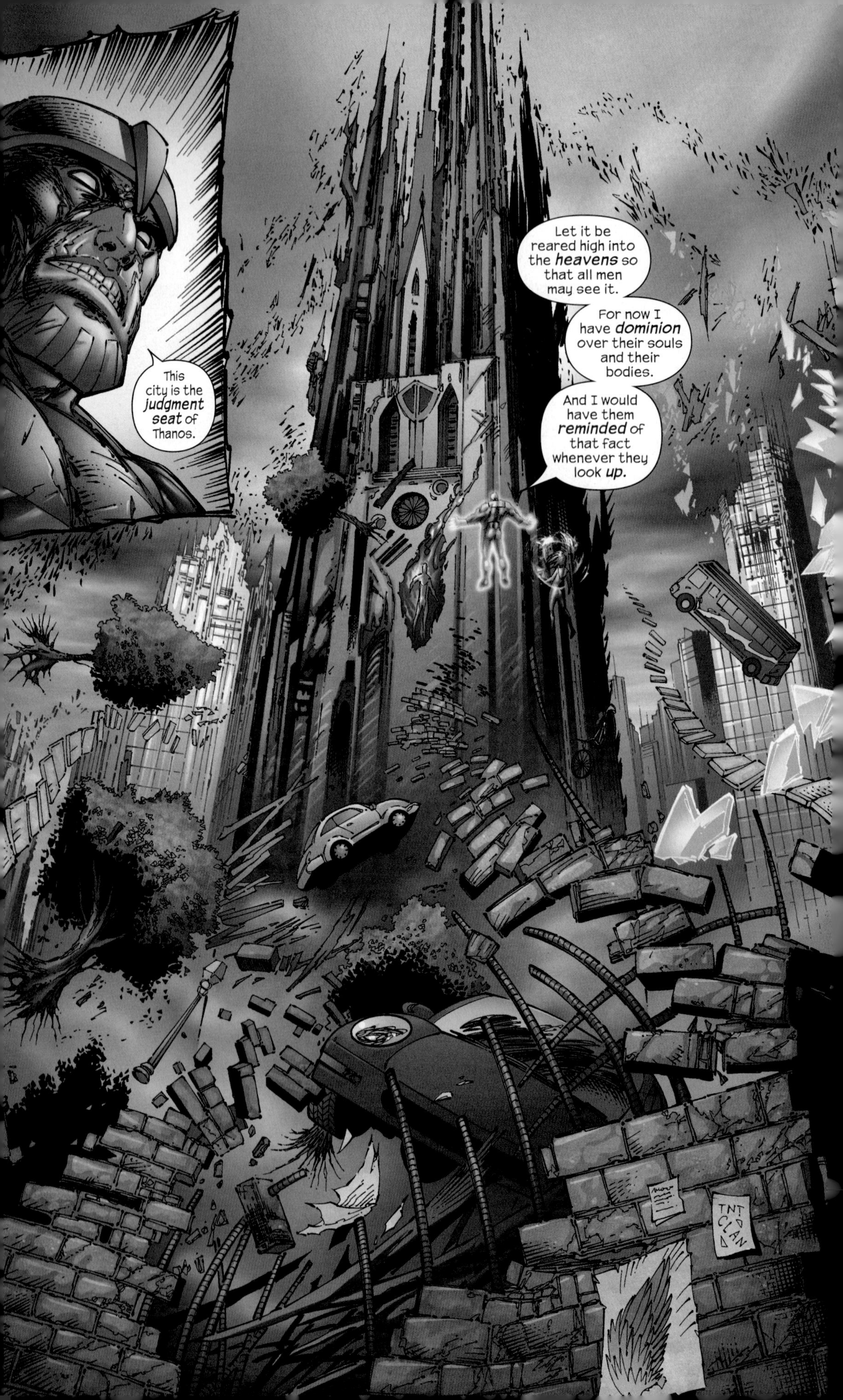

This city is the judgment seat of Thanos.
Let it be reared high into the heavens so that all men may see it.
For now I have dominion over their souls and their bodies.
And I would have them reminded of that fact whenever they look up.
TNT CLAN

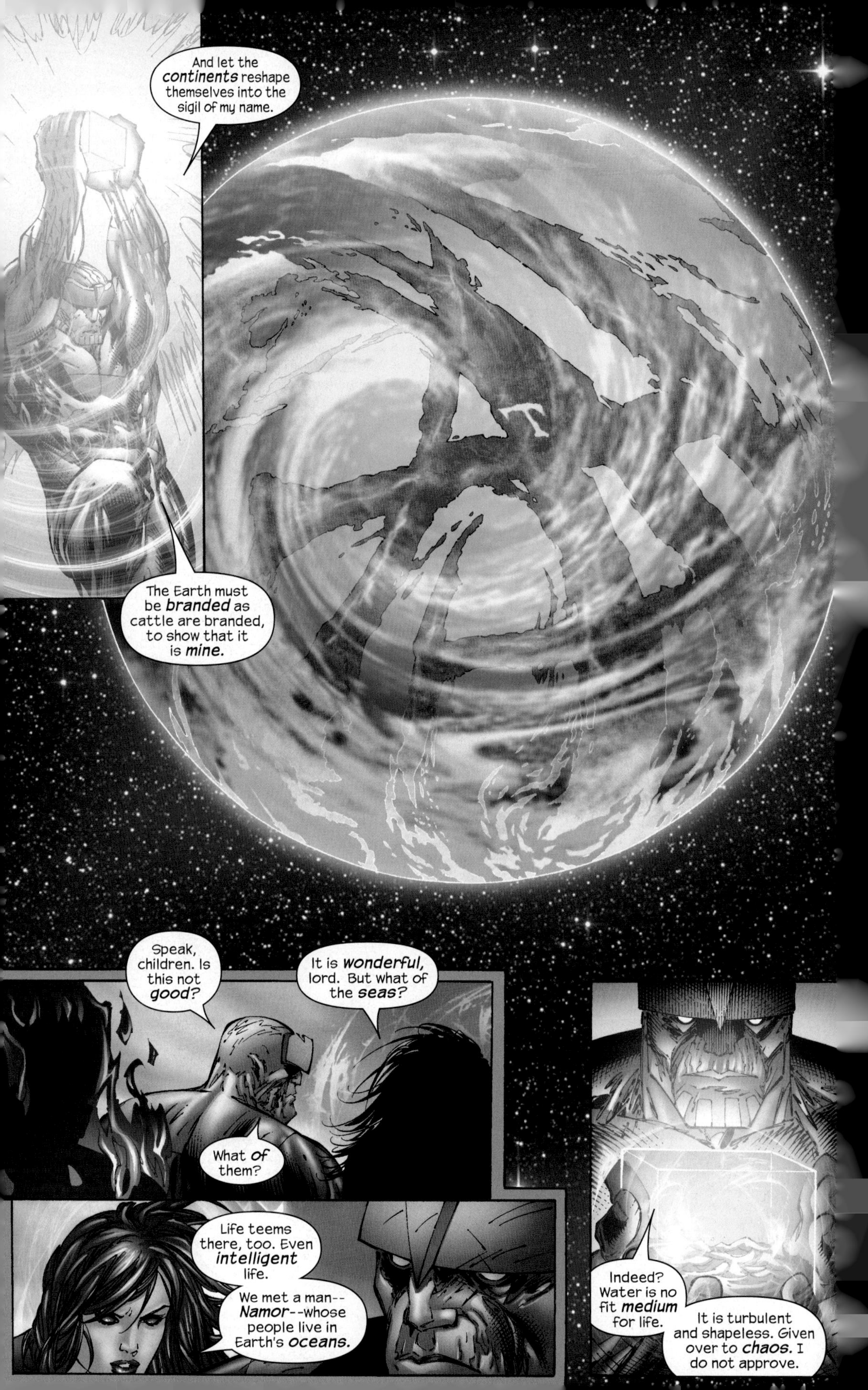

And let the *continents* reshape themselves into the sigil of my name.
The Earth must be *branded* as cattle are branded, to show that it is *mine.*
Speak, children. Is this not *good?*
It is *wonderful,* lord. But what of the *seas?*
What *of* them?
Life teems there, too. Even *intelligent* life.
We met a man-- *Namor*--whose people live in Earth's *oceans.*
Indeed? Water is no fit *medium* for life.
It is turbulent and shapeless. Given over to *chaos.* I do not approve.

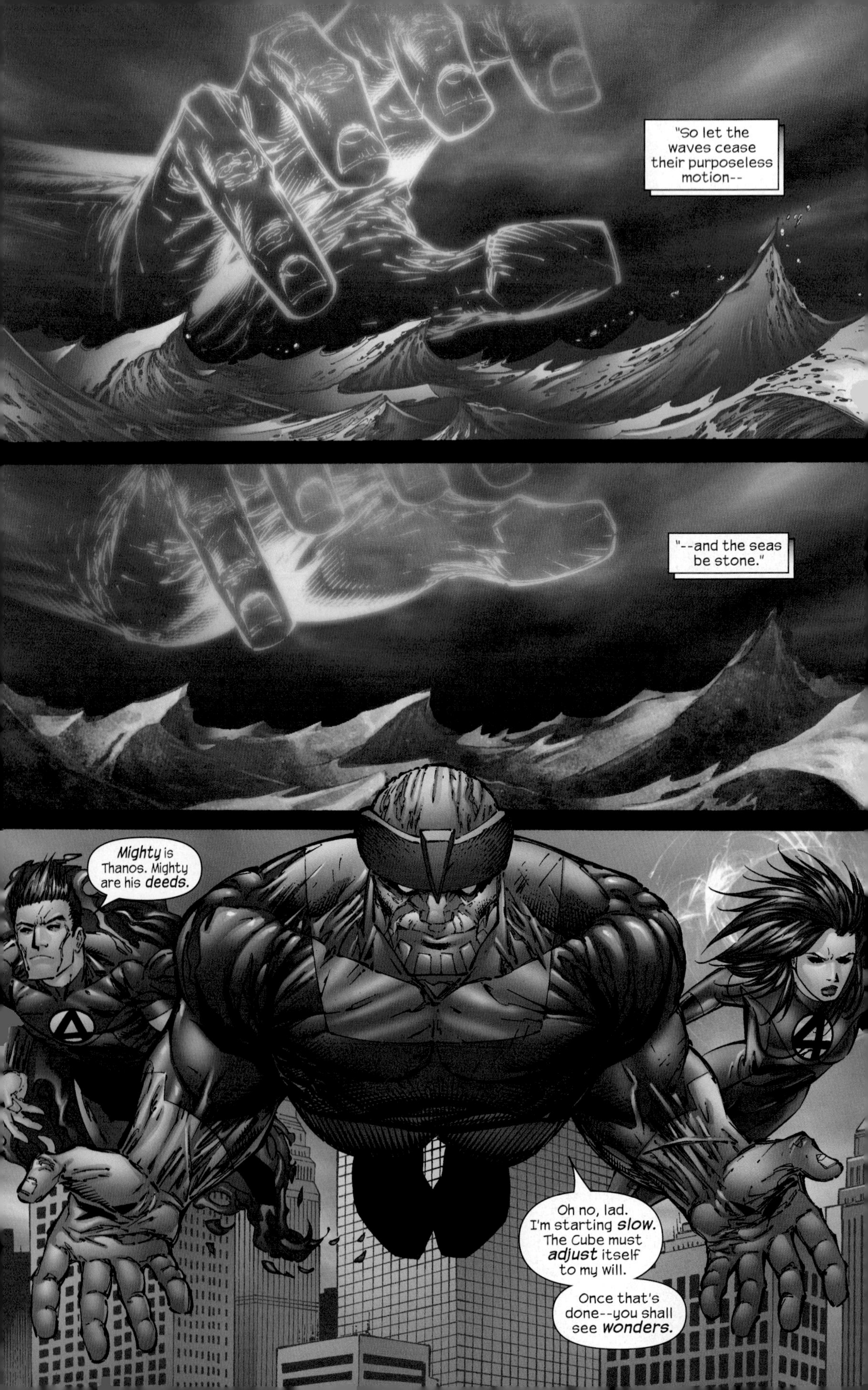
"So let the waves cease their purposeless motion--
"--and the seas be stone."
Mighty is Thanos. Mighty are his *deeds.*
Oh no, lad. I'm starting *slow.* The Cube must *adjust* itself to my will.
Once that's done--you shall see *wonders.*

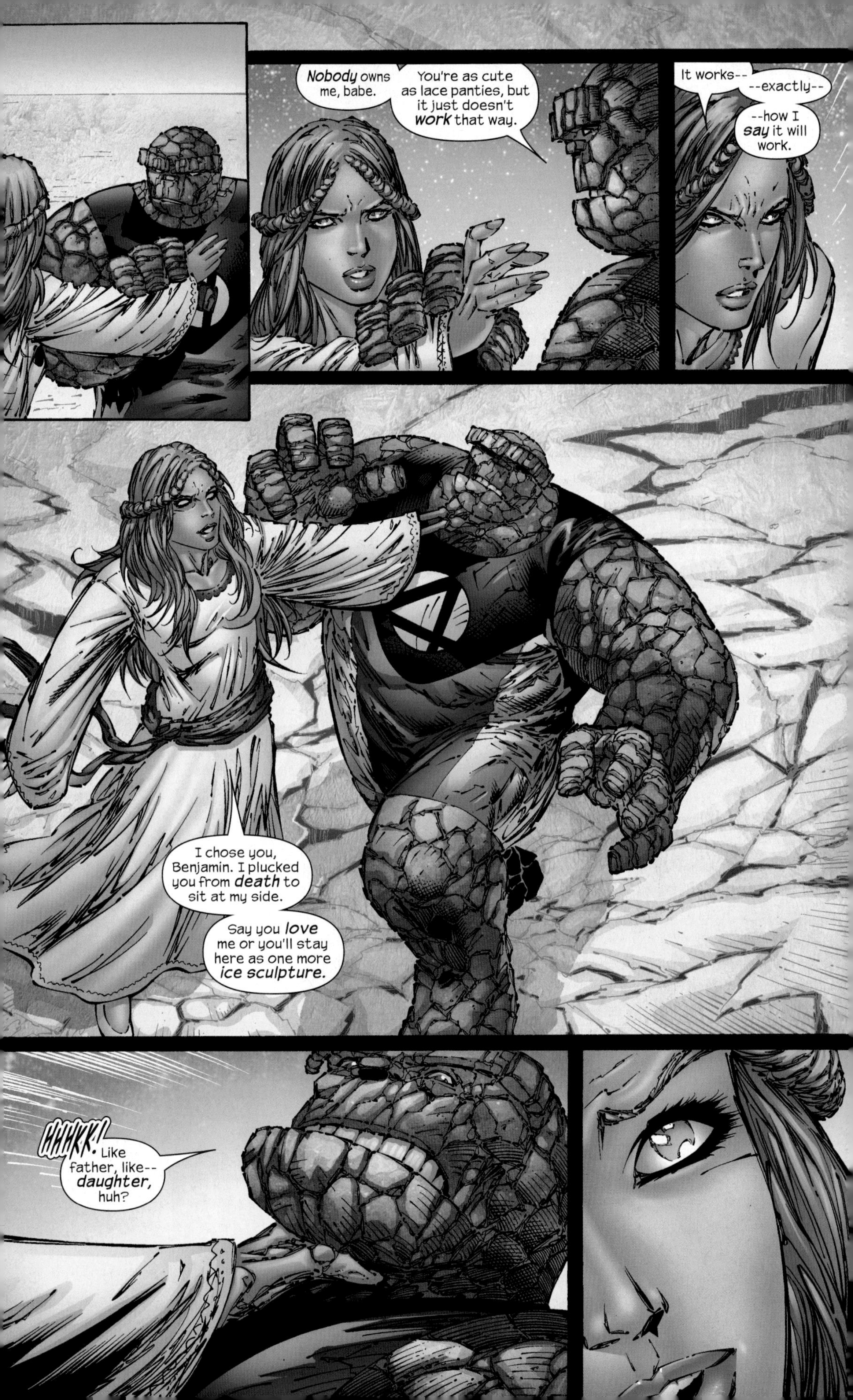
Nobody owns me, babe.
You're as cute as lace panties, but it just doesn't work that way.
It works--
--exactly--
--how I say it will work.
I chose you, Benjamin. I plucked you from death to sit at my side.
Say you love me or you'll stay here as one more ice sculpture.
CHHKK!
Like father, like-- daughter, huh?

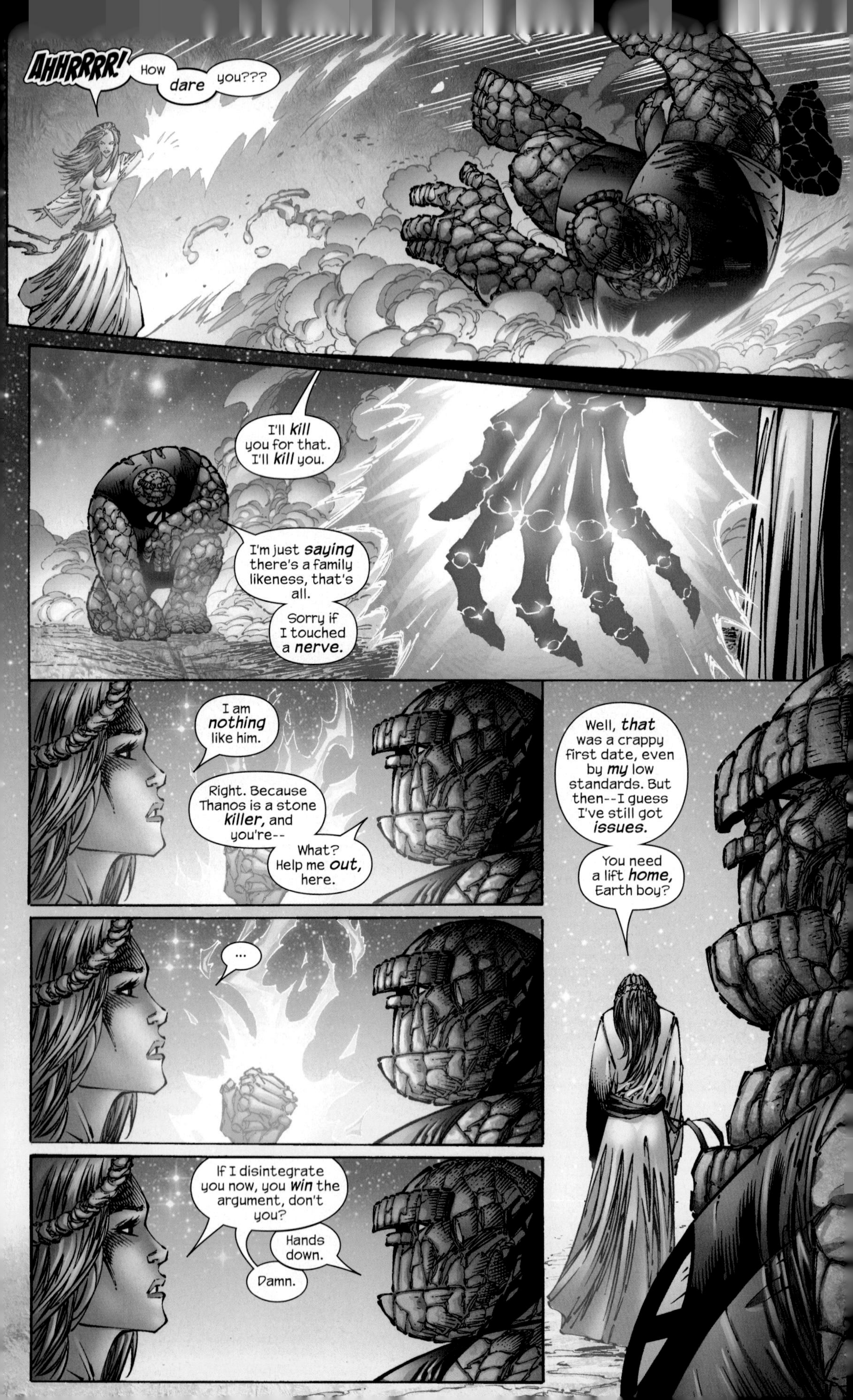
AHHRRRR!
How dare you???
I'll kill you for that. I'll kill you.
I'm just saying there's a family likeness, that's all.
Sorry if I touched a nerve.
I am nothing like him.
Right. Because Thanos is a stone killer, and you're--
What? Help me out, here.
...
If I disintegrate you now, you win the argument, don't you?
Hands down.
Damn.
Well, that was a crappy first date, even by my low standards. But then--I guess I've still got issues.
You need a lift home, Earth boy?

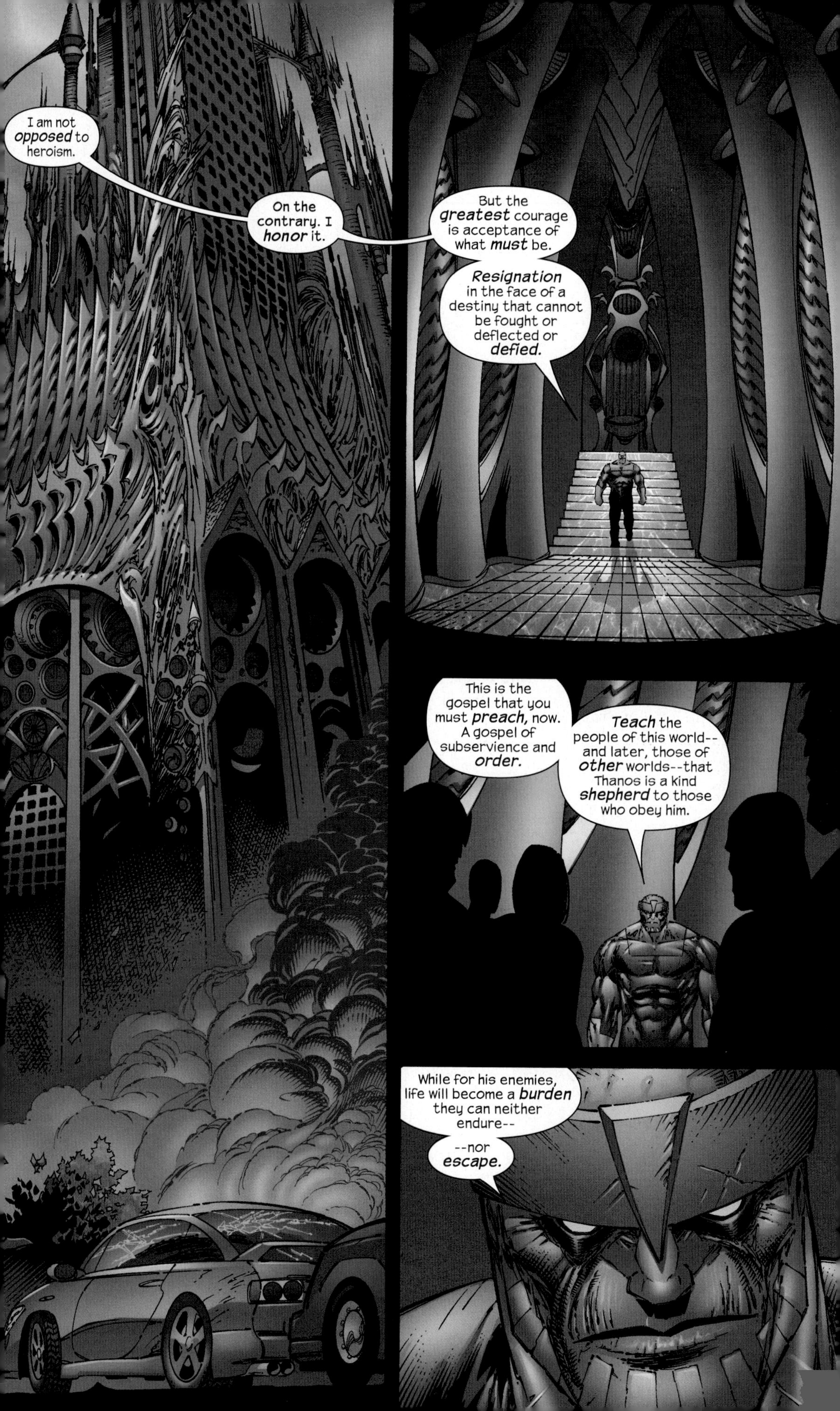
I am not opposed to heroism.
On the contrary. I honor it.
But the greatest courage is acceptance of what must be.
Resignation in the face of a destiny that cannot be fought or deflected or defied.
This is the gospel that you must preach, now. A gospel of subservience and order.
Teach the people of this world--and later, those of other worlds--that Thanos is a kind shepherd to those who obey him.
While for his enemies, life will become a burden they can neither endure--
--nor escape.

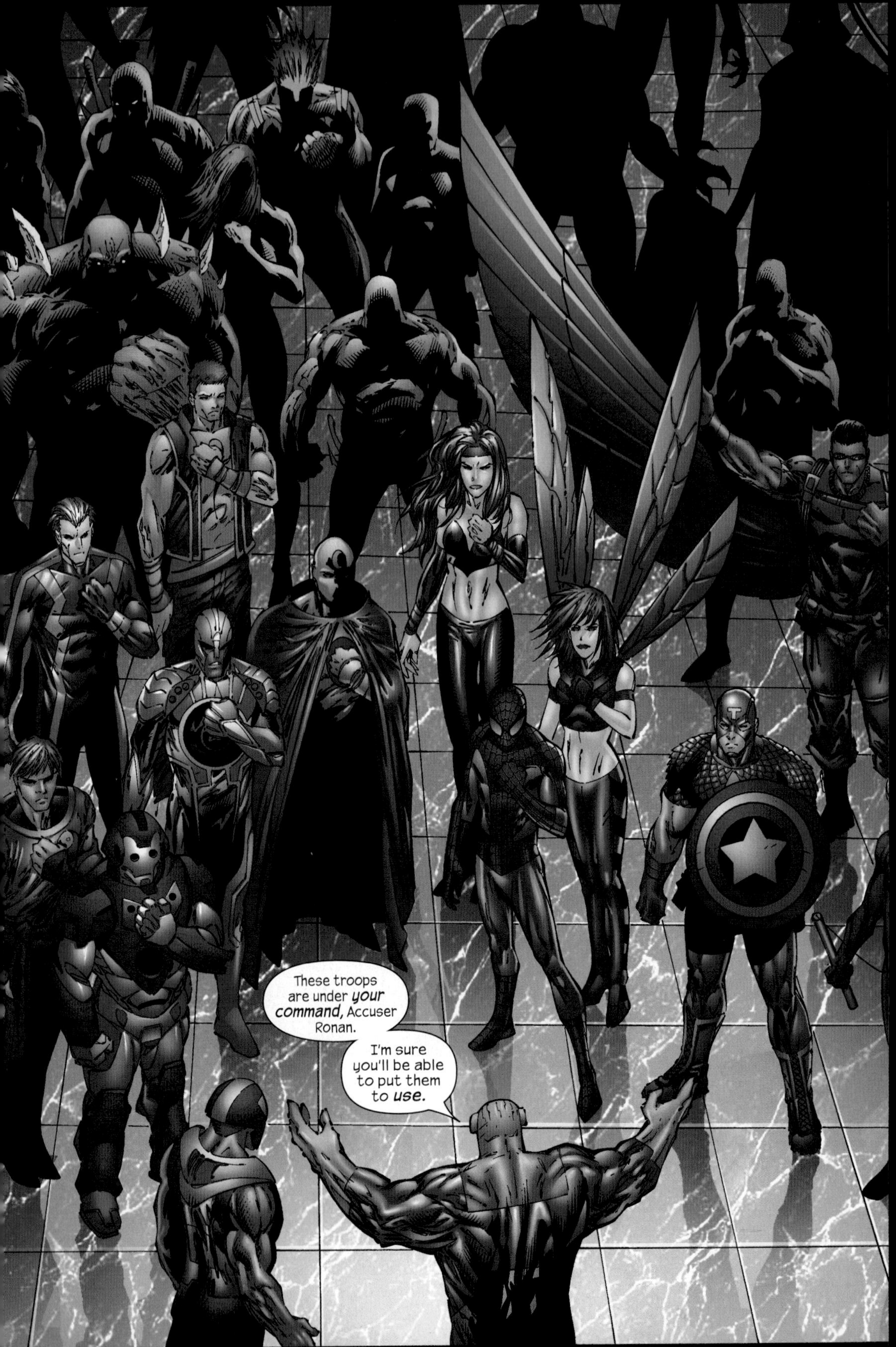
These troops are under your command, Accuser Ronan.
I'm sure you'll be able to put them to use.

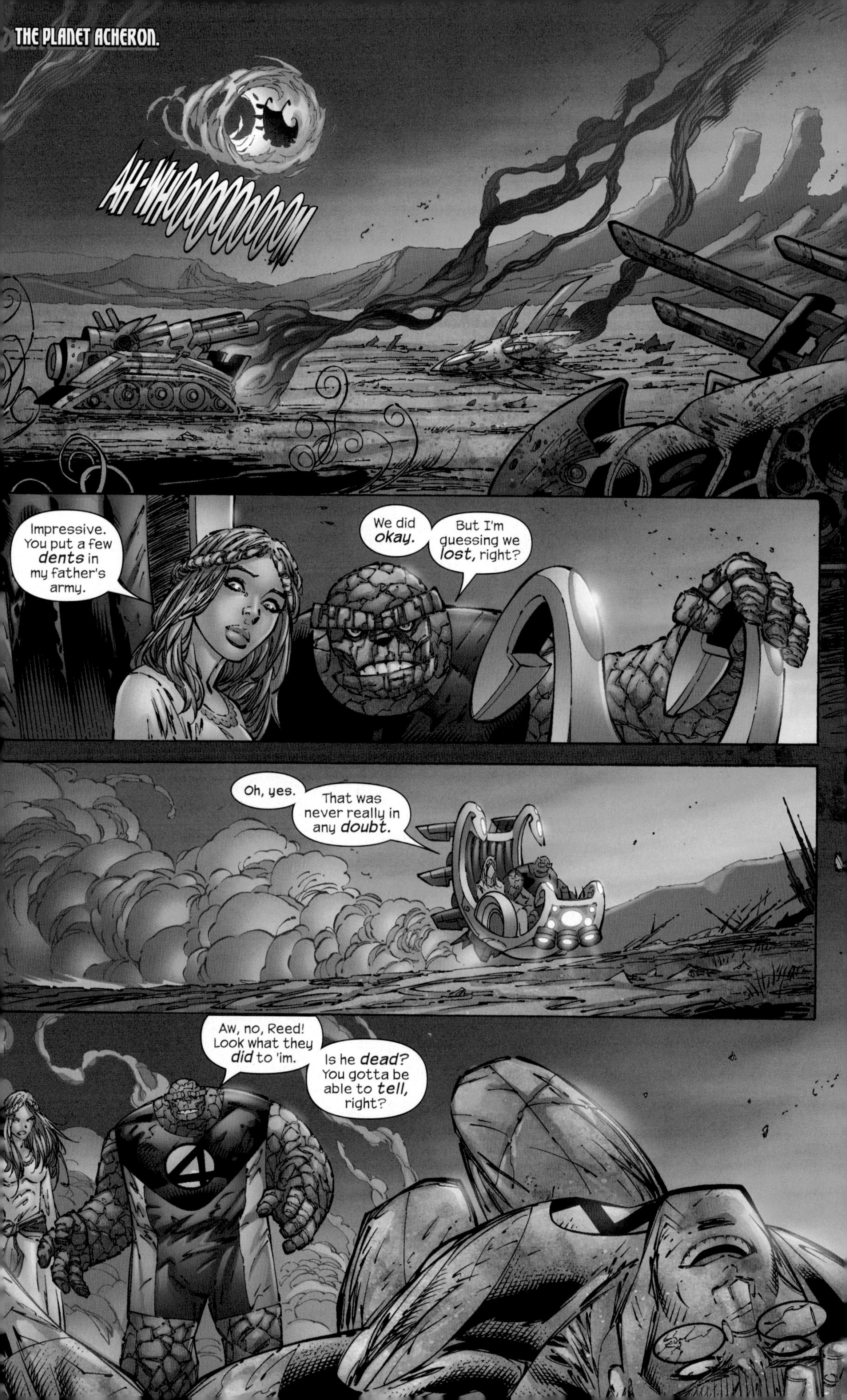
THE PLANET ACHERON.
AH-WHOOOOOOOOOM
Impressive. You put a few dents in my father's army.
We did okay.
But I'm guessing we lost, right?
Oh, yes.
That was never really in any doubt.
Aw, no, Reed! Look what they did to 'im.
Is he dead? You gotta be able to tell, right?

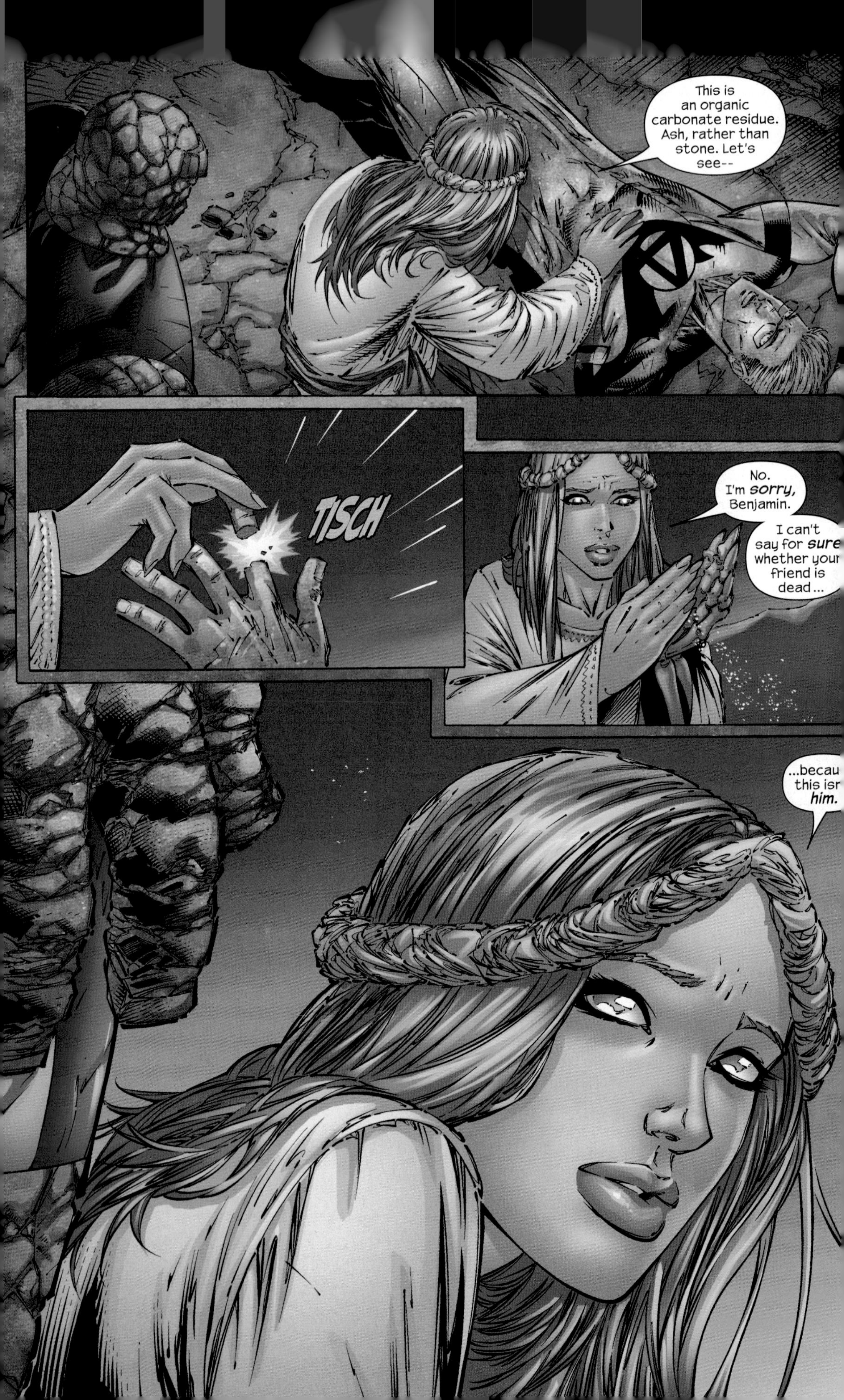
This is an organic carbonate residue. Ash, rather than stone. Let's see--
TISCH
No. I'm *sorry,* Benjamin.
I can't say for *sure* whether your friend is dead...
...becau this isn *him.*

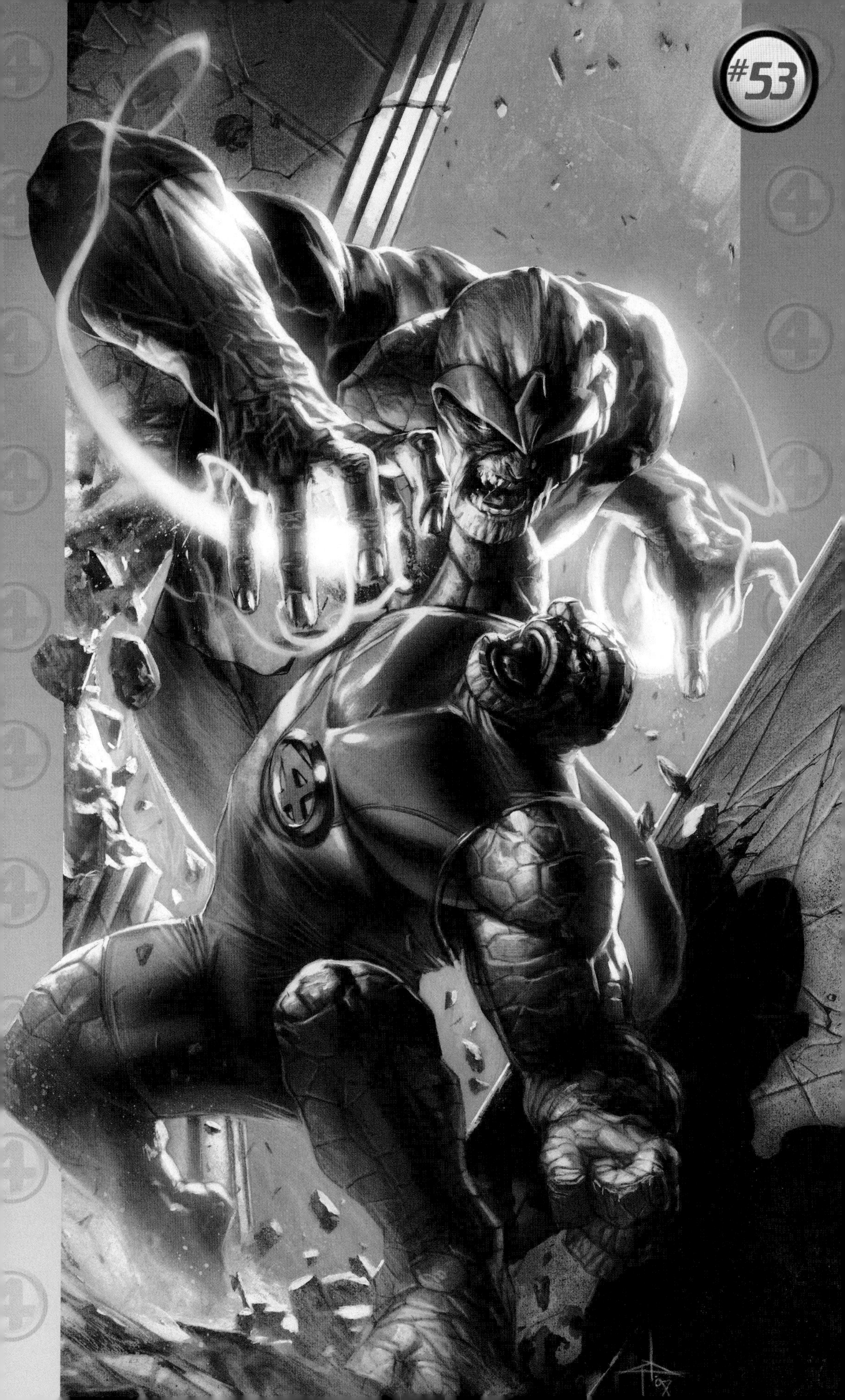
#53

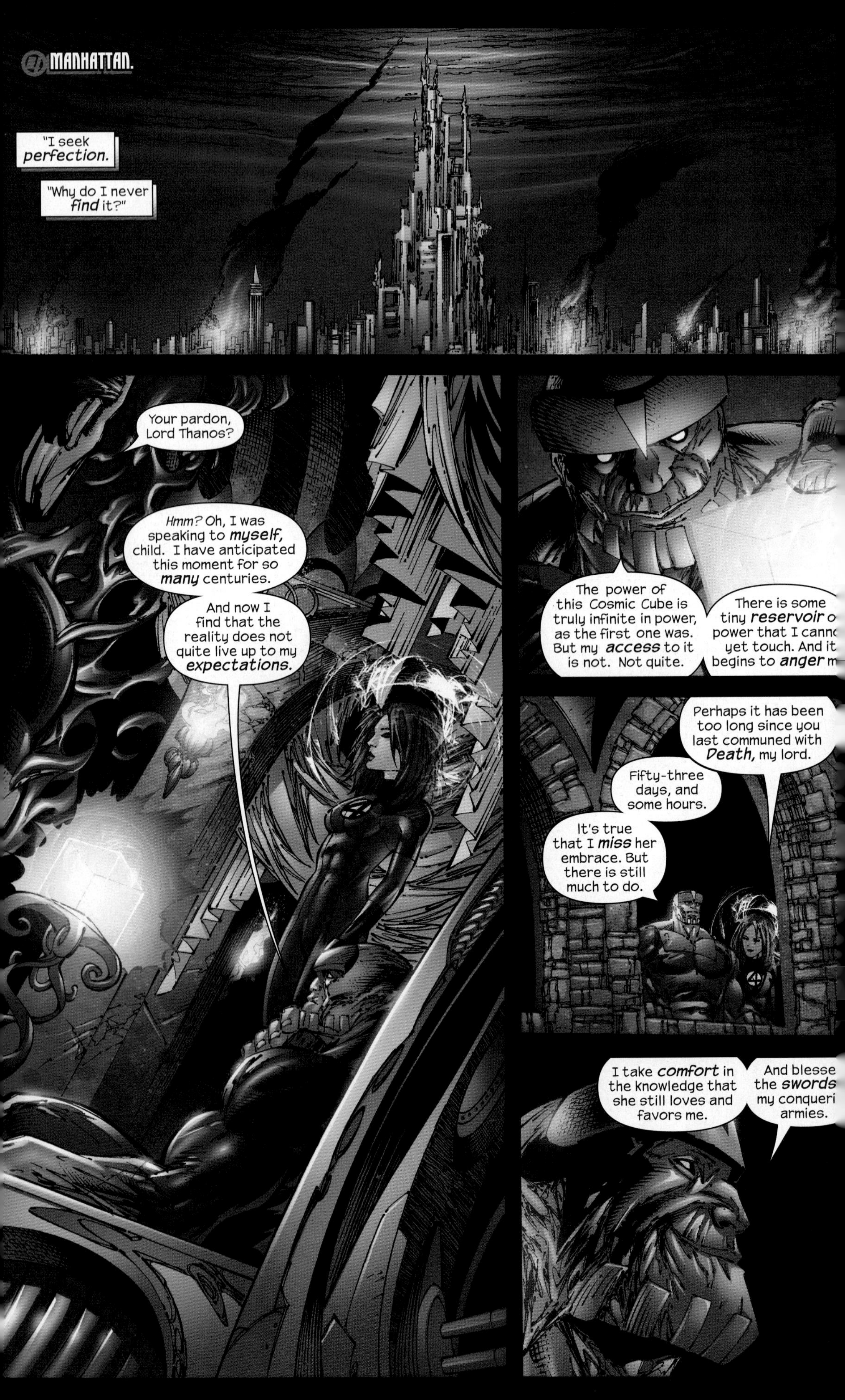
MANHATTAN.
"I seek perfection.
"Why do I never find it?"
Your pardon, Lord Thanos?
Hmm? Oh, I was speaking to myself, child. I have anticipated this moment for so many centuries.
And now I find that the reality does not quite live up to my expectations.
The power of this Cosmic Cube is truly infinite in power, as the first one was. But my access to it is not. Not quite.
There is some tiny reservoir o power that I cann yet touch. And it begins to anger m
Perhaps it has been too long since you last communed with Death, my lord.
Fifty-three days, and some hours.
It's true that I miss her embrace. But there is still much to do.
I take comfort in the knowledge that she still loves and favors me.
And blesse the swords my conqueri armies.

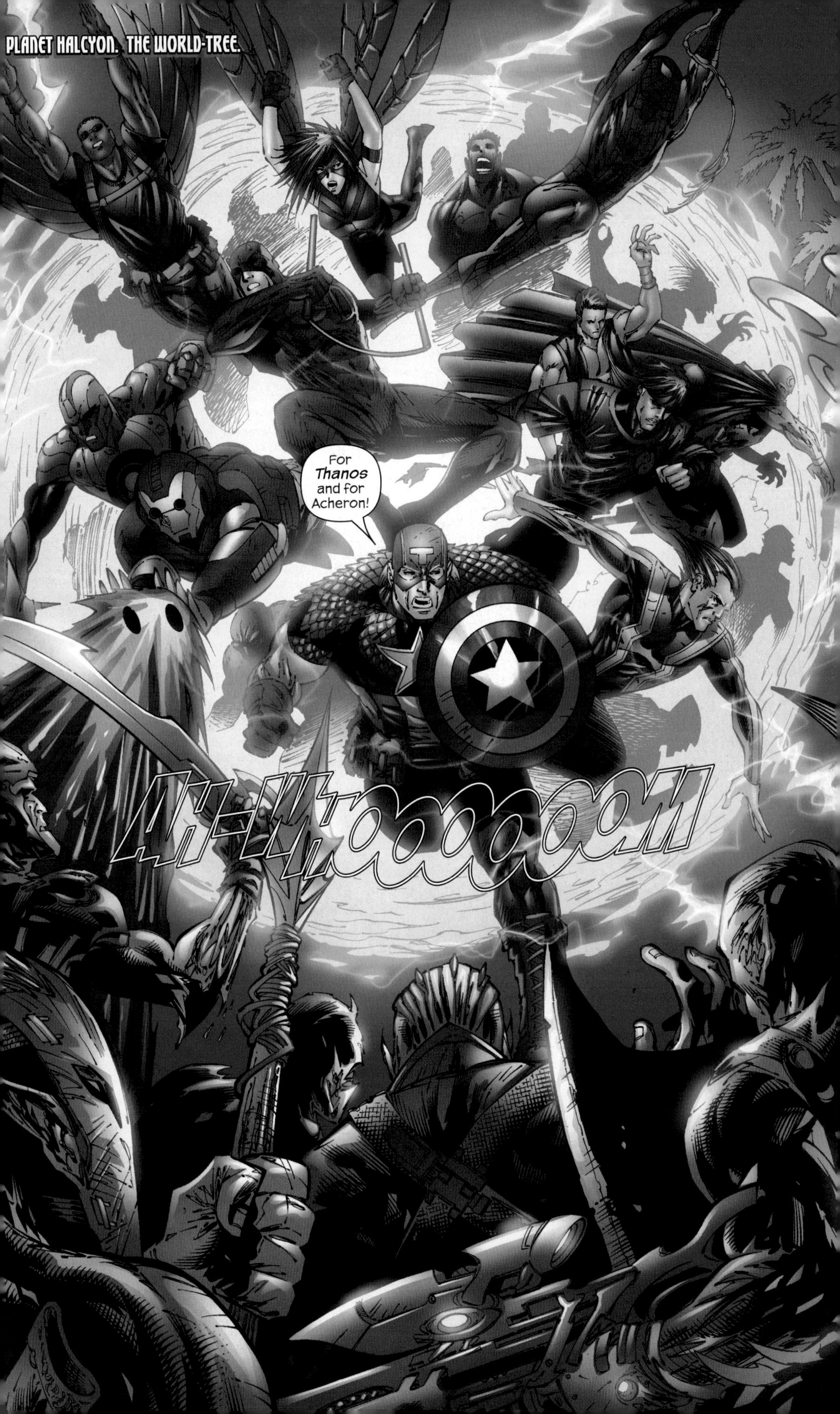
PLANET HALCYON. THE WORLD-TREE.
For *Thanos* and for Acheron!
AH-HOOOOOOM

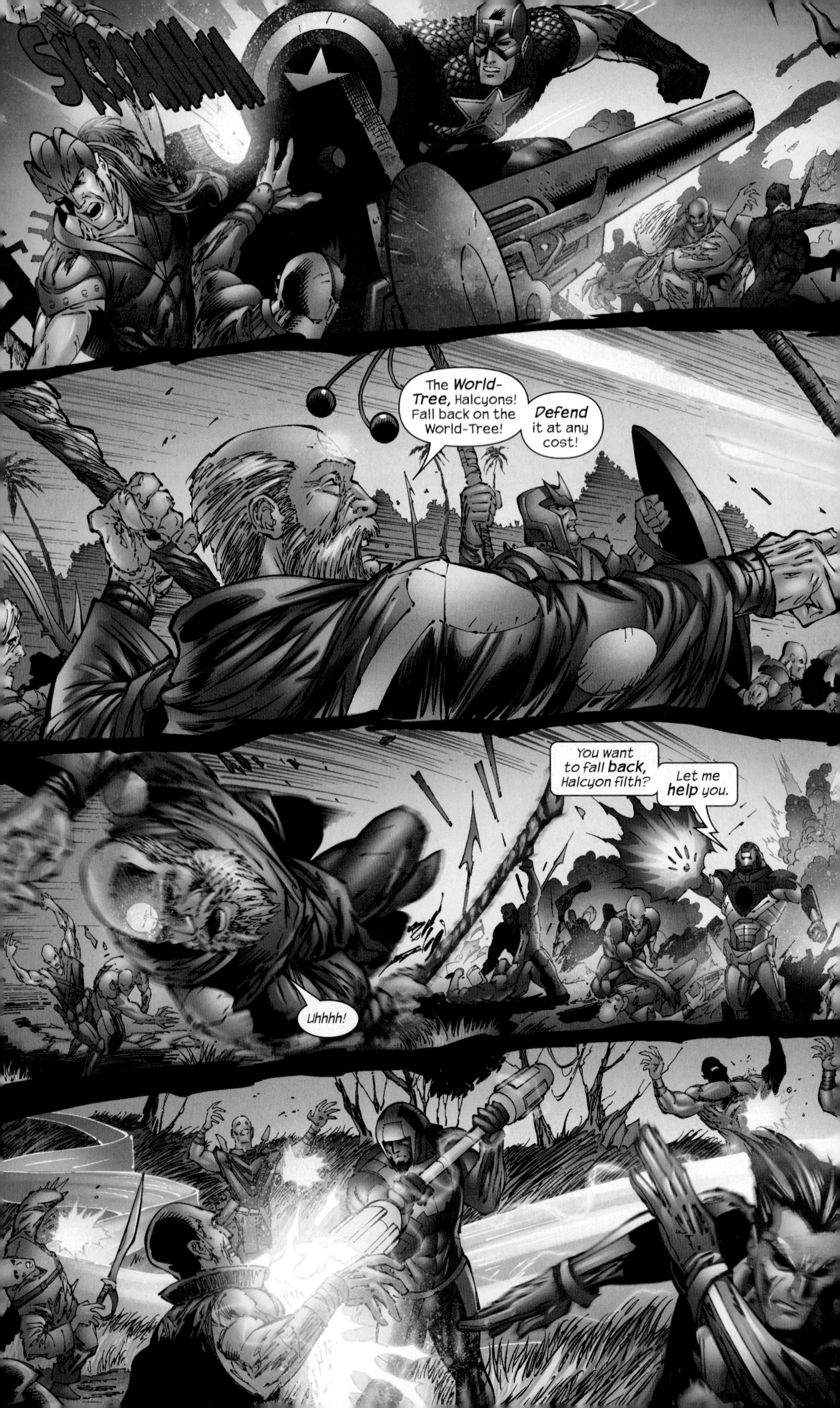
SKRAAMM
The World-Tree, Halcyons! Fall back on the World-Tree!
Defend it at any cost!
You want to fall back, Halcyon filth?
Let me help you.
Uhhhh!

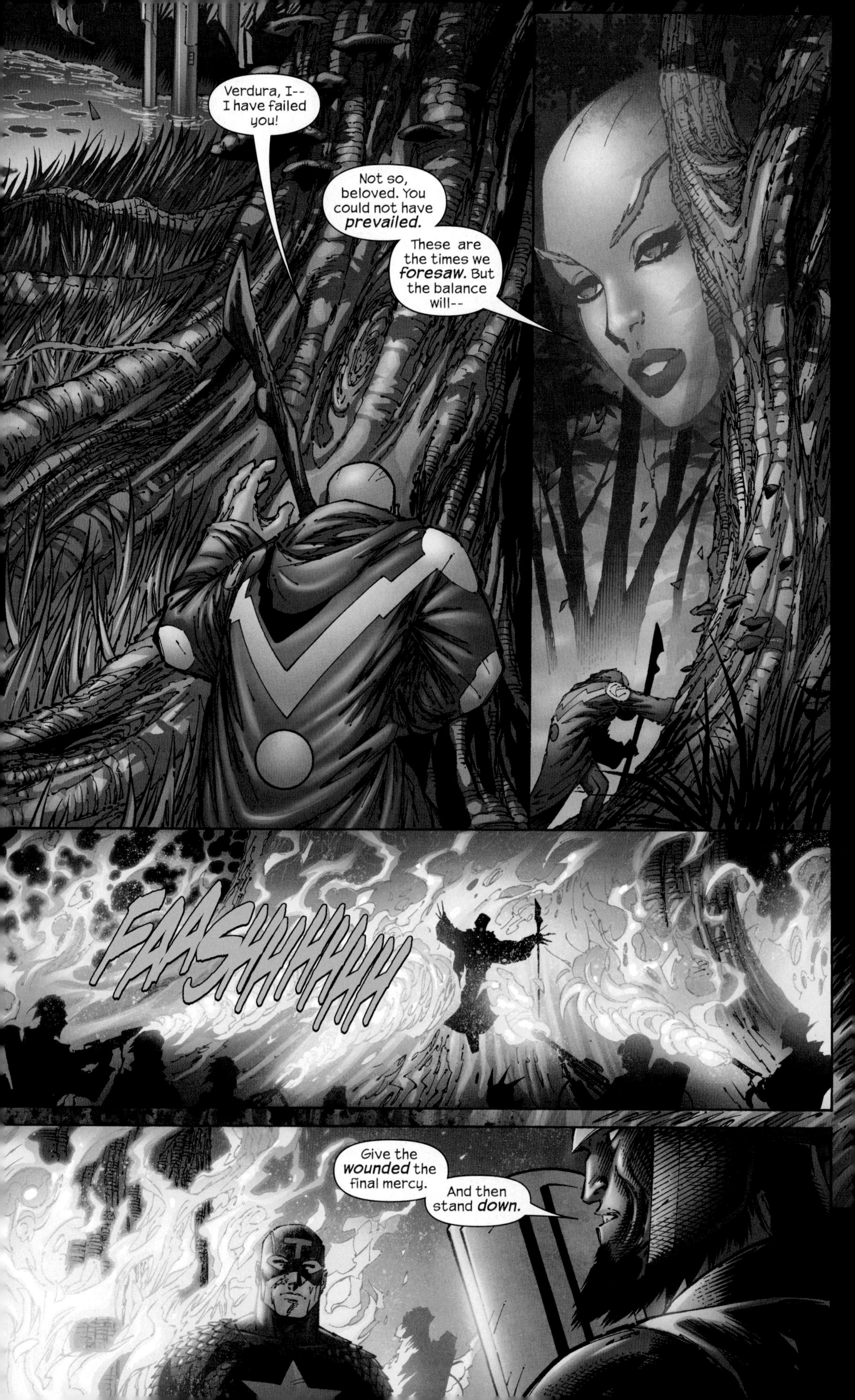
Verdura, I-- I have failed you!
Not so, beloved. You could not have *prevailed.*
These are the times we *foresaw.* But the balance will--
FAASHHHHHH
Give the *wounded* the final mercy.
And then stand *down.*

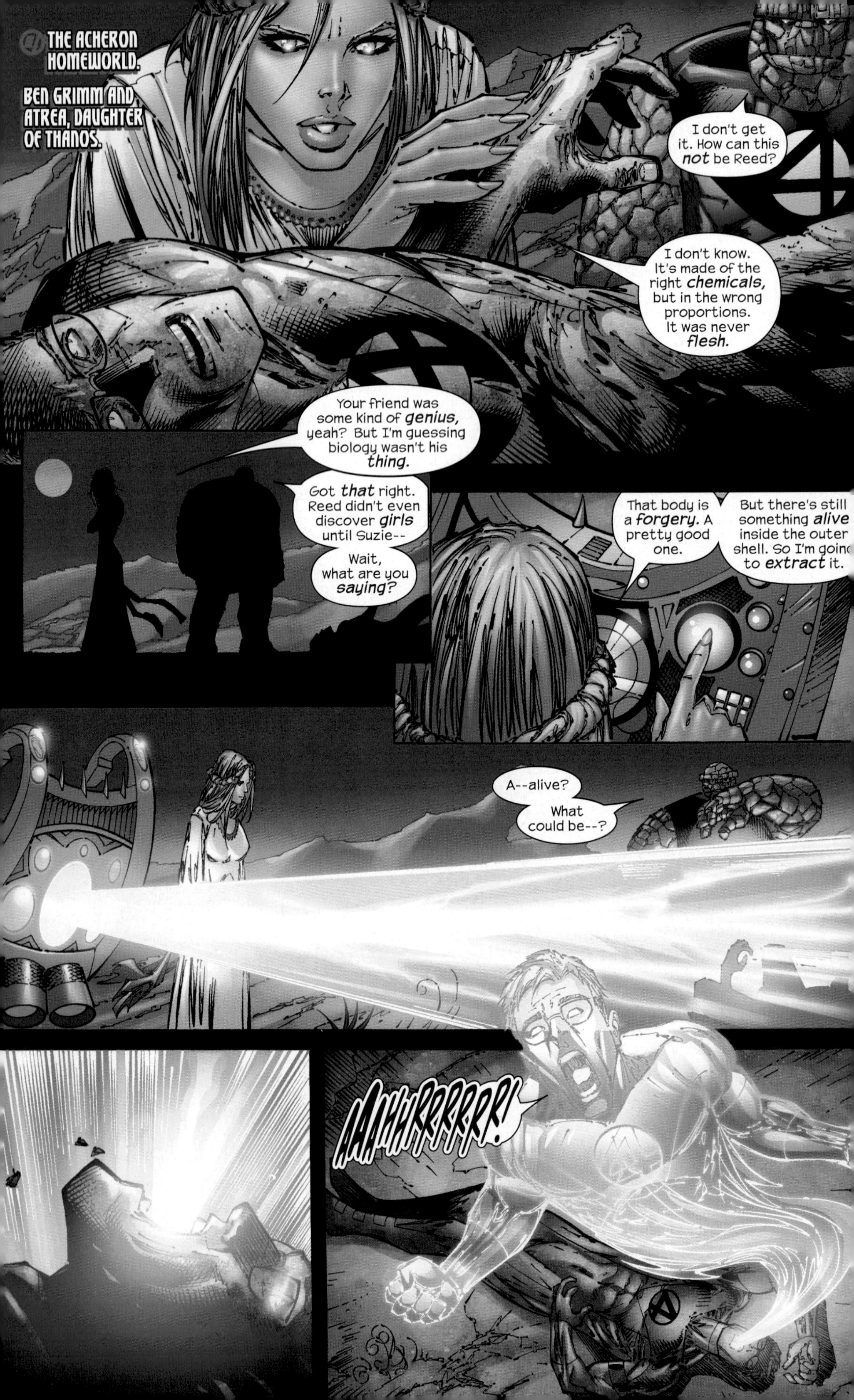
THE ACHERON HOMEWORLD.
BEN GRIMM AND ATREA, DAUGHTER OF THANOS.
I don't get it. How can this not be Reed?
I don't know. It's made of the right chemicals, but in the wrong proportions. It was never flesh.
Your friend was some kind of genius, yeah? But I'm guessing biology wasn't his thing.
Got that right. Reed didn't even discover girls until Suzie--
Wait, what are you saying?
That body is a forgery. A pretty good one.
But there's still something alive inside the outer shell. So I'm going to extract it.
A--alive?
What could be--?
AAAHHRRRRRR!

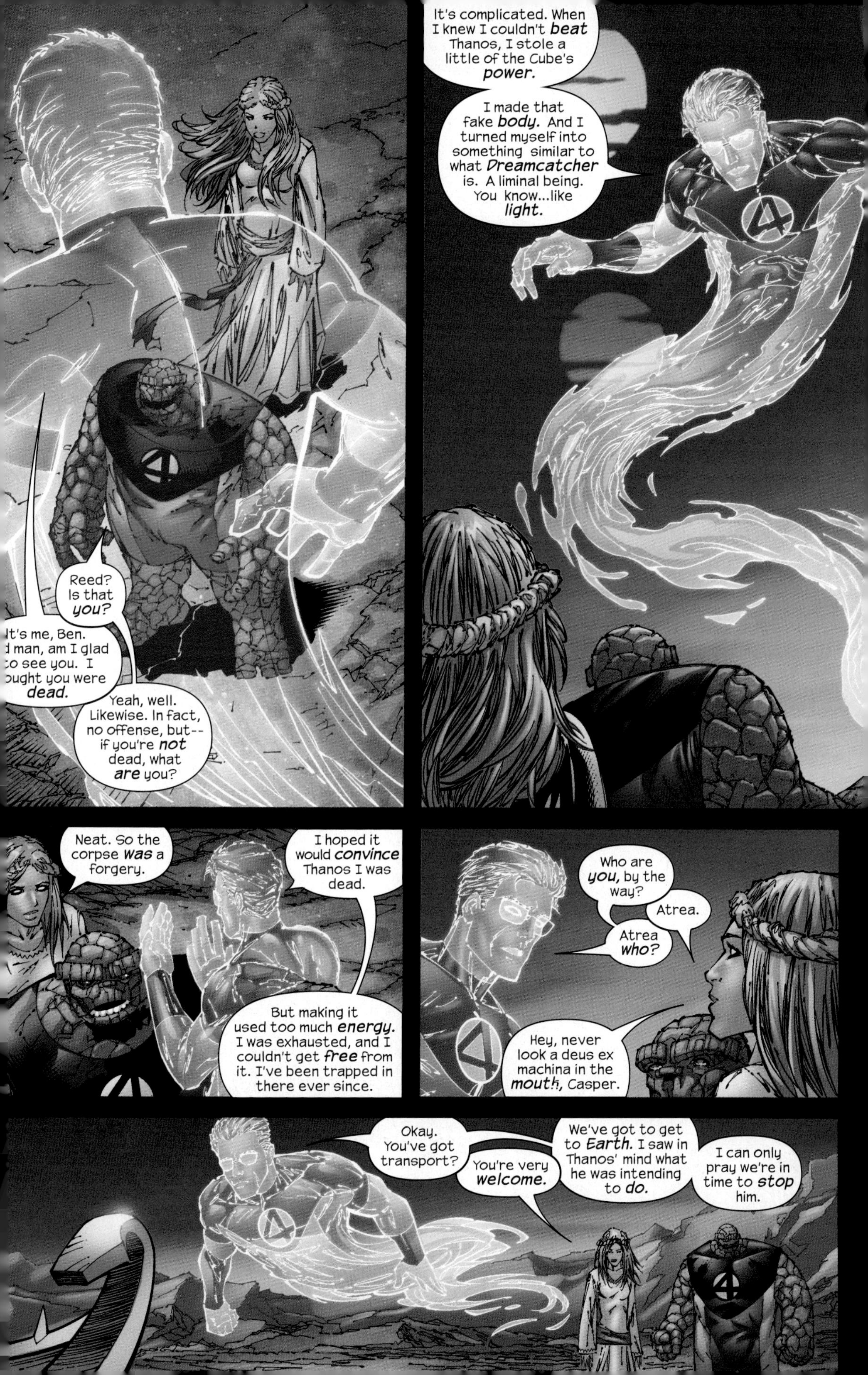
Reed? Is that you?
It's me, Ben. ...d man, am I glad to see you. I ...ought you were dead.
Yeah, well. Likewise. In fact, no offense, but-- if you're not dead, what are you?
It's complicated. When I knew I couldn't beat Thanos, I stole a little of the Cube's power.
I made that fake body. And I turned myself into something similar to what Dreamcatcher is. A liminal being. You know...like light.
Neat. So the corpse was a forgery.
I hoped it would convince Thanos I was dead.
But making it used too much energy. I was exhausted, and I couldn't get free from it. I've been trapped in there ever since.
Who are you, by the way?
Atrea.
Atrea who?
Hey, never look a deus ex machina in the mouth, Casper.
Okay. You've got transport?
You're very welcome.
We've got to get to Earth. I saw in Thanos' mind what he was intending to do.
I can only pray we're in time to stop him.

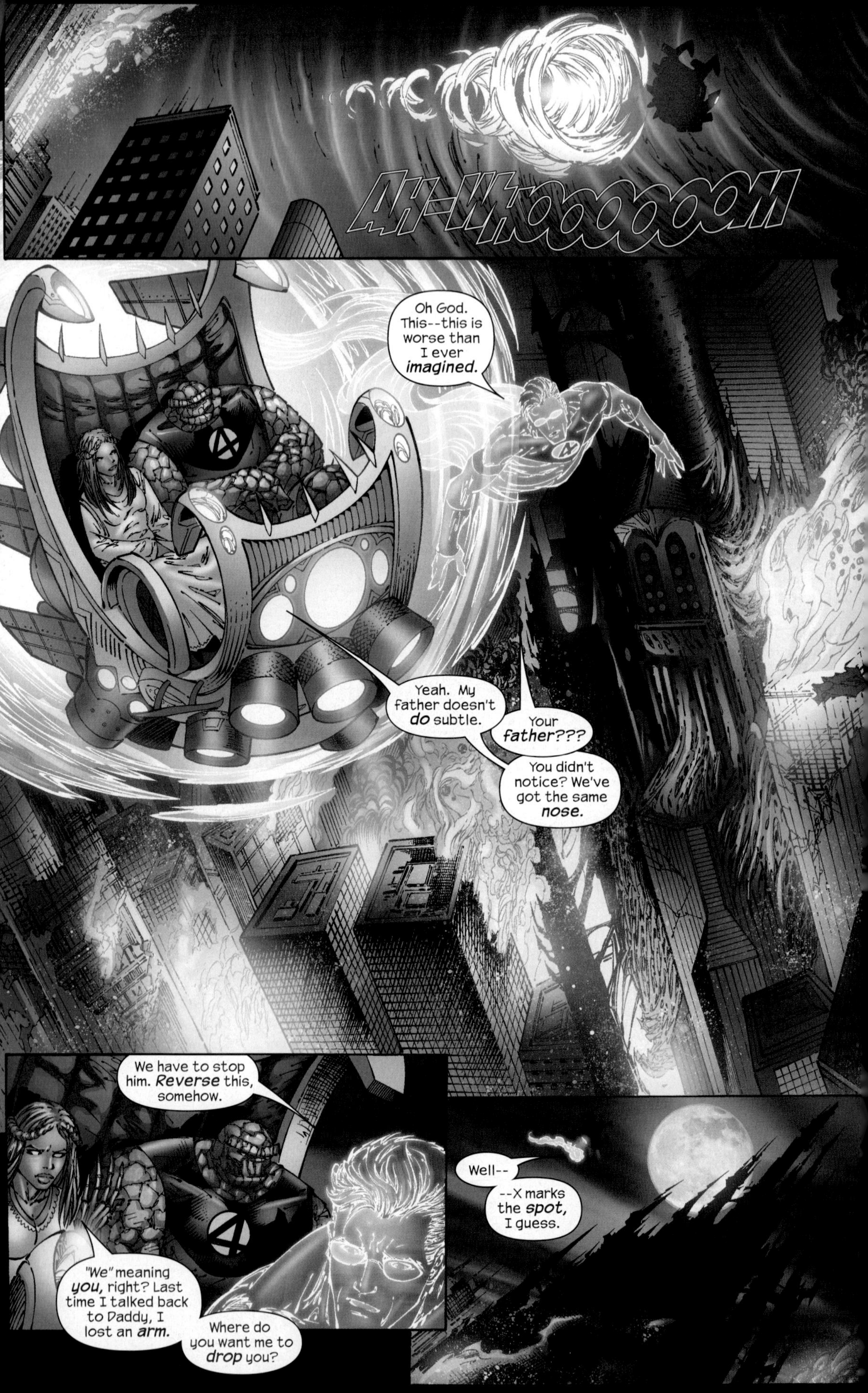
AH-WHOOOOOOM
Oh God. This--this is worse than I ever *imagined.*
Yeah. My father doesn't *do* subtle.
Your *father???*
You didn't notice? We've got the same *nose.*
We have to stop him. *Reverse* this, somehow.
"We" meaning *you,* right? Last time I talked back to Daddy, I lost an *arm.*
Where do you want me to *drop* you?
Well--
--X marks the *spot,* I guess.

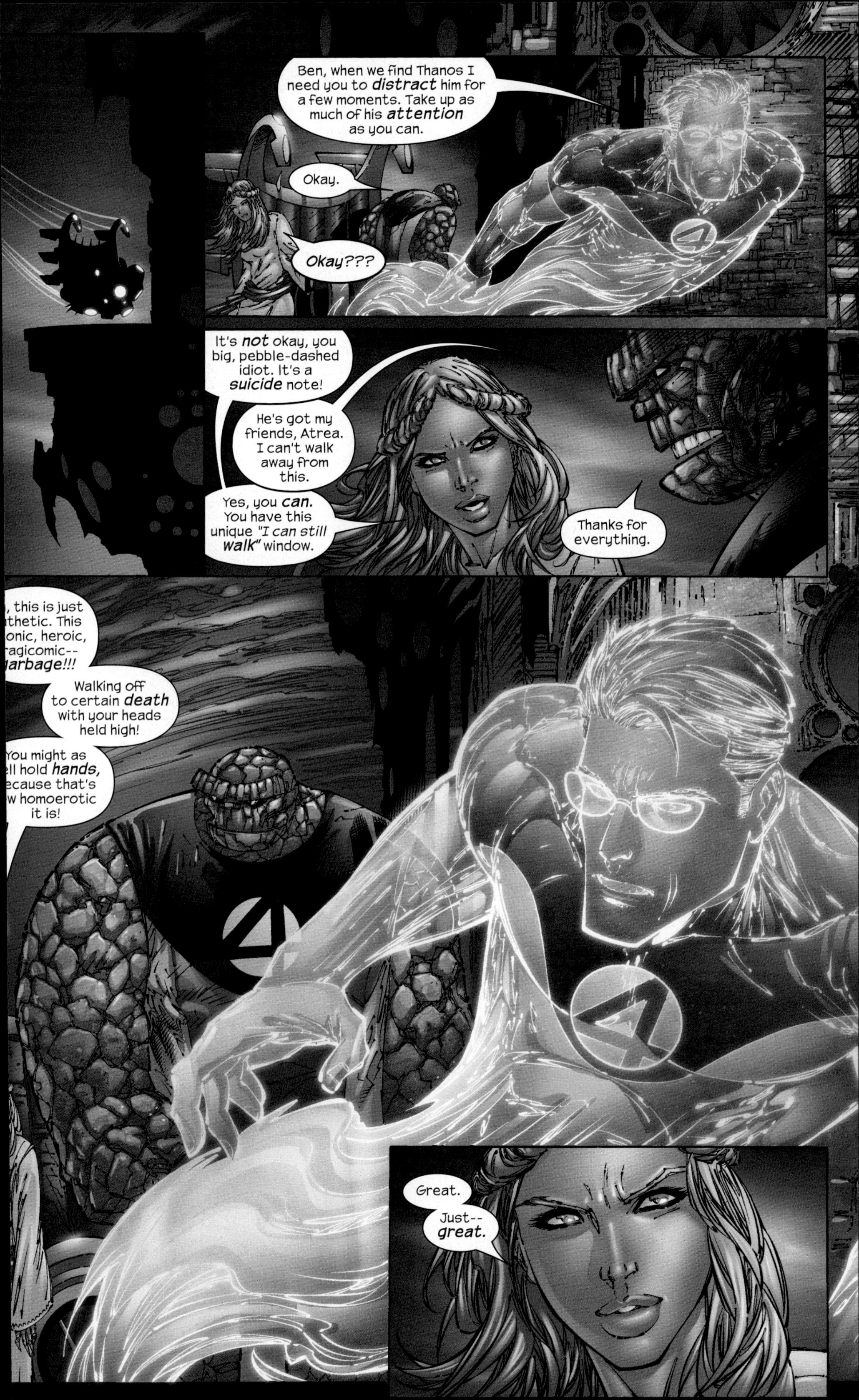

Ben, when we find Thanos I need you to *distract* him for a few moments. Take up as much of his *attention* as you can.
Okay.
Okay???
It's *not* okay, you big, pebble-dashed idiot. It's a *suicide* note!
He's got my friends, Atrea. I can't walk away from this.
Yes, you *can.* You have this unique *"I can still walk"* window.
Thanks for everything.
, this is just thetic. This onic, heroic, agicomic-- arbage!!!
Walking off to certain *death* with your heads held high!
You might as ll hold *hands,* ecause that's w homoerotic it is!
Great.
Just-- *great.*

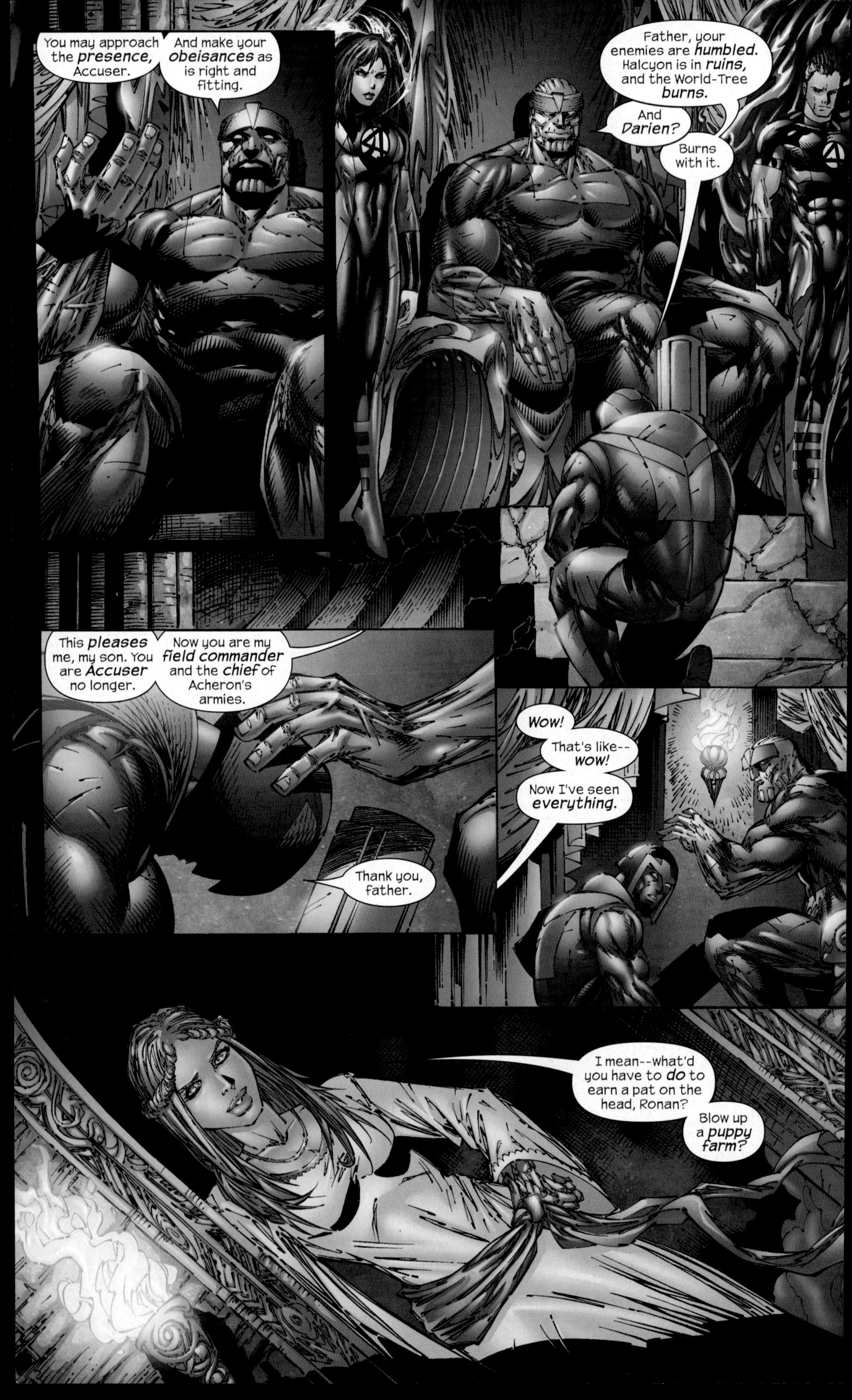
You may approach the presence, Accuser.
And make your obeisances as is right and fitting.
Father, your enemies are humbled. Halcyon is in ruins, and the World-Tree burns.
And Darien?
Burns with it.
This pleases me, my son. You are Accuser no longer.
Now you are my field commander and the chief of Acheron's armies.
Thank you, father.
Wow!
That's like-- wow!
Now I've seen everything.
I mean--what'd you have to do to earn a pat on the head, Ronan?
Blow up a puppy farm?

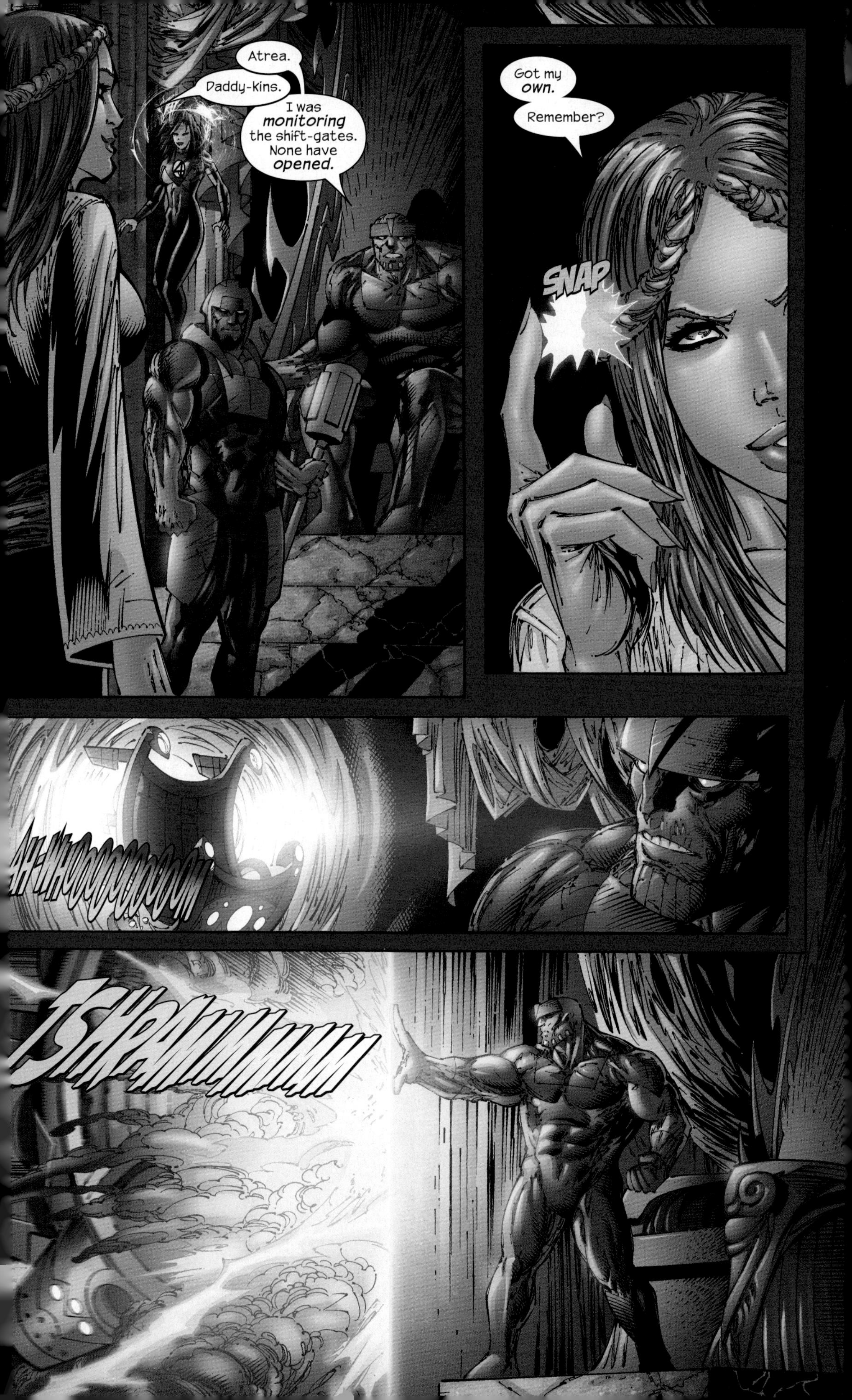
Atrea.
Daddy-kins.
I was *monitoring* the shift-gates. None have *opened.*
Got my *own.*
Remember?
SNAP
TSHPAHHHHHHHHHHH

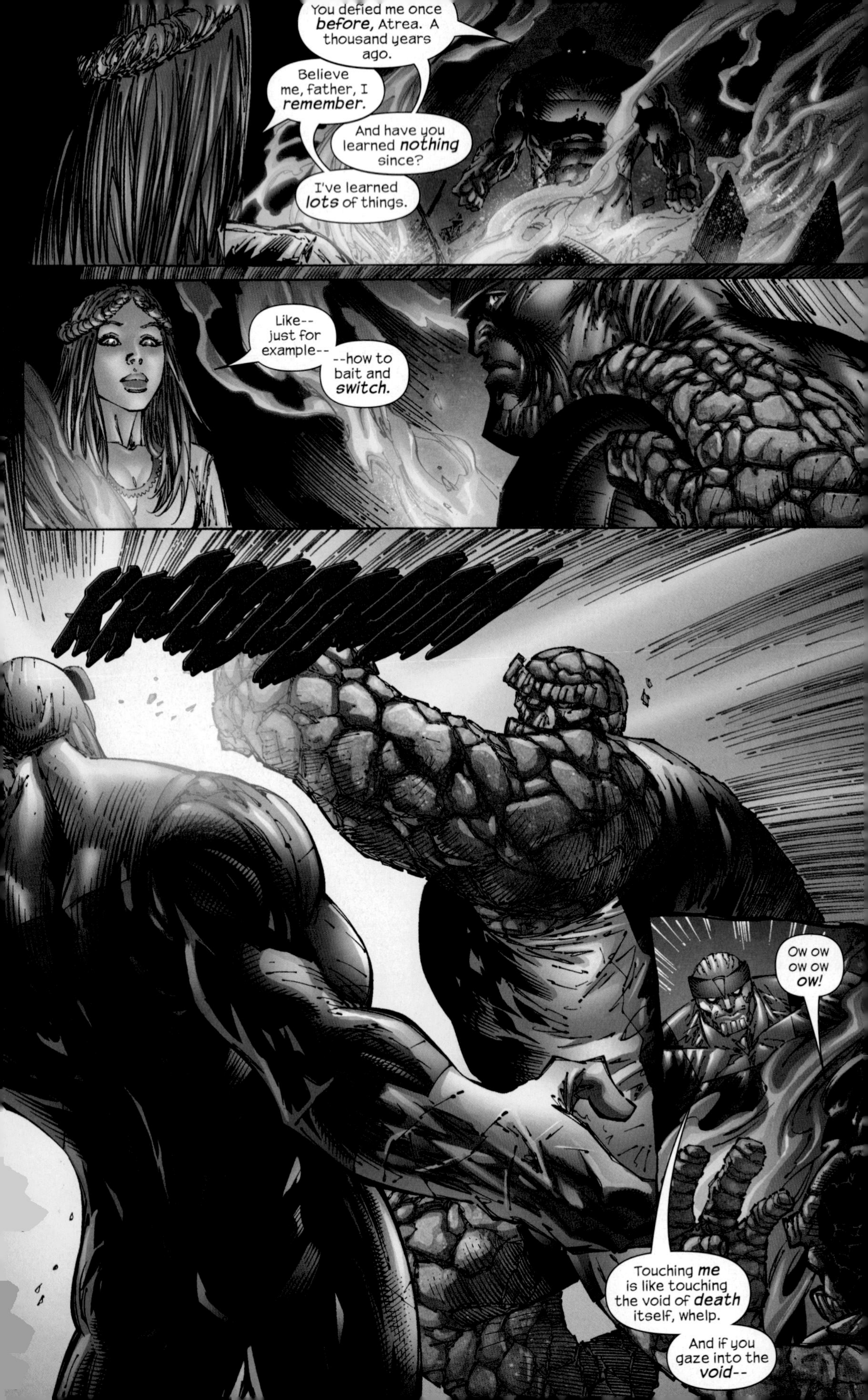
You defied me once before, Atrea. A thousand years ago.
Believe me, father, I remember.
And have you learned nothing since?
I've learned lots of things.
Like-- just for example--
--how to bait and switch.
Ow ow ow ow OW!
Touching me is like touching the void of death itself, whelp.
And if you gaze into the void--

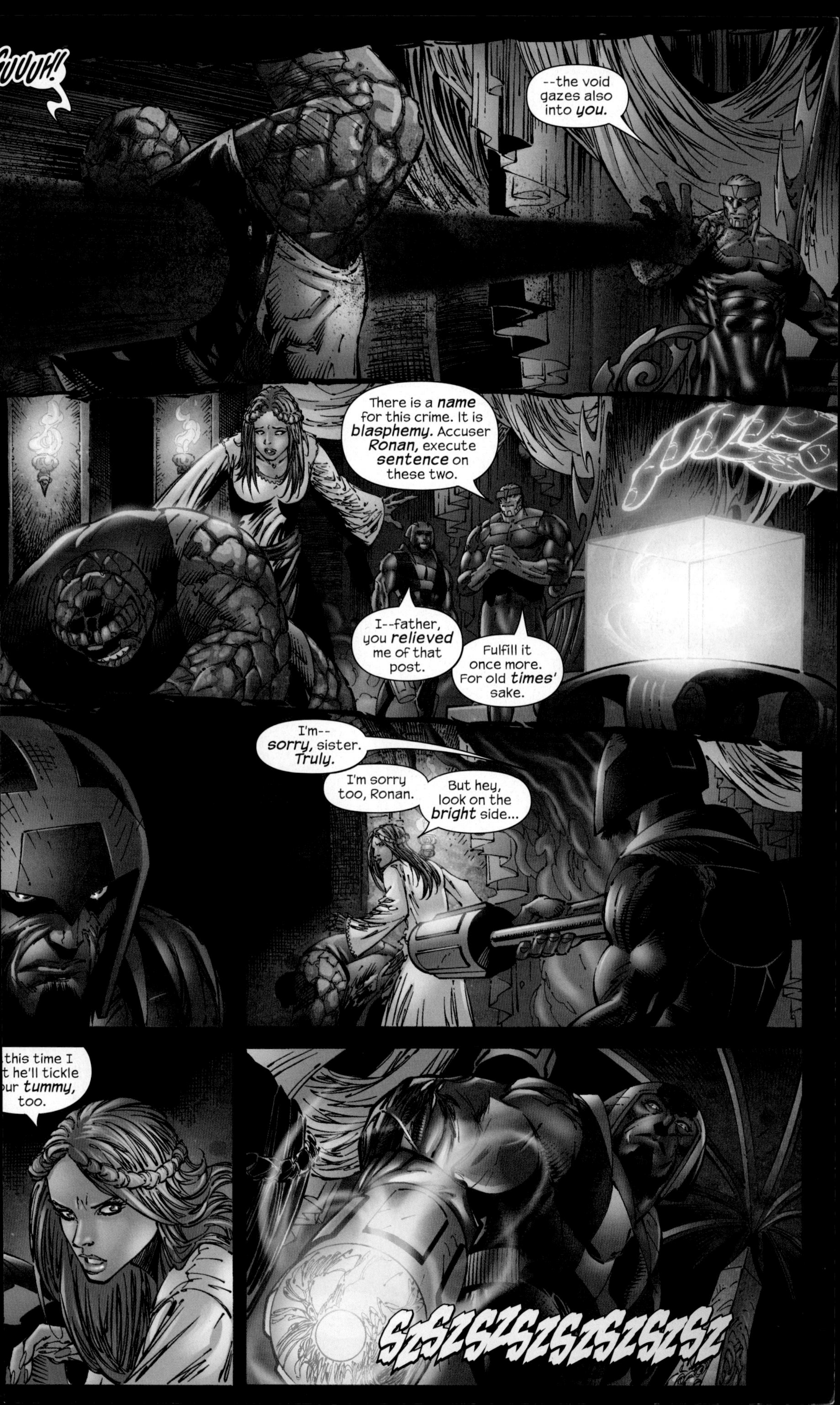

VUUUH!
--the void gazes also into *you.*
There is a *name* for this crime. It is *blasphemy.* Accuser *Ronan,* execute *sentence* on these two.
I--father, you *relieved* me of that post.
Fulfill it once more. For old *times'* sake.
I'm-- *sorry,* sister. *Truly.*
I'm sorry too, Ronan.
But hey, look on the *bright* side...
this time I t he'll tickle ur *tummy,* too.
SZSZSZSZSZSZSZSZSZSZ

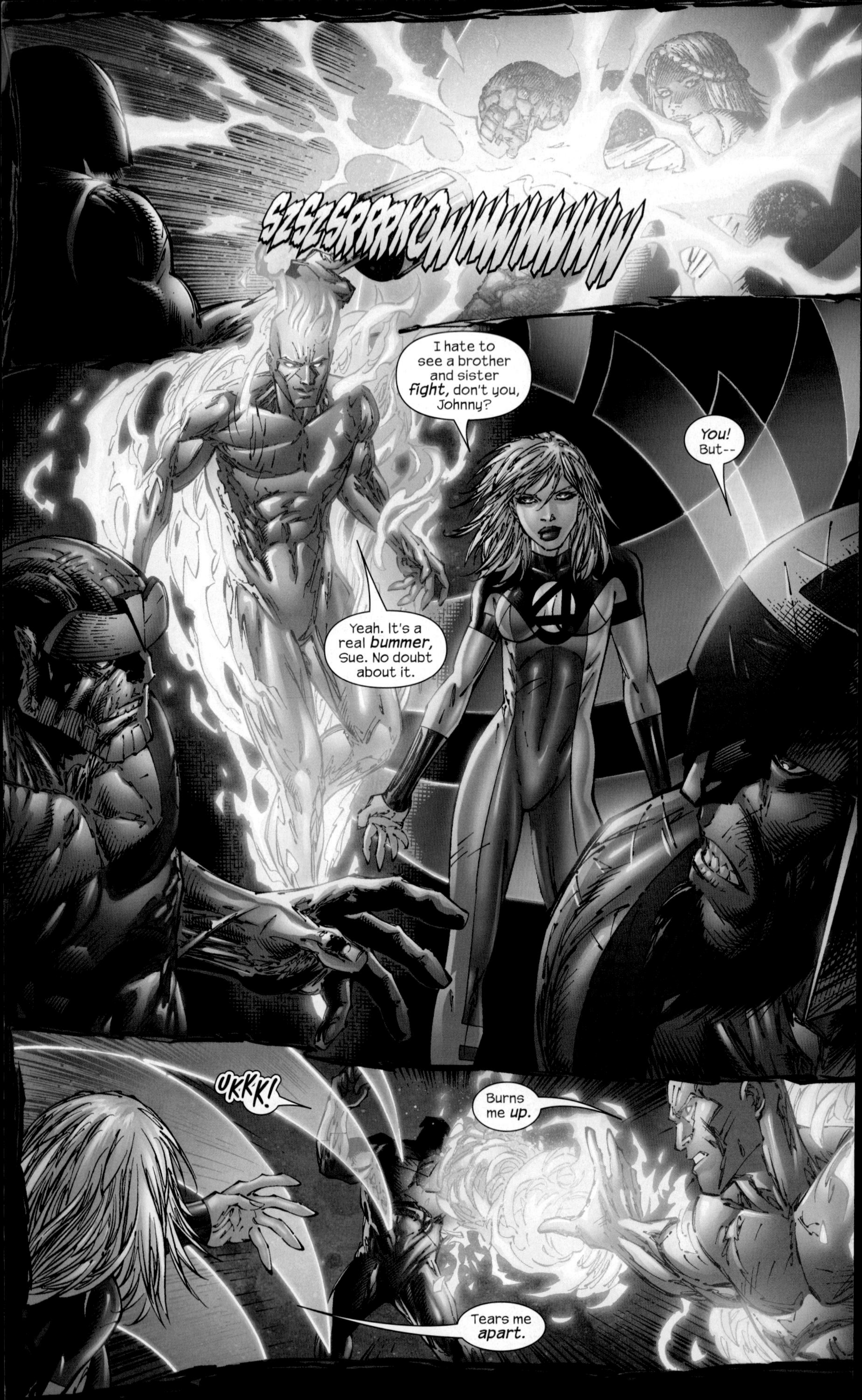
SZSZSRRRKOWWWWWWWW
I hate to see a brother and sister *fight,* don't you, Johnny?
You! But--
Yeah. It's a real ***bummer,*** Sue. No doubt about it.
UKKK!
Burns me *up.*
Tears me ***apart.***

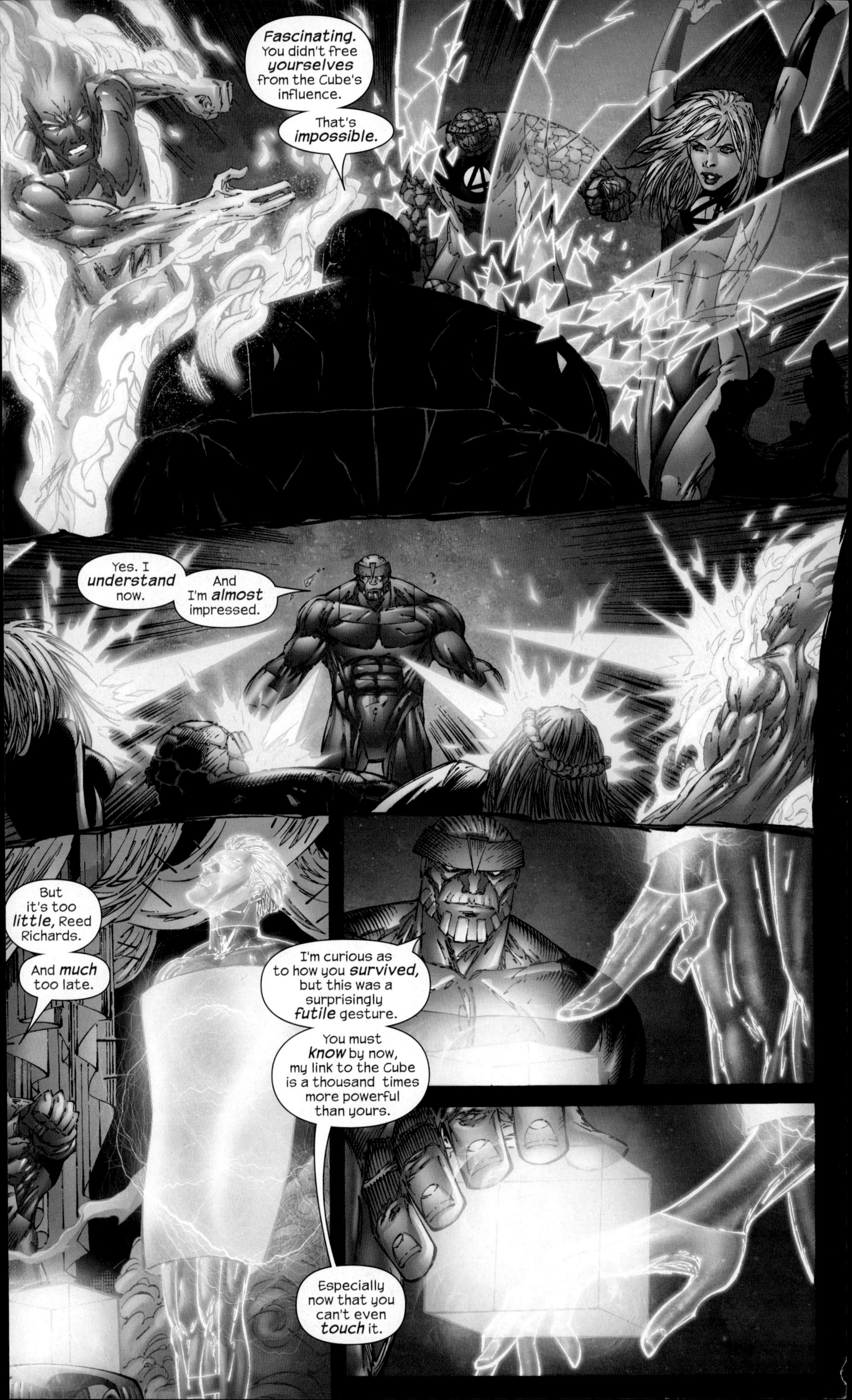
Fascinating. You didn't free yourselves from the Cube's influence.
That's impossible.
Yes. I understand now.
And I'm almost impressed.
But it's too little, Reed Richards.
And much too late.
I'm curious as to how you survived, but this was a surprisingly futile gesture.
You must know by now, my link to the Cube is a thousand times more powerful than yours.
Especially now that you can't even touch it.

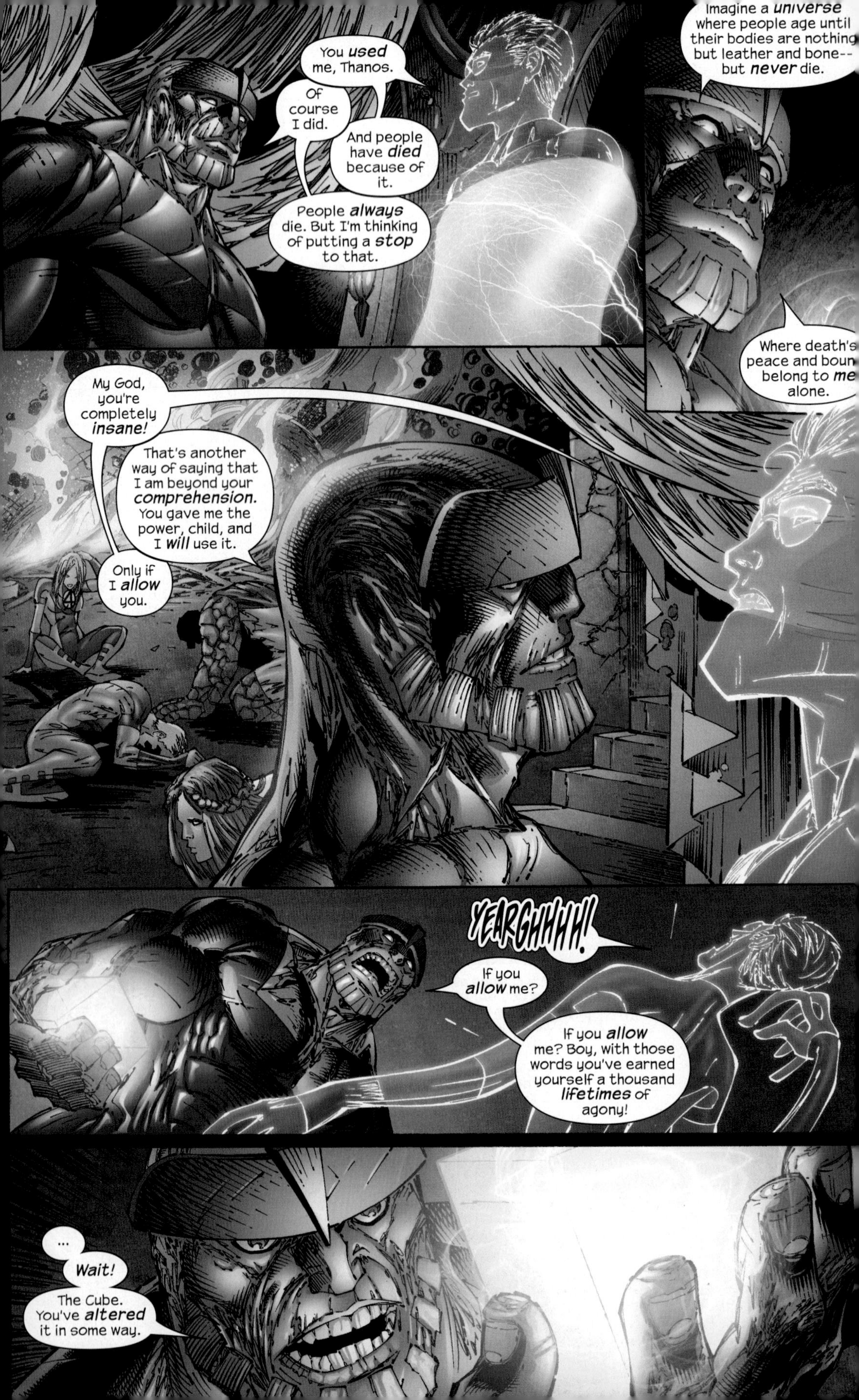
You used me, Thanos.
Of course I did.
And people have died because of it.
People always die. But I'm thinking of putting a stop to that.
Imagine a universe where people age until their bodies are nothing but leather and bone-- but never die.
Where death's peace and boun belong to me alone.
My God, you're completely insane!
That's another way of saying that I am beyond your comprehension. You gave me the power, child, and I will use it.
Only if I allow you.
YEARGHHHH!
If you allow me?
If you allow me? Boy, with those words you've earned yourself a thousand lifetimes of agony!
...
Wait!
The Cube. You've altered it in some way.

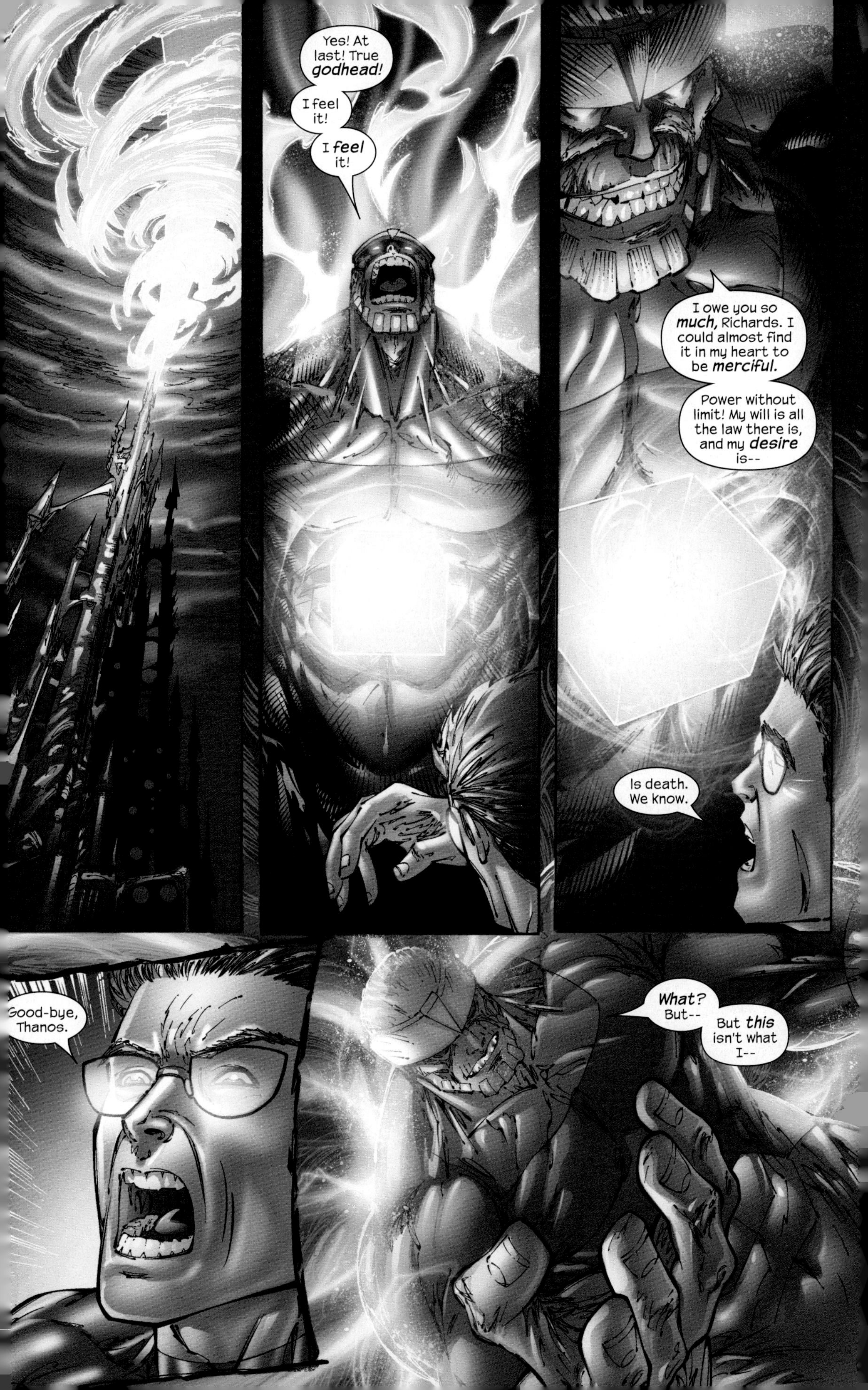
Yes! At last! True *godhead!*
I feel it!
I *feel* it!
I owe you so *much,* Richards. I could almost find it in my heart to be *merciful.*
Power without limit! My will is all the law there is, and my *desire* is--
Is death. We know.
Good-bye, Thanos.
What? But--
But *this* isn't what I--

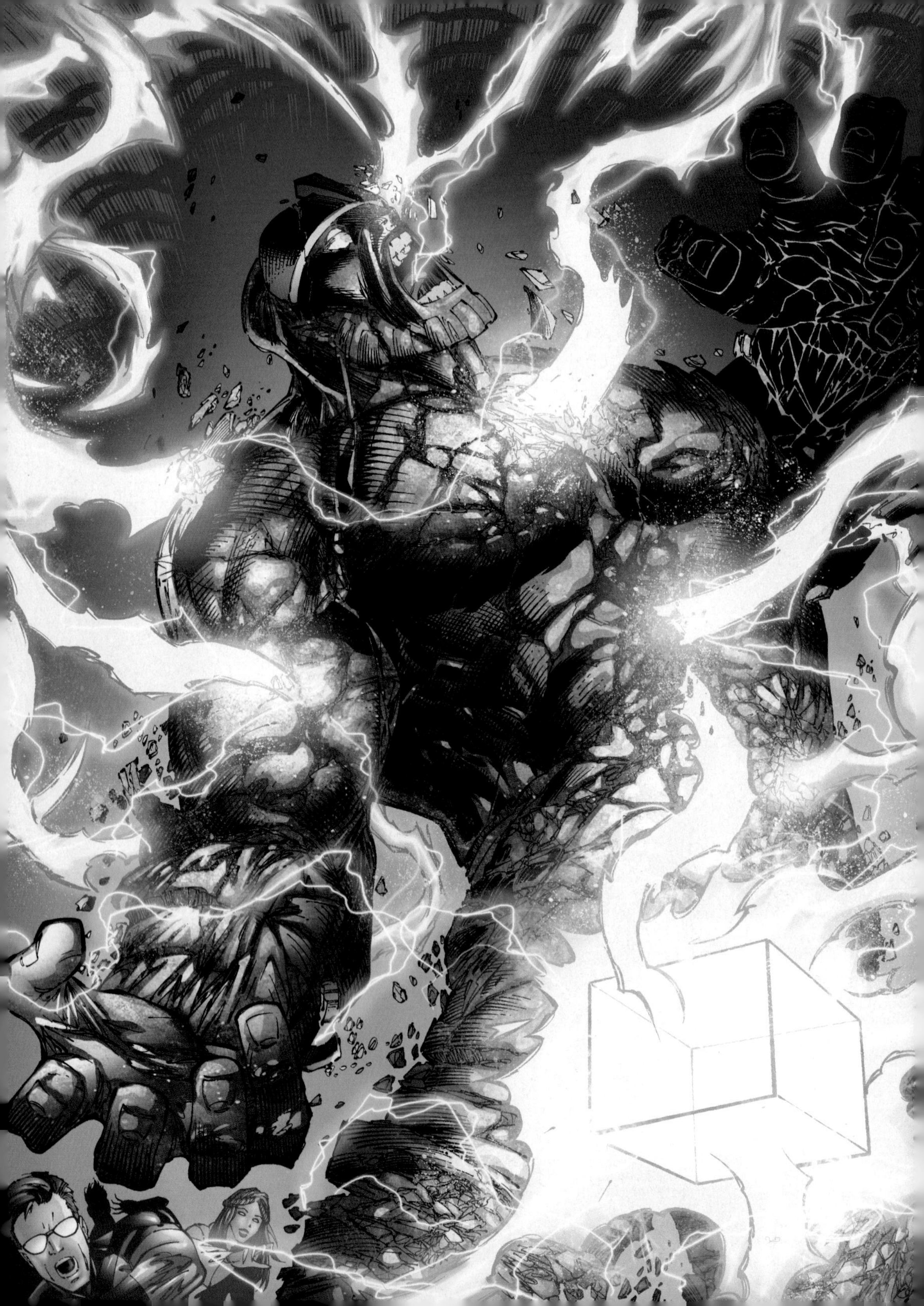

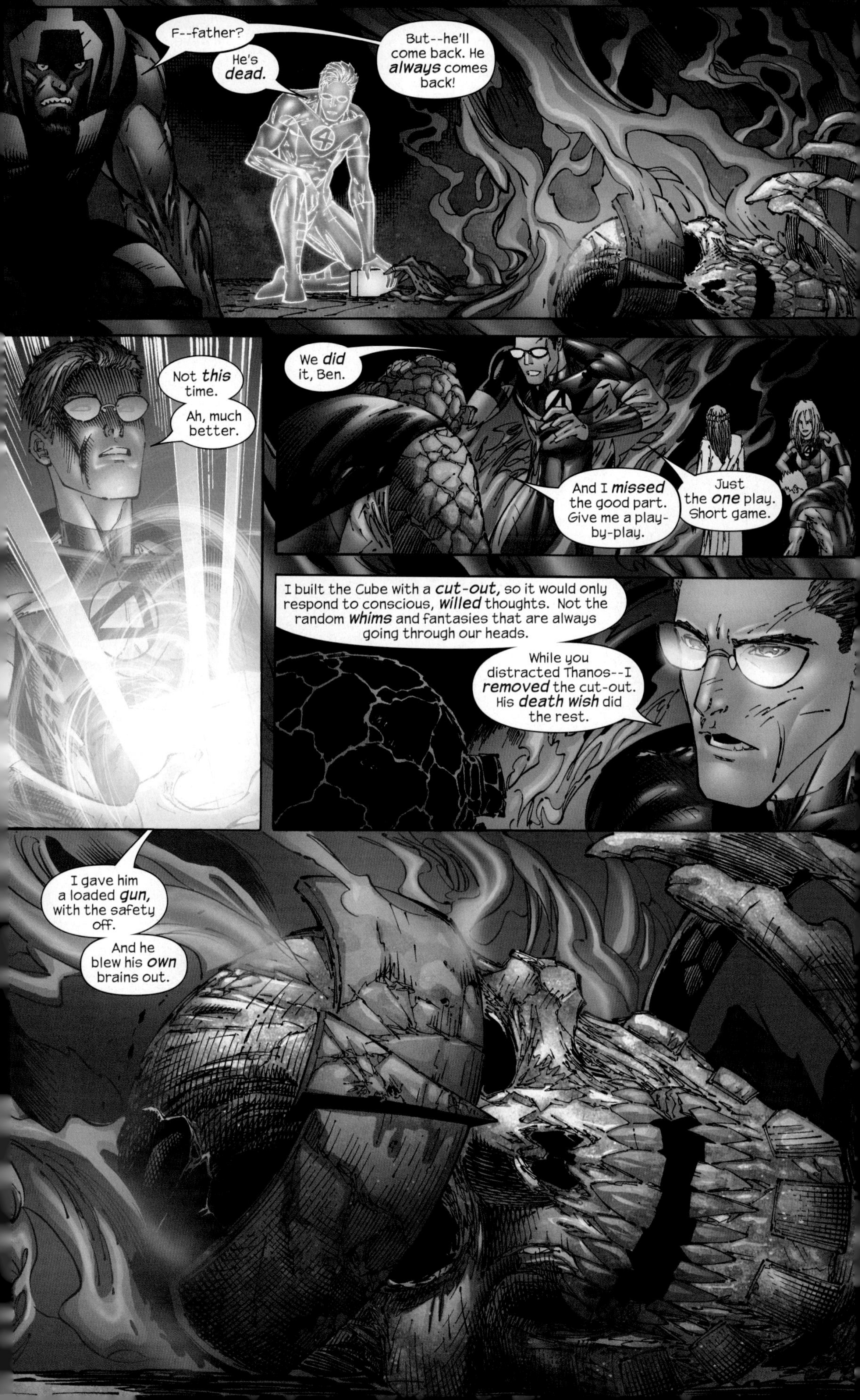
F--father?
He's *dead.*
But--he'll come back. He *always* comes back!
Not *this* time.
Ah, much better.
We *did* it, Ben.
And I *missed* the good part. Give me a play-by-play.
Just the *one* play. Short game.
I built the Cube with a *cut-out,* so it would only respond to conscious, *willed* thoughts. Not the random *whims* and fantasies that are always going through our heads.
While you distracted Thanos--I *removed* the cut-out. His *death wish* did the rest.
I gave him a loaded *gun,* with the safety off.
And he blew his *own* brains out.

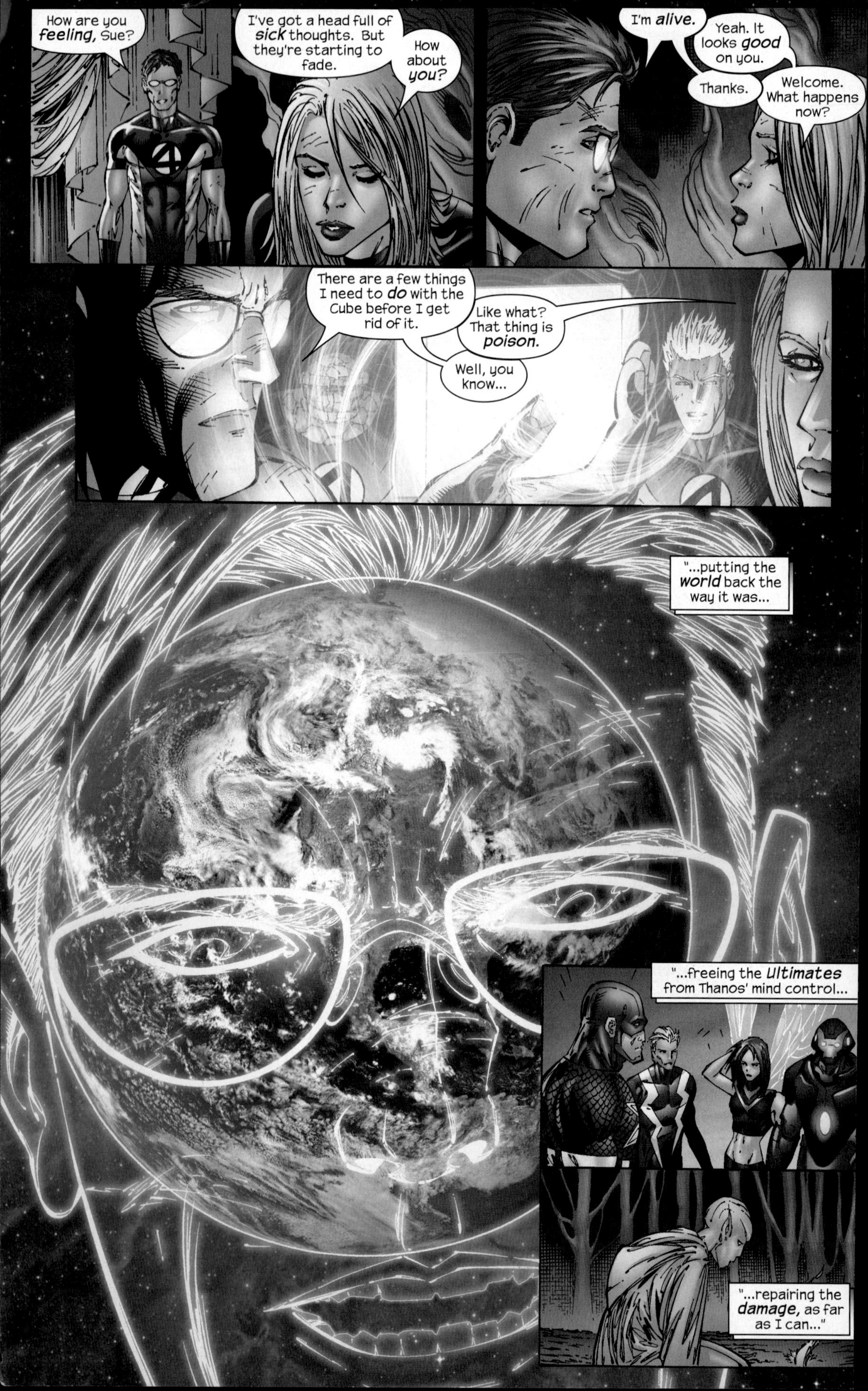
How are you *feeling,* Sue?
I've got a head full of *sick* thoughts. But they're starting to fade.
How about *you?*
I'm *alive.*
Yeah. It looks *good* on you.
Thanks.
Welcome. What happens now?
There are a few things I need to *do* with the Cube before I get rid of it.
Like what? That thing is *poison.*
Well, you know...
"...putting the *world* back the way it was...
"...freeing the *Ultimates* from Thanos' mind control...
"...repairing the *damage,* as far as I can..."

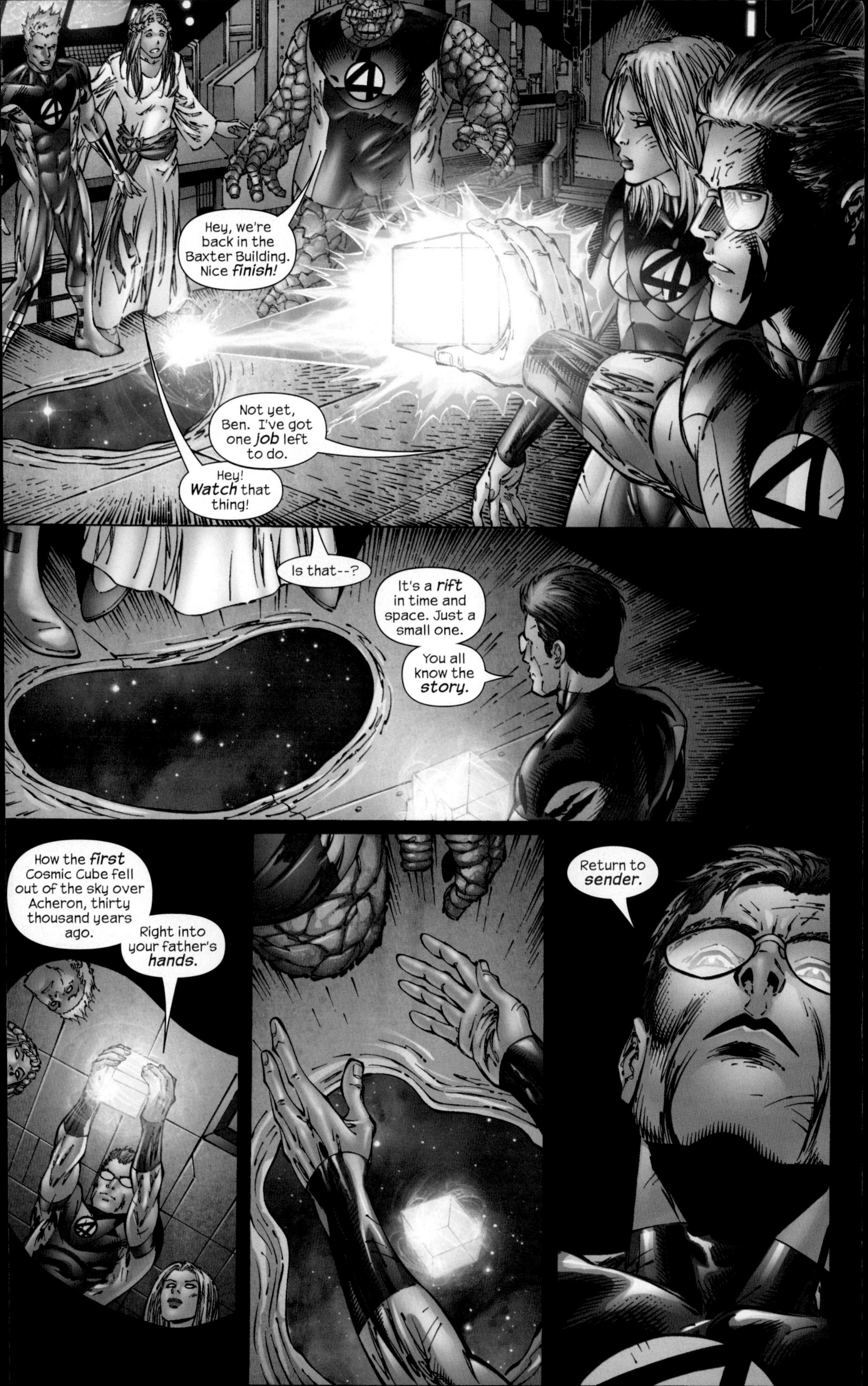
Hey, we're back in the Baxter Building. Nice finish!
Not yet, Ben. I've got one job left to do.
Hey! Watch that thing!
Is that--?
It's a rift in time and space. Just a small one.
You all know the story.
How the first Cosmic Cube fell out of the sky over Acheron, thirty thousand years ago.
Right into your father's hands.
Return to sender.

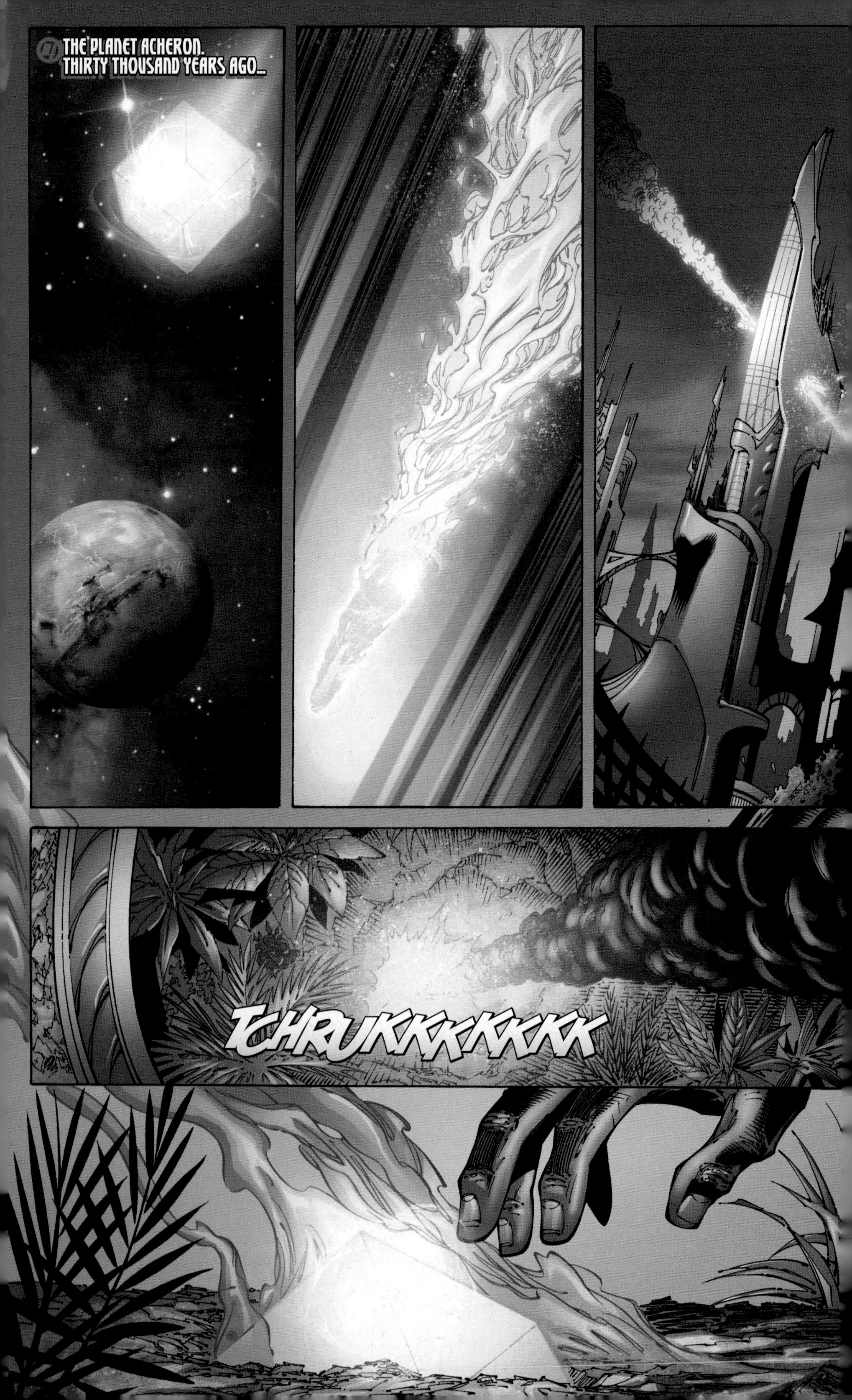
THE PLANET ACHERON.
THIRTY THOUSAND YEARS AGO...
TCHRUKKKKKKKK

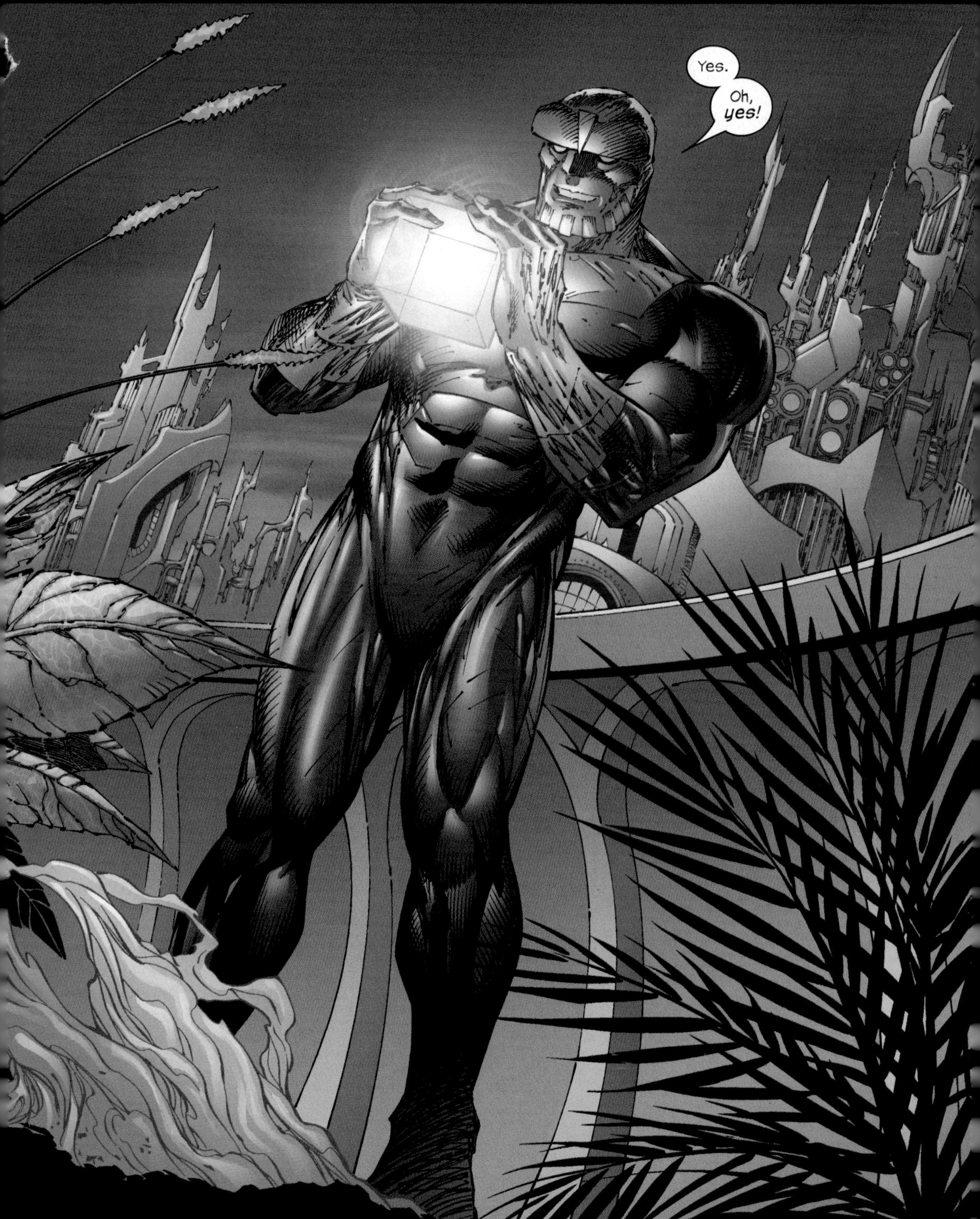
Yes.
Oh, yes!

CURRENT MEMBERS: Human Torch (Johnny Storm), Invisible Woman (Susan Storm), Mr. Fantastic (Reed Richards), Thing (Ben Grimm)
BASE OF OPERATIONS: Baxter Building, Manhattan

HISTORY: Over a decade ago, the U.S. government, under the auspices of the Director of Mainland Technology Development, began gathering international child prodigies at a Manhattan laboratory facility in the Baxter Building, giving them the best resources and teachers the project could afford. Headed by scientist William Storm and the U.S. military's General Ross, the project discovered the N-Zone, an otherdimensional space which paralleled our own. When 11-year-old Reed Richards independently accessed this zone and began sending small toys into it, the project recruited him to join their work. Over the following ten years, Reed Richards, Victor Van Damme, and other students and instructors worked on the project before the government ultimately constructed its N-Zone teleportational gate in the Nevada desert, intending to teleport an apple to a receptor in Guantanamo Bay, Cuba.

Unbeknownst to the others, Victor Van Damme altered the device's settings and, upon its activation, the five people on its steps vanished into Unbeknownst to the others, Victor Van Damme altered the device's settings and, upon its activation, the five people on its steps vanished into interdimensional space, returning altered. Reed Richards returned to the same spot, transformed into a mass of pliable cells. Ben Grimm, Reed's childhood friend, was transported to Mexico and transformed into the rockish Thing; Johnny Storm was transported to Paris, his skin converted to flame-emitting cells; Victor Van Damme was transported to an unrevealed location and acquired a mechanized skin; while Sue Storm was transported into the Nevada desert, acquiring invisibility powers.

Arthur Molekevic, a fired Baxter Building instructor who had covertly observed the experiment and its transformed subjects, sent his artificial ani-men after the five. Initially retrieving Susan while the government gathered Reed, Ben, and Johnny at the Baxter Building, Molekevic then sent what seemed to be an enormous monster after them. Defeating it, they followed it to Molekevic's underground laboratories and retrieved Susan, inadvertently destroying the underground chambers in the process and apparently burying Molekevic. The government relocated the remaining Baxter Building students to a secondary facility in Oregon, and dedicated the Manhattan facility to the quiet study of the altered four.

When Van Damme attacked the Baxter Building six months later, Reed tracked him to Copenhagen. Refused permission to go to Denmark by the government, the quartet went anyway in Reed's childhood "Fantasti-Car," knowing they needed Victor's knowledge to restore themselves. Battling Van Damme, they were unable to defeat him before the government arrived and were forced by international law to set him free.

The four used a reconstructed N-Zone transporter to pilot a decommissioned U.S. Space Shuttle, heavily modified by Reed Richards and awkwardly christened the "Awesome" by Johnny Storm, to explore the N-Zone itself. The quartet made contact there with the being known as Nihil, who tried to kill them and followed them back to Earth, where both ships crashed in Las Vegas. The Fantastic Four were officially "outed" as super-humans on the Sunset Strip while defeating Nihil and his alien crew. Returning to the Baxter Building, they were briefly attacked by a rejected Baxter thinker named Rhona Burchill who was jealous of Reed's status, and subsequently aided the Ultimates, with Ben and Johnny fighting beside Nick Fury, Carol Danvers, and the Ultimates' Thor and Black Widow against the Kree, while Reed and Sue went into space with Iron Man to investigate Gah Lak Tus. The quartet also investigated the mystery of a secret race known as the Inhumans, then pursued a group of Chrono-Bandits across time after they duplicated a time machine which Reed and Sue had co-created. Recently Reed made interdimensional contact with another universe's version of the Fantastic Four, bringing the team into conflict with an alien world afflicted with a zombie-creating virus.

After capturing their extradimensional zombie counterparts, the FF fought Namor, Dr. Doom, Arthur Molekevic, Thanos, the Squadron Supreme and Diablo, rescued the Earth's kidnapped population from Zenn-La, and battled Red Ghost alongside Crimson Dynamo in Russia.

HISTORY: Thanos is the ruler of the Endless Resurgence, an empire centered on the planet Acheron of over 1000 worlds. Their god as much as he is their ruler, Thanos controls his people through a combination of force and fear, viewing freedom as disorder, a hole in the universe which lets in randomness and chaos. Death is an end to uncertainty, and hence he loves it. Thanos views his rule as the natural order; fate and chance are at war, and fate must win, through everyone being subjugated to him. Long ago he possessed a cube which provided great power, which allowed him to erase the wills of his populace and overwrite them with his own, but under unspecified circumstances it was lost to him more than 1000 years ago, and ever since he has sought to replace it. Thanos claims his friendship with death grants him disposition over bodies and souls, offering those who obey him an improved existence in their next incarnation, and promising those who fail him pain and torment in this life and the next.

Despite this, some worlds still resist him, but dissent is ruthlessly put down by his soldiers, the Ravens and the Bombardiers, and his sons, such as Gallowglass and Ronan the Accuser. Known to be merciless, when the planet Pyx rose up against him, Thanos ordered Ronan to kill all males over the age of 10. Only one world successfully resists conquest, Halcyon, home of the "World Tree," where a peaceful people turned their children into warriors to preserve their way of life, forming into Seed Units with incredible powers. Eventually the Endless Resurgence captured Halcyon's greatest warrior and figurehead, Tesseract, but Seed Unit 19 rescued him during one of Thanos' deaths, escaping to far away Earth. Resurrecting shortly after they returned to Acheron space, Thanos sensed Seed 19 was accompanied by Earth's Fantastic Four, and specifically Reed Richards, whom Thanos instantly knew was capable of building a replacement for his lost cube. Aware Reed had landed on Pyx, Thanos ordered the garrison there to find and retrieve him, and sent Ronan to assist with this. Locating them, Thanos manifested himself through the body of Reed's friend, the Thing, and tried to commission Reed with creating the cube, but Reed demanded he depart Ben's mind before he would give an answer. Thanos offered to transfer the Thing from his monstrous form into a more humanoid one, but after confirming what Thanos would use it for, Reed refused. With bribery having failed, Thanos tried coercion, grabbing the head of Reed's other friend, Johnny Storm, and threatening to crush it; Johnny pleaded with Ben, whose consciousness began fighting back, weakening the connection enough for Seed 19's Dreamcatcher to break it. With Thanos seemingly gone, Reed and his friends soon escaped back to Earth, but were warned by Seed 19 that Thanos would not forget the injury they had inflicted and

REAL NAME: Thanos
ALIASES: None
IDENTITY: No dual identity
OCCUPATION: God ruler of the Endless Resurgence empire
CITIZENSHIP: Acheron
PLACE OF BIRTH: Unrevealed
KNOWN RELATIVES: Ronan (son), Gallowglass (son, deceased)
GROUP AFFILIATION: None
EDUCATION: Unrevealed
FIRST APPEARANCE: Ultimate Fantastic Four #35 (2006)

would seek them out. Back on Earth, Reed began trying to figure out how to construct the cube, claiming it might be their only defense if Thanos showed up, unaware that the tyrant's psychic presence seemed to be secretly assisting his research.

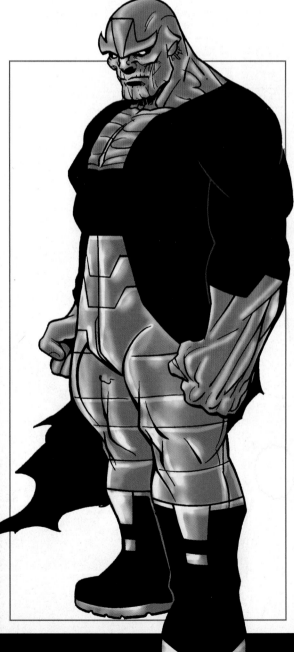

HEIGHT: 8'3"
WEIGHT: 2800 lbs.
EYES: Green
HAIR: None

ABILITIES/ACCESSORIES: Thanos possesses immense physical strength (lifting over 100 tons) and endurance. His psychic powers outstrip this; he is aware of events several star systems away, and can take over other's bodies, using them as conduits to channel his mind and power until his mind exhausts and kills the frail host form. He can rise from the dead, sacrificing other lives to resurrect his own body, recharging his energies to awaken more powerful the longer he stays dead; the longest he has remained dead seems to be a little over 49 days. He also claims he can transfer his followers' souls from one body to another, and control what form their next life will take after they die.

POWER GRID	1	2	3	4	5	6	7
INTELLIGENCE							
STRENGTH							
SPEED							
DURABILITY							
ENERGY PROJECTION							
FIGHTING SKILLS							

issue #51 cover sketches

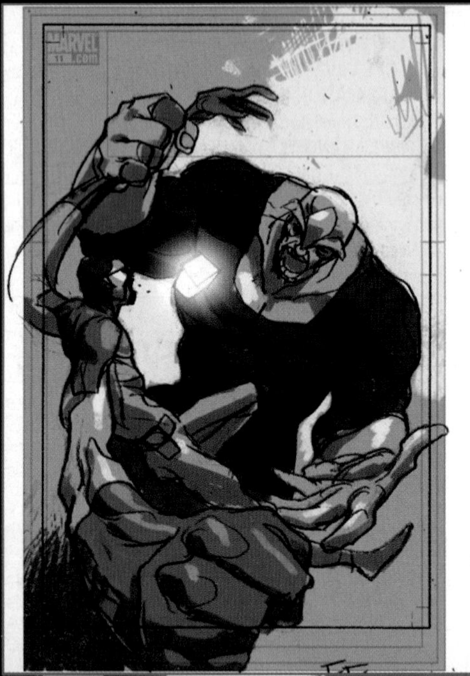

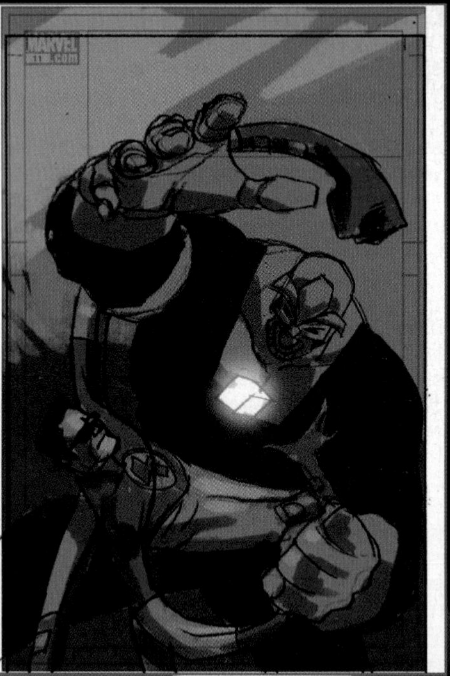

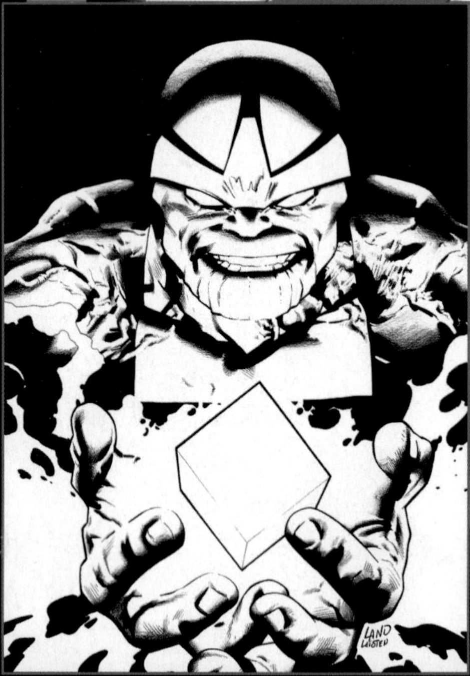

issue #52 cover inks

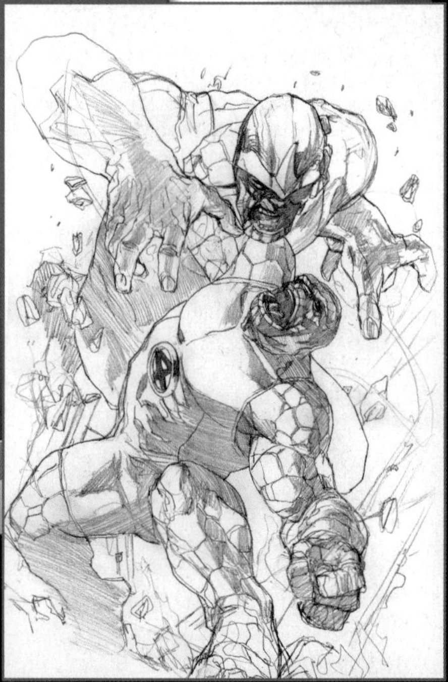

issue #53 cover sketch